NEVER GIVE IN!

The Best of Winston Churchill's Speeches

Selected and edited by his grandson

WINSTON S. CHURCHILL

PIMLICO

Published by Pimlico 2004

2 4 6 8 10 9 7 5 3 1

First published in Great Britain by Pimlico 2003

Paperback edition
Pimlico 2004

Pimlico
Random House, 20 Vauxhall Bridge Road,
London SW1V 2SA

Random House Australia (Pty) Limited
20 Alfred Street, Milsons Point, Sydney,
New South Wales 2061, Australia

Random House New Zealand Limited
18 Poland Road, Glenfield,
Auckland 10, New Zealand

Random House South Africa (Pty) Limited
Endulini, 5A Jubilee Road, Parktown 2193, South Africa

Random House UK Limited Reg. No. 954009

A CIP catalogue record for this book
is available from the British Library

ISBN 1-8441-3412-1

Papers used by Random House UK Limited are natural,
recyclable products made from wood grown in sustainable forests.
The manufacturing processes conform to the environmental
regulations of the country of origin

Printed and bound in Great Britain by William Clowes Ltd

Never give in, never give in,
never, never, never, never –
in nothing, great or small,
large or petty –
never give in
except to convictions of honour
and good sense!

Winston S. Churchill
Address to the boys of Harrow School, 29 October 1941

CONTENTS

3. The Wilderness Years 1930–39

ILLUSTRATIONS

ACKNOWLEDGMENTS

I wish, first and foremost, to express my thanks to my aunt, Lady Soames DBE, for sharing with me her recollections of the way her father worked when preparing his speeches. My thanks are also due to Allen Packwood, Director of the Churchill Archive Centre, Churchill College, Cambridge, as well as to Archives Assistants David Carter, Rachel Lloyd and Jude Brimer, for their unfailing help in providing original documents and tracking down photographs.

I am indebted to Sir Martin Gilbert, Sir Winston Churchill's official biographer, who completed with such distinction 'The Great Biography', on which my late father, Randolph Churchill, had embarked, for his guidance and advice. I am also most grateful to that veritable mine of knowledge regarding Churchill publications and quotations, Richard M. Langworth, CBE, Chairman of the Churchill Center of the United States (see Appendix).

I wish also to express my appreciation to Robert Crawford CBE, Director-General of the Imperial War Museum and to Hilary Roberts, Head of Collections Management of the Photograph Archive, for assisting in the provision of photographs, as well as to Esther Barry, Librarian of the BBC Photograph Library and Julie Snelling of the BBC Written Archives Centre.

I wish especially to record my indebtedness to my late friend and erstwhile parliamentary colleague, Robert Rhodes James, who, assisted by an army of researchers world-wide, published in 1974 his massive eight-volume work *Winston S. Churchill: The Complete Speeches 1897–1963* (Chelsea House Publishers in association with R.R. Bowker Company, New York and London), for the magisterial job he did in tracking down and assembling the overwhelming majority of my grandfather's speeches. His work has been invaluable in the preparation of this book and remains a treasure trove for universities, libraries and researchers. It contains twenty times the material that could be accommodated in this volume, and I commend it to anyone seeking a fuller text.

Finally, I must express my gratitude to James Rogers, for his encouragement, as well as for his painstaking assistance and advice in the checking of material and in the preparation of the text for the publishers. My special thanks are also due to my secretary, Penelope Tay, for her cheerful and untiring efforts in the preparation of the typescript. I also wish to record my appreciation to Jörg Hensgen of Random House UK for his help and advice.

Winston S. Churchill
Editor

EDITOR'S PREFACE

Winston Churchill's rendez-vous with destiny came on 10 May 1940, with his appointment as Prime Minister in Britain's hour of crisis. On that day Hitler launched his *blitzkrieg* against France, Belgium and the Low Countries, which was to smash all in its path. It was then that Winston Churchill, already 65 years of age and, as he put it, 'qualified to draw the Old Age Pension', deployed the power of his oratory. After years during which the British nation had heard only the voices of appeasement and surrender, suddenly a new note was sounded. In a broadcast to the nation on 19 May 1940, he declared: 'I speak to you for the first time as Prime Minister in a solemn hour in the life of our country, of our Empire, of our Allies and, above all, of the cause of Freedom.'

After a graphic account of the devastating advances by Nazi forces on the Continent he continued: 'We have differed and quarrelled in the past; but now one bond unites us all – to wage war until victory is won, and *never* to surrender ourselves to servitude and shame, whatever the cost and agony may be.'

The effect of his words was electric. Though the situation might appear hopeless, with the French and Belgian armies – which had held firm during four long years of slaughter in the First World War – crumbling in as many weeks in the face of the furious German assault, and the remnants of Britain's small, ill-equipped army preparing to retreat to Dunkirk, and when many, even of Britain's friends, believed that she, too, would be forced to surrender, Winston Churchill – in the memorable phrase of that great American war-correspondent, Edward R. Murrow, 'mobilised the English language and sent it into battle.'

With his innate understanding of the instincts and character of the British people, garnered from leading them in battle as a junior officer in conflicts on the North-West Frontier of India, in the Sudan and South Africa, as well as in the trenches of Flanders in the First World War, Churchill inspired the British nation to feats of courage and endurance, of which they had never known, or even imagined themselves capable. In his very first Address to the House of Commons, three days after becoming Prime Minister, he famously

The Orator with his editor, 10 Downing Street, 1952.

declared (13 May 1940): 'I have nothing to offer but blood, toil, tears and sweat.'

Nor was it only the British nation that was inspired and buoyed up during five long years of war but also, as I discovered, his words gave hope to the downtrodden nations of Occupied Europe. A few years ago I had the privilege of addressing a Service of Commemoration at London University, on the occasion of the 50th Anniversary of the Warsaw Ghetto Uprising. Afterwards a strikingly attractive lady came up and told me: 'Mr Churchill, I was a girl of just twelve, living in the Ghetto at the time of the Uprising, as the Nazi storm-troopers were attacking us to take us off to the concentration camps. Whenever your grandfather broadcast on the BBC, we would all crowd around the radio. I could not understand English, but I knew that, if my family and I were to have any hope of coming through this war, it depended entirely on this strong, unseen voice that I could not understand. We were all taken to Bergen Belsen – I was the only survivor. I was liberated by the British Army, in fact by the man you see standing beside me, who is today my husband.' I found it a profoundly proud, yet humbling, moment.

With his pugnacity and puckish sense of humour, Winston Churchill commanded the attention of the British nation and was successful in persuading his fellow countrymen that – though every other major nation of Europe had surrendered to the invading Nazi hordes – Britain could, and would, fight on alone. There may have been greater orators, in the traditional sense of an ability to stand up on a soapbox and – without a note or a microphone – command and move a crowd of 10 or 20,000. Most obviously the names of Gladstone and Lloyd George spring to mind, though even in that league Winston Churchill was in the forefront.

But where he came into his own was in his command of the House of Commons and, most of all, in his radio broadcasts on the BBC to the people of Britain and the wider world. Here technology came to his aid in the nick of time. For many centuries, ever since William Caxton invented his printing press in the year 1474, the only means of mass communication had been through newspapers which, by the early twentieth century, had fallen into the hands of a handful of media tycoons who, individually and collectively, wielded immense political power. However, in 1924 – just fifteen years before the outbreak of the Second World War – Stanley Baldwin became the first British Prime Minister ever to make a radio broadcast. At the time there were barely 125,000 radio sets in Britain. However by

1940 this number had risen to close on 10 million, almost one to every home and certainly to every pub in the land.

This technological breakthrough gave Churchill a direct link to the masses of the people, and proved invaluable. The style that he adopted, and which proved so effective, was to address them not as unseen masses, but as individuals – he envisioned his audience as a couple and their family, gathered round their coal fire in the 'cottage-home'. In this way he succeeded in forging a personal bond at grass-roots level with the ordinary man and woman in the street; and it was this that was to see him – and them – through five years of the cruellest war the world has ever known. Though, at the time, there were no facilities for the broadcasting of Parliament, the British Broadcasting Corporation would, in the case of his more important parliamentary speeches, arrange for him to redeliver them before their microphones, so that they could be heard, not only throughout Great Britain, but across Occupied Europe, as well as throughout the United States and the farthest outposts of the British Commonwealth and Empire.

In embarking on this work I have been anxious to draw together into a single manageable volume what I regard as the best and most important of my grandfather's speeches, spanning more than sixty years of his active political life, from his first political speech in 1897 to his acceptance of United States Honorary Citizenship from President John F. Kennedy in 1963. At the outset, I had no idea of the magnitude of the task upon which I was embarking. I knew that my grandfather was prolific as a writer, with some 30 volumes of history and biography to his credit. I was also aware of his phenomenal output as an artist, with nearly 500 completed canvases – some of a remarkably high quality – at his home at Chartwell in Kent by the time of his death.

However, I had no idea of the sheer scale of the speeches he painstakingly composed, rehearsed and delivered. The great majority were brought together by my late parliamentary colleague, Robert Rhodes James, in his *Winston Churchill: The Complete Speeches 1897–1963*, published in 1974, an 8-volume work comprising more than 8,000 closely printed pages – 12,500 pages in any self-respecting typeface – totalling some 5 million words.

Time and again on the American lecture circuit I have been asked: 'Who was your grandfather's speechwriter?' My reply is simple: 'He was a most remarkable man, by the name of Winston Spencer Churchill.' In an age when front-rank politicians, almost without exception, have a raft of speechwriters, my reply provokes amazement. My aunt, Mary Soames, the last survivor of my grandfather's children, recently told me:

> My father never, at any stage of his life, employed the services of a speechwriter. At various points in his career, in dealing with Departmental matters, he would be supplied by officials with various notes and statistics, especially in relation to technical or legal matters.
>
> Furthermore, there was a gentleman called George Christ (pronounced 'Krist') – whom my father insisted on summoning with the words: 'Send for Christ!' – who was an official at Conservative Central Office, and who would supply suggestions of points he might consider including in his Addresses to the Conservative Party Annual Conference, during the years he was Party Leader.
>
> But it was my father – and he alone – who drafted all his major speeches especially, of course, those to the House of Commons. Jane Portal (Lady Williams), who was one of his private secretaries at the time, tells of how my father, already 80 years old and in the final months of his second Premiership, delivered himself, in the space of 7 to 8 hours, of a lengthy and detailed speech on the Hydrogen Bomb.

The late Sir John Colville, one of my grandfather's private secretaries in the wartime years, told me shortly before his death: 'In the case of his great wartime speeches, delivered in the House of Commons or broadcast to the nation, your grandfather would invest approximately one hour of preparation for every minute of delivery.' Thus he would devote thirty hours of dictation, rehearsal and polishing to a half-hour speech. Therein, no doubt, lies the explanation as to how they came to move the hearts of millions in the greatest war of history and why, even to this day, they have such emotive power.

My task of reducing Churchill's phenomenal output of speeches – spanning his more than sixty years of active political life – to a single volume, thereby making many of them readily available for the first time to the general reader, has been a daunting one. I have had to be ruthless with the editing in order to reduce the corpus of his speeches to a mere 5 per cent of the whole. Some – especially the great war speeches – I reproduce in full; others have been pruned with varying degrees of severity, while a large number, for want of space, have had to be omitted entirely. My aim throughout has been to set before the reader the very best of Winston Churchill's speeches while, at the same time, setting them in the context of the long span of his roller-coaster career, with its deep troughs and dazzling peaks.

This work leads the reader through Winston Churchill's early career, from his election to Parliament at the age of 26, through his defection in 1904 from the Conservative to the Liberal Party and his meteoric rise to the front ranks of politics, becoming in rapid succession Colonial Under-Secretary (1906), President of the Board of Trade (1908), Home Secretary (1910). We see him as a political firebrand, proposing the abolition of the House of Lords, and then as a social reformer, laying the early foundation stones of the Welfare State, before becoming First Lord of the Admiralty (1911–15), where it fell to him to prepare the British Navy for war.

We trace the anguish of his resignation from the Admiralty, when he was made the scapegoat for the failure of the Dardanelles landings on Turkey's Gallipoli peninsula. Churchill saw this as the gateway, not only to defeating Germany's ally, Turkey, and sustaining Britain's ally, Russia, but as the means of attacking Germany from the rear, which he believed could shorten the war by one, or even two, years. It was probably the most brilliant strategic concept of the First World War. But for reasons largely outside his control, it failed and there was a general belief that he was finished politically. Weighed down with sorrow at being deprived of the chance to contribute his undoubted talents to directing the fortunes of war, he headed for the trenches of Flanders – that narrow stretch of land straddling the French and Belgian border, where one quarter of a million British and Commonwealth soldiers perished – to serve as a front-line soldier. If he could not have a post of power, then at least he would have a post of honour.

Reappointed to office as Minister of Munitions (1917–19) and Secretary of State for War and Air, under Lloyd George, he then became Colonial Secretary. In 1922 at the Cairo Conference he was responsible for the creation of the kingdoms of Jordan and Iraq and for setting the Hashemite rulers, Abdullah and Feisal, on their respective thrones in Amman and Baghdad, as well as for delineating, for the first time, the political boundaries of Biblical Palestine.

We follow him as he re-crosses the floor of the House of Commons to rejoin the Conservative Party, and through his tenure, under Prime Minister Stanley Baldwin, as Chancellor of the Exchequer. However it is only in the early 1930s, when he is out of office and launches his campaign to warn of the dangers of a rearmed Germany under the leadership of Adolf Hitler, that we reach the real 'meat' of this work. Churchill becomes ever more alarmed at the turn of events in Europe, as he was by the folly of the Baldwin Government to continue down the path of disarmament while, beyond 3,000 miles of Atlantic, the United States remained resolutely aloof from the unfolding crisis.

These were Winston Churchill's 'Wilderness Years', years when – despite the cogent arguments he presented to Parliament and his detailed marshalling of the facts drawing attention to the enormous scale of German rearmament – none would listen to his warnings, and the governments of Britain and France clung ostrich-like to their avowed policy of appeasement. By the time of the Munich crisis (September 1938) – when the governments of Britain and France sold down the river the liberties of the Czechoslovak peoples in a shameful attempt to buy time for themselves – Churchill could count on the fingers of one hand his true political friends and allies in Parliament.

Though 1940 and his wartime years as Prime Minister were, undoubtedly, his glory years, it is my belief that, in terms of moral courage and dogged determination, Winston Churchill's finest hour was in the late 1930s when, reviled by his Party, and denounced as a 'war monger', he continued his valiant though vain battle to alert the British people to the impending danger, convinced that united and decisive joint action by the former Allies – Britain, France and the United States – could stop Hitler in his tracks and, even as late as 1936, that it could do so without a shot being fired.

After Munich – the point at which Prime Minister Neville Chamberlain proudly proclaimed that he had in his hand a piece of paper, bearing the signatures of Herr Hitler and his own, vowing that Britain and Germany would never go to war again – the scales slowly fell off his fellow countrymen's eyes, as Hitler's brazen determination to tear up not only the Treaties that had ended the First World War, but all Agreements he had subsequently entered into, became increasingly apparent.

Finally, the tide of public opinion began to turn against the architects of Appeasement, and a growing ground swell of public opinion came to be heard, demanding Winston Churchill's return to high office. However it was not until 3 September 1939 – the very day the Second World War was declared and as Hitler's tank armies invaded and occupied Poland – that Winston Churchill was called back to his old post as First Lord of the Admiralty and charged with the task of preparing the Royal Navy for war with Germany for the second time in a quarter century. In the instant of his return to the Admiralty the signal was flashed to the Fleet: 'Winston is back.' As he himself recounted in his *War Memoirs*:

So it was that I came again to the room that I had quitted in pain and sorrow almost a quarter century before . . . Once again we must fight for life and honour against all the might and fury of the valiant, disciplined and ruthless German race. Once again! So be it.

How quickly the world forgets – and the younger generation almost certainly has no idea – that it was Britain and France who declared war on Nazi Germany, for the violation and invasion of Poland, with which they were bound by a treaty of alliance.

There followed the so-called 'phoney' war, in which on the Western Front there was no opening of hostilities on land, though at sea the war was very real. It was not until 10 May 1940 that Hitler felt strong enough to launch his *blitzkrieg* against France, Belgium and Holland. On that same day, as the rising political storm in Britain swept Chamberlain from office, Winston Churchill was invited to become Prime Minister.

Far from being daunted by the task that lay ahead, Churchill was exhilarated. As he confided in his *War Memoirs*:

As I went to bed at 3.00 am, I was conscious of a profound sense of relief. At last I had the authority to give directions over the whole scene. I felt as if I was walking with destiny, and that all my past life had been but a preparation for this hour and for this trial.

In the absence of any effective armaments, beyond the power of the Royal Navy at sea and the fledgling, but as yet untested, Royal Air Force in the skies, Winston Churchill deployed his powers of oratory in all their simplicity, majesty and eloquence. Those who had refused to heed his blunt warnings of harsh reality in the peace-time years of the 1930s became his avid listeners and partisans once battle was joined. Churchill was shocked by the speed with which, in quick succession, the Belgian and French governments surrendered to Hitler. He was utterly determined that Great Britain would not succumb in the same way.

I recall my late mother, Ambassador Pamela Harriman, telling me about those critical days in late May and early June of 1940, as the British Army fell back on Dunkirk and retreated across the Channel, France was falling and Hitler prepared to launch Operation 'Sealion' – codeword for his invasion of Britain. My mother, just 20 years old and six months pregnant with me, was living with her in-laws at 10 Downing Street. They would normally dine early, frequently just my mother and my grandparents together as, by 9.30 or 10.00 p.m., the first air raid warnings would sound and my mother and I would be sent to the basement.

She related how, one evening, the Prime Minister was brooding at the dinner table, preoccupied with his thoughts. Nothing was said. Suddenly he drew his eyes into sharp focus on to my mother's and growled fiercely: 'If the Hun comes, I am counting on each one of you to take one with you before you go!' 'But Papa,' exclaimed my mother, 'I don't have a gun and, even if I did, I would not know how to use it.' 'But, my dear,' rejoined my grandfather, his voice increasing in power and menace, and with his fist held high: 'You can go to the kitchen and grab a carving knife!' Though he never used such direct language in addressing the British people, it was with that same spirit that he inspired the nation.

Now, at last, the nation was eager to listen, and willing to follow his lead, as he evoked and proclaimed their innermost instincts. Though it might be against all reason, they came to share Churchill's conviction that, come what may, we could survive in our island, succoured by our Commonwealth and Empire across the seas and, soon, with the powerful material support of the United States under the Lend-Lease Agreement.

But Churchill was sufficient of a realist to know that, on her own, Britain did not have the strength to liberate the nations of Occupied Europe and defeat Nazi Germany. His game-plan was simple: to play for time and hold out until the 'Great Republic across the seas' as he fondly called America, the land of his mother's birth, could be persuaded to join the fray. Many of his speeches were aimed at engaging not only the material support but the active involvement of the United States.

In his Address to the House of Commons (18 June 1940) in what has come to be known as the 'Finest Hour' speech he famously declared:

> What General Weygand called the Battle of France is over. I expect that the Battle of Britain is about to begin. Upon this battle depends the survival of Christian civilisation. Upon it depends our own British life, and the long continuity of our institutions and our Empire. The whole fury and might of the enemy must very soon be turned on us. Hitler knows that he will have to break us in this island or lose the war.
>
> If we can stand up to him, all Europe may be free and the life of the world may move forward into the broad sunlit uplands. But if we fail, then the whole world, including the United States, including all that

we have known and cared for, will sink into the abyss of a new Dark Age made more sinister, and perhaps more protracted, by the lights of perverted science. Let us therefore brace ourselves to our duties and so bear ourselves that, if the British Empire and its Commonwealth last for a thousand years, men will still say '*this* was their finest hour!'

It would be difficult to exaggerate the sense of profound relief that swept over him when, some 18 months later, he heard of the Japanese attack on the US Fleet at Pearl Harbor, sure in the knowledge that America would now be engaged 'up to the neck and to the death'. From that moment onwards, Churchill never doubted the victorious outcome of the Allied cause but – already three years before the hour of victory – he had become deeply anxious about what would be the shape of post-war Europe with the Soviet Red Army at its heart.

Despite his rejection by the British electorate in the hour of victory in the summer of 1945, he launched new campaigns at Fulton, Missouri (5 March 1946), to warn America and the world to the mortal danger posed to the nations of Europe by the Russian Army occupying central and eastern Europe in the guise of liberators, but in reality with the intent of enslaving; and also to crusade for the building of a United Europe out of the ashes and ruins of the Second World War as he proclaimed at Zurich (19 September 1946), when he boldly declared:

> I am now going to say something that will astonish you. The first step in the recreation of the European family must be a partnership between France and Germany. In this way only can France recover the moral leadership of Europe. There can be no revival of Europe without a spiritually great France and a spiritually great Germany. The structure of the United States of Europe, if well and truly built, will be such as to make the material strength of a single state less important.

Amazingly, after six years as Leader of the Opposition, having rebuilt his political position and, through his labours as an author, rebuilt his financial fortunes, at the age of 76 he became Prime Minister for the second time. For four more years he laboured to try to secure a relaxation of tension between the heirs of Stalin and the Western Powers, in an attempt to avoid disaster in what became known as the 'Cold War'.

I conclude this work with Winston Churchill's speech, in which he accepted with pride the Honorary Citizenship conferred upon him by President John F. Kennedy and the Congress of the United States. My grandfather, already 88 years of age, and too frail to make the journey to Washington himself, asked his only son, Randolph, to deliver on his behalf what was to be his final speech. I accompanied my father on that memorable and proud occasion, as on 9 April 1963, President Kennedy, in a ceremony in the Rose Garden of the White House, proclaimed Winston Churchill an Honorary Citizen of the United States. Churchill's message concluded:

In this century of storm and tragedy I contemplate with high satisfaction the constant factor of the interwoven and upward progress of our peoples. Our comradeship and our brotherhood in war were unexampled. We stood together, and because of that fact the free world now stands.

Winston S. Churchill
30 November 2002

1. Young Statesman 1899–1915

When his father, Lord Randolph Churchill, died in 1895 at the early age of 46, Winston determined to quit the Army at the earliest opportunity in favour of a career in politics. He burned to vindicate the memory of his father, whom he hero-worshipped, despite the fact that he had treated him with so much coldness and disdain. Churchill's capture by the Boers in South Africa in November 1899, during the Anglo-Boer War, and his dramatic escape from captivity, catapulted him into the headlines and provided him with the basis, impecunious as he was, to launch his career in politics. Thus in October 1900, at the age of 25, he was elected Member of Parliament for Oldham in Lancashire and – with one brief interruption – was to serve in Parliament, under six sovereigns, until October 1964.

It was not long before Churchill found himself out of sympathy with the Conservative Party, most especially on the issue of Protection, to which he was strongly opposed and, in May 1904, he 'crossed the floor' to join the Opposition Liberals. Fortuitously the move was well timed: within two years the Conservatives had gone down to a landslide defeat and, soon afterwards, he was offered ministerial office as Under-Secretary for the Colonies in the Liberal Government of Herbert Asquith. Thereafter he enjoyed a meteoric rise to the front ranks of politics, becoming in quick succession President of the Board of Trade in 1908, Home Secretary in 1910 and First Lord of the Admiralty in 1911, where it fell to him to prepare the British fleet for war with Germany.

FIRST POLITICAL SPEECH:
'THE DRIED UP DRAIN-PIPE OF RADICALISM'

26 July 1897

Claverton Down, Bath

Twenty-two years old and still a serving officer, on leave from his regiment in India, the young Winston addressed his first public meeting, a summer fête of the Primrose League (founded in memory of Benjamin Disraeli), at the house which is today the American Museum in Britain. His speech – well prepared, rehearsed and memorised – already demonstrates his keen social conscience about the harsh conditions of life, and work, of the great mass of the people, which was to be a foremost feature of his early career. In My Early Life *he sets the scene:*

> *We repaired to our tent, and mounted the platform, which consisted of about four boards laid across some small barrels. There was neither table, nor chair; but as soon as about a hundred persons had rather reluctantly, as I thought, quitted their childish amusements in the park, the Chairman rose and in a brief speech introduced me to the audience.*

Though Parliament is dull, it is by no means idle. (*Hear, hear.*) A measure is before them of the greatest importance to the working men of this country. (*Cheers.*) I venture to hope that, if you think it presumptuous in one so young to speak on such a subject, you will put it down to the headstrong enthusiasm of youth. (*Hear, hear and laughter.*) This measure is designed to protect workingmen in dangerous trades from poverty if they become injured in the service of their employers. (*Hear, hear.*) When the Radicals brought in their Bill and failed, they called it an Employers' Liability Bill. Observe how much better the Tories do these things. (*Hear, hear.*) We call the Bill the Workmen's Compensation Bill, and that is a much nicer name. (*Laughter and hear, hear.*) This Bill is a great measure of reform. It grapples with evils that are so great that only those who are intimately connected with them are able to form any idea of them. (*Cheers.*) Every year it is calculated that 6,000 people are killed and 250,000 injured in trades in this country. That is a terrible total, larger than the greatest battle ever fought can show. (*Hear, hear.*) I do not say that workmen have not been treated well in the past by the kindness and consideration of their employers, but this measure removes the question from the shifting sands of charity and places it on the firm bedrock of law. (*Cheers.*) So far it is only applied to dangerous trades. Radicals, who are never satisfied with Liberals, always liberal with other people's money (*laughter*), ask why it is not applied to all. That is like a Radical – just the slap-dash, wholesale, harum-scarum policy of the Radical. It reminds me of the man who, on being told that ventilation is an excellent thing, went and smashed every window in his house, and died of rheumatic fever. (*Laughter and cheers.*) That is not Conservative policy. Conservative policy is essentially a tentative policy – a look-before-you-leap policy; and it is a policy of don't leap at all if there is a ladder. (*Laughter.*) It is because our progress is slow that it is sure and constant. (*Hear, hear.*) But this Bill might be taken as indicating the forward tendency of Tory legislation, and as showing to thousands of our countrymen engaged in industrial pursuits that the Tories are willing to help them, and besides having the inclination, that they also have the power (*hear, hear*), and that the British workman has more to hope for from the rising tide of Tory democracy than from the dried-up drain-pipe of Radicalism. (*Laughter and cheers.*) . . .

There are not wanting those who say that in this Jubilee year our Empire has reached the height of its glory and power, and that now we shall begin to decline, as Babylon, Carthage, Rome declined. Do not believe these croakers but give the lie to their dismal croaking by showing by our actions that the vigour and vitality of our race is unimpaired and that our determination is to uphold the Empire that we have inherited from our fathers as Englishmen (*cheers*), that our flag shall fly high upon the sea, our voice be heard in the councils of Europe, our Sovereign supported by the love of her subjects, then shall we continue to pursue that course marked out for us by an all-wise hand and carry out our mission of bearing peace, civilisation and good government to the uttermost ends of the earth. (*Loud cheers.*)

'ESCAPE!'

23 December 1899

Durban Town Hall, Natal, South Africa

In South Africa to report the Anglo-Boer War for the London
Morning Post, Churchill had been taken prisoner of war by the Boers
(Dutch settlers in South Africa) on 15 November 1899 in what came
to be known as 'The Armoured Train Incident'. He spent his 25th
birthday behind barbed wire in a prisoner-of-war camp in Pretoria,
plotting his escape. On the night of 12/13 December he escaped and,
after ten days on the run – including several nights concealed in a rat-
infested coal mine by an English mine-manager – he reached
Portuguese East Africa and freedom. (For a fuller account of his
capture and escape the reader should consult Winston Churchill's
My Early Life). He then made his way by ship to Durban, where
British settlers gave him a rapturous welcome. As he relates in My
Early Life:

> *I reached Durban to find myself a popular hero. I was received as if I*
> *had won a great victory. The harbour was decorated with flags. Bands*
> *and crowds thronged the quays. . . . Whirled along on the shoulders*
> *of the crowd, I was carried to the steps of the town hall, where*
> *nothing would content them but a speech, which after a becoming*
> *reluctance I was induced to deliver.*

By his capture and escape, Churchill had become the hero of the
hour and had made a name for himself sufficient to launch forth on a
political career, which was his ambition.

This is not the time for a long speech. We have got outside the region
of words: we have to go to the region of action. We are now in the
region of war, and in this war we have not yet arrived at the half-way
house. But with the determination of a great Empire, surrounded by
Colonies of unprecedented loyalty, we shall carry our policy to a
successful conclusion, and under the old Union Flag there will be an
era of peace, liberty, equality and good government in South Africa. I
thank you once again for your great kindness. I am sure I feel within
myself a personal measure of that gratitude which every Englishman

'Escape!' Durban Town Hall, South Africa, 23 December 1899.

who loves his country must feel towards the loyal and devoted Colonists of Natal.

'THE ANNIVERSARY OF MY ESCAPE'

13 December 1900

Waldorf Astoria Hotel, New York City

Elected Member of Parliament for Oldham, Lancashire, in the election of October 1900, Winston Churchill, who urgently needed to repair his finances, embarked on a six-week lecture tour of the USA and Canada on the subject of the Anglo-Boer War and his dramatic escape. He was disconcerted to discover the extent of American sentiment in favour of the Boers. Mark Twain, who chaired his inaugural meeting, introduced him to his New York audience with the elegant accolade: 'Mr Churchill by his father is an Englishman, by his mother he is an American, no doubt a blend that makes the perfect man.'

This is the anniversary of my escape, many accounts of which have been related here and in England, but none of which is true. I escaped by climbing over the iron paling of my prison while the sentry was lighting his pipe. I passed through the streets of Pretoria unobserved and managed to board a coal train on which I hid among the sacks of coal.

When I found the train was not going in the direction I wanted, I jumped off. I wandered about aimlessly for a long time, suffering from hunger, and at last I decided that I must seek aid at all risks. I knocked at the door of a kraal, expecting to find a Boer, and, to my joy, found it occupied by an Englishman named John Howard, who ultimately helped me to reach the British lines.

MAIDEN SPEECH: 'A CERTAIN SPLENDID MEMORY'

18 February 1901

House of Commons

The 26-year-old MP took his seat as a Tory in the new Parliament, which was opened by King Edward VII, following the death a month earlier of Queen Victoria. Just four days later he made his maiden speech, which he concluded with a becoming reference to his father, Lord Randolph Churchill, who had died six years earlier after a meteoric but doomed political career. The sketch-writer of the Tory Daily Telegraph *recorded the next day: 'He had a great opportunity, and he satisfied the highest expectations.' The* Daily Express *reported: 'He held a crowded House spellbound.'*

I understood that the hon. Member, to whose speech the House has just listened, had intended to move an Amendment to the Address. The text of the Amendment, which had appeared in the papers, was singularly mild and moderate in tone; but mild and moderate as it was, neither the hon. Member nor his political friends had cared to expose it to criticism or to challenge a division upon it, and, indeed, when we compare the moderation of the Amendment with the very bitter speech which the hon. Member has just delivered, it is difficult to avoid the conclusion that the moderation of the Amendment was the moderation of the hon. Member's political friends and leaders, and that the bitterness of his speech is all his own. It has been suggested to me that it might perhaps have been better, upon the whole, if the hon. Member, instead of making his speech without moving his Amendment, had moved his Amendment without making his speech. I would not complain of any remarks of the hon. Member were I called upon to do so. In my opinion, based upon the experience of the most famous men whose names have adorned the records of the House, no national emergency short, let us say, of the actual invasion of this country itself ought in any way to restrict or prevent the entire freedom of Parliamentary discussion. Moreover, I do not believe that the Boers would attach particular importance to the utterances of the hon. Member. No people in the world received so much verbal sympathy and so little practical support as the Boers. If I were a Boer fighting in the field – and if I were a Boer I hope I should be fighting in the field – I would not allow myself to be taken in by any message of sympathy, not even if it were signed by a hundred hon. Members. . . .

What ought to be the present policy of the Government? I take it that there is a pretty general consensus of opinion in this House that it ought to be to make it easy and honourable for the Boers to surrender, and painful and perilous for them to continue in the field. Let the Government proceed on both those lines concurrently and at full speed. I sympathise very heartily with my hon. friend the senior member for Oldham, who, in a speech delivered last year, showed great anxiety that everything should be done to make the Boers understand exactly what terms were offered to them, and I earnestly hope that the right hon. Gentleman the Colonial Secretary will leave nothing undone to bring home to those brave and unhappy men who are fighting in the field that whenever they are prepared to recognise that their small independence must be merged in the larger liberties of the British Empire, there will be a full guarantee for the security of their property and religion, an assurance of equal rights, a promise of representative institutions, and last of all, but not least of all, what the British Army would most readily accord to a brave and enduring foe – all the honours of war. I hope the right hon. Gentleman will not allow himself to be discouraged by any rebuffs which his envoys may meet with, but will persevere in endeavouring to bring before these people the conditions on which at any moment they may obtain peace and the friendship of Great Britain. Of course, we can only promise, and it rests with the Boers whether they will accept our conditions. They may refuse the generous terms offered them, and stand or fall by their old cry, 'Death or independence!' (*Nationalist cheers*). I do not see anything to rejoice at in that prospect, because if it be so, the war will enter upon a very sad and gloomy phase. If the Boers remain deaf to the voice of reason, and blind to the hand of friendship, if they refuse all overtures and disdain all terms, then, while we cannot help admiring their determination and endurance, we can only hope that our own race, in the pursuit of what they feel to be a righteous cause, will show determination as strong and endurance as lasting. . . .

I cannot sit down without saying how very grateful I am for the kindness and patience with which the House has heard me, and which have been extended to me, I well know, not on my own account, but because of a certain splendid memory which many hon. Members still preserve.

LIFTING AGAIN THE 'TATTERED FLAG'

13 May 1901

House of Commons

Not even three months after his maiden speech, Churchill mounted a major attack on St John Brodrick, the Secretary of State for War, over his plans for a reform of the Army. He assailed what he dubbed 'Mr Brodrick's Army', raising again the 'tattered flag of retrenchment and economy' – the cause in which his father had sacrificed his political career. It marked the first of a growing number of attacks on his own party, which culminated three years later in his 'crossing the floor' of the House of Commons and joining the Liberal Party.

I wish to complain very respectfully, but most urgently, that the Army Estimates involved by the scheme lately explained by the Secretary of State for War are much too high, and ought to be reduced, if not this year, certainly at the conclusion of the South African campaign. I regard it as a grave mistake in Imperial policy to spend thirty millions a year on the Army. I hold that the continued increase in Army expenditure cannot be viewed by supporters of the Government without the greatest alarm and apprehension, and by Members who represent working class constituencies without extreme dislike.

I desire to urge considerations of economy on His Majesty's Government, and as a practical step that the number of soldiers which they propose to keep ready for expeditionary purposes should be substantially reduced. First of all I exclude altogether from this discussion the cost of the South African War. Once you are so unfortunate as to be drawn into a war, no price is too great to pay for an early and victorious peace. All economy of soldiers or supplies is the worst extravagance in war. I am concerned only with the Estimates for the ordinary service of the year, which are increasing at such a rate that it is impossible to view them without alarm. Does the House realise what British expenditure on armaments amounts to? See how our Army Estimates have grown – seventeen millions in 1894, eighteen in 1897, nineteen in 1899, twenty-four in 1900, and finally in the present year no less than twenty-nine millions eight hundred thousand. . . .

If I might be allowed to revive a half-forgotten episode – it is half-forgotten because it has passed into that period of twilight which intervenes between the bright glare of newspaper controversy and the calm rays of the lamp of history – I would recall that once upon a time a Conservative and Unionist Administration came into power supported by a large majority, nearly as powerful, and much more cohesive, than that which now supports His Majesty's Government, and when the time came round to consider the Estimates the usual struggle took place between the great spending Departments and the Treasury. I say 'usual'; at least it used to be so, I do not know whether it is so now. The Government of the day threw their weight on the side of the great spending Departments, and the Chancellor of the Exchequer resigned. The controversy was bitter, the struggle uncertain, but in the end the Government triumphed, and the Chancellor of the Exchequer went down for ever, and with him, as it now seems, there fell also the cause of retrenchment and economy, so that the very memory thereof seems to have perished. . . . Wise words, Sir, stand the test of time, and I am very glad the House has allowed me, after an interval of fifteen years, to lift again the tattered flag of retrenchment and economy. . . .

I stand here to please the cause of economy. I think it is about time that a voice was heard from this side of the House pleading that unpopular cause; that someone not on the bench opposite, but a Conservative by tradition, whose fortunes are linked indissolubly to the Tory party, who knows something of the majesty and power of Britain beyond the seas, upon whom rests no taint of cosmopolitanism, should stand forward and say what he can to protest against the policy of daily increasing the public burden. If such a one is to stand forward in such a cause, then, I say it humbly, but with I hope becoming pride, no one has a better right than I have, for this is a cause I have inherited, and a cause for which the late Lord Randolph Churchill made the greatest sacrifice of any Minister of modern times. . . .

The Empire which has grown up around these islands is essentially commercial and marine. The whole course of our history, the geography of the country, all the evidences of the present situation, proclaim beyond a doubt that our power and prosperity alike and together depend on the economic command of markets and the naval command of the sea; and from the highest sentimental reasons, not less than from the most ordinary practical considerations, we must avoid a servile imitation of the clanking military empires of the European continent, by which we cannot obtain the military predominance and security which is desired, but only impair and vitiate the natural sources of our strength and vigour. There is a higher reason still. There is a moral force – the Divine foundation of earthly power – which, as the human race advances, will more and more strengthen and protect those who enjoy it; which would have protected the Boers better than all their cannon and brave commandos if, instead of being ignorant, aggressive, and corrupt, they had enjoyed that high moral reputation which protected us in the dark days of the war from European interference – for, in spite of every calumny and lie uttered or printed, the truth comes to the top, and it is known alike by peoples and by rulers that on the whole British influence is healthy and kindly, and makes for the general happiness and welfare of mankind. And we shall make a fatal bargain if we allow the moral force which this country has so long exerted to become diminished, or perhaps even destroyed for the sake of the costly, trumpery, dangerous military playthings on which the Secretary of State for War has set his heart.

'AN AGE OF GREAT EVENTS AND LITTLE MEN'

21 November 1901

Philomathic Society Dinner, Liverpool

Given that there was a Conservative Government in office, this speech is further evidence of the scant regard the new Member had for the leaders of his own Party.

One aspect of modern life which strikes me very much is the elimination of the individual. In trade, vast and formidable combinations of labour stand arrayed against even vaster and more formidable combinations of capital, and, whether they war with each other or cooperate, the individual in the end is always crushed under. Let us look into the political world and see how the combination grew and the individual steadily diminished. At one period the House of Commons possessed Pitt and Fox, Burke and Sheridan; at another, Peel and Bright, Disraeli and Gladstone. We are not quite so well off now, but Governments were never more stable and secure. I think the late Lord Randolph Churchill one of the last of the old school of politicians. . . . Nothing would be worse than that independent men should be snuffed out and that there should be only two opinions in England – the Government opinion and the Opposition opinion. The perpetually unanimous Cabinet disquiets me. I believe in personality. The House of Commons depends for its popularity, and consequently for its power, on the personality of its members.

We live in an age of great events and little men, and if we are not to become the slaves of our own systems or sink oppressed among the mechanism we ourselves created, it will only be by the bold efforts of originality, by repeated experiment, and by the dispassionate consideration of the results of sustained and unflinching thought.

'A NAVY . . . STRONG ENOUGH TO PRESERVE THE PEACE OF THE WORLD'

17 January 1903

Oldham, Lancashire

The young Member for Oldham renews his attack on 'Mr Brodrick's Army'.

The failure of this Army scheme is a very serious business, and it is a matter which Parliament will have to discuss. We have frittered away money. We have wasted time. Above all, we have exhausted that public interest in the Army which the war had excited, and which might have been made the driving power of great and beneficial and sorely needed reforms. But there is one consolation, though it is, perhaps, rather a grim consolation. It was a scheme all along unsuited to our needs; it never ought to have succeeded; it never could have succeeded. From the very beginning it deserved opposition, and was doomed to failure. We did not want to have in England three army corps or soldiers to sail away and attack anybody anywhere at a moment's notice. That is a dangerous and provocative provision. That is enough men to get us into trouble with a great European nation, and nothing like enough men to get us out again. (*Hear, hear.*) We do not want to have in England a large Regular Army for home defence. We do not want our Volunteers to remain a mere despised appendage of the War Office. (*Cheers.*)

There is scarcely anything more harmful to the British Army than this perpetual imitation of the German system (*hear, hear*), of German uniforms, and of methods. Sometimes I think the whole Cabinet has got a touch of German measles (*laughter*), but Mr Brodrick's case is much the worst. He is spotted from head to foot (*laughter*), and he has communicated the contagion to the Army.

Perhaps you would say to me, 'You are very ready to tell us what kind of an Army we do not want, but will you tell us what kind of an army we do?' Well, it is almost impossible for any one who has not got access to the machinery and knowledge of a great Department to make detailed positive propositions on such a very complicated question, but after what I have said I feel I ought to put forward some suggestions of a constructive character. First of all, the British Regular Army of the future would have to be, nearly all of it, serving abroad in the great garrisons of the Empire – India, Egypt, South Africa, and in the various fortresses and coaling stations which are so necessary to us; and for this reason we would only be able to have a very small Regular Army at home. It ought to be a very good Army (*hear, hear*) – perhaps much better paid and, I hope, better trained than at present; but, still, it could only be a very small Army – an Army big enough to send an expedition to fight the Mahdi or the Mad Mullah, and just the kind of Army to do that sort of thing very well, but not big enough to fight the Russians or the Germans or the French. Then we would have to entrust the defence of the soil of England from a foreign invasion to a great voluntary citizen army of Yeomanry, of Militia, and of Volunteers. (*Cheers.*) These would have to be our stand-by in the hour of need, as they have been in the South African war, and we would have to spend a great deal of money that we saved by reducing the number of Regular soldiers on making this citizen army worthy of our trust and equal to its responsibility. Last of all, and first of all, and in the middle all the time, we must place our faith and our money in the British Navy (*loud cheers*), which alone secures our island home from the foot of the spoiler, which alone safeguards the world-strewn commerce of our people and protects the wide-spread dominions of the King. (*Cheers.*) Some day, perhaps, the eminent statesmen who govern us – the men who really govern, I mean – will turn their minds to this tremendous question and will think it out with something of the care and labour and brain power, say, Mr Balfour devoted to the Education Bill or Mr Chamberlain devoted to the Workmen's Compensation Act. (*Hear, hear.*) And whenever that fortunate day should arrive I would make so bold as to prophesy that the ambitious dreams of renewed military glory to be won by British Regulars on the Continent of Europe which distort our present Army policy will be roughly brushed aside, and that in their place will come a true conception of our varied needs and circumstances and a wiser and more thrifty employment of our resources; a professional Army to garrison the Empire; a volunteer citizen Army to defend it; and over all a British Navy, of which I need only say this – that it must be strong enough to preserve the peace of the world. (*Cheers.*)

'THE MERE WASHPOT OF PLUTOCRACY'

4 June 1904

Alexandra Palace, London

On 31 May 1904 Churchill 'crossed the floor' of the House of Commons to take his place among the Liberal party on the Opposition benches. He did so on the issue of Free Trade which, bowing to Protectionist cartels, the Conservative party had abandoned. A few days later, in the company of the Leaders of the Liberal Party, Sir Henry Campbell-Bannerman and Lloyd George, he addressed a meeting to celebrate the centenary of Richard Cobden, the Liberal free-trader who founded the 'Manchester School' of economists.

And how is it with the Conservative party? They are not pleased with me. (*Laughter.*) They tell me I ought to join the Liberal party – (*Cheers.*) It is not a bad idea. (*Renewed cheers.*) I will consider it carefully. (*Laughter and cheers.*) I have a sincere respect for the Conservative party. They are an ancient party, and I believe that they will at intervals have a valuable and a useful function to fulfil in the government of the country. But the Conservative party has allowed itself to become the instrument of an ambitious man. It has allowed itself to advocate a reactionary and a dangerous policy. It has allowed itself to embark upon a gamble for another lease of power, a gamble with the food of the people. And in consequence the Conservative party will suffer, and will, I think, deservedly suffer, electoral defeat some day in a perhaps not too distant future. (*Cheers.*)

But a graver danger than defeat threatens the Conservative party. There are worse things than defeat – dishonour is worse. The Conservative party is threatened with a revolutionary change in its character and position, a change which will make it not a national party, not a constitutional party, not an Imperial party, not even an aristocratic party; it is in danger of becoming a capitalist party. (*Cheers.*) It is in great danger of becoming the mere washpot of the plutocracy, the engine of the tariff and the trust, and a hard confederation of interest and monopoly banded together to corrupt and to plunder the commonwealth. (*Loud cheers.*) That is the danger which many of the wisest men in the party are striving to save it from, and whatever our political opinions may be we must all hope that it may be preserved from that danger. What should we say of the statesman who is responsible for all this disturbance – Mr Chamberlain? How are the mighty fallen! (*Laughter.*) 'But yesterday the word of Caesar might have stood against the world' – now he has to sit next to Mr Chaplain. (*Laughter.*) Only a year ago Mr Chamberlain was going to sweep the country; now he dare not face a debate in the House of Commons. (*Cheers.*) Mr Chamberlain denies that he ran away from the debate in the House of Commons. I don't accuse him of running away. I saw a phrase in the war report this morning which expresses the situation exactly. He did not run away, he executed a strategic movement to the rear. (*Much laughter.*) Mr Chamberlain is very angry because Lord Hugh Cecil – (*cheers*) – accused him of cowardice. I don't accuse him of cowardice; I think he acted as a wise and prudent man – (*laughter*) – in shirking the debate, because the plain truth is that his supporters are so incompetent that his arguments are such rubbish, that his figures are such figures – (*laughter*) – that he dare not submit them to the free and unprejudiced debate of the House of Commons. (*Cheers.*) No, he will keep them for the meetings of the Tariff Reform League in the country, those meetings which are attended by carefully selected working men in dress clothes and unemployed who pay 15s. a piece for their tickets. (*Laughter.*)

We are here this afternoon to celebrate the centenary of Mr Cobden, and I am proud of the high and honourable duty which has been entrusted to me in moving this resolution. It is the fashion nowadays to speak with a great deal of contempt of the Manchester School, and no abuse seems to be bad enough for Mr Cobden. But I venture to think there will be some of you here who will believe it is very nearly time that the peaceful, philanthropic, socialising doctrines of Mr Bright and Mr Cobden were a little more considered by the statesmen who rule our land. (*Cheers.*) We do not pretend that everything Mr Cobden said was right, or that the political system of thought which he established was a complete and final revelation of worldly wisdom. But in the long stairway of human progress and achievement which the toil and sacrifice of generations are building it was Cobden's work to lay a mighty stone. (*Cheers.*) Other stones had been laid upon that stone, stones of social standards and social reform, stones of Imperial responsibility, and you have only got to walk about the streets of London to see that there is plenty more work waiting to be done by a master mason. (*Cheers.*) But we believe that the work which Cobden did was done for ever; that the stone he laid shall never be transplanted, that the heights he gained shall never be abandoned. (*Cheers.*) We may differ among ourselves, we probably do, as to how far, how fast, or in what direction we shall move forward, but on one point we are all agreed – we are not going back one inch. (*Loud and prolonged cheers.*) We are not going back because the principles we defend are principles which endure from one generation to another. Men change, manners change, customs change, Governments and Prime Ministers change, even Colonial Secretaries change – (*laughter*) – sometimes they change their offices, sometimes they change their opinions. (*Laughter.*) But principles do not change. Whatever was scientifically true in the economic proportions which were established 60 years ago in the controversy of a far greater generation than our own is just as true in 1904 as it was in 1846, and it will still be true as long as men remain trading animals on the surface of the habitable globe.

'FOR FREE TRADE'

16 June 1904

Cheetham Hill, Manchester

By now Churchill had thrown himself wholeheartedly into the battle against Protectionism and on the side of Free Trade.

We are gathered here and I stand here with Liberal support as the Free Trade candidate for North-west Manchester because a distinguished politician has changed his mind. Many people change their minds in politics. Some people change their minds to avoid changing their party. – (*Laughter.*) Some people change their party to avoid changing their mind. – (*Renewed laughter.*) There have been all sorts of changes in English politics, but I think that Mr Chamberlain's change is much the most remarkable of any that history records. – (*Hear, hear.*) When you think that the man who broke up or was breaking up the Liberal Government of 1885 by being more Radical than Mr Gladstone, and was driving the Duke of Devonshire out of the Liberal party and Liberal Government in 1885, is the man who is now breaking up the Conservative Government in 1904 by being more Tory and more reactionary than any Conservative in that government, I think you will agree with me that it is a world's record – (*laughter and cheers*), – that it is less like an ordinary political manoeuvre than like one of those acrobatic feats which are so popular in circuses and hippodromes. There is one particular feat of which I am forcibly reminded tonight – the novel and exciting spectacle of 'looping the loop'. – (*Laughter.*) It is a very dangerous and a very difficult performance. I don't know whether you have ever seen it. Sometimes it succeeds and sometimes it fails. When it succeeds great applause is accorded to the performer. When it fails he is usually carried away on a shutter. – (*Laughter.*) But whether it succeeds or whether it fails the performance always commands the attention and the interest of the audience. . . .

I hope in the autumn to lay before the electors a statement upon these subjects at greater length. When the election comes, it is on these points that I will ask for your support, and I will put on my bills –

Vote for Churchill, Cheap Food, Peace, Retrenchment, and Reform.

The Protectionists have failed to prove that this country is not prosperous; they have failed to prove that they have a remedy which will make us prosperous; and they have failed to prove that their remedy can be effectively applied. As the world goes, we are undoubtedly a prosperous nation, and, man for man, the most prosperous nation. But even if we were not prosperous, Protection would only accelerate our decline and exacerbate our misfortunes. Is it a strange thing that there has been some disorganisation of our commerce after the close of a great and costly war? Mr Chamberlain told a Birmingham audience two years ago that England was rich enough to fight just such another war. Ah! the Birmingham barrel-organ is playing a different tune today – (*Laughter.*) England is now bleeding to death, and we are told that the colonies will leave us unless Canadian loyalty is purchased at 2*s.* a quarter and Australian allegiance at a penny a pound. – (*Laughter.*)

Mr Chamberlain's motives no doubt are pure enough, but what about some of those who were supporting him – those rich landlords and wealthy manufacturers who jostled one another on his platforms? Was it all for the unity of the Empire; was it all for the good of the Empire? – (*Laughter.*) I will show by quotations that the working men of Spain, France, and Germany are more discontented than the English working men, and that a Free Trade movement is in progress both in Germany and America. I do not look upon foreign peoples as if they are our enemies. – (*Loud cheers.*) The King has gone from one European capital to another endeavouring to spread goodwill among the nations. What is the good of that if we have another lot of people with a distinguished man at their head going about appealing to every narrow, bigoted, insular prejudice, representing every foreigner as an enemy, spreading ill-will and dissension among the nations of the earth? – (*Cheers.*) The union of the Anglo-Saxon race is a great ideal, and if ever it is to be achieved it will be by increasing and not diminishing the friendly intercourse of trade between this country and the United States. Against such wanton folly as a tariff war with the United States, Free-traders appeal with confidence to Lancashire, and we hope that, as in years gone by, Lancashire will point the path of honour and wisdom to the people of the British islands. – (*Loud cheers.*)

'DEAR FOOD FOR THE MILLIONS: CHEAP LABOUR FOR THE MILLIONAIRE'

13 May 1905

Manchester

As Churchill's son and biographer, Randolph (the editor's father) observed: 'While Churchill reserved his invective largely for the public platform, he gave the House of Commons the best fruit of his thoughts and the most reasoned arguments in his power.' Here he castigates the Conservative party, which he rebrands the 'Protectionist' party, together with its leader Arthur Balfour, who was still Prime Minister.

The great leader of the Protectionist party, whatever else you may or may not think about him, has at any rate left me in no doubt as to what use he will make of his victory if he should win it. We know perfectly well what to expect – a party of great vested interests, banded together in a formidable confederation, corruption at home, aggression to cover it up abroad, the trickery of tariff juggles, the tyranny of a party machine; sentiment by the bucketful, patriotism by the imperial pint, the open hand at the public exchequer, the open door at the public-house, dear food for the millions, cheap labour for the millionaire.

'BRITISH HOSPITALITY'

9 October 1905

Cheetham Hill, Manchester

By now Churchill had firmly moved his political attentions to North-West Manchester in England's industrial North, where he was to stand with Liberal support as the Free Trade candidate in the General Election three months later.

If the Unemployment Bill was a sham, the Aliens Bill was a sham with lunacy superimposed upon it. (*Laughter.*) I am not going to argue the merits of legislation against the admission of aliens into the country. But the Act as it was forced through the House of Commons by the closure contains absurdities which would make a deaf mute roar with laughter. The object of the bill was to keep out undesirables, but any undesirable, whether he was a thief, or a diseased man, or an idiot, might come in if he came in as a third-class passenger and not by steerage. A poverty line was drawn for the first time; a few shillings made the difference between desirability and undesirability. Moreover, the alien who chose to travel in a ship where there were not more than nineteen other aliens might come in freely. The Act will not in any degree alter the situation in England. On the other hand, it may inflict hardship and vexation upon many deserving people who seek a refuge on our shores, and it violates that tradition of British hospitality of which we have been proud and from the practice of which we have at more than one period reaped marked and permanent advantage. (*Cheers.*)

'NO MORE GARTERS FOR DUKES'

14 December 1905

City Liberal Club, Manchester

On 4 December Arthur Balfour's Conservative Government resigned, hoping to exploit divisions in the ranks of the Liberal party, which had been out of office for twenty years. However the prospect of office proved a firm stimulant to unity and Sir Henry Campbell-Bannerman formed a Liberal administration in which Winston Churchill was offered his first ministerial post as Under-Secretary to the Colonies. In the General Election which followed he won the Manchester North-West seat by a majority of 1,241 votes.

Mr Balfour at Manchester said that his resignation was received ungratefully by those who had so long demanded it. Sir Henry Campbell-Bannerman had no reason to be grateful to Mr Balfour. It was not out of any consideration for him that Mr Balfour resigned. Nothing but the bluntest compulsion procured his retirement. (*Cheers.*)

In what condition has he left the public estate? The property is heavily mortgaged, the banking account overdrawn, the annual charges are vastly increased, and national credit has been gravely impaired. The philanthropy of the late government made Consols cheap enough to be within the range of the comparatively poor people. (*Laughter.*) Sir Henry Campbell-Bannerman came to the counsels of a Sovereign who was deserted at an awkward moment in the interests of a party manoeuvre. He will find nothing in the condition of the public business, legislative, administration, Parliamentary, or financial, to make him indebted to his predecessor. (*Cheers.*) Indeed the change of Government that has just taken place is less like an ordinary transfer of power from one great party to another than the winding up of an insolvent concern which had been conducted by questionable and even shady methods to a ruinous conclusion. (*Cheers.*) The firm Balfour, Balfour, and Co. has stopped payment. The managing director, a Birmingham man of large views and unusual versatility, absconded two years ago, leaving heavy outstanding liabilities, and he is believed to have since devoted himself mainly to missionary work. (*Loud laughter.*) Ever since, the business has been going downhill; it is now in liquidation. (*Cheers.*) Its paper is no longer accepted in the City and it has been 'hammered' on Change. (*Cheers and laughter.*) No more sinecures for guinea pigs, no more garters for dukes, no more peerages for the faithful press – (*laughter*); – the crash has come at last. Sir Henry Campbell-Bannerman presented himself in the capacity of the official receiver, to secure the rights of the creditors and safeguard the interests of the shareholders, according to the regular law of the land.

'THE GIFT OF ENGLAND'

31 July 1906

House of Commons

Five years after Britain's decisive, but costly, victory over the Boers in South Africa it fell to Churchill to draw up the constitution giving them self-government. The measure of his success was to be shown by the fact that, in two World Wars, the Boers overwhelmingly sided with Britain. In this speech, Churchill makes a vain plea to the Conservatives to support the government and make the Transvaal constitution not the gift of a party, but 'the gift of England'.

I have now finished laying before the House the constitutional settlement, and I should like to say that our proposals are interdependent. They must be considered as a whole; they must be accepted or rejected as a whole. I say this in no spirit of disrespect to the Committee, because evidently it is a matter which the Executive Government should decide on its own responsibility, and if the policy which we declare were changed new instruments would have to be found to carry out another plan. We are prepared to make this settlement in the name of the Liberal Party. That is sufficient authority for us; but there is a higher authority which we should earnestly desire to obtain.

I make no appeal, but I address myself particularly to the right hon. Gentlemen who sit opposite, who are long versed in public affairs, and not able to escape all their lives from a heavy South African responsibility. They are the accepted guides of a Party which, though in a minority in this House, nevertheless embodies nearly half the nation. I will ask them seriously whether they will not pause before they commit themselves to violent or rash denunciations of this great arrangement. I will ask them, further, whether they will not consider if they cannot join with us to invest the grant of a free Constitution to the Transvaal with something of a national sanction. With all our majority we can only make it the gift of a party; they can make it the gift of England. And it that were so, I am quite sure that all those inestimable blessings which we confidently hope will flow from this decision will be gained more surely and much more speedily; and the first real step taken to withdraw South African affairs from the arena of British party politics, in which they have inflicted injury on both political parties and in which they have suffered grievous injury themselves. I ask that that may be considered; but in any case we are prepared to go forward alone, and Letters Patent will be issued in strict conformity with the settlement I have explained this afternoon if we should continue to enjoy the support of a Parliamentary majority.

'THE CAUSE OF THE LEFT-OUT MILLIONS'

11 October 1906

St Andrew's Hall, Glasgow

Though born the grandson of a duke, the young Churchill had a keen social conscience and was deeply shocked by the very real poverty which afflicted many millions of the population. This prompted him to espouse what, at the time, was regarded as radical causes, such as unemployment insurance, a minimum wage, and better working conditions, especially for those who laboured in the mines.

The cause of the Liberal Party is the cause of the left-out millions; and because we believe that there is in all the world no other instrument of equal potency and efficacy available at the present time for the purposes of social amelioration, we are bound in duty and in honour to guard it from all attacks, whether they arise from violence or from reaction.

There is no necessity tonight to plunge into a discussion of the philosophical divergencies between Socialism and Liberalism. It is not possible to draw a hard-and-fast line between individualism and collectivism. You cannot draw it either in theory or in practice. That is where the Socialist makes a mistake. Let us not imitate that mistake. No man can be a collectivist alone or an individualist alone. He must be both an individualist and a collectivist. The nature of man is a dual nature. The character of the organisation of human society is dual. Man is at once a unique being and a gregarious animal. For some purposes he must be collectivist, for others he is, and he will for all time remain, an individualist. Collectively we have an Army and a Navy and a Civil Service; collectively we have a Post Office, and a police, and a government; collectively we light our streets and supply ourselves with water; collectively we indulge increasingly in all the necessities of communication. But we do not make love collectively, and the ladies do not marry us collectively, and we do not eat collectively, and we do not die collectively, and it is not collectively that we face the sorrows and the hopes, the winnings and the losings of this world of accident and storm. . . .

I look forward to the universal establishment of minimum standards of life and labour, and their progressive elevation as the increasing energies of production may permit. I do not think that Liberalism in any circumstances can cut itself off from this fertile field of social effort, and I would recommend you not to be scared in discussing any of these proposals, just because some old woman comes along and tells you they are Socialistic. If you take my advice, you will judge each case on its merits. Where you find that State enterprise is likely to be ineffective, then utilise private enterprises, and do not grudge them their profits.

The existing organisation of society is driven by one mainspring – competitive selection. It may be a very imperfect organisation of society, but it is all we have got between us and barbarism. It is all we have been able to create through unnumbered centuries of effort and sacrifice. It is the whole treasure which past generations have been able to secure, and which they have been able to bequeath; and great and numerous as are the evils of the existing condition of society in this country, the advantages and achievements of the social system are greater still. Moreover, that system is one which offers an almost indefinite capacity for improvement. We may progressively eliminate the evils; we may progressively augment the goods which it contains. I do not want to see impaired the vigour of competition, but we can do much to mitigate the consequences of failure. We want to draw a line below which we will not allow persons to live and labour, yet above which they may compete with all the strength of their manhood. We want to have free competition upwards; we decline to allow free competition to run downwards. We do not want to pull down the structures of science and civilisation: but to spread a net over the abyss; and I am sure that if the vision of a fair Utopia which cheers the hearts and lights the imagination of the toiling multitudes should ever break into reality it will be by developments through, and modifications in, and by improvements out of, the existing competitive organisation of society; and I believe that Liberalism mobilised, and active as it is today, will be a principal and indispensable factor in that noble evolution.

I have been for nearly six years, in rather a short life, trained as a soldier, and I will use a military metaphor. There is no operation in war more dangerous or more important than the conduct of a rear-guard action and the extrication of a rear-guard from difficult and broken ground. In the long war which humanity wages with the elements of nature the main body of the army has won its victory. It has moved out into the open plain, into a pleasant camping ground by the water springs and in the sunshine, amid fair cities and fertile fields. But the rear-guard is entangled in the defiles, the rear-guard is still struggling in mountainous country, attacked and assailed on every side by the onslaughts of a pitiless enemy. The rear-guard is encumbered with wounded, obstructed by all the broken vehicles that have fallen back from the main line of the march, with all the stragglers and weaklings that have fallen by the way and can struggle forward no farther. It is to the rear-guard of the army that attention should be directed. There is the place for the bravest soldiers and the most trusted generals. It is there that all the resources of military science and its heaviest artillery should be employed to extricate the rear-guard – not to bring the main army back from good positions which it occupies, not to throw away the victory which it has won over the brute forces of nature – but to bring the rear-guard in, to bring them into the level plain, so that they too may dwell in a land of peace and plenty.

That is the aim of the Liberal Party, and if we work together we will do something for its definite accomplishment.

GEORGE BERNARD SHAW: 'A VOLCANO'

22 October 1906

Free Trade Hall, Manchester

The Socialist-leaning playwright and author was not Churchill's most favourite person, but here he indulges in some light-hearted banter at his expense.

We had yesterday in Manchester Mr George Bernard Shaw, who has been favouring us with his views on methods of human and social regeneration. Mr Bernard Shaw is rather like a volcano. There is a great deal of smoke; there are large clouds of highly inflammable gas. There are here and there brilliant electrical flashes; there are huge volumes of scalding water, and mud and ashes cast up in all directions. Among the mud and ashes of extravagance and nonsense there is from time to time a piece of pure gold cut up, ready smelted from the central fires of truth. I do not myself dislike this volcano. It is not a very large volcano, though it is in a continual state of eruption. What is his remedy for the evil conditions which we see before us. It is very simple and drastic – he proposes to cut off the Lord Mayor's head. – (*Laughter.*) I have had the pleasure of meeting the Lord Mayor several times during his tenure of office, and although I do not doubt that a capital sentence hanging over his head would stimulate him to even greater exertions, yet I am inclined to think the work you have done deserves some better reward.

'MY AFRICAN JOURNEY'

18 January 1908

National Liberal Club, London

Relishing his position as Colonial Under-Secretary, Churchill used the Parliamentary recess as the opportunity to visit Britain's colonies in East Africa. He had returned just the day before and was filled with enthusiasm for all he had seen.

If you ask what is my prevailing impression – my prepondering impression – in the journey I have taken, I would say frankly it is one of astonishment. It is not the first time I have travelled abroad. I have had the opportunity of examining Africa from both ends – from the Sudan and from the South, – and I have travelled very widely over India. But I confess I have never seen countries so fertile and so beautiful outside Europe as those to which I have travelled on the journey from which you welcome me back tonight. There are parts of the East African Protectorate which in their beauty, in the coolness of the air, in the richness of the soil, in their verdure, in the abundance of running water, in their fertility – parts which absolutely surpass any of the countries which I have mentioned, and challenge comparison with the fairest regions of England, France, or Italy. (*Cheers.*) I have seen in Uganda a country which from end to end is a garden – inexhaustible, irrepressible, and exuberant fertility upon every side – and I cannot doubt that the great system of lakes and waterways, which you cannot fail to observe if you look at the large map of Africa, must one day become the great centre of tropical production, and play a most important part in the economic development of the whole world.

SOCIALISM: 'ALL YOURS IS MINE!'

22 January 1908

Cheetham, Manchester

The fledgling Labour Party were junior partners in the Liberal administration, which constituted what would today be called a 'Lib-Lab Pact'. In the ranks of the Labour Party there were to be found many hard-line Socialists, to whose presence in the Liberal coalition Churchill took the strongest exception, while anxious not to alienate the working-class vote.

The Socialists – the extreme and revolutionary party of Socialists – are very fond of telling us they are reviving in modern days the best principles of the Christian era. They consider they are the political

Electioneering in Manchester, 1908.

embodiment of Christianity, though, to judge by the language which some of them use and the spirit of envy, hatred, and malice with which they go about their work, you would hardly imagine they had studied the teaching of the Founder of Christianity with the attention they profess to have given to the subject. – (*Hear, hear.*)

But there is one great difference between Socialists of the Christian era and those of which Mr Victor Grayson is the apostle. The Socialism of the Christian era was based on the idea that 'all mine is yours', but the Socialism of Mr Grayson is based on the idea that 'all yours is mine'. – (*Cheers.*) And I go so far as to say that no movement will ever achieve any real advantage for the mass of the people that is based upon so much spite and jealousy as is the present Socialist movement in the hands of its extreme men.

THE PEN: 'LIBERATOR OF MAN AND OF NATIONS'

17 February 1908

Author's Club, London

Having moonlighted as a war-correspondent during his years in the Army, on the North-West frontier of India, on the Afghan border, in the Sudan and South Africa, Churchill had already published six significant works, including a major biography of his late father.

The fortunate people in the world – the only really fortunate people in the world, in my mind, – are those whose work is also their pleasure. The class is not a large one, not nearly so large as it is often represented to be; and authors are perhaps one of the most important elements in its composition. They enjoy in this respect at least a real harmony of life. To my mind, to be able to make your work your pleasure is the one class distinction in the world worth striving for; and I do not wonder that others are inclined to envy those happy human beings who find their livelihood in the gay effusions of their fancy, to whom every hour of labour is an hour of enjoyment, to whom repose – however necessary – is a tiresome interlude, and even a holiday is almost deprivation. Whether a man writes well or ill, has much to say or little, if he cares about writing at all, he will appreciate the pleasures of composition. To sit at one's table on a sunny morning, with four clear hours of uninterruptible security, plenty of nice white paper, and a Squeezer pen – (*laughter*) – that is true happiness. The complete absorption of the mind upon an agreeable occupation – what more is there than that to desire? What does it matter what happens outside? The House of Commons may do what it likes, and so may the House of Lords. – (*Laughter.*) The heathen may rage furiously in every part of the globe. The bottom may be knocked clean out of the American market. Consols may fall and suffragettes may rise. – (*Laughter.*) Never mind, for four hours, at any rate, we will withdraw ourselves from a common, ill-governed, and disorderly world, and with the key of fancy unlock that cupboard where all the good things of the infinite are put away. – (*Cheers.*)

I often fortify myself amid the uncertainties and vexations of political life by believing that I possess a line of retreat into a peaceful and fertile country where no rascal can pursue and where one need never be dull or idle or even wholly without power. It is then, indeed, that I feel devoutly thankful to have been born fond of writing. It is then, indeed, that I feel grateful to all the brave and generous spirits who, in every age and in every land, have fought to establish the now unquestioned freedom of the pen. – (*Cheers.*)

And what a noble medium the English language is. It is not possible to write a page without experiencing positive pleasure at the richness and variety, the flexibility and the profoundness of our mother-tongue. If an English writer cannot say what he has to say in English, and in simple English, depend upon it it is probably not worth saying. What a pity it is that English is not more generally studied. . . .

Now, I am a great admirer of the Greeks, although, of course, I have to depend upon what others tell me about them – (*laughter*), – and I would like to see our educationists imitate in one respect, at least, the Greek example. How is it that the Greeks made their language the most graceful and compendious mode of expression ever known among men? Did they spend all their time studying the languages which had preceded theirs? Did they explore with tireless persistency the ancient root dialects of the vanished world? Not at all. They studied Greek. – (*Cheers.*) They studied their own language. They loved it, they cherished it, they adorned it, they expanded it, and that is why it survives a model and delight to all posterity. Surely we, whose mother-tongue has already won for itself such an unequalled empire over the modern world, can learn this lesson at least from the ancient Greeks and bestow a little care and some proportion of the years of education to the study of a language which is perhaps to play a predominant part in the future progress of mankind.

'WHAT IS SOCIETY?'

4 May 1908

Kinnaird Hall, Dundee

On 8 April Herbert Asquith succeeded Sir Henry Campbell-Banner-man as Prime Minister. The same day he appointed Churchill, at the young age of 33, to be President of the Board of Trade with a seat in the Cabinet. At the time it was still the practice that newly appointed Cabinet Ministers had to seek re-election by their constituencies before they could accept an office of profit under the Crown. Churchill's constituents were not minded to endorse him and he was defeated by 429 votes. But the Scottish city of Dundee provided him with a haven, and shortly after this speech, returned him in a by-election with a large majority. Later that summer, on 12 September, he married Miss Clementine Hozier.

And what is society? I will tell you what society is. Translated into concrete terms, Socialistic 'society' is a set of disagreeable individuals who obtained a majority for their caucus at some recent election, and whose officials in consequence would look on humanity through innumerable grills and pigeon-holes and across innumerable counters, and say to them, 'Tickets, please.' (*Laughter.*) Truly this grey old world has never seen so grim a joke. (*Applause.*) Now, ladies and gentlemen, no man can be either a collectivist or an individual. He must be both; everybody must be both a collectivist and an individualist. For certain of our affairs we must have our arrangements in common. Others we must have sacredly individual and to ourselves. (*Cheers.*) We have many good things in common. You have the police, the Army, the Navy, and officials – why, a President of the Board of Trade you have in common. (*Applause.*) But we don't eat in common; we eat individually. (*Laughter.*) And we don't ask the ladies to marry us in common. (*Laughter.*) And you will find the truth lies in these matters, as it always lies in difficult matters, midway between extreme formulae. It is in the nice adjustment of the respective ideas of collectivism and individualism that the problem of the world and the solution of that problem lie in the years to come. (*Applause.*) But I have no hesitation in saying that I am on the side of those who think that a greater collective element should be introduced into the State and municipalities. I should like to see the State undertaking new functions, particularly stepping forward into those spheres of activity which are governed by an element of monopoly. (*Applause.*) Your tramways and so on; your great public works, which are of a monopolistic and privileged character – there I see a wide field for State enterprise to embark upon. But when we are told to exalt and admire a philosophy which destroys individualism and seeks to replace it by collectivism, I say that is a monstrous and imbecile conception which can find no real foothold in the brains and hearts – and the hearts are as trustworthy as the brains – in the hearts of sensible people. (*Loud cheers.*)

'I *AM* THE BOARD OF TRADE'

4 February 1909

Chamber of Commerce dinner, Newcastle-upon-Tyne

If there is any office in the Government which should claim a friendly reception it is the Board of Trade. In a sense I am the Board of Trade. (*Laughter.*) I preside over a Board which for centuries has not met. One constitutes a quorum. I am that quorum. But in a larger sense the Board of Trade is a great apparatus of beneficent Government organisation, a great accumulation of knowledge, and it has a staff which is quite equal to the very finest flavour of the Civil Service. Its attitude is non-partisan. It has relations with all parties and with the leaders not only of industrial enterprise but of the trade unions, and both sides are willing to give the Board the best information they have when any important question arises. The statutory powers of the Board are large, and the amount of work done that is outside the statutory powers, by goodwill and conciliation, is also great. Both sides know that they will get fair treatment, and that there will be no hanky-panky or jerrymandering in dealing with different interests and different classes. This undoubtedly gives the Board in its larger aspect an influence far outside any power that is conferred upon it by Parliament. (*Cheers.*) Its three great principles, enunciated by my predecessor, are 'Confer, Conciliate, and Compromise'.

THE BUDGET: 'CANNOT AFFORD TO LIVE OR DIE'

22 May 1909

Free Trade Hall, Manchester

Considering that you have all been ruined by the Budget – (*laughter*), – I think it very kind of you to receive me so well. When I remember all the injuries you have suffered – how South Africa has been lost – (*laughter*); – how the gold mines have been thrown away; how all the splendid army which Mr Brodrick got together – (*laughter*) – has been reduced to a sham; and how, of course, we have got no navy of any kind whatever – (*laughter*), – not even a fishing smack, for all the 35 millions a year we give the Admiralty; and when I remember that in spite of all these evils the taxes are so oppressive and so cruel that any self-respecting Conservative will tell you he cannot afford either to live or die – (*laughter*), – when I remember all this, Mr Chairman, I think it remarkable that you should be willing to give me such a hearty welcome back to Manchester. Yes, gentlemen, when I think of the colonies we have lost, of the Empire we have alienated, of the food we have left untaxed – (*laughter*), – and the foreigners we have left unmolested – (*laughter*), – and the ladies we have left outside – (*laughter*) – I confess I am astonished you are glad to see me here again.

'A VIOLENT RUPTURE OF CONSTITUTIONAL CUSTOM'

4 September 1909

Palace Theatre, Leicester

A constitutional crisis was looming in consequence of the threat of the House of Lords, which at the time represented the landed aristocracy, to reject the Liberal Chancellor of the Exchequer, David Lloyd George's, 'People's Budget'. The Chancellor sought an extra £4 million to enable him to introduce retirement pensions for the elderly and to build seven new Dreadnoughts (battleships) for the Royal Navy. He proposed doing this by increasing taxation on the wealthier sections of society, especially the property owners. Churchill's defiant threat to the House of Lords earned him an amazing rebuke from the King, in the form of an unprecedented letter to The Times *from the King's Private Secretary.*

A general election consequent upon the rejection of the Budget by the Lords would not, ought not, and could not be fought upon the Budget alone. – (*Cheers.*) Budgets come, as the late Lord Salisbury said in 1894, and Budgets go. Every Government has its own expenditure for each year. Every Government has hitherto been entitled to make its own provision to meet that expenditure. There is a Budget every year. Memorable as the Budget of my right hon. friend may be, far-reaching as is the policy dependent upon it, the Finance Bill, after all, is only in its character an annual affair. But the rejection of the Budget by the House of Lords would not be an annual affair. – (*Loud and prolonged cheering.*) It will be a violent rupture of constitutional custom and usage extending over 300 years, and recognised during all that time by the leaders of every party in the State. It would involve a sharp and sensible breach with the traditions of the past. And what does the House of Lords depend upon if not upon the traditions of the past? – (*Cheers.*) It would amount to an attempt at revolution, not by the poor but by the rich, not by the masses but by the privileged few, not in the name of progress but in that of reaction, not for the purpose of broadening the framework of the State, but greatly narrowing it. Such an attempt, whatever you may think of it, would be historic in its character, and the results of the battle fought upon it, whoever won, must inevitably be not of an annual but of a permanent and final character – (*Cheers.*) The result of such an election must mean an alteration of the veto of the House of Lords. – (*More cheers.*) If they win – (*Voices: 'They won't' and 'Never'*) – they will have asserted their right not merely to reject the legislation of the House of Commons but to control the finances of the country. And if they lose we will smash to pieces their veto. – (*Loud and prolonged cheers.*)

I say to you that we do not seek the struggle. We have our work to do. But if it is to come it could never come better than now. – (*Loud cheers.*) Never again, perhaps not for many years in any case, will such an opportunity be presented to the British democracy. Never will the ground be more favourable. Never will the issues be more clearly or more vividly defined. – (*Cheers.*) Those issues will be whether taxation, which is admitted on all sides to be necessary, shall be imposed upon luxuries, superfluities, and monopolies, or upon the prime necessaries of life, whether you shall put your tax upon the unearned increment in land or upon the daily bread of labour, whether the policy of constructive social reform on which we are embarked and which expands and deepens as we advance, shall be carried through and given a fair chance, or whether it shall be brought to a dead stop, and all the energies and attention of the State devoted to Jingo armaments and senseless foreign adventure. And lastly, the issue will be whether the British people in the year of grace 1909 are going to be ruled through a representative Assembly elected by six or seven millions of voters and about which everyone in the country has a chance of being consulted, or whether they are going to allow themselves to be dictated to and domineered over by a miserable minority of titled persons – (*laughter*), – who represent nobody, who are responsible to nobody, and who only scurry up to London to vote in their party interests, in their class interests, and in their own interests. These will be the issues of the struggle, and I am glad that the responsibility for such a struggle, if it should come, will rest with the House of Lords themselves. – (*Hear, hear.*) But if it is to come we do not need to complain. We will not draw back from it. – (*Hear, hear.*) We will engage in it with all our hearts, it being always clearly understood that the fight will be a fight to the finish – (*loud cheers*), – and that the fullest forfeits which are in accordance with the national interests shall be exacted from the defeated foe. – (*Loud cheers.*)

'THE MOST ANCIENT AND THE MOST GLORIOUS MONARCHY'

4 December 1909

Empire House, Southport, Lancashire

Churchill – the subject of fierce criticism from the Tories, who regarded him not only as a renegade, but a traitor to his class – was at pains to make clear his strong support for the institution of an hereditary monarchy, while all the while heaping scorn and ridicule upon the Upper Chamber of Parliament, which was based on the same principle.

There is no difficulty in vindicating the principle of an hereditary Monarchy. The experience of every country, and of all the ages, the practical reasonings of common sense, arguments of the highest theory, arguments of the most commonplace experience, all unite to show the profound wisdom which places the supreme leadership of the State beyond the reach of private ambition and above the shocks and changes of party strife. (*Hear, hear.*) And, further, let it not be forgotten that we live under a limited and Constitutional Monarchy. The Sovereign reigns, but does not govern. That is a maxim we were all taught out of our schoolbooks. The powers of government are exercised upon the advice of Ministers responsible to Parliament, and those Ministers are capable of being displaced, and are frequently displaced, by a House of Commons freely elected by millions of voters. The British Monarchy has no interests divergent from those of the British people. (*Cheers.*) It enshrines only those ideas and causes upon which the whole British people are united. It is based upon the abiding and prevailing interests of the nation, and thus through all the swift changes of the last hundred years, through all the wide developments of a democratic State, the English Monarchy has become the most secure, as it is the most ancient and the most glorious, Monarchy in the whole of Christendom. (*Cheers.*)

'THE UPKEEP OF THE ARISTOCRACY'

17 December 1909

Victoria Opera House, Burnley, Lancashire

The previous day Lord Curzon, speaking in Churchill's former constituency of Oldham, had stoutly defended the hereditary principle of the role of the unelected House of Lords. This was Churchill's mocking rejoinder.

When I began my campaign in Lancashire I challenged any Conservative speaker to come down and say why the House of Lords, composed as the present House of Lords is, should have the right to rule over us, and why the children of that House of Lords should have the right to rule over our children. – (*Cheers.*) My challenge has been taken up with great courage – (*laughter*) – by Lord Curzon. – (*Groans.*) No, the House of Lords could not have found any more able and, I will add, any more arrogant defender, and at Oldham on Wednesday – you have heard of Oldham – (*laughter*), – so have I. – (*Laughter.*) Well, at Oldham Lord Curzon treated a great public meeting to what I can only call a prize essay on the Middle Ages. . . .

The claim of the House of Lords is not that if the electors like the sons of distinguished men they may have legislative functions entrusted to them; it is that, whether they like it or not, the sons and the grandsons and the great-grandsons, and so on till the end of time, of distinguished men shall have legislative functions entrusted to them. That claim resolves itself into this, that we should maintain in our country a superior class, with law-giving functions inherent in their blood, transmissible by them to their remotest posterity, and that these functions should be exercised irrespective of the character, the intelligence, or the experience of the tenant for the time being – (*laughter*), – and utterly independent of the public need and the public will. That is a proposition which only needs to be stated before any average British jury to be rejected with instantaneous contempt. – (*Cheers.*) Why has it never been rejected before? In my opinion it has never been rejected because the House of Lords has never before been taken seriously by the democratic electorate, which has been in existence since 1885. They have never been taken seriously because they were believed to be in a comatose and declining condition, upon which death would gradually supervene. Now we see the House of Lords stepping into the front rank of politics; not merely using their veto over any legislation sent up by any majority, however large, from any House of Commons, however newly elected, but also claiming new powers over the whole of the finances – powers which would make them the main governing centre in the State. (*Cheers.*) That is why we are forced to examine their pretensions very closely; and when we have examined them, I venture to think there will not be much left of them. . . .

Now I come to the third great argument of Lord Curzon. 'All civilisation,' he said – he was quoting a great French writer, an Agnostic, Renan – 'all civilisation has been the work of aristocracies.' – (*Laughter.*) They liked that in Oldham. – (*Laughter.*) There was not a duke, not an earl, not a marquis, not a viscount in Oldham who did not feel that a compliment had been paid to him. – (*Loud laughter.*) What does Lord Curzon mean by aristocracy? It is quite clear from the argument of his speech that he did not mean Nature's aristocracy, by which I mean the best and most gifted beings in each generation in each country, the wisest, the bravest, the most generous, the most skilful, the most beautiful, the strongest, and the most active. If he had meant that I think we should probably agree with him. Democracy properly understood means the association of all through the leadership of the best, but the context of Lord Curzon's quotation and the argument of his speech, which was designed entirely to prove that the House of Lords was a very desirable institution for us to maintain in its present form, clearly shows that by aristocracy he meant the hereditary legislator, the barons, earls, dukes, etc. – I do not mean anything disrespectful by the etc. – (*laughter*), – and their equivalents in other countries. That is what he meant by aristocracy in the argument he employed at Oldham. Well, again I say this has only to be dismissed as absurd. – (*Cheers.*)

'All civilisation has been the work of aristocracies.' Why, it would be much more true to say the upkeep of the aristocracy has been the hard work ·of all civilisations. – (*Loud cheers and 'Say it again.'*) Nearly all great ideas and the energy by which all the great services by which mankind has been benefited have come from the mass of the people.

'FOR SOLDIERS TO FIRE ON THE PEOPLE WOULD BE A CATASTROPHE'

7 February 1911

House of Commons

By now Churchill was Home Secretary and the outbreak of violence and destruction of property in the mining valleys of South Wales, as a result of the miners' strike, led to his being criticised by the Conservatives for not deploying troops sufficiently quickly, and by the Socialists for using excessive force. Arthur Balfour, Leader of the Opposition, led the Conservative attack on the Home Secretary's handling of the crisis.

I was yesterday the subject of attack from no less a person than the Leader of the Opposition, and he has attacked me, not for the excessive amount of force employed, but for not employing sufficient force – for not sending military instead of police – for not sending military soon enough, and the right hon. Gentleman devoted so much time in the important speech which he delivered at the beginning of this Session to this subject that I am really surprised that in the course of this Debate, though I waited to give full opportunity for it, no Member of the Opposition has risen to support the charges which were made against the Government and the Secretary of State for Home Affairs. Let me just read to the House what the right hon. Gentleman says. He said:

> Many of these deplorable occurrences might have been avoided had he not at a critical moment refused to carry out decisively and effectively the measures which he contemplated. Had he not held back the military and not shown some doubt and hesitation at a critical moment, much destruction of property, many unhappy incidents, and many circumstances which all, whatever their opinions, must look upon as a great blot on the procedure of civilised society, might have been wholly avoided.

That is, I am sure, a very serious charge. . . .

I should like to point out to the House upon this point that the forces which the Government sent at the request of the Chief

Constable and the local authorities in the Rhondda Valley were in every respect more suitable to the work which they were likely to have to do than the force of infantry which had been asked for in the morning. Policemen accustomed to handle crowds are from every point of view more effective in these matters than soldiers, especially infantry, and we were sending as many foot constables and a considerable number of mounted constables as well in place of the two companies of infantry which had been asked for, and we were sending in addition, to be in support, two squadrons of cavalry. Therefore, no charge could be made against the Government that adequate forces were not sent to the scene, or that suitable forces were not sent to the scene. On the contrary, the forces sent were larger and more suitable than those which were asked for. . . .

Whatever we were guilty of, there was no vacillation. Obstinacy perhaps, but vacillation, no. The decision was never departed from to use the police as a cover and shield for the military. What I had in my mind as the principal subject of apprehension was the idea of the arrival in the night of a body of soldiers hurriedly sent by train from a long distance, disembarking under conditions of excitement at a station and moved out of the station into direct collision with an angry mob, who were not at all accustomed to see the soldiers and were perhaps not at all acquainted with the weapons they carried or with the limitations attendant upon military action. That I was resolved to guard against, if it were possible to do so, while maintaining law and order. . . .

The mining population of South Wales are, as the House knows, a well-educated, peaceful, intelligent and law-abiding class of men, and have often, I may express the personal opinion here, been very hardly tried in more ways than one during these troubles, for which, in my judgment, they are not the only people to blame. In my opinion the riots were largely caused by rowdy youths and roughs from outside, foreign to the district, and I think it only just to place that on record in fairness to the miners of South Wales, who have been attacked in a general way by people who know nothing at all about the matter. Local authorities and private employers are very ready sometimes, and from insufficient cause, to call for troops. Troops cost them nothing, police cost money to the local authorities; and there is a very general disposition in some quarters to suppose that the whole British Army is always to be available, irrespective of the circumstances, upon the demand of any local authority. The local authority sends for troops, and they think that troops should always be sent, very often not thinking of the effect of military weapons or the

difficulty which surrounds military action. Law and order must be
preserved, but I am confident that the House will agree with me that
it is a great object of public policy to avoid a collision between
soldiers and crowds of persons engaged in industrial disputes. All
such collisions attended, as they must be, by loss of life and by the
use of firearms, do great harm to the Army, which is a volunteer
Army, and whose relation with the civil forces of the country must be
carefully safeguarded, and they also cause feuds and resentments
which last for a generation. For soldiers to fire on the people would
be a catastrophe in our national life. Alone among the nations, or
almost alone, we have avoided for a great many years that
melancholy and unnatural experience. And it is well worth while, I
venture to think, for the Minister who is responsible to run some risk
of broken heads or broken windows, to incur expense and an
amount of inconvenience in the police arrangements, and to accept
direct responsibility in order that the shedding of British blood by
British soldiers may be averted, as, thank God, it has been
successfully averted in South Wales.

UNEMPLOYMENT INSURANCE

22 May 1911

House of Commons

*Churchill felt passionately the need to provide the breadwinners in
every family in Britain with a safeguard against the risk of
unemployment. He and the Chancellor of the Exchequer, David
Lloyd George, were the principal architects of this far-reaching
measure of social reform.*

There is no proposal in the field of politics that I care more about
than this great insurance scheme, and what I should like to say is that
there must be no delay in carrying the unemployment insurance any
more than in carrying the invalidity insurance. Strong as are the
arguments for bringing forward invalidity insurance, they are no less
strong – in fact, they are even stronger – for unemployment
insurance. A few years ago everybody was deeply impressed with the
unsatisfactory condition of affairs which left our civilisation open to

challenge in this respect, namely, that a man who was willing to work, and who asked that his needs might be met, could not find the means either of getting work or being provided for. That could not but make thinking men uncomfortable and anxious. Providence has ordained that human beings should have short memories, and pain and anxiety are soon forgotten. But are we always to oscillate between panic and torpor?

People talk of the improvidence of the working man. No doubt he has to bear his responsibility, but how can you expect a working man who has few pleasures and small resources, and with the constant strain that is put upon him, to scan trade cycles and to discern with the accuracy of Board of Trade officials the indications and fluctuations of world-wide markets. His failure to do so is excusable. But what can be said of the House of Commons? We have the knowledge and the experience, and it is our duty to think of the future. It is our duty to prepare and to make provision for those for whom we are responsible. What could be said for us, and what could excuse our own improvidence if the next depression found us all unprepared? There is something to be said for the working man who does not provide against unemployment. It may not fall upon him. The great majority of working men will not become unemployed in the insured trades. A working man may escape, but the State will not escape, and the House of Commons will not escape. The problem will come back to the House of Commons as sure as death and quite as cruel, and then it will be too late. It is no use attempting to insure against unemployment when it is upon you and holds you in its grip. There is no use going round then to unemployed working men and asking them to insure against unemployment. It is only in those good years that we can make provision to secure the strength of the fund which will enable us to face the lean years. All our calculations are based upon taking good years with the bad. We must begin now while unemployment is not a feature of our political life and discussion. We must begin now if the fund is to begin strong. We owe a great deal to the Chancellor of the Exchequer in connection with this great scheme. He has devised it and made it possible in the public life of this country. He has afforded us something which does give common ground for all our best efforts, and I think it will be found one of the strongest forces for the country to unite upon. There is exhilaration in the study of insurance questions because there is a sense of elaborating new and increased powers which have been devoted to the service of mankind. It is not only a question of order in the face of confusion. It is not only a question of collective strength of the nation to render effective the thrift and the exertions of the individual, but we bring in the magic of averages to the aid of the million.

NATIONAL RAIL STRIKE

22 August 1911

House of Commons

Industrial unrest continued, but now the Home Secretary and the Government found themselves confronted not by a localised dispute as in the South Wales mines at the beginning of the year, but by a nation-wide strike that theatened to disrupt the entire means of distribution of food and vitally needed supplies to maintain the life of the country. Troops were deployed and in one incident, at Llanelli in Wales, four people were killed.

I have a right to ask the House to look at the emergency with which we were faced, and which alone would justify the strong and unusual measures which we thought it necessary to take. Let the House realise it. In that great quadrilateral of industrialism, from Liverpool and Manchester on the west to Hull and Grimsby on the east, from Newcastle down to Birmingham and Coventry in the south – in that great quadrilateral which, I suppose, must contain anything between 15 to 20 millions of persons, intelligent, hard-working people, who have raised our industry to the forefront of the world's affairs – it is practically certain that a continuance of the railway strike would have produced a swift and certain degeneration of all the means, of all the structure, social and economic, on which the life of the people depends. If it had not been interrupted it would have hurled the whole of that great community into an abyss of horror which no man can dare to contemplate. . . .

I was criticised very severely at the beginning of the year for trying to deal with the difficulties and troubles on the South Wales coal field without using the military forces. I think the House will admit that on that occasion, at any rate, I strained every effort in my power, ran considerable risk, and put the country to considerable expense, to try to substitute other means of maintaining order for the employment of the military forces. I can assure the House that the feelings with which I acted then have never departed from my mind. But Tonypandy was a small affair and produced no great national reaction, and when that took place we had other resources available. I had it within my power – by a very unusual step, I admit – to send a thousand, or, if necessary, two thousand Metropolitan Police to South Wales to stand between the people and the troops, and to put off the employment of the military to the last minute. But on this occasion, with the whole country in a state of disturbance, with disorder actually breaking out in scores of places, the Metropolitan Police would have been totally inadequate to render any assistance to the local forces. Even if they had been adequate, not one single man could be spared from his duty in the Metropolis. . . .

It is quite idle for anyone to pretend that the strike was conducted peacefully and without violence. Even in the forty-eight hours which it lasted serious riots occurred in four or five places, and minor riots in twenty or more places. There were six or more attacks on railway stations, and a very great many on signal-boxes all along the line. I need not enlarge on the peril of driving people out of the signal-boxes at a time when even a few trains were running. There were nine attempts to damage the permanent way, of which we have a record at present, or to wreck trains, or to tamper with points. There were a great number of cases, almost innumerable in fact, of attempts to stop trains, and to stone them. I do not suppose the people of this country realise that these are a class of offences that the law says are punishable with penal servitude, up to penal servitude for life. There were many cases of telegraph and signal wires being cut. . . .

The policy which we have pursued throughout was wherever soldiers were sent to send plenty, so that there could be no mistake about the obvious ability of the authorities to maintain order, and so that the soldiers themselves could be in sufficient force to do what was necessary without taking advantage of the terrible weapons which modern science had placed in their hands. That decision has been taken with a view to the prevention of loss of life. I believe that it has achieved the results which we had in view. Some loss of life has, unhappily, occurred. In what the hon. Gentleman the Member for Leicester calls 'the reckless employment of force', about twenty shots, carefully counted, have been fired with serious intent. Four or five persons have been killed by the military. The House sees these instances chronicled everywhere today. Their painful effect is fresh in our minds. What is not seen, what cannot be measured, is how many lives were saved and how many tragedies and sufferings were averted

– that can never be known! But there are some things which indicate how great are the benefits which have been derived from the maintenance of order by the military forces. We know that people die from many causes. The death-rate in Liverpool has doubled during the course of these troubles. It is a death-rate which has not fallen upon those who live in the Toxteth district. It is contributed by the working-class children, who have suffered in the course of these disputes, and who would have suffered if the evils of the cessation of industry and of the stoppage of food supplies had been added to those of anarchy and riot.

The House should remember that the Llanelli rioters, left to themselves, with no intrusion of the police, and no assistance from the military for some hours, in a few streets of the town during the evening wrought in their drunken frenzy more havoc to life and limb, shed more blood, produced more serious injury among themselves, than all the 50,000 soldiers who have been employed on strike duty all over the country during the last few days. That is the answer which I make to the criticisms and the attacks of the hon. Gentleman the Member for Leicester. I say on behalf of the Government that we will cheerfully, confidently, face any reproaches, attacks or calumniations which anger may create, or malice may keep alive, because, as trustees for the people, responsible for their welfare and for their safety, thinking only of that and of their vital needs, we tried to do our duty.

'THE MAINTENANCE OF NAVAL SUPREMACY IS OUR WHOLE FOUNDATION'

9 November 1911

The Lord Mayor's Banquet, The Guildhall, London

Deteriorating relations between France and Germany, combined with a major expansion of the German Navy and the unexpected appearance of the German gunboat Panther *off the Moroccan port of Agadir in July, prompted anxieties in London. Winston Churchill, who had circulated to Cabinet colleagues a remarkable and detailed memorandum entitled 'Military Aspects of the Continental Problem', was, in late October abruptly moved to the post of First Lord of the*

Admiralty, where for the next four years he would have full charge of the Royal Navy.

The navy is strong – we have got to keep it strong – (*loud and prolonged cheers*), – strong enough, that is, to use for all that it may have to do. And not only strong but ready, instantly ready, to put forth its greatest strength to the best possible advantage. . . . But here let me say a few words of the utmost plainness. Our naval preparations are necessarily based upon the naval preparations of other Powers. It would be affectation – and quite a futile kind of affectation – to pretend that the sudden and rapid growth of the German navy is not the main factor in our determination whether in regard to expenditure or new construction. To disguise this would be to do less than justice to the extraordinary and prodigious develop-ments which have resulted from German energy and German science in recent years. It would further be foolish to deny the plain truth that naval competition between these two mighty Empires – who all the time have such enormous common interests, who all the time have no natural cause for quarrel – it would be foolish to deny that naval competition between them lies at the foot and in the background of almost every difficulty which has baffled the earnest efforts which are repeatedly made – and in which the city of London has taken a noble part – to arrive at really friendly feelings between the two countries. While that competition continues every element of distrust and unrest is warm and active, and one evil leads to another in a long and ugly concatenation. We are not so arrogant as to suppose that the blame and the error which follow so often on human footsteps lies wholly on one side. But the maintenance of naval supremacy is our whole foundation. Upon it stands not the Empire only, not merely the great commercial prosperity of our people, not merely a fine place in the world's affairs. Upon our naval supremacy stands our lives and the freedom we have guarded for nearly a thousand years.

Next year the Navy Law – which when completed will give Germany a magnificent and formidable fleet, second only to our own – next year the law prescribes that the limit of expansion has been reached and that the annual quota of new ships added to the German navy will fall to a half the quota of recent years. Hitherto that law, as fixed by Parliament, has not been in any way exceeded, and I gladly bear witness to the fact that the statements of the German Ministers about it have been strictly borne out by events. Such is the state of affairs in the world that the mere observance of that law without an increase would come to Europe as a great and sensible relief. We should feel that heavy as naval expenditure will undoubtedly be, the high-water mark at any rate has been reached, and all over the world men would breathe more freely and the nations would enter upon a more trustful and more genial climate of opinion. In this we should readily associate ourselves; and if, on the other hand, my Lord Mayor, the already vast programmes of other Powers for war upon the sea should be swollen by the new and added expansions, that would be a matter of extreme regret to us and other States. But I am bound to say on behalf of His Majesty's Government that of all the states and nations of the world Britain will be found the best able to bear the strain and the last to fail at the call of duty. – (*Cheers.*)

'WHY SHOULD NOT IRELAND HAVE HER CHANCE?'

8 February 1912

Celtic Park Football Ground, Belfast

For more than a generation the 'Irish Question' had been a battleground that bedevilled and, not infrequently, dominated British politics, souring relations between the island of Ireland and the rest of the British Isles. The Liberal Government was determined to grant the Irish 'Home Rule' or self-government, with their own Parliament within the British Empire. Winston Churchill was a foremost proponent of this policy, while the fiercely Protestant Ulstermen of the north of Ireland were strenuously opposed to being placed under the rule of Catholic Dublin. Never shy of going into the lion's den, Churchill – to the fury of the Protestants – addressed a crowd of over 5,000 in the Catholic area of Belfast. Feelings were running so high within the Protestant community that an entire battalion of the Brigade of Guards had to be deployed to ensure his safety.

I am glad to be with you today. Contact with Ireland is contact with history. And how can we tell that this great meeting which is assembled here under circumstances of such peculiar significance this afternoon may not in future years be looked back to as a beneficent landmark in Irish and in British history? (*Cheers.*) I come before you as the representative of a Government which for more than six years has directed the affairs of the State, which has presided over six years of peaceful progress and the six best years in trade which these islands have ever known, and a Government which has passed great legislation, which has had to deal with powerful antagonists, and which has usually succeeded in its undertakings. And I come to you on the eve of a Home Rule Bill. (*Loud and prolonged cheers.*) We intend to place before Parliament our plan for the better government of Ireland. It will be a plan harmonious with Imperial interests – (*hear, hear*), – and we are resolved that it shall be a plan creditable to its authors. (*Cheers.*) We do not desire to be responsible for the fortunes of a measure not seriously intended to become the law of the land. (*Hear, hear.*) We have consulted, and we shall consult fully, with the leaders of Irish public opinion, but the decision rests with us. The bill which we shall introduce, and I believe carry into law – (*cheers*), – will be a bill of a British Government designed to smooth the path of the British Empire, and liberate new forces for its services. (*Hear, hear.*) In making this clear we put no strain upon the confidence of our Irish friends. For more than twenty-five years Home Rule has been the adopted child of the Liberal party – (*cheers*), – and during a whole generation, in office and in Opposition, in good luck or in bad, Liberals have been taught by Mr Gladstone – (*cheers*) – to believe that the best solution of Irish difficulties lies in the establishment of an Irish Parliament with an Executive responsible to it – (*hear, hear*), – and every year the reasons upon which they have relied have been strengthened by new facts and by new experiences, and have marched forward with the general march of events. . . .

A settlement of the long quarrel between the British Government and the Irish people would be to the British Empire a boon and a blessing, a treasure-ship, a wonderful reinforcement, precious beyond compare. . . .

The main argument which all these years has sustained the Home Rule cause has been the continuous and unalterable demand of the Irish people, in an overwhelming majority, through every recognised channel of the national will, for the establishment of an Irish Legislature. The Irish claim has never been fairly treated by the statesmen of Great Britain. They have never tried to deal with Ireland in the spirit in which both great parties face the large problems of the British Empire. And yet, why should not Ireland have her chance? Why should not her venerable nationhood enjoy a recognised and respected existence? Why should not her own distinctive point of view obtain a complete expression? Why should the Empire, why should the world at large, be deprived of a new contribution to the sum of human effort? History and poetry, justice and good sense, alike demand that this race, gifted, virtuous, and brave, which has lived so long and has endured so much, should not, in view of her passionate desire, be left out of the family of nations, and should not be lost forever among the indiscriminated multitudes of men. – (*Cheers.*) What harm could Irish ideas and Irish sentiments and Irish dreams, if given their free play in the Irish Parliament, do to the strong structure of the British power? Would not the arrival of an Irish Parliament upon the brilliantly lighted stage of the modern world be an enrichment and an added glory to the treasures of the British Empire? – (*Cheers.*) . . .

I appeal to Ulster to step forward with noble courage, and by a supreme act of generosity and public spirit to win the great prize of Irish peace for themselves and the world. I have been reminded often and again in the last few weeks of the words Lord Randolph Churchill used more than a quarter of a century ago. The reverence which I feel for his memory and the care with which I have studied his public life make me quite content to leave it to others to judge how far there is continuity between his work and any I have tried to do. I am sure the Liberal party will never become an instrument of injustice and of oppression to the Protestants of Ulster. I know this is a duty in which the people of Ulster must not fail. It is a task and a trust placed upon them in the name of Ireland, in the name of the British Empire, in the name of justice and goodwill to help us all to settle the Irish question wisely and well for ever now. There is the task which history has assigned to them, and it is in a different sense that I accept and repeat Lord Randolph Churchill's words, 'Ulster will fight and Ulster will be right.' Let Ulster fight for the dignity and honour of Ireland. Let her fight for the reconciliation of races and for the forgiveness of ancient wrongs. Let her fight for the unity and consolidation of the British Empire. Let her fight for the spread of charity, tolerance, and enlightenment among men. Then, indeed, 'Ulster will fight and Ulster will be right.' – (*Loud cheers.*)

'WE LIVE IN AN AGE OF INCIPIENT VIOLENCE'

18 March 1912

House of Commons

Churchill took to the Admiralty like a duck to water. Though barely three years before he had been conspiring with Lloyd George in Cabinet to cut back the Admiralty's naval building programme, now that a German threat was evident, he threw himself into the task with relish, making sure that, should war come, the Navy would be ready. In this detailed and masterly speech, he proposes a 'Naval holiday' to Germany, undertaking that Great Britain would lay down no new ships if Germany did the same. If Germany continued building, Britain would outbuild her by 60 per cent each year.

I propose, with the permission of the House, to lay bare to them this afternoon, with perfect openness, the naval situation. It is necessary to do so mainly with reference to one Power. I regret that necessity, but nothing is to be gained by using indirect modes of expression. On the contrary, the Germans are a people of robust minds, whose strong and masculine sense and high courage does not recoil from, and is not offended by, plain and blunt statements of fact, if expressed with courtesy and sincerity. Anyway, I must discharge my duty to the House and the country. The time has come when both nations ought to understand, without ill-temper or disguise, what will be the conditions under which naval competition will be carried on during the next few years. The cost and strength of a navy depend upon two main things: first of all, there is the establishment of ships and men maintained in the various scales of commission; secondly, the rate and amount of new construction by which the existing fleets are renewed or augmented. An increase in the establishment of great Navies like the British and the German Navies does not involve such heavy additions to the annual expenditure as an increase in the new construction. On the other hand, the cost of increases in new construction is confined to the years in which it takes place and comes to an end with the completion of the ships, while increases in the number of men, although comparatively small so far as the cost is concerned in one year, involve charges in pay and pensions which recur year after year for a whole generation. . . .

We have no longer to contemplate as our greatest potential danger, the alliance, junction, and co-operation of two naval Powers of approximately equal strength, with all the weakness and uncertainty inherent in such combinations, but we have had for some time to consider the growth and development of a very powerful homogeneous Navy, manned and trained by the greatest organising people of the world, obeying the authority of a single Government, and concentrated within easy distance of our shores. . . . The actual standard in new construction – I am not speaking of men or establishment – which the Admiralty has, in fact, followed during recent years, has been to develop a 60 per cent superiority in vessels of the 'Dreadnought' type over the German navy on the basis of the existing Fleet Law. There are other and higher standards for the smaller vessels, with which I will not complicate the argument, as they do not greatly affect finance. . . .

Applying the standard which I have outlined to the existing German navy law without any addition, that is to say, two ships a year for the next six years, for that is what the law prescribes, and guarding ourselves very carefully against developments in other countries which cannot now be foreseen, it would appear to be necessary to construct for the next six years four ships, and three ships in alternate years, beginning this year with four. . . .

Let me make clear, however, that any retardation or reduction in German construction will, within certain limits, be promptly followed here, as soon as it is apparent, by large and fully proportioned reductions. For instance, if Germany elected to drop out any one, or even any two, of these annual quotas and to put her money into her pocket for the enjoyment of her people and the development of her own prosperity, we will at once, in the absence of any dangerous development elsewhere not now foreseen, blot out our corresponding quota, and the slowing down by Germany will be accompanied naturally on our larger scale by us. Of course both Great Britain and Germany have to consider, among other things, the building of other Powers, though the lead of both these countries is at present very considerable over any other Power besides each other. Take, as an instance of this proposition which I am putting forward for general consideration, the year 1913. In that year, as I apprehend, Germany will build three capital ships, and it will be necessary for us to build five in consequence. Supposing we were both to take a holiday for that year. Supposing we both introduced a blank page in the book of misunderstanding; supposing that Germany were to build no ships in that year, she would save herself between £6,000,000 and

£7,000,000 sterling. But that is not all. We should not in ordinary circumstances begin our ships until she has started hers. The three ships that she did not build would therefore automatically wipe out no fewer than five British potential super-'Dreadnoughts', and that is more than I expect them to hope to do in a brilliant naval action. As to the indirect results, even from a single year, they simply cannot be measured, not only between our two great brother nations, but to all the world. They are results immeasurable in their hope and brightness. This, then, is the position which we take up, that the Germans will be no gainers, so far as naval power is concerned, over us by any increases they may make, and no losers for the basis I have laid down by any diminution. Here, then, is a perfectly plain and simple plan of arrangement whereby without diplomatic negotiation, without any bargaining, without the slightest restriction upon the sovereign freedom of either Power, this keen and costly naval rivalry can be at any time abated. It is better, I am sure, to put it quite frankly, for the Parliaments and peoples to judge for themselves. . . .

The consequence of defeat at sea are so much greater to us than they would be to Germany or France. There is no similarity between our naval needs and those of the two countries I have mentioned. There is no parity of risk. Our position is highly artificial. We are fed from the sea; we are an unarmed people; we possess a very small Army; we are the only Power in Europe which does not possess a large Army. We cannot menace the independence or the vital interest of any great continental State; we cannot invade any continental State. We do not wish to do so, but even if we had the wish we have not got the power.

These are facts which justify British naval supremacy in the face of the world. If ever any single nation were able to back the strongest fleet with an overwhelming army, the whole world would be in jeopardy, and a catastrophe would swiftly occur. People talk of the proportion which the navies of different countries should bear to the commercial interests of the different nations – the proportion of France, the proportion of Italy, the proportion of Germany – to their respective mercantile marines; but when we consider our naval strength we are not thinking of our commerce, but of our freedom. We are not thinking of our trade, but our lives. Nothing, of course, can make us absolutely safe against combinations which the imagination can summon up. We have faced combinations again and again in the past, and sometimes at heavy odds, but we must never conduct our affairs so that the navy of any single Power would be able to engage us at any single moment, even our least favourable moment, with any reasonable prospect of success. If this is insular arrogance, it is also the first condition of our existence. I am glad to be able to assure the House that no difficulty will be experienced in making arrangements to maintain our relative positions in the near future, and to secure as quickly as we need them adequate margins of safety. I am glad also that these measures will not involve any excessive or disproportionate expense. We do not, of course, require to build any more ships other than those I have referred to under the head of 'new construction'. All we should need to do is to bring, as we require it, and no sooner, a larger proportion of our existing Fleet into a higher status of commission, and consequently of greater readiness. We propose also at the present time, in view of the increases which are in progress, to recast completely the organisation of the Fleet. Under the new organisation the ships available for home defence will be divided into first, second, and third Fleets, the whole three Fleets, comprising eight battle squadrons of eight ships each, together with their attendant cruiser squadrons, flotillas, and all auxiliaries. . . .

I hope the House will discern from the account I have given the general principle of naval administration to which we adhere – homogeneity of squadrons; simplicity of types and classes; modernity of material; concentration in the decisive theatres; constant and instant readiness for war; reliance upon gun power; reliance upon speed; and, above all, reliance upon 136,000 officers and seamen, the pride of our race, and bred from their boyhood up to the permanent service of the sea. These are the principles which we ask the House of Commons to approve. For the rest I have only a word to say.

The spectacle which the naval armaments of Christendom afford at the present time will no doubt excite the curiosity and the wonder of future generations. Here are seen all the polite peoples of the world, as if moved by spontaneous impulse, devoting every year an immense and ever-growing proportion of their wealth, their manhood, and their scientific knowledge to the construction of gigantic military machinery, which is obsolescent as soon as it is created; which falls to pieces almost as soon as it is put together; which has to be continually renewed and replenished on a larger scale; which drains the coffers of every Government; which denies and stints the needs of every people; and which is intended to be a means of protection against dangers which have perhaps no other origin than in the mutual fears and suspicions of men. The most hopeful interpretation which can be placed upon the strange phenomenon is that naval and military rivalries are the modern substitute for what in earlier ages would have been actual wars; and just as credit transactions have in the present day so largely superseded cash payments, so the jealousies and disputes of nations are more and more decided by the mere possession of war power without the necessity for its actual employment. If that were true the grand folly of the twentieth century might be found to wear a less unamiable aspect. Still we cannot conceal from ourselves the fact that we live in an age of incipient violence and strong and deep-seated unrest. The utility of war even to the victor may in most cases be an illusion. Certainly all wars of every kind will be destitute of any positive advantage to the British Empire, but war itself, if ever it comes, will not be an illusion – even a single bullet will be found real enough. The Admiralty must leave to others the task of mending the times in which we live, and confine themselves to the more limited and more simple duty of making quite sure that whatever the times may be our Island and its people will come safely through them.

'AIR POWER!'

10 November 1913

The Lord Mayor's Banquet, The Guildhall, London

Churchill was one of the very first to understand the potential of air power, not just as spotter-aircraft for naval artillery, but on the battlefield as well. He founded the Royal Naval Air Service and, indeed, became an impassioned aviator himself, proud to share the dangers of the early aviators when the art of flying was in its infancy.

Our hearts should go out tonight to those brilliant officers – Commander Samson and his band of brilliant pioneers – to whose enterprise and to whose devotion it is due that in an incredibly short space of time our naval aeroplane service has been raised to that primacy from which it must never be cast down. (*Cheers.*) But that is not enough, and I have come here tonight to tell you that it is not only in naval aeroplanes that we must have superiority. I would venture to submit to this great company assembled that the enduring safety of this country will not be maintained by force of arms unless over the whole sphere of aerial development we are able to make ourselves the first nation. Many difficulties have to be overcome. Other countries have started sooner. The native genius of France, the indomitable perseverance of Germany, have produced results which we at present cannot equal. In order to achieve the position which is necessary the War Office and the Admiralty will have to work together, as they are now working, in the closest intimacy and cooperation. In order to achieve that position you will have to make up your minds to spend year after year your money, and month after month to pay your toll in precious lives. The keenest eye, the surest hand, the most undaunted heart, must be offered and risked and sacrificed in order that we may attain – as we shall undoubtedly attain – that command and perfection in aerial warfare which will be an indispensable element, not only in naval strength, but in national security. (*Loud cheers.*)

'UNCONQUERABLE AND INCOMPARABLE'

4 March 1914

Royal Aero Club dinner, Savoy Hotel, London

At a time that the British War Office's principal thinking still revolved around sending men to war on horseback, the First Lord of the Admiralty, with his boundless energy, was driving forward military aviation and encouraging the development of what he called his 'Land Battleships', later to be known as the 'Tank'. Indeed it was to the tank that Field Marshal Ludendorff was to credit the defeat of the German Armies in 1918.

The progress which has been made in this country in the last few years, and especially in the last year, has been very great. Though we started last we have profited to the full by all that has been discovered in other lands, and we have contributed ourselves, in some important particulars, to the sum of knowledge. Not only with aeroplanes but with airships things are done today which nobody would have thought right or prudent to do twelve months or even nine or six months ago. ... This new art and science of flying is surely one in which Great Britain ought to be able to show herself – I do not say supreme in numbers, but supreme in quality. Perhaps flying is one of the best tests of nationality which exists. It is a combination of science and skill, of organisation and enterprise. The forces in our country are unconquerable and incomparable if they are only properly directed. It has been reserved for us to see flying a commonplace and ordinary event. That is a great fact, because no one can doubt that the development and discovery of the flying art definitely enlarges the boundaries of human activity. One cannot doubt that flying, to judge from the position which it has reached even today, must in the future exercise a potent influence, not only upon the habits of men, but upon the military destinies of states. (*Cheers.*)

'THE WORLD IS ARMED
AS IT WAS NEVER ARMED BEFORE'

17 March 1914

House of Commons

This speech, introducing the Naval Estimates, lasted for over two hours. It was remarkable for its detail, its power and for Churchill's complete mastery both of the subject and the House. The Tory Daily Telegraph, *no friend to the First Lord, described it as 'the longest and perhaps also the most weighty and eloquent speech to which the House of Commons have listened during the present generation'.*

We must begin by recognising how different is the part played by our Navy from that of the navies of every other country. Alone among the great modern States, we can neither defend the soil upon which we live nor subsist upon its produce. Our whole Regular Army is liable to be ordered abroad for the defence of India. The food of our people, the raw material of our industries, the commerce which constitutes our wealth, have to be protected as they traverse thousands of miles of sea and ocean from every quarter of the globe. Here we must consider the disparity of risks and stakes between us and other naval Powers. Defeat to Germany at sea means nothing but loss of the ships sunk or damaged in battle. Behind the German 'Dreadnoughts' stand four and a half million soldiers, and a narrow sea-front bristling with fortresses and batteries. Nothing we could do, after a naval victory, could affect the safety or freedom of a single German hamlet.

Behind the British line of battle are the long, light-defended stretches of the East Coast, our endless trade routes and food routes, our small Army and our vast peaceful population, with their immense possessions. The burden of responsibility laid upon the British Navy is heavy, and its weight increases year by year. All the world is building ships of the greatest power, training officers and men, creating arsenals, and laying broad and deep the foundations of future permanent naval development and expansion. In every country powerful interests and huge industries are growing up, which will render any check or cessation in the growth of navies increasingly difficult as time goes by. Besides the Great Powers, there are many small States who are buying or building great ships of war, and whose vessels may, by purchase, by some diplomatic combination or by duress, be brought into the line against us. None of these Powers need, like us, navies to defend their actual independence or safety. They build them so as to play a part in the world's affairs. It is sport to them. It is life and death to us. These possibilities were described by Lord Crewe in the House of Lords last year. It is not suggested that the whole world will turn upon us, or that our preparations should contemplate such a monstrous contingency. By a sober and modest conduct, by a skilful diplomacy, we can in part disarm and in part divide the elements of potential danger. But two things have to be considered: First, that our diplomacy depends in great part for its effectiveness upon our naval position, and that our naval strength is the one great balancing force which we can contribute to our own safety and to the peace of the world. Secondly, we are not a young people with a blank record and a scanty inheritance. We have won for ourselves, in times when other powerful nations were paralysed by barbarism or internal war, an exceptional share of the wealth and traffic of the world.

We have got all we want in territory, but our claim to be left in undisputed enjoyment of vast and splendid possessions, largely acquired by war and largely maintained by force, is one which often seems less reasonable to others than to us. Further, we have intervened regularly, as it was our duty to do, and as we could not help doing, in the affairs of Europe and of the world, and great advantage to European peace has resulted, even in this last year, from our interference. We have responsibilities in many quarters today. We are far from being detached from the problems of Europe. We have passed through a year of continuous anxiety, and, although

His Majesty's Government believe the foundations of peace among the Great Powers have been strengthened, yet the causes which might lead to a general war have not been removed and often remind us of their presence. There has not been the slightest abatement of naval and military preparation. On the contrary, we are witnessing this year increases of expenditure by Continental Powers in armaments beyond all previous experience. The world is armed as it was never armed before. Every suggestion or arrest or limitation has so far been ineffectual. From time to time awkward things happen, and situations occur which make it necessary that the naval force at our immediate disposal, now in this quarter, now in that, should be rapidly counted up. On such occasions the responsibilities which rest on the Admiralty come home with brutal reality to those who are responsible, and unless our naval strength were solidly, amply, and unswervingly maintained, the Government could not feel that they were doing their duty to the country.

'THE WAR WILL BE LONG AND SOMBRE'

11 September 1914

National Liberal Club, London

On 25 July word reached London of the Austrian ultimatum to Serbia. The next day orders were signalled to the Home Fleet not to disperse following the test mobilisation in which, fortuitously, they had been engaged. By 1 August the Royal Navy was at its battle stations. The critical event came on 3 August with Germany's invasion of Belgium and France. The British Government issued an ultimatum to Germany to respect Belgian neutrality. When the ultimatum expired at midnight on 4 August, the order was flashed from the Admiralty to the British Fleet: 'Commence hostilities against Germany!'

We meet here together in serious times, but I come to you tonight in good heart (*cheers*), and with good confidence for the future and for the task upon which we are engaged. It is too soon to speculate upon the results of the great battle which is waging in France. Everything that we have heard during four long days of anxiety seems to point to a marked and substantial turning of the tide.

We have seen the forces of the French and British Armies strong enough not only to contain and check the devastating avalanche which had swept across the French frontier, but now at last, not for an hour or for a day, but for four long days in succession, it has been rolled steadily back. (*Cheers.*) With battles taking place over a front of 100 or 150 miles one must be very careful not to build high hopes on results which are achieved even in a great area of the field of war. We are not children looking for light and vain encouragement, but men engaged upon a task which has got to be put through. Still, when every allowance has been made for the uncertainty with which these great operations are always enshrouded, I think it only fair and right to say that the situation tonight is better, far better, than cold calculation of the forces available on both sides before the war should have led us to expect at this early stage. (*Cheers.*)

It is quite clear that what is happening now is not what the Germans planned (*laughter*), and they have yet to show that they can adapt themselves to the force of circumstances created by the military power of their enemies with the same efficiency that they have undoubtedly shown in regard to plans long preferred, methodically worked out, and executed with the precision of deliberation.

The battle, I say, gives us every reason to meet together tonight in good heart. But let me tell you frankly that if this battle had been as disastrous as, thank God, it appears to be triumphant, I should come before you with unabated confidence and with the certainty that we have only to continue in our efforts to bring this war to the conclusion which we wish and intend. (*Cheers.*)

We did not enter upon the war with the hope of easy victory; we did not enter upon it in any desire to extend our territory, or to advance and increase our position in the world; or in any romantic desire to shed our blood and spend our money in Continental quarrels. We entered upon this war reluctantly after we had made every effort compatible with honour to avoid being drawn in, and we entered upon it with a full realisation of the sufferings, losses, disappointments, vexations, and anxieties, and of the appalling and sustaining exertions which would be entailed upon us by our action. The war will be long and sombre. It will have many reverses of fortune and many hopes falsified by subsequent events, and we must derive from our cause and from the strength that is in us, and from the traditions and history of our race, and from the support and aid of our Empire all over the world the means to make this country

Winston visits Clementine's munition workers' canteen,
Enfield, North London, 1915.

overcome obstacles of all kinds and continue to the end of the furrow, whatever the toil and suffering may be.

But though we entered this war with no illusions as to the incidents which will mark the progress, as to the ebb and flow of fortune in this and that part of the gigantic field over which it is waged, we entered it, and entered it rightly, with the sure and strong hope and expectation of bringing it to a victorious conclusion. (*Cheers.*) I am quite certain that if we, the people of the British Empire, choose, whatever may happen in the interval, we can in the end make this war finish in accordance with out interests and the interests of civilisation. (*Cheers.*) Let us build on a sure foundation. Let us not be the sport of fortune, looking for victories here and happy chances there; let us take measures, which are well within our power, which are practical measures, measures which we can begin upon at once and carry through from day to day with surety and effect. Let us enter upon measures which in the long run, whatever the accidents and incidents of the intervening period may be, will secure us that victory upon which our life and existence as a nation not less than the fortune of our Allies and of Europe absolutely depends. (*Cheers.*)

THE DARDANELLES

5 June 1915

Dundee

Appalled at the prospect of British soldiers dying in their hundreds of thousands to gain a few hundred yards on the Western Front, where the trenches stretched from the Swiss Alps to the North Sea, Churchill was convinced there must be some better way of attacking Germany than 'chewing barbed wire' in Flanders. Accordingly he set his naval experts to work to devise a plan for seizing the Dardanelles on the Gallipoli Peninsula in the Eastern Mediterranean with the aim of knocking Germany's ally, Turkey, out of the war, linking up with Russia and mounting a joint attack on Germany from the east. However, due to inadequate military support by the War Office, the attack stalled and Churchill's deputy, the volatile Admiral Lord Fisher, resigned in May 1915, triggering a ministerial crisis. The

Government was reconstituted as a coalition, including the Conserva-
tives. Their price was the removal of the First Lord from his post at
the Admiralty. Churchill was devastated. He later remarked, 'At a
moment when every fibre of my being was inflamed to action, I was
forced to remain a spectator of the tragedy.'

I thought it right to take an opportunity of coming here to my
constituency in view of all the events which have recently taken
place, and also of the fact that considerably more than a year has
passed since I have had the opportunity of speaking in Dundee. I
have not come here to trouble you with personal matters, or to
embark on explanations or to indulge in reproaches or recrimina-
tions. In wartime a man must do his duty as he sees it, and take his
luck as it comes or goes. I will not say a word here or in Parliament
which I cannot truly feel will have a useful bearing upon the only
thing that matters, upon the only thing I care about, and the only
thing I want you to think about – namely, the waging of victorious
war upon the enemy. (*Cheers.*)

I was sent to the Admiralty in 1911, after the Agadir crisis had
nearly brought us into war, and I was sent with the express duty laid
upon me by the Prime Minister to put the Fleet in a state of instant
and constant readiness for war in case we were attacked by
Germany. (*Cheers.*) Since then, for nearly four years, I have borne the
heavy burden of being, according to the time-honoured language of
my patent, 'responsibile to Crown and Parliament for all the business
of the Admiralty', and when I say responsible, I have been
responsible in the real sense, that I have had the blame for everything
that has gone wrong. (*Laughter and cheers.*) These years have
comprised the most important period in our naval history – a period
of preparation for war, a period of vigilance and mobilisation, and a
period of actual war under conditions of which no man has any
experience. I have done my best – (*cheers*) – and the archives of the
Admiralty will show in the utmost detail the part I have played in all
the great transactions that have taken place. It is to them I look for
my defence.

I look also to the general naval situation. The terrible dangers of
the beginning of the war are over. The seas have been swept clear: the
submarine menace has been fixed within definite limits; the personal
ascendancy of our men, the superior quality of our ships on the high
seas, has been established beyond doubt or question. (*Cheers.*) Our
strength has greatly increased, actually and relatively from what it
was in the beginning of the war, and it grows continually every day

by leaps and bounds in all the classes of vessels needed for the special purpose of the war. Between now and the end of the year, the British Navy will receive reinforcements which would be incredible if they were not actual facts. Everything is in perfect order. Nearly everything has been foreseen, all our supplies, stores, ammunition, and appliances of every kind, our supplies and drafts of officers and men – all are there. Nowhere will you be hindered. You have taken the measure of your foe, you have only to go forward with confidence. (*Cheers.*) On the whole surface of the seas of the world no hostile flag is flown. (*Loud cheers.*)

In that achievement I shall always be proud to have had a share. My charge now passes to another hand, and it is my duty to do everything in my power to give to my successor loyal support in act, in word, and in thought. (*Cheers.*). . .

The Army of Sir Ian Hamilton, the Fleet of Admiral de Robeck, are separated only by a few miles from a victory such as this war has not yet seen. When I speak of victory, I am not referring to those victories which crowd the daily placards of any newspapers. I am speaking of victory in the sense of a brilliant and formidable fact, shaping the destinies of nations and shortening the duration of the war. Beyond those few miles of ridge and scrub on which our soldiers, our French comrades, our gallant Australians, and our New Zealand fellow-subjects are now battling, lie the downfall of a hostile empire, the destruction of an enemy's fleet and army, the fall of a world-famous capital, and probably the accession of powerful Allies. The struggle will be heavy, the risks numerous, the losses cruel; but victory when it comes will make amends for all. There never was a great subsidiary operation of war in which a more complete harmony of strategic, political, and economic advantages has combined, or which stood in truer relation to the main decision which is in the central theatre. Through the narrows of the Dardanelles and across the ridges of the Gallipoli Peninsula lie some of the shortest paths to a triumphant peace.

'TAKE CONSTANTINOPLE ... WHILE TIME REMAINS'

15 November 1915

House of Commons

On 11 November the Dardanelles Committee was replaced by a War Committee, from which Churchill was excluded. The Government favoured evacuating the Gallipoli Peninsula. Accordingly, Churchill resigned from the Government. Just 40 years old and convinced that his political career was over, he announced his intention to join the Army in Flanders and fight in the trenches as a soldier. His wife, Clementine, remarked, 'I thought he would never get over the Dardanelles; I thought he would die of grief.' Here he defends his actions at the Admiralty.

The essence of an attack upon the Gallipoli Peninsula was speed and vigour. We could reinforce from the sea more quickly than the Turks could reinforce by land, and we could, therefore, afford to renew our attacks until a decision was obtained. To go slow, on the other hand – to leave long intervals between the attacks, so as to enable the Turks to draw reinforcements from their whole Empire, and to refresh and replace their troops again and again – was a great danger. Secondly, on the Gallipoli Peninsula, our Army has stood all the summer within a few miles of a decisive victory. There was no other point on any of the war fronts, extending over hundreds of miles, where an equal advance would have produced an equal, or even a comparable, strategic result. It has been proved in this war that good troops, properly supported by artillery, can make a direct advance of two or three miles in the face of any defence. The advance, for instance, which took Neuve Chapelle, or Loos, or Souchez, if it had been made on the Gallipoli Peninsula would have settled the fate of the Turkish Army on the promontory, would probably have decided the whole operations, might have determined the attitude of the Balkans, might have cut Germany from the east, and might have saved Serbia.

All through this year I have offered the same counsel to the Government – undertake no operation in the west which is more costly to us in life than to the enemy; in the east, take Constantinople; take it by ships if you can; take it by soldiers if you must; take it by whichever plan, military or naval, commends itself to your military experts, but take it, and take it soon, and take it while time remains. The situation is now entirely changed, and I am not called upon to offer any advice upon its new aspects. But it seems to me that if there were any operations in the history of the world which, having been begun, it was worth while to carry through with the utmost vigour and fury, with a consistent flow of reinforcements, and an utter disregard of life, it was the operations so daringly and brilliantly begun by Sir Ian Hamilton in the immortal landing of the 25th April.

2. Oblivion and Redemption 1916–29

Following the failure of the Dardanelles landings in the Eastern Mediterranean, for which Churchill was made the scapegoat, he was in May 1915 forced to stand down as First Lord of the Admiralty, where he had been at the heart of the direction of Britain's war effort on the high seas. Convinced his political career was in ruins and describing himself as 'the escaped scapegoat', in early 1916 he forsook the House of Commons for the trenches of Flanders, to serve as a soldier in the front line, where he commanded the 6th Battalion of the Royal Scots Fusiliers. It was not until July 1917 that he returned to Cabinet office, when appointed Minister of Munitions by the new Prime Minister, David Lloyd George. Thereafter he served as Secretary of State for War and Air, as well as Colonial Secretary.

However, increasingly out of sympathy with the Liberal Party over its ever closer alignment with the fledgling Labour Party, he decided to forsake their ranks and 'cross the floor' for a second time.

Churchill was amazed when, in October 1924, the newly elected Conservative Prime Minister, Stanley Baldwin, invited him to become Chancellor of the Exchequer, an office which his father had previously held. Soon thereafter he returned to the Conservative fold. His tenure at the Treasury was most notable for Britain's return to the Gold Standard, but the timing proved unfortunate, given the impending Great Crash of 1929 and the Great Depression that was to follow.

'THE HARDEST OF TESTS MEN HAVE
EVER BEEN CALLED UPON TO BEAR'

23 May 1916

House of Commons

After spending several months in the trenches of Flanders under the fire of the enemy, Churchill returned to the House of Commons to give a soldier's-eye view of the conflict. But he sat isolated on the Opposition benches, facing the Liberal-Conservative coalition and his words went largely unheeded.

The first thing that strikes a visitor to our Armies in France or in Flanders – and I make no doubt that our armies in the East exhibit a similar condition – is the very large number of officers and men in the prime of their military manhood who never, or only very rarely, go under the fire of the enemy. In fact, you perceive one of the clearest and grimmest class distinctions ever drawn in this world – the distinction between the trench and the non-trench population. All our soldiers, all our officers, are brave and honest men. All are doing their duty, a necessary duty, and are ready to do any other duty which they may be asked to perform. But the fact remains that the trench population lives almost continuously under the fire of the enemy. It returns again and again, after being wounded twice and sometimes three times, to the front and to the trenches, and it is continually subject, without respite, to the hardest of tests that men have ever been called upon to bear, while all the time the non-trench population scarcely suffers at all, and has good food and good wages, higher wages in a great many cases than are drawn by the men under fire every day, and their share of the decorations and rewards is so disproportionate that it has passed into a byword. I wish to point out to the House this afternoon that the part of the Army that really counts for ending the war is this killing, fighting, suffering part.

This war proceeds along its terrible path by the slaughter of infantry. It is this infantry which it is most difficult to replenish, which is continually worn away on both sides, and though all the other services of the Army are necessary to its life, and to its maintenance – and I am not in the least disparaging their importance and their value – it is this fighting part that is the true measure of your military power, and the only true measure. All generals in the field make their calculations in rifles, but my right hon. friend knows well how immense is the disparity between rifle strength and rations strength. We have suffered together disappointment in hearing that armies, so imposing on paper, so large in numbers when they left our shores, were whittled down by calculations of rifle strength by the generals on the spot to two-thirds or even a lesser fraction of their total number. Like him, I have rebelled against that calculation in the past, but, nevertheless, I have become convinced that it is really the true and proper method of computing your war effort at a given moment. Every measure which you can take to increase the proportion of rifle strength to rations strength will be a direct addition to your war power, and will be just as direct an addition to your war power as if you ordered new classes of recruits to join the Colours. Nay, more, it will be a net addition and not a gross addition to your war power. If I may use the language of business – and after all this war is becoming in many aspects to resemble a vast though hideous business – I would say that the rifle strength actually under the fire of the enemy is the dividend. Everything else of the whole vast military effort may be classed as working expenditure, the result of which is the production of war power. The object of the Army is to produce war power. Everything else that takes place leading to the lining up of men in battle is the preliminary steps by which the final result is achieved.

'GRAPPLING WITH THE MOST TERRIBLE FOE'

31 May 1916

House of Commons

Just one month later the Battle of the Somme was to begin. On the first day – 1 July 1916 – the British Army sustained its greatest ever single-day loss: 55,000 men dead or wounded, and that was just the beginning. Churchill was proud to share the dangers of those courageous men in the front line, but he was bitter at having no hand

*in the direction either of policy or strategy. The 9th Scottish Division,
to which he makes reference, was the one in which he commanded
the 6th Battalion of the Royal Scots Fusiliers.*

At one end of our military system we have the country yielding
willingly, though not without great difficulty, inconvenience, real
hardship, much dislocation and risk, its whole manhood, its last
reserves, or almost its last reserve, including men who have hitherto
been kept back in some cases through very good reasons, but who
must now go in spite of their reasons. You have that at one end of
your military system. At the other end you have a comparatively, I
would almost say an astonishingly, small proportion of war-worn
soldiers who compose the fighting battalions, and they are heavily
burdened, severely tried and short-handed, who go back again and
again month after month, almost year after year, and between these
two you have an enormous multitude of khaki figures collected with
great difficulty, maintained at heavy expense; the greater part of
them willing and eager to take part in the war, but through want of
management or organisation, or defective organisation, are prevented from being useful either in industry or in the field. That is the
broad outline of my case, and it is so important that I am bound to
press it and labour it in bringing it before the House of Commons.

What is the proportion of rifle strength to ration strength? The
Under-Secretary said euphemistically that there was some disparity
between ration and rifle strength, and there always must be. Let us
see what it is a little more closely. I shall keep on very broad and
general lines in this respect, but I think it is absolutely necessary that
the House and the country should follow the main outlines of Army
organisation. After all, the electorate and hon. Members who
represent it ought to be as familiar with the details of Army
organisation as we used to be in peace-time with the details of any of
the old political controversies here. Broadly speaking, I believe the
following to be correct. I am speaking very broadly, allowing large
margins for everything I say. Half the total ration strength of the
British Army is at home, and half abroad. Of the half abroad, half of
it fights and half does not fight. Of the half that fights about three-
quarters fights as infantry in the trenches and in the assaults, and
nearly all the losses fall on them. That is three-quarters of the half of
the half, and the other quarter may consist of the artillery and other
services who come under fire and who render the most effective
service against the enemy, but who do not suffer to anything like the
same extent. In other words, on this calculation, which is a very

liberal one, very much on the other side, for every five men who are taken from the nation at one end – I would almost say out of every six men who are taken from the nation at one end – one effective infantry rifle is produced over the parapet at the other end. . . .

Two bold conclusions may be drawn which I will submit to the Committee. First of all, that the number and proportion of those who actually fight ought to be greatly raised, and that it should be greatly raised by a comparatively small addition to the total aggregate; and secondly, that so far as possible able-bodied men, and especially young men employed in all those other much more numerous parts of the military organisation, ought to take their turn at the front, and not leave it to the same lot to go on continuously, and come back wounded time after time, until they are finally knocked out. In my own experience it happened to my battalion to receive a draft of thirty-five men, out of which twenty-six had been previously wounded, some of them very severely wounded, and this at a time when you can see with your own eyes going about this country that there are millions of men here and elsewhere who have never yet heard the whistle of a bullet. There are more than a million – at any rate, I should think more than two millions – of men who have not heard the whistle of a bullet. . . .

I will tell the House the story of the 9th Scottish Division. This division was the premier division of Scotland, the first division of the New Army to be raised by Scotland at the beginning of the war. In the Battle of Loos, this division, with the other Scottish division, the 15th, played a very notable part. Out of the 9,500 infantry who advanced to the attack 6,000 were killed and wounded in the battle. Some of the battalions lost three-fourths of their strength, but nearly all succeeded in achieving the task which was set them of gaining the positions – some of the most important positions – and they were only lost when they were subsequently handed over at a later stage to other troops. One battalion of this division – a battalion of the Cameron Highlanders – went into action about 850 strong. Thirty officers, the colonel, the Cameron of Lochiel, the adjutant, and 110 men, the survivors alone out of that 850, took and held the objective which they were set to take. Four successive lines were swept away, but the fifth line went on without the slightest hesitation. With these troops shattered in the first day's battle, the remnant of 1,200, collected out of the brigade of 4,000, were asked two days afterwards to make another attack, and they went over the parapet and renewed the attack with the utmost *élan* and good spirit.

You talk about the charge of Balaclava and the charge of the

Fusiliers at Albuera, but those deeds pale before the deeds which have been done by the new divisions raised in the British Army. . . .

There can be no justification for retaining great masses of troops in this country either in divisional formations or as coast watchers. A reasonable provision must be made for a mobile and central force – that is a matter, of course, entirely for the Executive – but for the rest, cannot the Volunteers be made to play their part in subsidiary duties, and release men of military age wherever they may be found for the purpose of supplementing the fighting battalions?

To sum up, I submit to the Government, which has absolute power in all these matters – for after all the House of Commons has very little power and can only place matters before the Administration – that with a proper use of our resources in manpower it would be possible immediately to raise all fighting units to full strength. It would be possible in a few months to raise all infantry battalions in the field to 1,200 strong, thus adding at a stroke 40 per cent or 50 per cent to the rifle strength, and at the same time it would be possible to arrange for a regular system of rotation – I do not say a universal system, but a regular instituted system of rotation by which every young man so far as possible took his share with the fighting battalion and every worn-out soldier had a turn of rest. Next year it would be possible with a proper use of our resources – if the military situation renders it necessary, and if you look far enough ahead and act in time – to increase the scale of our military operations and either to add an extra infantry brigade to each division, or to embark upon that greater task which we must not exclude from the possibility of practical politics of raising the total number of divisions from seventy to the ideal at which we should aim of a hundred. We cannot survey the field of war today without profound realisation of the magnitude of the task before us. The continuing power of the enemy, which I mentioned on another occasion, on every front is proved to us by every telegram that comes in. We feel ourselves grappling with the most terrible foe that ever menaced freedom. Our whole life energies are required. We are trying our best, but are we at present developing the full results of the great effort made by the nation? I cannot think so. . . . No one who subjects the present organisation of the Army, either in the field or at home, to searching and dispassionate scrutiny can believe that every measure to that end is being taken at the present time.

'PERILS, SORROWS AND SUFFERINGS
WE HAVE NOT DESERVED'

10 December 1917

Corn Exchange, Bedford

The year 1917 was the grimmest of the Great War. The morale of the French Army was damaged by the failure of the Nivelle offensive and the British Army's attack at Passchendaele had become bogged down in mud and barbed wire. On the Eastern front, the great Russian Army had collapsed, undermined by the Communist October Revolution. The only bright prospect was the entry into the war of the United States.

Two months ago I stated in London that the war was entering upon its sternest phase, but I must admit that the situation at this moment is more serious than it was reasonable two months ago to expect. The country is in danger. It is in danger as it has not been since the Battle of the Marne saved Paris and the Battle of Ypres and of the Yser saved the Channel ports. The cause of the Allies is now in danger. The future of the British Empire and of democracy and of civilisation hangs and will continue to hang for a considerable period in a balance and an anxious suspense.

It is impossible, even if it were desirable, to conceal these facts from our enemies. It would be folly not to face them boldly ourselves. Indeed, I am inclined to think that most people in this country, in this wonderful island, are already facing squarely and resolutely the facts of the situation. We read in the newspapers and in some speeches which are delivered of appeals to the Government to tell the truth about the war, to tell the truth about our war aims, but as a matter of fact the great bulk of the British people have got a very clear idea of how we stand and a still clearer idea of what we are aiming at. (*Hear, hear.*)

Anyone can see for himself what has happened in Russia. Russia has been thoroughly beaten by the Germans. Her great heart has been broken not only by German might but by German intrigue, not only by German steel but by German gold. Russia has fallen on the ground prostrate, in exhaustion and in agony. No one can tell what fearful vicissitudes will come to Russia or how or when she will arise, but arise she will. (*Cheers.*)

It is this melancholy event which has prolonged the war, that has robbed the French and the British and the Italian armies of the prize that was perhaps almost within their reach this summer. It is this event, and this event alone, that has exposed us to the perils and sorrows and sufferings which we have not deserved, which we cannot avoid, but under which we shall not bend. . . .

Our people are war-hardened and not war-weary. We have all the means of doing our part in bringing about victory. (*Cheers.*) But there is something much greater than all this. If Russia has, for the time being, fallen out of our ranks, the United States of America have entered them. (*Cheers.*) The great Republic of the West, more than a hundred millions, of the most educated and scientific democracy in the world are coming to our aid, marching along all the roads of America, steering across the ocean, organising their industries for war, spending their wealth like water, developing slowly but irresistibly and unceasingly the most gigantic, elemental forces ever yet owned and applied to the triumph of a righteous cause. The appearance of this mighty champion at the other end of the world has restored to us the fortunes of the war, and has repaired and more than repaired all that we have suffered in the loss of Russia. (*Cheers.*)

The intervention of America means the uniting of practically the whole world, and the whole of its resources against the German Power. It cannot fail in the end to be decisive. (*Cheers.*) It will secure us victory.

'THE WAR IS WON!'

16 December 1918

Australia and New Zealand Luncheon Club,
Connaught Rooms, London

Just five weeks earlier, on 11 November 1918, the greatest war in the history of the world had come to an end. Churchill thanks the loyal Dominions of the Commonwealth and Empire, from Canada to India, South Africa to Australia and New Zealand, each one of which without being asked, had rallied to the defence of the

Motherland. Here he salutes the 'Anzacs', the Australia/New Zealand Army Corps.

The war is won. (*Cheers.*) All our dreams have come true. We have reached the end of the long, long trail. And what a victory! I do not know what your feelings are, but I can tell you for myself that in the five weeks which have passed since firing stopped on the Western front I have felt a new and fresh inward satisfaction every day in contemplating the magnitude and the splendour of our achievement and our success. (*Cheers.*) It grows upon one like a living fire burning within. It fills our hearts with pride and with thankfulness that we have lived in such a time and belong to such a race. (*Cheers.*)

When we look back on the time before the war, we see how easy it was for foreigners to think that the British Empire was only a figment of the imagination – we see how easy it was for them to think that we were given over to ease, slothfulness, luxury, and party politics, that we were a great people whose climax had been reached at the battles of Trafalgar and Waterloo, and that we were now passing placidly down the slope which so many other great Empires and nations had trod. I do not blame them. I do not blame these foreign nations, friends, neutrals, or foes, for their great miscalculation. But what a miscalculation it was! This war has proved the soundness of the British race at every point. There has been no test to which they have not been subjected – and extraordinarily varied those tests have been – but there has been no test in which the stock has not been found absolutely sound. We see the victories and the prodigies performed by our armies; the great work of the British Navy, on which all depended. (*Cheers.*) But it is British institutions that have triumphed just as much as martial deeds by flood and field and in the air. All over the world, in every country, it is to the British way of doing things that they are looking now.

Of all the tests of the soundness of our institutions nothing can equal that proof which was given when the great communities, the Dominions of the Crown over the seas, so many thousands of miles from the area of conflict, enjoying absolute freedom, enjoying in all senses an absolute practical independence, under no pressure of any kind, but with a pure, spontaneous feeling, obeying no call but that of the blood – when these great Dominions, without a moment's hesitation, entered a quarrel, as to the beginning of which they could not necessarily have been consulted, and hastened to pour out their blood and treasure, and raise themselves in the struggle of arms to a foremost place. That gift which came back to us in this old land, in this small island, from the principles of freedom, that is one of the great and amazing proofs of the soundness of British institutions which the Great War has revealed.

'BOLSHEVIST ATROCITIES'

11 April 1919

Aldwych Club Luncheon, Connaught Rooms, London

As a civil war raged in Russia between the 'White' (or Tsarist) Russians and the 'Reds' (Communists), Churchill did what he could to get munitions and supplies to the anti-Soviet forces. He later admitted that he had 'tried to strangle Bolshevism in its cradle'.

The British Government has issued a White-book giving a vivid picture, based on authentic evidence, of Bolshevist atrocities. Tyranny presents itself in many forms. The British nation is the foe of tyranny in every form. That is why we fought Kaiserism and that is why we would fight it again. That is why we are opposing Bolshevism. Of all tyrannies in history the Bolshevist tyranny is the worst, the most destructive, and the most degrading. It is sheer humbug to pretend that it is not far worse than German militarism. The miseries of the Russian people under the Bolshevists far surpass anything they suffered even under the Tsar. The atrocities by Lenin and Trotsky are incomparably more hideous, on a larger scale, and more numerous than any for which the Kaiser himself is responsible. There is this also to be remembered – whatever crimes the Germans have committed, and we have not spared them in framing our indictment, at any rate they stuck to their Allies. They misled them, they exploited them, but they did not desert, or betray them. It may have been honour among thieves, but that is better than dishonour among murderers.

Lenin and Trotsky had no sooner seized on power than they dragged the noble Russian nation out of the path of honour and let loose on us and our Allies a whole deluge of German reinforcements, which burst on us in March and April of last year. Every British and French soldier killed last year was really done to death by Lenin and Trotsky, not in fair war, but by the treacherous desertion of an ally without parallel in the history of the world. There are still Russian Armies in the field, under Admiral Koltchak and General Deniken, who have never wavered in their faith and loyalty to the Allied cause, and who are fighting valiantly and by no means unsuccessfully against that foul combination of criminality and animalism which constitutes the Bolshevist régime. We are helping these men, within the limits which are assigned to us, to the very best of our ability. We are helping them with arms and munitions, with instructions and technical experts, who volunteered for service. It would not be right for us to send our armies raised on a compulsory basis to Russia. If Russia is to be saved it must be by Russian manhood. But all our hearts are with these men who are true to the Allied cause in their splendid struggle to restore the honour of united Russia, and to rebuild on a modern and democratic basis the freedom, prosperity, and happiness of its trustful and good-hearted people.

FAREWELL TO 'THE BEER OF OLD ENGLAND'

18 July 1919

Mansion House, London

In thanking General Pershing and his fellow Americans for their contribution to securing victory, Churchill commiserates that these gallant men will be returning to a land of Prohibition.

We are all delighted to see General Pershing and his gallant Americans over here. (*Cheers.*) We are passing through a phase of intense rejoicing almost reaching the extremes to which human beings are capable, and the rejoicings after the great war are like everything else in that great war – on a scale and in a degree of intensity in proportion to this unique period. But in all of this rejoicing there is no occasion which has given more real and genuine pleasure to those who have taken part in it than being present here today in the Guildhall and coming here to the hospitable board of the Lord Mayor to welcome General Pershing and the distinguished American General's staff, officers and others whom he has brought with him. (*Cheers.*)

We hope that they will carry away very pleasant memories of their all too brief visit to England. I am emboldened in this hope by a reflection, which came across my mind this morning, when I had the honour of being present at the parade of the American Regiment and of following the Prince of Wales along the line of that magnificent infantry. The solemn thought came across my mind that not one of these magnificent men would in a few weeks have a drop to drink again. (*Laughter.*) And I could not help feeling that among other memories which they will carry back from Europe there will be at least some of them who will preserve an affectionate sentiment for the estaminets and the red wine of France, and perhaps also for the beer of Old England. (*Laughter.*) I even hope, if it is not too sanguine, that in the future some at least of them will be drawn back to this country again and may resume with us, assuming we are still in a state of freedom and independence, the relaxation and indulgences which cheered their lives during the hard days of the war.

'THE JEWS SHOULD HAVE A NATIONAL HOME'

31 March 1921

Reply to a Muslim delegation, Government House, Jerusalem

Churchill, who had returned to Cabinet office as Minister of Munitions at the end of the war, was now Colonial Secretary. In that capacity he had just convened and chaired the Cairo Conference at which, from the ruins of the Ottoman Empire (which had allied itself with Germany), the states of Jordan and Iraq were established under the Hashemite Emirs Abdullah and Feisal. At the same time the boundaries of Biblical Palestine were delineated for the first time. A staunch supporter of the 'Balfour Declaration', Churchill made clear his view that Palestine should be a National Home for the Jews, but not to the exclusion of the Palestinians.

I consider your address partly partisan and incorrect. You ask me to repudiate the Balfour Declaration and stop immigration. This is not in my power and is not my wish. . . . Moreover it is manifestly right that the scattered Jews should have a national centre and a national home in which they might be reunited, and where else but in

Palestine, with which the Jews for 3,000 years have been intimately and profoundly associated? We think it is good for the world, good for the Jews, and good for the British Empire, and it is also good for the Arabs dwelling in Palestine, and we intend it to be so. They shall not be supplanted nor suffer but they shall share in the benefits and the progress of Zionism.

I draw your attention to the second part of the Balfour Declaration emphasising the sacredness of your civil and religious rights. I am sorry you regard it as valueless. It is vital to you, and you should hold and claim it firmly. If one promise stands, so does the other. We shall faithfully fulfil both. . . . Examine Mr Balfour's careful words, Palestine to be 'a national home' not 'the national home', a great difference in meaning.

The establishment of a national home does not mean a Jewish Government to dominate the Arabs. Great Britain is the greatest Muslim State in the world, and is well disposed to the Arabs and cherishes their friendship. . . . You need not be alarmed for the future. Great Britain has promised a fair chance for the Zionist movement, but the latter will succeed only on its merits. . . . We cannot tolerate the expropriation of one set of people by another. The present form of Government will continue for many years. Step by step we shall develop representative institutions, leading to full self-government, but our children's children will have passed away before that is completed.

LENIN

8 June 1921

Chamber of Commerce Luncheon, Manchester

The scale of the wholesale slaughter of millions of their fellow Russians by the Bolshevist rulers of Russia was slowly filtering through to the West.

Some people consider Lenin clever, but we will all agree that he has had the most expensive education. (*Laughter.*) I do not suppose that any man since the beginning of the world has had such a costly education as this gentleman. Probably seven or eight million have lost their lives, and many more have had their lives utterly ruined, in order to teach Monsieur Lenin the rudiments of political economy. (*Laughter.*) He was a backward pupil. He was told that private property existed as the reward of human toil and thrift. He did not believe it. He killed many thousands of people with whom he disagreed, and caused the deaths of many thousands more, in order to find out the truth of that proposition before he came to the conclusion that they were right and he was wrong. After all a man must learn, and it was no doubt a very interesting experiment from his point of view. Monsieur Lenin then turned his attention to currency, and, seeing machines making bank notes, he had a flash of pure Communistic genius. (*Laughter.*) He thought that all he had to do to solve the social problem was to keep the machine going as fast as possible. (*Laughter.*) He thought he had thus found a way of making everybody rich, and of paying every workman several thousands a year. He has destroyed the currency of Russia to such an extent that it is said that if you take a cab in Moscow you have to take another cab to take the bank notes that represented the cabman's fare – (*laughter*) – and he has thus destroyed the vital factor in the means of commerce and exchange between town and country, so that the people of the towns are being starved because they have no products to give to the peasants in exchange for the food they grow. This starvation of the cities of Russia made a great impression on Monsieur Lenin. It ought to have made a great impression on the cities. But he is a backward pupil, and his education is only improving very slowly. He has not started yet on the Ten Commandments – 'Thou shalt not steal', and 'Thou shalt do no murder.' (*Laughter.*) That belongs to a later phase in his education, and, no doubt, it will cost thousands more of lives. As we watch this terrible panorama of Russian misery, let us abstract a moral which should be a guidance and an aid. Russia cannot save herself by her exertion, but she may at least save other nations by her example. The lesson from Russia, writ in glaring letters, is the utter failure of this Socialistic and Communistic theory, and the ruin which it brings to those subjected to its cruel yoke.

'THE CULTURE AND GLORIES OF THE ARAB RACE'

14 June 1921

House of Commons

Even in these early days, Churchill sees the dangers posed by the extremism of Saudi Arabia's Wahabi sect, which in recent decades has been responsible for the spread throughout the Muslim world of thousands of 'madrassas' (religious seminaries) dedicated to the propagation of extremist Muslim fundamentalism, combined with virulent hatred of Western values and culture.

Broadly speaking, there are two policies which can be adopted towards the Arab race. One is the policy of keeping them divided, of discouraging their national aspirations, of setting up administrations of local notables in each particular province or city, and exerting an influence through the jealousies of one tribe against another. That was largely, in many cases, the Turkish policy before the war, and, cynical as it was, it undoubtedly achieved a certain measure of success. The other policy, and the one which, I think, is alone compatible with the sincere fulfilment of the pledges we gave during the war to the Arab race and to the Arab leaders, is an attempt to build up around the ancient capital of Baghdad, in a form friendly to Britain and to her Allies, an Arab State which can revive and embody the old culture and glories of the Arab race, and which, at any rate, will have a full and fair opportunity of doing so if the Arab race shows itself capable of profiting by it. Of these two policies we have definitely chosen the latter.

If you are to endeavour so to shape affairs in the sense of giving satisfaction to Arab nationality, you will, I believe, find that the very best structure around which to build, in fact, the only structure of this kind which is available, is the house and family and following of the Sherif of Mecca. It was King Hussein who, in the crisis of the war, declared war upon the Turks and raised the Arab standard. Around that standard gathered his four capable sons – of whom the Emir Feisal and the Emir Abdulla are the two best known in this country – and many of the principal chiefs and notabilities of the Arab world. With them at our side we fought, and with their aid as a valuable auxiliary Lord Allenby hurled the Turks from Palestine.

Both the Emir Abdulla and the Emir Feisal have great influence in Iraq among the military and also among the religious classes, both Sunni and Shiah. The adherents of the Emir Feisal have sent him an invitation to go to Mesopotamia and present himself to the people and to the assembly which is soon to gather together, and King Hussein has accorded his son permission to accept the invitation. The Emir Abdulla, the elder brother, has renounced his rights and claims. I have caused the Emir Feisal to be informed, in answer to his inquiry, that no obstacle will be placed in the way of his candidature, that he is at liberty to proceed forthwith to Mesopotamia, and that, if he is chosen, he will receive the countenance and support of Great Britain. In consequence, the Emir Feisal has already left Mecca on the 12th of this month, and is now on his journey to Mesopotamia, where he will arrive in about 10 days. We must see how opinion forms itself and what is the view of the National Assembly when it is elected. I cannot attempt to predict the course of events, but I do not hesitate to say that, if the Emir Feisal should be acceptable to the people generally, and to the Assembly, a solution will have been reached which offers, in the opinion of the highest authorities on whom I am relying, the best prospects for a happy and a prosperous outcome.

There has, however, lately arisen in Iraq and particularly in the Province of Basra, a considerable movement in the direction of continuing direct British rule. People always seem to want something different from what is actually being done. When we were giving them direct British rule a few years ago they rebelled against it. Now that we offer them the Arab State which was then demanded so ardently, there is a considerable feeling that perhaps after all British rule will be found to be most stable. It is one of the comparatively few compliments that we have been receiving in this part of the world. I think it reflects very much credit upon Sir Percy Cox that in so short a time he has effected such a considerable change in the public sentiment towards us. But I can hold out no hope that we shall be found willing to continue these direct responsibilities. Our object and our policy is to set up an Arab Government, and to make it take the responsibility, with our aid and our guidance and with an effective measure of our support, until they are strong enough to stand alone, and so to foster the development of their independence as to permit the steady and speedy diminution of our burden. I cannot say in regard to Mesopotamia that there are primary, direct, strategic British interests involved. The defence of India can be better conducted from her own strategic frontier. Mesopotamia is not, like

Egypt, a place which in a strategic sense is of cardinal importance to our interests, and our policy in Mesopotamia is to reduce our commitments and to extricate ourselves from our burdens while at the same time honourably discharging our obligations and building up a strong and effective Arab Government which will always be the friend of Britain and, I will add, the friend of France.

We are leaning strongly to what I may call the Sherifian solution, both in Mesopotamia, to which the Emir Feisal is proceeding, and in Trans-Jordania, where the Emir Abdulla is now in charge. We are also giving aid and assistance to King Hussein, the Sherif of Mecca, whose State and whose finances have been grievously affected by the interruption of the pilgrimage, in which our Mohammedan country-men are so deeply interested, and which we desire to see resumed. The repercussion of this Sherifian policy upon the other Arab chiefs must be carefully watched. In the vast deserts of Arabia, which stretch eastward and north-eastward from the neighbourhood of Mecca to the Persian Gulf and to the boundaries of Mesopotamia, there dwell the peoples of Nejd, powerful nomadic tribes, at the head of whom the remarkable chief Bin Saud maintains himself. This Arab chief has long been in a state of warfare, raid, and reprisal with King Hussein and with his neighbours generally. A large number of Bin Saud's followers belong to the Wahabi sect, a form of Mohammed-anism which bears, roughly speaking, the same relation to orthodox Islam as the most militant form of Calvinism would have borne to Rome in the fiercest times of the religious wars. The Wahabis profess a life of exceeding austerity, and what they practise themselves they rigorously enforce on others. They hold it as an article of duty, as well as of faith, to kill all who do not share their opinions and to make slaves of their wives and children. Women have been put to death in Wahabi villages for simply appearing in the streets. It is a penal offence to wear a silk garment. Men have been killed for smoking a cigarette, and as for the crime of alcohol, the most energetic supporter of the temperance cause in this country falls far behind them. Austere, intolerant, well-armed, and bloodthirsty, in their own regions the Wahabis are a distinct factor which must be taken into account, and they have been, and still are, very dangerous to the holy cities of Mecca and Medina, and to the whole institution of the pilgrimage, in which our Indian fellow-subjects are so deeply concerned.

The Emir Bin Saud has shown himself capable of leading and, within considerable limits, of controlling these formidable sectaries.

'THE DREARY STEEPLES OF FERMANAGH AND TYRONE'

16 February 1922

House of Commons

The Irish Free State Bill, which divided Ireland between 'Loyalist' Ulster in the north and what was to become the Irish Republic in the south, produced great animosity, both in Ireland and in the House of Commons.

Then came the Great War. Every institution, almost, in the world was strained. Great empires have been overturned. The whole map of Europe has been changed. The position of countries has been violently altered. The modes of thought of men, the whole outlook on affairs, the grouping of parties, all have encountered violent and tremendous changes in the deluge of the world, but as the deluge subsides and the waters fall short we see the dreary steeples of Fermanagh and Tyrone emerging once again. The integrity of their quarrel is one of the few institutions that has been unaltered in the cataclysm which has swept the world. That says a lot for the persistency with which Irishmen on the one side or the other are able to pursue their controversies. It says a great deal for the power which Ireland has, both Nationalist and Orange, to lay their hands upon the vital strings of British life and politics, and to hold, dominate, and convulse, year after year, generation after generation, the politics of this powerful country.

CONSERVATIVE ONCE MORE

16 September 1925

Midlands Conservative Club Dinner, Birmingham

In 1922 the wartime coalition government, led by Lloyd George, had been driven from office by the Conservatives, who went on to win a

Electioneering on the way back to Westminster, 1924.

resounding victory. However, just a year later, the new leader of the
Conservative Party called a further election, which led to the
formation of the first Labour Government. Meanwhile Churchill, by
a 10,000-vote margin majority, lost his Dundee seat to a Prohibi-
tionist by the name of Scrimgeour, whom Churchill described as
'possessed of all the virtues I despise and none of the sins that I
admire'. He was to be out of Parliament for a whole year, in the
course of which he gravitated back to the Conservative Party, which
he saw as the most effective bulwark against Socialism. In October of
1924 he was returned for the Conservative seat of Epping and the
Conservative Party, under its new leader, Stanley Baldwin, won an
overwhelming victory. As Churchill commented in his memoirs: 'I
was surprised, and the Conservative Party dumbfounded, when he
[Prime Minister Stanley Baldwin] invited me to become Chancellor
of the Exchequer.' Thus, in the space of twenty tumultuous years he
had 'crossed the floor' for a second time and was once again back in
the Conservative fold. He later commented: 'Anyone can rat, but it
takes a certain amount of ingenuity to re-rat.'

It is almost a quarter of a century since I was president of the
Midland Conservative Club, and addressed its members in this room.
Twenty-five years is a long period in our brief lives, and an
appreciable period in the history of a nation. But what a period is
this twenty-five years, through which we have passed! Never have
there been so many gigantic and terrible events crowded into an
equal span, and never have there been so many changes, and such
deep changes, in the same period in the social, political and economic
structure of Britain, of Europe, and of the world. Five great Empires
– the German Empire, the Austrian Empire, the Russian Empire, the
Turkish Empire, and the Chinese Empire – have been overwhelmed
by various forms of destruction.

When we survey this tremendous and frightful panorama which
has unfolded itself before us, it seems almost miraculous that our
small island, with its crowded population and widespread possessions, should have survived intact, united, safe; and it ought to
arouse in us feelings of deep thankfulness about the past and inspire
us with confidence and courage in the difficulties of the present and
of the future. (*Cheers.*)

But, even here in England, where the thread of historical continuity
has alone among ancient states remained unbroken, immense
changes, some good, some bad, have swept across our national and
political life. The old order of government and society has largely

passed away. Women have begun to play a part in our public life hitherto unexampled in the world. The union between Great Britain and Ireland has been repealed, and the Irish question has sunk in a grim yet hopeful solution. Thirdly, and not the least among supreme domestic events, millions of electors, who were or whose fathers were accustomed to seek progress under the direction of the Liberal Party, have transferred their allegiance to Socialist standards, and are now, poor fellows, mouthing the dreary fallacies of Karl Marx. (*Laughter.*)

Finally, there has been erected in Moscow a vast organisation of revolutionary propaganda, directed by a sect of able, ruthless men, armed with the remaining resources of a once mighty Empire, whose avowed purpose is to involve all other countries in the same ruin and enslavement which they have meted out to Russia. (*Cheers.*) I said 'all other countries', but can we be blind to the fact that British interests and the British Empire and Britain herself have been singled out as the first and main object of their malice. This island community of ours, which in all the great quarrels of the last 400 years has always defended, and hitherto always successfully defended, the cause of ordered freedom, stands as a massive obstacle in the path of the Bolshevist revolutionaries. To lay it low, to shatter it to pieces, to grind it to powder by every resource of violence or cunning – that is their task. They have recognised it. Let us recognise it too. (*Cheers.*)

These are the principal immense changes which have come into our British political life, and I think you will agree with me that they make it necessary for us, each and all, to choose with resolution the path we must take. . . .

The present Conservative Government and its Prime Minister stand as a solid central body of stalwart common sense and moderation. After three General Elections in three years, with all their waste and worry, with governments rising and falling like houses of cards, the nation, a year ago, returned a new House of Commons containing an overwhelming Conservative majority, elected on what is practically universal suffrage, and entitled, under the Constitution, to a five years' term of office. The wish of the nation, unmistakably expressed, was that there should be a period of stability and tranquillity, during which law and order should be firmly maintained and constitutional practices strictly observed: during which, also, a policy of peace, patience and perseverance should be given a fair chance over a number of years.

'THE FOLLIES OF SOCIALISM'

11 December 1925

Town Hall, Battersea

The follies of Socialism are inexhaustible. They talk of comradeship and preach the brotherhood of men. What are they? They are the most disagreeable people. Talk about worldwide common brotherhood! Even among themselves they have twenty discordant factions who hate one another even more than they hate you and me. Their insincerity! Can you not feel a sense of disgust at the arrogant presumption of superiority of these people? Superiority of intellect! 'We are looking forward,' they say, 'to a state of humanity far better than the present squalid human race will ever attain.' Then when it comes to practice, down they fall with a wallop not only to the level of ordinary human beings but to a level which is even far below the average. (*Laughter and cheers.*)

Then there is this foreign element in Socialism, which I think deserves to awaken a sense of repulsion in every British breast. Why, they never thought of one single idea for themselves! They borrow all their ideas from Russia and Germany. They always sit adulating every foreign rascal and assassin who springs up for the moment. All their economics are taken from Karl Marx and all their politics from the actions of Lenin. With feelings of indignation I sometimes contemplate the harm the Socialists have done in corrupting and perverting great masses of our fellow-countrymen with their absurd foreign-imported doctrines. (*Cheers.*) If they want to speed up a movement of social reform is it necessary to teach people to dance to their ugly tune?

Behind Socialism stands Communism. Behind Communism stands Moscow, that dark, sinister, evil power which has made its appearance in the world – a band of cosmopolitan conspirators gathered from the underworld of Europe and America – which has seized the great Russian people by the hair of their heads and holds them in a grip, robbing them of victory, of prosperity, of freedom. This plaguish band of conspirators are aiming constantly to overthrow all civilised countries and reduce every nation to the level of misery to which they have plunged the great people of Russia. They strike everywhere, by every method, through every channel which is open to them, but there is no country at which they strike so much as at this island of ours.

'ARTFUL DODGER'!

22 April 1926

House of Commons

The rules of what constitutes 'Parliamentary language' were evidently more liberally interpreted in the 1920s than in more modern times. Certainly the barrage of epithets cast at the Chancellor of the Exchequer must constitute something of a record.

A great deal of hard and strong language has been used in these Debates, and I shall claim, as I am sure I shall be accorded, the fullest liberty and latitude of debate in replying to the serious charges that have been made. I asked a gentleman very kindly to look through the Debates and let me have a statistical appreciation of the strength of the language used, and his analysis is very interesting. The word 'robbery' or 'robbed' was used 67 times; 'confiscation', 10; 'plunder', 10; 'steal', 3 – and once more by the right hon. Gentleman the Member for Derby in his last remarks, but that arrived after the list was closed; 'Raid', 11; 'theft', 2; 'filch', 1; 'grab', 1; and there was one 'cheat'. The right hon. Gentleman the Member for Spen Valley (Sir J. Simon) is entitled to the credit of that. 'Breach of faith', 19; 'betrayal', 5; 'outrage', 1; 'infamy', 1; 'rascality', 1; 'perfidy', 1; 'mean', 15; 'paltry', 1; 'despicable', 1; 'shabby', 1; and 'dastardly', 3. I received the following compliments: 'the villain of the piece', 'robber', 'marauder', 'cat-burglar' and 'artful dodger'. I think that is rather complimentary having regard to the quarter from which it emanated. The more exuberant Members of the party opposite have for some years, at elections at any rate, been accustomed to salute me by the expression 'murderer', and from that point of view 'robber' is a sort of promotion. It shows that I am making some headway in their esteem. Words which are on proper occasions the most powerful engines lose their weight and power and values when they are not backed by fact or winged by truth, when they are obviously the expression of a strong feeling, and are not related in any way to the actual facts of the situation.

'THE BLUSHING LIBERAL BRIDE'

22 October 1928

Chingford

When the General Election came in May 1929, the Liberals gained a slim majority over the Socialists. The Conservative Government resigned, a minority Labour Government under Ramsay MacDonald came to office with Liberal Party support, as Churchill had predicted in this address to his constituents. This marked the end of Churchill's career as Chancellor of the Exchequer. His decision to return Britain to the Gold Standard was controversial and the timing, coming shortly before the 'Great Crash' of 1929, proved unfortunate. The Annual Register for 1929 records: 'Mr Churchill had proved himself the most able debater in the party, if not in the House, but as a financier his success has been questionable.'

There can be only one issue at the General Election: whether there should be a Socialist Government in power or not. I am astounded at the levity with which this dire choice seems to be contemplated in some quarters. Mr Lloyd George will perhaps be allowed to join the Socialist Government, to give them stability – financial stability – and to teach them Parliamentary tactics. Some of the newspapers are busy arranging a Liberal–Socialist pact. The blushing Liberal bride is to be wedded to the somewhat reluctant Socialist swain. Lord Rothermere will apparently present himself in the guise of the heavy father giving his blessing to the happy pair: 'Increase and multiply, my children. Be virtuous and you will be happy. Be economical and you will be rich.' The Wedding March, played on organs of a million horse-power, will be 'We all go the same way home.' (*Laughter.*)

'A DISARMAMENT FABLE'

24 October 1928

Aldersbrook

In 1925 Germany had been brought back into the comity of nations and became a signatory of the Locarno Pact, under the terms of which the European victors of the Great War, Great Britain and France, obliged themselves to disarm. But all the discussion of arms and disarmament only served to make the nations involved view one another with heightening suspicion and distrust – a situation to which Churchill alludes in his mocking allegory.

The discussion of the last two years has tended to bring naval, military, and air matters into a position of international consequence and prominence which is not at all warranted by anything in the present peaceable state of the world. Governments have been forced to examine all sorts of imaginary and immature possibilities which will never be translated into reality if any of the great and free democracies of the world are able to make their opinion prevail.

In order not to give offence to anyone, I will use a parable: Once upon a time all the animals in the Zoo decided that they would disarm, and they arranged to have a conference to arrange the matter. So the Rhinoceros said when he opened the proceedings that the use of teeth was barbarous and horrible and ought to be strictly prohibited by general consent. Horns, which were mainly defensive weapons, would, of course, have to be allowed. The Buffalo, the Stag, the Porcupine, and even the little Hedgehog all said they would vote with the Rhino, but the Lion and the Tiger took a different view. They defended teeth and even claws, which they described as honourable weapons of immemorial antiquity. The Panther, the Leopard, the Puma, and the whole tribe of small cats all supported the Lion and the Tiger. Then the Bear spoke. He proposed that both teeth and horns should be banned and never used again for fighting by any animal. It would be quite enough if animals were allowed to give each other a good hug when they quarrelled. No one could object to that. It was so fraternal, and that would be a great step towards peace. However, all the other animals were very offended with the Bear, and the Turkey fell into a perfect panic.

The discussion got so hot and angry, and all those animals began thinking so much about horns and teeth and hugging when they argued about the peaceful intentions that had brought them together that they began to look at one another in a very nasty way. Luckily the keepers were able to calm them down and persuade them to go back quietly to their cages, and they began to feel quite friendly with one another again.

3. The Wilderness Years 1930–39

In May 1929, when the Liberals returned to office, in support of a minority Labour Government, Churchill found himself out of office for more than ten years. From the early 1930s, first over India, then over Appeasement in the face of a re-arming Germany, Churchill found himself ever more alienated from the leadership and mainstream of the Conservative Party, to the point where, by the late 1930s, when Hitler was on the rampage in Europe, Churchill could count his political friends and allies in Parliament on the fingers of one hand.

With prescience and clarity, he saw that the world was heading for catastrophe. Convinced that the disaster could be averted, he did all in his power to warn the peoples of Britain, the United States and Western Europe of the dangers, but none would listen. Repudiated and reviled as a 'war-monger', these were the years when he was most sternly put to the test. From the point of view of sheer moral courage and dogged determination, I have no doubt that this was Winston Churchill's 'Finest Hour'.

The Munich crisis, in which the British and French Governments shamefully betrayed the independence of Czechoslovakia in the hope of appeasing Hitler's appetite for aggression, proved the turning point. Initially the Prime Minister, Neville Chamberlain, was hailed as the man who saved the peace. But, as the months slipped by, not only Chamberlain but, increasingly, the British public came to see they had been duped and that Churchill had been right all along. Thereafter, there was an ever more insistent demand for Churchill's return to office.

'A SEDITIOUS MIDDLE TEMPLE LAWYER'

23 February 1931

Winchester House, Epping

One of the Labour Government's first actions was to propose, with Conservative support, Dominion status – including self-government – for India, something to which Churchill was firmly opposed. This speech with its fierce attack on the Hindu nationalist leader Mahatma Gandhi caused offence and was much criticised, not only in India, but in Britain as well.

Now I come to the administration of India. In my opinion we ought to dissociate ourselves in the most public and formal manner from any complicity in the weak, wrong-headed and most unfortunate administration of India by the Socialists and by the Viceroy acting upon their responsibility. It is alarming and also nauseating to see Mr Gandhi, a seditious Middle Temple lawyer, now posing as a fakir of a type well known in the East, striding half-naked up the steps of the viceregal palace, while he is still organising and conducting a defiant campaign of civil disobedience, to parley on equal terms with the representative of the King-Emperor. Such a spectacle can only increase the unrest in India.

'ABANDONING INDIA'

18 March 1931

Royal Albert Hall, London

Churchill, who had had many years' experience of India as a soldier, was firmly convinced that the effective removal of British power would lead, not only to the demise of the British Empire, but to large scale inter-communal violence and bloodshed between

Hindus and Muslims. Tragically, he was to be proved right in this. Nonetheless, by his stand he alienated a large element of the Conservative Party, at a time when, shortly, he would need every friend and political ally he could muster.

To abandon India to the rule of the Brahmins would be an act of cruel and wicked negligence. It would shame for ever those who bore its guilt. These Brahmins who mouth and patter the principles of Western Liberalism, and pose as philosophic and democratic politicians, are the same Brahmins who deny the primary rights of existence to nearly sixty millions of their own fellow-countrymen whom they call 'untouchable', and whom they have by thousands of years of oppression actually taught to accept this sad position. They will not eat with these sixty millions, nor drink with them, nor treat them as human beings. They consider themselves contaminated even by their approach. And then in a moment they turn round and begin chopping logic with John Stuart Mill, or pleading the rights of man with Jean-Jacques Rousseau.

While any community, social or religious, endorses such practices and asserts itself resolved to keep sixty millions of fellow-countrymen perpetually and eternally in a state of sub-human bondage, we cannot recognise their claim to the title-deeds of democracy. Still less can we hand over to their unfettered sway those helpless millions they despise. Side by side with this Brahmin theocracy and the immense Hindu population – angelic and untouchable castes alike – there dwell in India seventy millions of Muslims, a race of far greater physical vigour and fierceness, armed with a religion which lends itself only too readily to war and conquest. While the Hindu elaborates his argument, the Muslim sharpens his sword. Between these two races and creeds, containing as they do so many gifted and charming beings in all the glory of youth, there is no intermarriage. The gulf is impassable. If you took the antagonisms of France and Germany, and the antagonisms of Catholics and Protestants, and compounded them and multiplied them ten-fold, you would not equal the division which separates these two races intermingled by scores of millions in the cities and plains of India. But over both of them the impartial rule of Britain has hitherto lifted its appeasing sceptre. Until the Montagu–Chelmsford reforms began to raise the question of local sovereignty and domination, they had got used to dwelling side by side in comparative toleration. But step by step, as it is believed we are going to clear out or be thrust out of India, so this tremendous rivalry and hatred of races springs into life again. It is becoming more acute every day. Where we to wash our hands of all responsibility and divest ourselves of all our powers, as our sentimentalists desire, ferocious civil wars would speedily break out between the Muslims and the Hindus. No one who knows India will dispute this.

PROHIBITION

November/December 1931

Lecture Tour of the United States

Having lost, in the Great Crash of 1929, the greater part of all he had earned by his writing and lecturing in the first thirty years of his adult life, Churchill launched forth on a major Lecture Tour of the United States. The excerpt quoted here is from his speech notes.

He took the strongest exception to Prohibition, both on political grounds, as well as those of personal inconvenience. The Editor's father, Randolph, who two years earlier, as an 18-year-old student, had accompanied his father on a similar tour of Canada and the United States, had been made responsible for several variously shaped 'medicine' bottles, containing a brownish liquid originating not a million miles from Scotland!

We have on the other hand, I think, been more successful than you in attacking the frightful social evils of intemperance. In our country, as in yours, an enormous amount of misery, poverty and crime, of broken lives and ruined homes arose from alcohol. . . . But we have used different weapons. We have used the weapon of taxation and regulation. We have not hesitated to handle the evil thing . . . treating it as a practical matter, like a disease, rather than as a moral issue.

'BANDS OF STURDY TEUTONIC YOUTHS'

23 November 1932

House of Commons

1932 marks the start of Churchill's campaign to warn his fellow-countrymen and the world of the dangers of Allied disarmament in the face of relentless German rearmament. The Nazi 'Blackshirts' and 'Brownshirts' were already throwing their weight around and, a bare ten weeks after this speech, Adolf Hitler was elected Chancellor of Germany.

On the other side there is Germany, the same mighty Germany which so recently withstood almost the world in arms; Germany which resisted with such formidable capacity that it took between two and three Allied lives to take one German life in the four years of the Great War; Germany which has also allies, friends and associates in her train, powerful nations, who consider their politics as associated to some extent with hers; Germany whose annual quota of youth reaching the military age is already nearly double the youth of France; Germany where the Parliamentary system and the safeguards of the Parliamentary system which we used to be taught to rely upon after the Great War are in abeyance. I do not know where Germany's Parliamentary system stands today, but certainly military men are in control of the essentials.

Germany has paid since the war an indemnity of about one thousand millions sterling, but she has borrowed in the same time about two thousand millions sterling with which to pay that indemnity and to equip her factories. Her territories have been evacuated long before the stipulated time – I rejoice in it – and now she has been by Lausanne virtually freed from all those reparations which had been claimed from her by the nations whose territories have been devastated in the war, or whose prosperity, like ours, has been gravely undermined by the war. At the same time, her commercial debts may well prove ultimately to be irrecoverable. I am making no indictment of Germany. I have respect and admiration for the Germans, and desire that we should live on terms of good feeling and fruitful relations with them; but we must look at the fact that every concession which has been made – many concessions have been made, and many more will be made and ought to be made – has been followed immediately by a fresh demand.

Now the demand is that Germany should be allowed to rearm. Do not delude yourselves. Do not let His Majesty's Government believe – I am sure they do not believe – that all that Germany is asking for is equal status. I believe the refined term now is equal qualitative status, or, as an alternative, equal quantitative status by indefinitely deferred stages. That is not what Germany is seeking. All these bands of sturdy Teutonic youths, marching through the streets and roads of Germany, with the light of desire in their eyes to suffer for their Fatherland, are not looking for status. They are looking for weapons, and, when they have the weapons, believe me they will then ask for the return of lost territories and lost colonies, and when that demand is made it cannot fail to shake and possibly shatter to their foundations every one of the countries I have mentioned, and some other countries I have not mentioned.

Besides Germany, there is Russia. Russia has made herself an Ishmael among the nations, but she is one of the most titanic factors in the economy and in the diplomacy of the world. Russia, with her enormous, rapidly increasing armaments, with her tremendous development of poison gas, aeroplanes, tanks and every kind of forbidden fruit; Russia, with her limitless manpower and her corrosive hatreds, weighs heavily upon a whole line of countries, some small, others considerable, from the Baltic to the Black Sea, all situated adjacent to Russian territory. These countries have newly gained their independence. Their independence and nationhood are sacred to them, and we must never forget that most of them have been carved, in whole or in part, out of the old Russian Empire, the Russian Empire of Peter the Great and Catherine the Great. In some cases these countries are also in deep anxiety about Germany.

I am sure that I have not overdrawn the picture. I have marshalled the facts, but I have not overdrawn the picture. Can we wonder, can any reasonable, fair-minded, peace-loving person wonder, in the circumstances, that there is fear in Europe, and, behind the fear, the precautions, perhaps in some cases exaggerated precautions, which fear excites? We in these islands, with our heavy burdens and with our wide Imperial responsibilities, ought to be very careful not to meddle improvidently or beyond our station, beyond our proportionate stake, in this tremendous European structure. If we were to derange the existing foundations, based on force though they may be, we might easily bring about the very catastrophe that most of all we desire to avert. What would happen to us then? No one can predict. But if by the part we had played in European affairs we had precipitated such a catastrophe, then I think our honour might be engaged beyond the limitations which our treaties and agreements prescribe.

We must not forget, and Europe and the United States must not forget, that we have disarmed. Alone among the nations we have disarmed while others have rearmed.

'PONTIFICAL, ANONYMOUS MUGWUMPERY'

22 February 1933

House of Commons

Here Churchill seeks to debunk the claim of the British Broadcasting Corporation to speak for Britain. Throughout the greater part of the 1930s the BBC unashamedly supported the appeasement policies of the Government and, with rare exception, did their best to deny Churchill access to the airwaves.

These well-meaning gentlemen of the British Broadcasting Corporation have absolutely no qualifications and no claim to represent British public opinion. They have no right to say that they voice the opinions of English or British people whatever. If anyone can do that it is His Majesty's Government; and there may be two opinions about that. It would be far better to have sharply contrasted views in succession, in alternation, than to have this copious stream of pontifical, anonymous mugwumpery with which we have been dosed so long. I am very much encouraged by this Debate. I think there is a general feeling in the House, even among the Liberals, a minority, and it may be an increasing minority, that I am championing fair play and free speech. This Debate, if it is properly interpreted and enforced, may mean the opening of a new, wider and freer use of this great instrument, which if it is opened to the political life of the nation can only bring enhancement to the strength of the State, and set upon more permanent foundations the institutions which this small island has evolved.

'ENGLAND'

24 April 1933

Royal Society of St George, London

So as not to be cut off in mid-sentence by the controllers of the BBC, Churchill uses the allegory of the tale of St George (England's Patron Saint) and the Dragon to mock and heap scorn on the Government's efforts to appease Germany, which he casts in the role of the Dragon.

I am a great admirer of the Scots. I am quite friendly with the Welsh, especially one of them. I must confess to some sentiment about Old Ireland, in spite of the ugly mask she tries to wear. But this is not their night. On this one night in the whole year we are allowed to use a forgotten, almost a forbidden word. We are allowed to mention the name of our own country, to speak of ourselves as 'Englishmen', and we may even raise the slogan 'St George for Merrie England'.

We must be careful, however. You see these microphones? They have been placed on our tables by the British Broadcasting Corporation. Think of the risk these eminent men are running. We can almost see them in our mind's eye, gathered together in that very expensive building, with the questionable statues on its front. We can picture Sir John Reith, with the perspiration mantling on his lofty brow, with his hand on the control switch, wondering, as I utter every word, whether it will not be his duty to protect his innocent subscribers from some irreverent thing I might say about Mr Gandhi, or about the Bolsheviks, or even about our peripatetic Prime Minister. But let me reassure him. I have much more serious topics to discuss. I have to speak to you about St George and the Dragon. I have been wondering what would happen if that legend were repeated under modern conditions.

St George would arrive in Cappadocia, accompanied not by a horse, but by a secretariat. He would be armed not with a lance, but with several flexible formulas. He would, of course, be welcomed by the local branch of the League of Nations Union. He would propose a conference with the dragon – a Round Table Conference, no doubt – that would be more convenient for the dragon's tail. He would make a trade agreement with the dragon. He would lend the dragon a lot of money for the Cappadocian taxpayers. The maiden's release would be referred to Geneva, the dragon reserving all his rights meanwhile. Finally St George would be photographed with the dragon (inset – the maiden).

There are a few things I will venture to mention about England. They are spoken in no invidious sense. Here it would hardly occur to anyone that the banks would close their doors against their depositors. Here no one questions the fairness of the courts of law and justice. Here no one thinks of persecuting a man on account of his religion or his race. Here everyone, except the criminals, looks on the policeman as the friend and servant of the public. Here we provide for poverty and misfortune with more compassion, in spite of all our burdens, than any other country. Here we can assert the rights of the citizen against the State, or criticise the Government of the day, without failing in our duty to the Crown or in our loyalty to the King. This ancient, mighty London in which we are gathered is still the financial centre of the world. From the Admiralty building, half a mile away, orders can be sent to a Fleet which, though much smaller than it used to be, or than it ought to be, is still unsurpassed on the seas. More than 80 per cent of the British casualties of the Great War were English. More than 80 per cent of the taxation is paid by the English taxpayers. We are entitled to mention these facts, and to draw authority and courage from them.

Historians have noticed, all down the centuries, one peculiarity of the English people which has cost them dear. We have always thrown away after a victory the greater part of the advantages we gained in the struggle. The worst difficulties from which we suffer do not come from without. They come from within. They do not come from the cottages of the wage-earners. They come from a peculiar type of brainy people always found in our country, who, if they add something to its culture, take much from its strength.

Our difficulties come from the mood of unwarrantable self-abasement into which we have been cast by a powerful section of our own intellectuals. They come from the acceptance of defeatist doctrines by a large proportion of our politicians. But what have they to offer but a vague internationalism, a squalid materialism, and the promise of impossible Utopias?

Nothing can save England if she will not save herself. If we lose faith in ourselves, in our capacity to guide and govern, if we lose our will to live, then indeed our story is told. If, while on all sides foreign nations are every day asserting a more agressive and militant nationalism by arms and trade, we remain paralysed by our own theoretical doctrines or plunged into the stupor of after-war exhaustion, then indeed all that the croakers predict will come true, and our ruin will be swift and final. Stripped of her Empire in the Orient, deprived of the sovereignty of the seas, loaded with debt and taxation, her commerce and carrying trade shut out by foreign tariffs and quotas, England would sink to the level of a fifth-rate Power, and nothing would remain of all her glories except a population much larger than this island can support.

Why should we break up the solid structure of British power, founded upon so much health, kindliness and freedom, for dreams which may some day come true, but are now only dreams, and some of them nightmares? We ought, as a nation and Empire, to weather any storm that blows at least as well as any other existing system of human government. We are at once more experienced and more truly united than any people in the world. It may well be that the most glorious chapters of our history are yet to be written. Indeed, the very problems and dangers that encompass us and our country ought to make English men and women of this generation glad to be here at such a time. We ought to rejoice at the responsibilities with which destiny has honoured us, and be proud that we are guardians of our country in an age when her life is at stake.

'WARS COME VERY SUDDENLY'

7 February 1934

House of Commons

This speech represents the opening barrage of Churchill's five-year offensive calling for Britain to rearm in the face of clear evidence that Hitler and the Nazis were determined to trample underfoot the disarmament clauses of the Treaty of Versailles, which had ended the Great War. Churchill's key theme was the vulnerability of British cities to air attack and the need to establish an Air Force at least as powerful as that of any potential enemy.

Wars come very suddenly. I have lived through a period when one looked forward, as we do now, with great anxiety and great uncertainty to what would happen in the future. Suddenly something did happen – tremendous, swift, overpowering, irresistible. Let me remind the House of the sort of thing that happened in 1914. There was absolutely no quarrel between Germany and France. One July afternoon the German Ambassador drove down to the Quai d'Orsay and said to, I think, M. Viviani, the French Prime Minister: 'We have been forced to mobilise against Russia, and war will be declared. What is to be the position of France?' The French Prime Minister made the answer, which his Cabinet had agreed upon, that France would act in accordance with what she considered to be her own interests. The Ambassador said, 'You have an alliance with Russia, have you not?' 'Quite so,' said the French Prime Minister. And that was the process by which, in a few minutes, the area of the struggle, already serious in the East, was enormously widened and multiplied by the throwing in of the two great nations of the West on either side. But sometimes even a declaration of neutrality does not suffice. On this very occasion, as we now know, the German Ambassador was authorised by his Government, in case the French did not do their duty by their Russian ally, in case they showed any disposition to back out of the conflict which had been resolved on by the German nation, to demand that the fortresses of Toul and Verdun should be handed over to German troops as a guarantee that the French, having declared neutrality, would not change their mind at a subsequent moment.

That is how the great thing happened in our own lifetime, and I am bound to say that I canot see in the present administration of Germany any assurance that they would be more nice-minded in dealing with a vital and supreme situation than was the Imperial Government of Germany, which was responsibile for this procedure being adopted towards France. No, Sir, and we may, within a measurable period of time, in the lifetime of those who are here, if we are not in a proper state of security, be confronted on some occasion with a visit from an ambassador, and may have to give an answer in a very few hours; and if that answer is not satisfactory, within the next few hours the crash of bombs exploding in London and the cataracts of masonry and fire and smoke will warn us of any inadequacy which has been permitted in our aerial defences. We are vulnerable as we have never been before. I have often heard criticisms of the Liberal Government before the war. It is said that its diplomacy was not sufficiently clear and precise, that it wrapped things up in verbiage, that it ought to have said downright and plain what it would do, and there were criticisms about its lack of preparation, and so forth. All I can say is that a far graver case rests upon those who now hold power if, by any chance, against our wishes and against our hopes, trouble should come – a far graver case.

Not one of the lessons of the past has been learned, not one of them has been applied, and the situation is incomparably more dangerous. Then we had the Navy, and no air menace worth speaking of. Then the Navy was the 'sure shield' of Britain. As long as it was ready in time and at its stations we could say to any foreign Government: 'Well, what are you going to do about it? We will not declare ourselves. We will take our own line, we will work out our own course. We have no wish or desire to hurt anyone, but we shall not be pressed or forced into any hasty action unless we think fit or well.' We cannot say that now. This cursed, hellish invention and development of war from the air has revolutionised our position. We are not the same kind of country we used to be when we were an island, only 20 years ago. That is the thing that is borne in upon me more than anything else. It is not merely a question of what we like and what we do not like, of ambitions and desires, of rights and interests, but it is a question of safety and independence. That is what is involved now as never before. . . .

I cannot conceive how, in the present state of Europe and of our position in Europe we can delay in establishing the principle of having an Air Force at least as strong as that of any Power that can get at us. I think that is a perfectly reasonable thing to do. It would only begin to put us back to the position in which we were brought up. We have lived under the shield of the Navy. To have an Air Force as strong as the air force of France or Germany, whichever is the stronger, ought to be the decision which Parliament should take, and which the National Government should proclaim.

'GERMANY IS ARMING'

8 March 1934

House of Commons

Churchill's insistent demand for parity in air power with Germany prompted Stanley Baldwin, in reply, to assure the House that the Government 'would see to it that in air strength and air power this country shall no longer be in a position inferior to any country within striking distance of our shores'. In the years that followed, as the Prime Minister's assertion was shown to be ever more hollow, Churchill would remind the House of his – dishonoured – promise.

I dread the day when the means of threatening the heart of the British Empire should pass into the hands of the present rulers of Germany. I think we should be in a position which would be odious to every man who values freedom of action and independence, and also in a position of the utmost peril for our crowded, peaceful population, engaged in their daily toil. I dread that day, but it is not, perhaps, far distant. It is, perhaps, only a year, or perhaps eighteen months, distant. Not come yet – at least, so I believe, or I hope and pray. But it is not far distant. There is still time for us to take the necessary measures, but it is the measures we want. Not this paragraph in this White Paper; we want the measures. It is no good writing that first paragraph and then producing £130,000. We want the measures to achieve parity. The hon. Gentleman opposite who spoke so many words of wisdom seemed to me to mar the significance and point of his argument when he interposed in it the statement that he was not committing himself to any increase.

Mr Mander: At this stage.

Mr Churchill: But this *is* the stage. I do not say today, but within the next week or so. The turning-point has been reached, and the new steps must be taken. . . . The scene has changed. This terrible new fact has occurred. Germany is arming – she is rapidly arming – and no one will stop her. None of the grievances between the victors and the vanquished have been redressed. The spirit of aggressive nationalism was never more rife in Europe and in the world. Far away are the days of Locarno, when we nourished bright hopes of the reunion of the European family and the laying in the tomb of that age-long quarrel between Teuton and Gaul of which we have been the victims in our lifetime.

That hope is gone, and we must act in accordance with the new situation.

'WE LIE WITHIN A FEW MINUTES' STRIKING DISTANCE . . .'

16 November 1934

Broadcast, London

This was one of those rare occasions during Churchill's 'Wilderness Years' when the BBC authorities – exercising a monopoly of the airwaves, heavily biased towards appeasement and ever fearful of broadcasting anything that might make Herr Hitler angry – allowed Churchill's lone voice airtime.

As we go to and fro in this peaceful country, with its decent orderly people going about their business under free institutions, and with so much tolerance and fair play in their laws and customs, it is startling and fearful to realise that we are no longer safe in our island home. For nearly a thousand years England has never seen the camp fires of an invader. The stormy seas and our Royal Navy have been our sure defence. Not only have we preserved our life and freedom through the centuries, but gradually we have come to be the heart and centre of an Empire which surrounds the globe. It is indeed with a pang of stabbing pain that we see all this in mortal danger.

> A thousand years scarce serve to form a State,
> An hour may lay it in the dust. . . .

Only a few hours away by air there dwells a nation of nearly seventy millions of the most educated, industrious, scientific, disciplined people in the world, who are being taught from childhood to think of war and conquest as a glorious exercise, and death in battle as the noblest fate for man. There is a nation which has abandoned all its liberties in order to augment its collective might. There is a nation which, with all its strength and virtues, is in the grip of a group of ruthless men preaching a gospel of intolerance and racial pride, unrestrained by law, by Parliament or by public opinion. It is but twenty years since these neighbours of ours fought almost the whole world, and almost defeated them. Now they are rearming with the utmost speed, and ready to their hands is this new lamentable weapon of the air, against which our Navy is no defence, before which women and children, the weak and frail, the pacifist and the jingo, the warrior and the civilian, the front line trenches and the cottage home, lie in equal and impartial peril.

Nay worse still, for with the new weapon has come a new method, or rather has come back the most brutish methods of ancient barbarism, namely the possibility of compelling the submission of races by terrorising and torturing their civil population. And worst of all – the more civilised a country is, the larger and more splendid its cities, the more intricate the structure of its social and economic life; the more is it vulnerable, the more it is at the mercy of those who may make it their prey.

At present we lie within a few minutes' striking distance of the French, Dutch, and Belgian coasts, and within a few hours of the great aerodromes of Central Europe. We are even within canon-shot of the Continent. So close as that! Is it prudent, is it possible, however we might desire it, to turn our backs upon Europe and ignore whatever may happen there? Everyone can judge this question for himself, and everyone ought to make up his mind about it without delay. It lies at the heart of our problem. For my part I have come to the conclusion – reluctantly I admit – that we cannot get away. Here we are and we must make the best of it. But do not underrate the risks – the grievous risks – we have to run.

I hope, I pray, and on the whole, grasping the larger hope, I believe, that no war will fall upon us. But if in the near future the Great War of 1914 is resumed again in Europe after the Armistice – for that is what it may come to – under different conditions no doubt – no one can tell where and how it would end, or whether sooner or later we should not be dragged into it, as the United States were dragged in against their will in 1917. Whatever happened and whatever we did, it would be a time of frightful danger for us. . . . Therefore it seems to me that we cannot detach ourselves from Europe, and that for our own safety and self-preservation we are bound to make exertions and run risks for the sake of keeping peace.

There are some who say – indeed it has been the shrill cry of the hour – that we should run the risk of disarming ourselves in order to set an example to others. We have done that already for the last five years, but our example has not been followed. On the contrary, it has produced the opposite result. All the other countries have armed only the more heavily; and the quarrels and intrigues about disarmament have only bred more ill-will between the nations.

'A CORRIDOR OF DEEPENING
AND DARKENING DANGER'

31 May 1935

House of Commons

I agree with Sir Herbert Samuel when he says that it is impossible for us, in the world in which we live, to treat with blank distrust the utterances of the Leader of so vast a State as Germany. To represent everything that has been said by Herr Hitler as only designed for the purposes of political manoeuvre would be to destroy the very means of contact and of parley between one great nation and another.

I agree with him also in feeling that the Air Locarno, as it has been called, is in itself an eminently desirable objective towards which we should work, and which, if concluded, will be a matter of real substance and importance. I welcome, with him, any steps which may be taken to achieve, if possible, air parity at levels lower than those which are now mentioned. But it is not going to be very easy. I welcome also, and perhaps most keenly, what has been said by the German Chancellor stigmatising the vile crime of indiscriminate bombing of civilian populations. Naturally the Government will be encouraged by all sections in the House to pursue these matters with patience and not without hope. But do not let us underrate the difficulties which attach to them. There may be many more complications in what is called an Air Locarno than would appear at first sight. Still, for what it is worth, the union of great countries putting their names to a document pledging them all to bomb the bomber would be an event which everyone would hail.

Even more difficulties attend the limitation of air armaments. Air armaments are not expressed merely by the air squadrons in existence or the aeroplanes which have been made; they cannot be considered apart from the capacity to manufacture. If, for instance, there were two countries which each had 1000 first-line aeroplanes, but one of which had the power to manufacture at the rate of 100 a month and the other at the rate of 1000 a month, it is perfectly clear that air parity would not exist between those two countries very long.

One would imagine, sitting in this House today, that the dangers were in process of abating. I believe that the exact contrary is the truth – that they are steadily advancing upon us, and that no one can be certain that a time may not be reached, or when it will be reached, when events may have passed altogether out of control. We must look at the facts. Nourish your hopes, but do not overlook realities.

The Secretary of State for Foreign Affairs [Sir John Simon] dropped out a phrase today which really is in keeping with what I call the illusion basis on which much of this discussion has proceeded. It was one of those casual phrases which nevertheless reveal an altogether unsound conception of the facts. He referred to countries with whom you feel it your absolute duty to remain on terms of air equality. Look at that. A 'duty to remain on terms of air equality.' We have not got equality. Speeches are made in the country by leading Ministers saying that we have decided that we must have air equality, that we cannot accept anything less. We have not got it. We are already decidedly inferior to Germany, and, it must be said, of course to France. All that lies before us for many months is that this inferiority becomes more and more pronounced. In the autumn of this year, in November, when we are supposed to be 50 per cent stronger, I hazard the melancholy prediction that we shall not be a third, possibly not a quarter, of the German air strength. What is the use of saying 'the countries with whom we consider it our absolute duty to remain on terms of air equality'? This is one of the terrible facts which lie before us and which will not be swept away merely by following the very natural inclination which we all have to say that they do not exist.

The German Army, already developed to twenty-one or twenty-two divisions, is working up to thirty-six as fast as it can, a division a month or something like that coming into full mobilisation capacity, tanks and the whole business. There is the Navy, and submarines have been made. Some are actually, I believe, practising, training their crews in that difficult art. Let me tell the House that submarines can be manufactured very quickly. I remember in November 1914 arranging for Mr Schwab, of Bethlehem, to make twenty submarines in what was then considered the incredibly short period of six months. Although these vessels had to be shifted from the United States to a Canadian dockyard for reasons of neutrality, it was possible to put sections on the railway-trucks and to deliver them in time. How do you know what progress has been made in constructing such sections? The arms production has the first claim on the entire industry of Germany. The materials required for the production of armaments are the first charge on the German exchange. The whole of their industry is woven into an immediate readiness for war. You have a state of preparedness in German industry which was not attained by our industry until after the late war had gone on probably for two years.

Besides this, there is tremendous propaganda, beginning with the schools and going right through every grade of youth to manhood, enforced by the most vigorous and harsh sanctions at every stage. All this is taking place. It is a very nice comfortable world that we look out on here in this country. It has found an apt reflection in this Debate today, but it has no relation whatever to what is going forward, and going forward steadily. Mark you, in time of peace, in peace politics, in ordinary matters of domestic affairs and class struggles, things blow over, but in these great matters of defence, and still more in the field of actual hostilities, the clouds do not roll by. If the necessary measures are not taken, they turn into thunderbolts and fall on your heads. The whole of this great process of psychological, moral, material and technical mobilisation of German war power is proceeding ceaselessly and with ever-increasing momentum.

It is the growth of German armaments which has fascinated and petrified nation after nation throughout Europe. Just look at what has happened in the last few weeks since we were last engaged in a serious discussion on foreign affairs. We know perfectly well that Poland continues in the German system. The Czechoslovakian elections have created a new Nazi party in Czechoslovakia, which is, I believe, the second party in the State. [19 May.] That is a very remarkable fact, having regard to the energy which the German people, when inspired by the Nazi spirit, are able to exercise. The Austrian tension increases. Many people talk about guaranteeing the independence of Austria, but guaranteeing that Austria will be kept separate from Germany is a different thing. You may at any time be faced with the position that the will of the Austrian people will be turned in the reverse direction from that which our policy has hitherto proclaimed. There is the Danubian tour of General Goering. He has been to Yugoslavia, Bulgaria and to Hungary. He has, in Hungary and Bulgaria, been renewing those old ties of comradeship and confidence which existed between them and Germany in the days of the war. In Yugoslavia undoubtedly his presence has exercised a very important influence there as a counter-influence to others that may be brought to bear. Everywhere these countries are being made to look to Germany in a special way, and let me say that I read in *The Times* on the 30th of May a significant telegram from Vienna dealing with this tour of General Goering, which finished up with these words: 'In the circumstances the strength and clarity of German policy gains by contrast' – that is, to the Allied policy – 'and the waverers among the smaller States are closely watching events.'

There is the question of the relations between Germany and Japan. It seems to me that that is a matter which must be in the thoughts of everyone who attempts to make an appreciation of the foreign situation. There are the difficulties of Italy's preoccupation with Abyssinia. There are the obvious stresses through which France is passing, not, indeed, in the matter of national defence, but in almost every other aspect of the life of that people. There is our own weakness in the air which is to become worse and worse month after month. All this is going forward.

It is easy, then, for Herr Hitler and the German Government to pursue a policy which I have heard described as 'power diplomacy'. What a transformation has taken place in the last two or three years! Two or three years ago it was considered sentimental, intellectual, liberally minded, to speak words of encouragement and compassion, and even to speak patronisingly of the German people, and to seek opportunities of making gestures to raise them up to more and greater equality with other countries. Now we see them with their grievances unredressed, with all their ambitions unsatisfied, continuing from strength to strength, and the whole world waits from week to week to hear what are the words which will fall from the heads of the German nation. It is a woeful transformation which has taken place.

It would be folly for us to act as if we were swimming in a halcyon sea, as if nothing but balmy breezes and calm weather were to be expected and everything were working in the most agreeable fashion. By all means follow your lines of hope and your paths of peace, but do not close your eyes to the fact that we are entering a corridor of deepening and darkening danger, and that we shall have to move along it for many months and possibly for years to come. While we are in this position, not only have we our own safety to consider, but we have to consider also whether the Parliamentary Governments of Western Europe, of which there are not many that function in the real sense of the word, are going to be able to afford to their subjects the same measure of physical security, to say nothing of national satisfaction, as is being afforded to the people of Germany by the dictatorship which has been established there. It is not only the supreme question of self-preservation that is involved in the realisation of these dangers, but also the human and the world cause of the preservation of free Governments and of Western civilization against the ever-advancing forces of authority and despotism.

'YOU HAVE UNSETTLED EVERYTHING – YOU HAVE SETTLED NOTHING'

5 June 1935

House of Commons

This fierce attack on the Conservative Administration (his own party) marks the end of Churchill's long battle over India, described by Sir Samuel Hoare, who, as Secretary of State for India (1931–35), had responsibility for piloting the Indian Bill through the Commons, as 'Churchill's Seven Years' War'. He was convinced that the settled 'scuttle and run' policy of the Conservative, Labour and Liberal Parties would bring only tragedy and bloodshed to the teeming millions of the Indian sub-continent, sharply divided as they were between Hindu and Muslim.

You have unsettled everything. You have settled nothing. Those whom you have sought to conciliate are those whom you have most offended. Those to whom your mission is most necessary are those whom you have most entirely abandoned. Those on whom you have to count most are those whom you are teaching least of all to count on you.

You must ask one final question – the greatest of all these questions. Does this Bill mean a broadening of Indian life, a widening and elevation of Indian thought? Does it mean that the Indian toiler when he rises to his daily task will have a better chance of, in the words of the American Constitution, 'life, liberty and the pursuit of happiness'? India is a country, almost a continent, which responded to the influence of British peace, order and justice and all the applications of modern science, only by an increase of population. There has been a tremendous increase of population there. New wealth, new food, new facilities for locomotion, new hygiene, new canals, improvement in forestry and agriculture have not made the Indian masses better off. They have only brought into being in the last 50 years 100,000,000 more souls in India. A gigantic population has remained, upon the whole, at a very low level of human subsistence, but has become much more numerous.

Such a vast helpless mass requires extra British guidance, higher efficiency of government, more British civil servants and a stricter and more vigorous administration in all technical matters. All you offer them are liberal formulas, administrative relaxation and decline. The huge machine of Indian government is to be allowed to slow down, just at the time when the inhabitants of India have multiplied far beyond the limit of their basic food supply, just at the time when they require, above all things, a far higher measure of disinterested and enlightened autocracy. Just at that very time you offer this bouquet of faded flowers of Victorian Liberalism which, however admirable in themselves, have nothing to do with Asia and are being universally derided and discarded throughout the continent of Europe.

Mr Isaac Foot: So much the worse for Europe.

Mr Churchill: For this bouquet they have to pay a heavy price. Money raised by taxes in India which, like the salt tax, draw exactions from the poorest of the poor, from people whose poverty is inconceivable even to the poorest of the poor in this country – this money is needed and its extraction is only justified if it is used for hospitals, for plague prevention, for technical education, for improved irrigation and other modern apparatus. Only in this way can a population which is one-sixth of the human race be kept at its present artificial level of numbers. In the standard of life they have nothing to spare. The slightest fall from the present standard of life in India means slow starvation, and the actual squeezing out of life, not only of millions but of scores of millions of people who have come into the world at your invocation and under the shield and protection of the British power. . . .

You have decided and you have the power. You have shown you have the power to force this through, and no doubt you have the power to force it upon the people of India. But it now appears that even these political classes are not satisfied with the government which you are going to give to them, with the constitution which you offer, or with the sacrifice which the Indian masses are to be asked to give. By every organ through which they can express their views, they reject your government and they spit upon your ill-conceived generosity, if generosity it be. Even the very classes of wealthy, small, unrepresentative minorities for whom you have set out to cater, have rejected the dish which you proffer to them.

This, then, is your plan for the better Government of India. We thank God that we have neither part nor lot in it. You have done what you like. You have now a harder thing before you, and that is to like what you have done. Only the years can make their proof of whether you will be successful in that or not. What has astounded me is that the Government should have pressed forward so obstinately with this Indian policy, which causes so much distress to many important elements in the Conservative party, at a time when the domestic political situation is so uncertain, when the Continent of Europe is drifting steadily nearer to the brink of catastrophe, when we have before us for so many months to come that awful hiatus in our air strength and in the vital defences of Great Britain. I should have thought that common prudence alone would have led them to make some modification of their plans which are admittedly makeshift, which conform to no logic or symmetry, which are not fixed by any agreement or treaty with any elements in Indian public life. It has astonished me that that has not occurred to them. . . .

I think it is a shortsighted Act. I am sure it is a wrongful Act. It is, to use the words of my Noble Friend, a fraud upon power and a malversation of political trust.

'I AM A TREATY MAN'

10 July 1935

House of Commons

As a signatory of the Treaty which brought the Irish Free State – later the Republic of Ireland – into being Churchill deplored the weakness with which the British Government accepted repeated repudiations of key elements of the Treaty by the Irish Prime Minister, Eamon de Valera.

I am a Treaty man. I am one of the signatories to the Irish Treaty. We have the great advantage that we are a self-contained British Parliament, but there were terrible arguments on the other side. At any rate, we signed this Treaty and Irishmen died to make it good and to keep it as a great instrument guiding our future relations. No one can possibly impugn the conduct of Great Britain. But what has happened to the Treaty now? It has been broken and repudiated. My right hon. Friend and the Dominions Secretary unfolded to the House part of that dismal catalogue of repudiation which has marked the last four years – the oath of allegiance, the abolition of the Senate, the last remaining vestige of the action of the Crown and the Governor-General, the right of appeal to the Privy Council, and the new law which makes a British subject a foreigner in the Free State if a proclamation is made under the Act.

The whole of this great transition has speedily transformed the Ireland we settled with as a Dominion within the Empire but with the full rights of the Canadian Dominion into an alien republic. The whole of that great transition has taken place during these four years in which we have had our own troubles to worry about, and no one has concerned himself with it. But there it is. It is not complete. There are a few remaining steps to be taken but not many. They are going to be taken. The whole of this thing is going to happen. Let me point out that it has been perfectly legal. When you passed that Statute of Westminster and when the Chief Whip assembled for the first time his mighty legions returned at the General Election and rolled them through the Lobby over the 50 who stood out on that occasion, when that happened and a refusal was made by the Government to exempt the Irish Treaty from the operations of the Statute, when that happened you regularised every necessary step, every necessary step that has been taken and may be taken in the future, to destroy and sweep away every vestige of the Treaty made between the two countries.

I have no doubt that we shall hear from the hon. and learned Gentleman speaking from the benches of the Labour party that de Valera has acted only within his legal rights. He may have broken every kind of good faith between nation and nation, and every kind of agreement between man and man, and made it quite clear that the word of Ireland entered into by people who were his colleagues and with whom he worked in bygone days is not of consequence to him, and that he has been the injured party for all time and that the small nations and the good faith of small nations has been impugned. But that is not a matter that affects the issue. He is legally entitled, as I understand, according to highest authority, to take all the steps he has done, and when we were advised he would not be so legally advised, we were voted down when we did not accept that.

I do not hesitate to draw a moral, which the House will quite readily accept from me, that in this great Indian Constitution Bill there are a great many things on which you have been advised by legal authority and of which the House has accepted the opinion which, when you come to look at their working out in practice year after year, will be found equally fallacious and equally injurious to what has occurred in Ireland, and injurious upon a far more immense scale in the history of the world and in the wealth and strength of this country. We are bound to draw attention to the past because it is the guide, and the only guide we have, to the immediate future, and we are bound to say that Ministers who were giving all these airy assurances about Ireland have repeated them during the whole course of this vast Indian Constitution Bill.

'NAVAL SECURITY'

24 July 1935

Harlow

We are approaching a General Election of the utmost consequence. If a wrong decision is taken it would certainly be disastrous and might be fatal. The election might result in a Socialist Government, and I cannot think of anything that would be more disastrous. In 1931 they reduced a wealthy, powerful Empire to the appearance of bankruptcy and ran away from their duty in the hour of need.

The Government have been aroused to take action with the air policy, and they also propose to build a larger Navy. I was present at the recent naval review and it was a fine sight, but it was an extraordinary experience to me, who, as First Lord, was at another naval review 20 years ago. Out of 17 ships, including two aircraft-carriers, 14 were ships for which I was responsible during the years in which I was in office. Both in the air and in the Navy we will have to make substantial preparations to put ourselves in a state of security.

'ABYSSINIA HAS BEEN INVADED'

8 October 1935

Chingford

On 3 October the Italian Armies of the Fascist Dictator, Benito Mussolini, invaded the ancient East African kingdom of Abyssinia

(Ethiopia). The League of Nations branded Italy the aggressor and imposed economic sanctions, except in the one field where it might have been effective: oil.

Since I spoke in the City of London things have become more serious, but also more simple. The outlook is lamentable, but we can discern its features more plainly. We know where we are and what we are going to do, and we also know what we are not going to do.

We can see the limits of our immediate commitments and dangers. The overwhelming mass of the nation and all parties in it are broadly agreed in supporting the policy of his Majesty's Government. The Ministers have explained it so clearly that no one can be in any doubt.

Let us see, then, what that policy is. First, we stand by all our obligations under the Covenant of the League of Nations. We will bear our part to the utmost of our ability in any measure which the Council of the League of Nations may prescribe against the declared aggressor in the present war.

The Government have, very rightly and very wisely, taken all the necessary precautions to put the British fleets and squadrons in the Mediterranean and the Red Sea in a condition of security during what may be a protracted period of tension. There is no reason to suppose that our historic control of the Mediterranean will be challenged. On the other hand, we have declared that we will not take single-handed action or go farther than the other countries are ready to go. I believe the great mass of the British people are profoundly agreed both upon our policy and its limitations.

No one can suggest that his Majesty's Government have not fulfilled every obligation into which they have entered not only in the letter but also in the spirit. Indeed, we have gone beyond our strict obligations. We have taken the lead, and we are taking the lead, in urging the League of Nations to assert its authority in the most effective way; and we have, no doubt, incurred a great deal of odium in Italy in consequence.

Whether we ought to have taken the lead as we have done is a matter for argument. It is certainly the course with which the most generous elements in British public life will sympathise. But no one can accuse us of having failed in the slightest degree in our international duty. On the contrary, we have, as usual, been better than our word, and I hope our friends in France will weigh and ponder over that pregnant and far-reaching truth.

Having taken our course and made up our minds, there is nothing to do but to carry it out with composure and consistency. It is very difficult to see far ahead. War has begun between Italy and Abyssinia. Abyssinia has been invaded. Abyssinian tribesmen are being attacked by very large Italian armies equipped with all the most terrible weapons of modern science. They are being bombed from the air, bombarded by cannon, trampled down by tanks, and they are fighting as well as they can in their primitive way to defend their hearths and homes, their rights and freedom.

It would be very rash to predict how the war will go. The accounts in the newspapers are very full, very interesting, and very obscure. It does not seem that much has happened so far. We shall be able to judge better when the Italian invasion has penetrated more deeply into the heart of this very rugged and difficult country, and when the Italian line of communication extends to over 150 miles. Until then it is wiser to suspend judgment on the military problem.

Neither do we know what degree of sanctions the League of Nations will prescribe against the aggressor. Whatever happens we shall do our bit. But this is a most painful question for France, and it is important that we should understand the anxious and cruel nature of the issue presented to the French people.

They see the Germans arming night and day, spending at least £700,000,000 or £800,000,000 in borrowed money in a single year on warlike preparations. They know that Germany has nearly twice their manpower, and that this enormous martial population is being organised and equipped at a speed and at a cost never yet equalled in time of peace. In fact Germany is, at this moment, living and working under war conditions, except that there is no actual fighting going on.

'NAZIDOM ... WITH ALL ITS HATREDS AND ALL ITS GLEAMING WEAPONS'

24 October 1935

House of Commons

I bear no grudge, I have no prejudice against the German people. I have many German friends, and I have a lively admiration for their splendid qualities of intellect and valour, and for their achievements in science and art. The re-entry into the European circle of a Germany at peace within itself, with a heart devoid of hate, would be the most precious benefit for which we could strive, and a supreme advantage which alone would liberate Europe from its peril and its fear, and I believe that the British and French democracies, the ex-service men, would go a long way in extending the hand of friendship to realise such a hope.

But that is not the position which exists today. A very different position exists today. We cannot afford to see Nazidom in its present phase of cruelty and intolerance, with all its hatreds and all its gleaming weapons, paramount in Europe at the present time. . . .

It is quite certain that the British Empire will never fight another war contrary to the League of Nations. Any attempt to embark upon a war of aggrandisement, or pride or ambition would break the British Empire into fragments and any Government that was even suspected of such a motive would be chased from power long before its machinations could become effective. Therefore, if ever the British Empire is called upon to defend itself, its cause and the cause of the League of Nations will be one. Where, then, is the difference? The fortunes of the British Empire and its glory are inseparably interwoven with the fortunes of the world. We rise or we fall together. Indeed, if we survive today the extraordinary situation it is because even in bygone times our ancestors so managed that in the main the special interests of Britain conformed to the general interests of the world. (*Interruption.*) Read history and find there anything which can contradict what I have said. I, therefore, make no secret of the fact that personally I regard the British Navy and its sister services and all that is implied in the Covenant of the League of Nations as allied insurances for our peace and safety, and I am sure we need them both, and we need, besides, all our wit and wisdom, and all our patience and common sense in order to escape ourselves and to help the modern world out of the dangers which encompass us.

What is the great new fact about the League of Nations? What is the change that has taken place since we separated last August? It is this. The League of Nations is alive. It is alive and in action. It is fighting for its life. Probably it is fighting for all our lives. But it is fighting. No one can ever pretend that without the United States the League of Nations could be a supreme authority, but the question has been for a long time whether it was not dead and a sham. People were despairing of the League of Nations. They pointed, and my right hon. Friend the Member for Sparkbrook [Mr Amery] still points, with accusing and wounding finger to its powerlessness in the Far East and to its indifference in the Chaco War. When we separated in August the League of Nations was becoming a byword. Look at what has happened since. Here are 50 sovereign States solemnly sitting down together to devise and concert hostile economic action against a great Power, prohibiting the export of arms to Italy, encouraging such export to Italy's enemy, taking concerted measures to destroy Italian credit and financial strength in every quarter of the globe, laying an embargo on many kinds of exports to Italy and even attempting a complete boycott of Italian imports into each country. When we are told that there are leakages and loopholes, that difficulties will arise and disputes will break out between the boycotters and so forth, that may all be true, but these are, to anyone who views things in their due proportion, only the exceptions which are proving a most impressive rule. Such a system of pains and penalties has never been proclaimed against a single State, as far as I am aware, in the whole history of the world. If we could get away a little further from the scene and take a more general view than is possible to us living through events from day to day, I am sure we should see that we are already in the presence of a memorable event.

Still more remarkable is the Italian acceptance of these sanctions. When we separated in August, the story was, when these matters were viewed in an academic light, that economic sanctions meant war, and certainly the original attitude of Italy was that any attempt to apply sanctions would be treated as an unfriendly act and an affront. But what has happened? All this has proved to be untrue. Signor Mussolini – I think it is a sign of his commanding mind; to my mind it is one of the strongest things he has done – has submitted to these invidious sanctions and still preserved his contact with the League of Nations. Instead of saying 'Italy will meet them with war,' he says 'Italy will meet them with discipline, with frugality and with sacrifice.' That is a great saying in the setting, in the difficulties, in which he stands. So I say that we are not only in the presence of an assertion of the public law of Europe but of its recognition by the State affected and by the historic figure at the head of that State. That is also a truly remarkable fact, and one that is full of hope.

What does the House suppose has been the underlying cause of the transformation in the activity and force of the League of Nations which we have seen operative in the short time that we have been absent from this House? The right hon. Gentleman the Member for Darwen [Sir H. Samuel] seemed to be entirely unconscious of it. He seemed to suppose that it is simply the moral force of public opinion and the many good arguments used by the Liberal party and by Liberal writers which have produced this transformation. One is quite sorry to undeceive him. One would like him to have nursed his delusion for a little longer. But the reason is so apparent that it cannot be concealed. The reason why the League of Nations is now a reality and is now gripping all men's minds and inspiring loyalties in we know not what other countries which have hitherto regarded it as an academic apparition is because there has been behind it, as there was behind so many causes vital to human progress and freedom, the Royal Navy.

How did this arise? Let us see exactly in what context it arose. As I understand it, when the Government determined to take a strong line upon the League of Nations Council it was certain that it would bring us into antagonism with Italy in the Mediterranean. We have ancient and valuable naval and military establishments in the Mediterranean. We have a fleet, a vital part of our own main fleet, in the Mediterranean. No doubt, all these have been allowed to fall into a very easy peacetime state and the Government would have been greatly to blame if they had pursued the course on which they had decided at Geneva without at the same time making our defences safe in the Mediterranean. So the great machine was set in motion, and after an interval of a few weeks the impressive effect of superior sea power became manifest. That power has not been transferred to the League of Nations. Nevertheless it lies in a certain sense behind it, and it has invested every decision and every debate at Geneva with a gravity and a significance which it never otherwise could have possessed.

'GERMANY . . . FEARS NO ONE'

March 1936

*Conservative Backbench Foreign Affairs Committee,
House of Commons*

Though remaining in the ranks of the Conservative Party, Churchill had already for five years found himself out of sympathy with the leadership and mainstream of the Party. His public disagreements

*over India and now over the failure of the Government to rearm in
the face of the mounting threat from Nazi Germany had left him
almost completely isolated. Undaunted, he battled on.*

For four hundred years the foreign policy of England has been to
oppose the strongest, most aggressive, most dominating Power on
the Continent, and particularly to prevent the Low Countries falling
into the hands of such a Power. Viewed in the light of history, these
four centuries of consistent purpose amid so many changes of names
and facts, of circumstances and conditions, must rank as one of the
most remarkable episodes which the records of any race, nation,
state, or people can show. Moreover, on all occasions England took
the more difficult course. Faced by Philip II of Spain, against Louis
XIV under William III and Marlborough, against Napoleon, against
William II of Germany, it would have been easy and must have been
very tempting to join with the stronger and share the fruits of his
conquest. However, we always took the harder course, joined with
the less strong Powers, made a combination among them, and thus
defeated and frustrated the Continental military tyrant whoever he
was, whatever nation he led. Thus we preserved the liberties of
Europe, protected the growth of is vivacious and varied society, and
emerged after four terrible struggles with an ever-growing fame and
widening Empire, and with the Low Countries safely protected in
their independence. Here is the wonderful unconscious tradition of
British foreign policy. All our thoughts rest in that tradition today. I
know of nothing which has occurred to alter or weaken the justice,
wisdom, valour, and prudence upon which our ancestors acted. I
know of nothing that has happened to human nature which in the
slightest degree alters the validity of their conclusions. I know of
nothing in military, political, economic, or scientific fact which
makes me feel that we might not, or cannot, march along the same
road. I venture to put this very general proposition before you
because it seems to me that if it is accepted, everything else becomes
much more simple.

Observe that the policy of England takes no account of which
nation it is that seeks the overlordship of Europe. The question is not
whether it is Spain, or the French Monarchy, or the French Empire,
or the German Empire, or the Hitler régime. It has nothing to do
with rulers or nations; it is concerned solely with whoever is the
strongest or the potentially dominating tyrant. Therefore, we should
not be afraid of being accused of being pro-French or anti-German. If
the circumstances were reversed, we could equally be pro-German

and anti-French. It is a law of public policy which we are following, and not a mere expedient dictated by accidental circumstances, or likes and dislikes, or any other sentiment.

The question, therefore, arises which is today the Power in Europe which is the strongest, and which seeks in a dangerous and oppressive sense to dominate. Today, for this year, probably for part of 1937, the French Army is the strongest in Europe. But no one is afraid of France. Everyone knows that France wants to be let alone, and that with her it is only a case of self-preservation. Everyone knows that the French are peaceful and overhung by fear. They are at once brave, resolute, peace-loving, and weighed down by anxiety. They are a liberal nation with free parliamentary institutions.

Germany, on the other hand, fears no one. She is arming in a manner which has never been seen in German history. She is led by a handful of triumphant desperadoes. The money is running short, discontents are arising beneath these despotic rulers. Very soon they will have to choose, on the one hand, between economic and financial collapse or internal upheaval, and, on the other, a war which could have no other object, and which, if successful, can have no other result than a Germanised Europe under Nazi control. Therefore, it seems to me that all the old conditions present themselves again, and that our national salvation depends upon our gathering once again all the forces of Europe to contain, to restrain, and if necessary to frustrate, German domination. For, believe me, if any of those other Powers, Spain, Louis XIV, Napoleon, Kaiser Wilhelm II, had with our aid become the absolute masters of Europe, they could have despoiled us, reduced us to insignificance and penury on the morrow of their victory. We ought to set the life and endurance of the British Empire and the greatness of this island very high in our duty, and not be led astray by illusions about an ideal world, which only means that other and worse controls will step into our place, and that the future direction will belong to them.

It is at this stage that the spacious conception and extremely vital organisation of the League of Nations presents itself as a prime factor. The League of Nations is, in a practical sense, a British conception, and it harmonises perfectly with all our past methods and actions. Moreover, it harmonises with those broad ideas of right and wrong, and of peace based upon controlling the major aggressor, which we have always followed. We wish for the reign of law and freedom among nations and within nations, and it was for that, and nothing less than that, that those bygone architects of our repute, magnitude, and civilisation fought, and won. The dream of a reign of international law and of the settlement of disputes by patient discussion, but still in accordance with what is lawful and just, is very dear to the British people. You must not underrate the force which these ideals exert upon the modern British democracy. One does not know how these seeds are planted by the winds of the centuries in the hearts of the working people. They are there, and just as strong as their love of liberty. We should not neglect them, because they are the essence of the genius of this island. Therefore, we believe that in the fostering and fortifying of the League of Nations will be found the best means of defending our island security, as well as maintaining grand universal causes with which we have very often found our own interests in natural accord.

My three main propositions are: First, that we must oppose the would-be dominator or potential aggressor. Secondly, that Germany under its present Nazi régime and with its prodigious armaments, so swiftly developing, fills unmistakably that part. Thirdly, that the League of Nations rallies many countries, and unites our own people here at home in the most effective way to control the would-be aggressor. I venture most respectfully to submit these main themes to your consideration. Everything else will follow from them.

It is always more easy to discover and proclaim general principles than to apply them. First, we ought to count our effective association with France. That does not mean that we should develop a needlessly hostile mood against Germany. It is a part of our duty and our interest to keep the temperature low between these two countries. We shall not have any difficulty in this so far as France is concerned. Like us, they are a parliamentary democracy with tremendous inhibitions against war, and, like us, under considerable drawbacks in preparing their defence. Therefore, I say we ought to regard our defensive association with France as fundamental. Everything else must be viewed in proper subordination now that the times have become so sharp and perilous. Those who are possessed of a definite body of doctrine and of deeply rooted convictions upon it will be in a much better position to deal with the shifts and surprises of daily affairs than those who are merely taking short views, and indulging their natural impulses as they are evoked by what they read from day to day. The first thing is to decide where you want to go. For myself, I am for the armed League of all Nations, or as many as you can get, against the potential aggressor, with England and France as the core of it. Let us neglect nothing in our power to establish the great international framework. If that should prove to be beyond our strength, or if it breaks down through the weakness or wrongdoing of others, then at least let us make sure that England and France, the two surviving free great countries of Europe, can together ride out any storm that may blow with good and reasonable hopes of once again coming safely into port.

THE JEWS: 'THEIR BLOOD AND RACE DECLARED DEFILING AND ACCURSED'

24 March 1936

House of Commons

Churchill who, as Colonial Secretary, had defined the borders of Biblical Palestine and placed Emir Abdullah on the throne of Jordan, remained a constant champion of the Zionist cause and upholder of the Balfour Declaration, which proclaimed Palestine a 'National Home' for the Jews.

The right hon. Gentleman has assured us that the Mandate and the Balfour Declaration are safe, but I personally feel great doubts about that. If you have an Arab majority, undoubtedly you will have continued friction between the principle of the Balfour Declaration and the steps that must be taken day by day and month by month to give effect to that Declaration and the wishes of the Arab majority. I should have thought it would be a very great obstruction to the development of Jewish immigration into Palestine and to the development of the national home of the Jews there.

I have no hostility for the Arabs. I think I made most of the settlements over 14 years ago governing the Palestine situation. The Emir Abdullah is in Transjordania, where I put him one Sunday afternoon at Jerusalem. I acted upon the advice of that very great man Colonel Lawrence, who was at my side in making the arrangements, which I believe have stood the test of time and many changes of government throughout the Middle East. But I cannot conceive that you will be able to reconcile, at this juncture and at this time, the development of the policy of the Balfour Declaration with an Arab majority on the Legislative Council. I do not feel a bit convinced of it, even though Sir Andrew Walker may be of that opinion. I do not feel convinced when I see so many other people who have studied the matter, and who are friends of Palestine, friends of the Arabs, friends of the Jews, who view this departure at the present moment with the very greatest misgiving.

We are doing very fine work in Palestine at the present moment. When I travelled through the country a little more than a year ago I was enormously impressed with the order and smoothness with which the administration was being conducted. If you go into neighbouring countries, like Syria, you see that there is also order and progress, but enormous military forces are used. Scores of thousands of troops are maintained in the country. I always consider that our administration must be judged, in comparison with these countries, not by the fact that they can govern with overwhelming military forces – anyone can do that – but that we can conduct progressive administration with the comparatively small forces that we employ in those areas.

Do not be in a hurry to overturn the existing system. It is working very well. It is not as though it had got into such a state that you said that you could not go on any more with the present administration, and that, although your local government institutions have completely failed up to date, or have made no success of their experiment, nevertheless you must plunge into the larger field. That is not the position. You are in the full tide of a successful experiment in British administration and your local government is moving forward in a very slow manner. Surely, therefore, you can afford to wait for some other time. Does the right hon. Gentleman mean to say that if, under the advice of Parliament or under the persuasion which reaches him from any quarter, he decided that this matter could not go forward this year or next year, but that he would wait for some other time – does he suggest that he would feel himself guilty of a breach of faith, of a breaking of the pledge given to the League of Nations? It is absurd. I have not the slightest doubt that, if our representatives at Geneva explained the position as it has been explained in this House from every bench, they would get cordial support for not taking this step at the present moment, from the authority whom they have a right to consult.

I have been speaking of this matter in connection with Palestine, but, of course, there is in our minds an added emphasis upon this question of Jewish migration which comes from other quarters, at a time when the Jewish race in a great country is being subjected to most horrible, cold, scientific persecution, brutal persecution, a cold 'pogrom' as it has been called – people reduced from affluence to ruin, and then, even in that position, denied the opportunity of earning their daily bread, and cut out even from relief by grants to tide the destitute through the winter; their little children pilloried in the schools to which they have to go; their blood and race declared defiling and accursed; every form of concentrated human wickedness cast upon these people by overwhelming power, by vile tyranny. I say that, when that is the case, surely the House of Commons will not allow the one door which is open, the one door which allows some relief, some escape from these conditions, to be summarily closed, nor even allow it to be suggested that it may be obstructed by the course which we take now.

'GREAT HAMMERS DESCENDING DAY AND NIGHT IN GERMANY'

26 March 1936

House of Commons

On 7 March Hitler's armies invaded the Rhineland in stark defiance of the Treaties of Versailles and Locarno – an event accepted with barely a protest by the British and French Governments. To Churchill it was confirmation of his warnings of the aggressive nature of Nazi Germany.

The violation of the Rhineland is serious from the point of view of the menace to which it exposes Holland, Belgium and France. It is also serious from the fact that when it is fortified – and I listened with apprehension to what the Secretary of State said about the Germans declining even to refrain from entrenching themselves during the period of negotiations; I listened with sorrow to that – when there is there a line of fortifications, as I suppose there will be in a very short time, it will produce great reactions on the European situation. It will be a barrier across Germany's front-door, which will leave her free to sally out eastward and southward by the back door.

In spite of the seriousness which I attach to this reoccupation of the Rhineland, I must say that it seems to me the smallest part of the whole problem. What is the real problem, the real peril? It is not the reoccupation of the Rhineland, but this enormous process of the rearmament of Germany. There is the peril. My right hon. Friend opposite says that in the election I seemed to be haunted by this idea. I confess that I have been occupied with this idea of the great wheels revolving and the great hammers descending day and night in Germany, making the whole industry of that country an arsenal, making the whole of that gifted and valiant population into one great disciplined war machine. There is the problem that lies before you. There is what is bringing the war. This Rhineland business is but a step, is but a stage, is but an incident in this process. I agree very much with the spokesman of the official Labour Opposition when he said there was fear. There is fear, in every country, all round. Even here, in this country, with some protection from distance, there is fear, deep fear. It takes a deep fear to make the hon. Member for West Fife (Mr Gallacher) speak in terms which commend themselves to almost every one who was in the House. What is the fear and what is the question which arises from that fear? It is, 'How are we going to stop this war which seems to be moving towards us in so many ways?'

There are, of course, two practical foreign policies for our country. The first is an alliance between Great Britain and France, the two surviving liberal democracies of the West, who, strongly armed, rich, powerful, with the seas at their disposal, with great air forces and great armies, would stand with their backs to the ocean and allow the explosion which may come in Europe to blast its way eastward or southward. There is a practical foreign policy, but I do hope that we shall not resign ourselves to that, without first an earnest effort to persevere in the other policy, namely, the establishment of real collective security under the League of Nations and of the reign of law and respect for international law throughout Europe. I venture to make a suggestion which I feel will not be entirely repugnant to those who sit opposite, namely, that, apart from this particular emergency and apart from the measures which the Foreign Secretary has taken, we should endeavour now with great resolution to establish effective collective security. In my view, all the nations and States that are alarmed at the growth of German armaments ought to combine for mutual aid, in pacts of mutual assistance, approved by the League of Nations and in accordance with the Covenant of the League.

We hear talk of the encirclement of Germany. I thought that the last speaker quite justly said that war encirclement would be intolerable, but peaceful, defensive encirclement may be inevitable, before the alarms of the nations are allayed. I say we would impose no encirclement on Germany that we would not submit to ourselves. It is not a case of the encirclement of Germany but of the encirclement of the potential aggressor. If we are the aggressors, let us be encircled and brought to reason by the pressure of other countries. If France is the aggressor, let her be restrained in the same way; and if it be Germany, let Germany take the measures meted out to her by countries who submit themselves to the law which they are prepared to take a share in enforcing. The first thing we ought to do is to make these pacts of mutual aid and assistance. My right hon. Friend the Member for Carnarvon Boroughs (Mr Lloyd George), who is not here now, spoke grave words of warning about military conventions. But you cannot have effective arrangements for mutual aid in contingencies of peril unless you have conventions. That is the first thing.

In the second place, I agree with what was said by the right hon. Gentleman who opened the Debate for the Opposition, that the Powers, once they are woven into this strong confederacy for defence and peace, should give to Germany an absolute guarantee of the inviolability of German soil and a promise that, if anyone invades her, all will turn against the offender and if she strikes at anyone, all will stand by and defend the victim. I am looking for peace. I am looking for a way to stop war, but you will not stop it by pious sentiments and appeals. You will only stop it by making practical arrangements. When you have these two conditions established firmly, when you have linked up the forces at the disposal of the League for defence, and when you have given that guarantee to Germany, then is the first moment when you should address Germany collectively, not only upon the minor question of the Rhine but upon the supreme question of German rearmament in relation to other countries – and they must not shirk presenting themselves to that test also. Further, at that moment you must invite Germany to state her grievances, to lay them on the council board and to let us have it out. But do not let us have it out as if we were a rabble flying before forces we dare not resist. Let us have it out on the basis that we are negotiating from strength and not from weakness; that we are negotiating from unity and not from division and isolation; that we are seeking to do justice, because we have power.

The whole history of the world is summed up in the fact that when nations are strong they are not always just, and when they wish to be just they are often no longer strong. I desire to see the collective forces of the world invested with overwhelming power. If you are going to run this thing on a narrow margin and to depend on a very slight margin, one way or the other, you are going to have war. But if you get five or ten to one on one side, all bound rigorously by the Covenant and the conventions which they own, then, in my opinion, you have an opportunity of making a settlement which will heal the wounds of the world. Let us have this blessed union of power and of justice:

Agree with thine adversary quickly while thou art in the way with him.

Let us free the world from the approach of a catastrophe, carrying with it calamity and tribulation, beyond the tongue of man to tell.

'HITLER HAS TORN UP THE TREATIES AND GARRISONED THE RHINELAND'

6 April 1936

House of Commons

As Hitler's actions became more brazen and the British and French Governments more craven, Churchill's warnings took on an added stridency and urgency.

Herr Hitler has torn up treaties and has garrisoned the Rhineland. His troops are there, and there they are going to stay. All this means that the Nazi régime has gained a new prestige in Germany and in all the neighbouring countries. But more than that. Germany is now fortifying the Rhine zone, or is about to fortify it. No doubt it will take some time. We are told that in the first instance only field entrenchments will be erected, but those who know to what perfection the Germans can carry field entrenchments like the Hindenburg Line, with all the masses of concrete and the underground chambers there included – those who remember that will realise that field entrenchments differ only in degree from permanent fortifications, and work steadily up from the first cutting of the sods to their final and perfect form.

I do not doubt that the whole of the German frontier opposite to France is to be fortified as strongly and as speedily as possible. Three, four or six months will certainly see a barrier of enormous strength. What will be the diplomatic and strategic consequences of that? I am not dealing with the technical aspect, but with the diplomatic reactions. The creation of a line of forts opposite to the French frontier will enable the German troops to be economised on that line, and will enable the main forces to swing round through Belgium and Holland. That is for us a danger of the most serious kind. Suppose we broke with France. Suppose these efforts to divide the last surviving free democracies of the Western world were successful and they were sundered, and suppose that France, isolated, could do no more than defend her own frontier behind Belgium and Holland by prolonging her fortress line, those small countries might very speedily pass under German domination, and the large colonial empires which they possess would no doubt be transferred at the same time. These are matters that ought not to escape our attention.

I thought that the Prime Minister's remark which he made some years ago about our frontier being the Rhine [30 July 1934] was liable at the time to be misunderstood; but if he meant that it was a mortal danger to Britain to have the Low Countries in the fortified grip of the strongest military power upon the Continent, and now, in these days, to have all the German aviation bases established there, he was only repeating the lesson taught in four centuries of history. That danger will be brought definitely and sensibly nearer from the moment that this new line of German fortifications is completed. But then, look East. There the consequences of the Rhineland fortification may be more immediate. That is to us a less direct danger, but is a more imminent danger. The moment those fortifications are completed, and in proportion as they are completed, the whole aspect of Middle Europe is changed. The Baltic States, Poland, and Czechoslovakia, with which must be associated Yugoslavia, Rumania, Austria and some other countries, are all affected very decisively the moment that this great work of construction has been completed.

Some of those nations, but not all, are now balancing in deep perplexity what course they should take. Should they continue in their association with the League of Nations and with what is called collective security and the reign of law? Or should they make the best terms they can with the one resolute, warlike Power which is stirring in Europe at the present time? That is the question they have to ask themselves. If nothing satisfactory has been achieved by the negotiations and conferences which no doubt will occupy a large part of this year, we may see many powerful nations, with armies and air forces, associated with the German Nazi system, and the other nations who are opposed to that system isolated and practically helpless. It is idle to say that these are not matters which the House of Commons should view with vigilance and attention. It is idle to pretend that these are only matters affecting the obscurities, the politics and the hatreds of Central Europe.

'THANK GOD FOR THE FRENCH ARMY'

24 September 1936

Théâtre des Ambassadeurs, Paris

Next to the English Channel, the French Army – many times the size of Britain's – was the principal bulwark standing between Britain and the armoured might of Nazi Germany. Here Churchill does what he can to put some backbone and resolve into the government of France. Sadly, his faith in the French Army was to prove misplaced.

There are three kinds of nations in the world at the present time. There are the nations which are governed by the Nazis; there are the nations which are governed by the Bolshevists, and there are the nations which govern themselves. It is this third class of nations in which the French and English peoples are most interested. We are interested in the nations which govern themselves through Parliaments freely elected under a democratic franchise. These are the nations where the people have the right to criticise the Ministers and functionaries of State. They can choose the complexion of the Government they wish to manage their affairs. They can hold public meetings to express all their different opinions. The individual citizen has the right if aggrieved to sue the State at law, and impartial Courts are provided which pronounce whether he or the executive power is in the right. In these countries the State exists to protect the rights of the individual, to enable him to make the best of himself, and to secure the free development of family life within the cottage home. We live in countries where the people own the Government and not in countries where the Government owns the people. Thought is free;

speech is free; religion is free; no one can say that the Press is not free; in short, we live in a liberal society, the direct product of the great advances in human dignity, stature, and well-being which will ever be the glory of the nineteenth century.

We have also the feeling that in France, England, the United States, in Switzerland, Belgium, Holland, and Scandinavia we not only have liberal constitutions which secure our rights, but we have been able to produce a greater material prosperity more widely diffused among the masses of the people than any form of despotism has yet been able to show. In these self-governing countries we may also claim to lead the world alike in accumulated wealth and in compassionate treatment of misfortune.

We must recognise that we have a great treasure to guard; that the inheritance in our possession represents the prolonged achievement of the centuries; that there is not one of our simple uncounted rights today for which better men than we are have not died on the scaffold or the battlefield. We have not only a great treasure; we have a great cause. Are we taking every measure within our power to defend that cause?

I am sure that the French, British, or American democracies would be very miserable if they were suddenly put under Nazi or Bolshevist rule. France and England are the chief architects of modern civilisation, and the United States is the heir and champion of our ideas. How could we bear, nursed as we have been in a free atmosphere, to be gagged and muzzled; to have spies, eavesdroppers, and delators at every corner; to have even private conversation caught up and used against us by the secret police and all their agents and creatures; to be arrested and interned without trial; or to be tried by political or party courts for crimes hitherto unknown to civil law? How could we bear to be treated like schoolboys when we are grown-up men; to be turned out on parade by tens of thousands to march and cheer for this slogan or for that; to see philosophers, teachers, and authors bullied and toiled to death in concentration camps; to be forced every hour to conceal the natural normal workings of the human intellect and the pulsations of the human heart? Rather than submit to such oppression there is no length we would not go. Our cause is good. Our rights are good. Let us make sure that our arms are good. Let us make sure that our conduct is wise. Let us make sure that it is governed by forethought and statesmanship.

The French Republic and the British Empire should stand shoulder to shoulder against aggression. After all we are not so weak and helpless as some people make out. Four years ago when things were very different I exclaimed to the House of Commons, 'Thank God for the French Army.' I repeat it here today with the instructed conviction that that Army is today the finest in the world. The future is not so certain – there are grave anxieties about the future – but it is something to speak with confidence of today. Of the British Fleet I can speak with particular assurance. It is certainly far stronger in relation to any fleet or combination of fleets in Europe than it was in 1914, and by the arrangements which are now being made by his Majesty's Government its preponderance will certainly be maintained in the future. There remains the problem of the Air, which requires the most urgent study of the Western democracies and greater exertions than either of them has yet made. But at any rate it would be a great mistake to suppose that we are either of us defenceless in this new arm at the present time. Here at any rate are means of defence which leave us still masters of our fortunes.

But good defences alone would never enable us by themselves to survive in the modern grim gigantic world. There must be added to those defences the sovereign power of generous motives and of high ideals, in fact, that cause of freedom, moral and intellectual, which I have endeavoured to describe. We must trust something to the power of enlightened ideas. We must trust much to our resolve not to be impatient or quarrelsome or arrogant. We seek peace. We long for peace. We pray for peace. We seek no territory. We aim at no invidious monopoly of raw materials. Our hearts are clean. We have no old scores to repay. We submit ourselves whole-heartedly, nay proudly, to the Covenant of the League of Nations. We desire faithfully and fairly to bear our part in building up a true collective security which shall not only lighten the burden of the toiling millions, but also provide the means by which the grievances of great dissatisfied nations, if well-founded, can be peacefully adjusted.

Another Great War would extinguish what is left of the civilisation of the world, and the glory of Europe would sink for uncounted generations into the dark abyss. We wish to prevent this war. We can only do so if we are armed and strong, if we are united upon fundamental principles, if we serve with equal loyalty side by side for the same high purpose, for no selfish purpose, no narrowly national purpose, no reactionary purpose, but a purpose known to us all, comprehended by us all, a purpose worthy of the genius of mankind.

It is the nature of extremists to be violent and furious, whereas the great central mass of temperate, tolerant, good-natured humanity is apt to be feeble in action and leadership. But if the cause of ordered freedom, of representative government, of the rights of the individual against the State is worth defending, it is surely worth defending efficiently. If we are to be drawn into such a competition let us make sure we win. Let us make sure that the force of right is not in the last resort deprived of the right of force. In Britain as in France the great mass of good people mean the right thing. Let those who have the responsibility of leadership make sure that they get it.

When we speak of representative or Parliamentary government we mean a system which faithfully and punctually gives those guarantees of law and order, or justice, tolerance, and fair play without which no Parliament or parley is possible. A Parliamentary régime must not become a mere fraudulent pretence to cover the advances of Nazi-ism or Communism. It was a grave fault in the Spanish Ministers that they continued to accept responsibility after they had ceased to have power. Their names stood for Parliamentary government; but others were acting in their names. That is a betrayal of trust. And this feature has justified, nay imposed upon us, a strict neutrality.

When we speak of collective security we mean a real collective security. We do not mean merely that one or two Powers should run great risks while others fail to play their part according to their strength; we certainly do not mean a multiplication of risks for some without equal or even any compensating protection. We do not mean that the peace-seeking nations should disarm while those who glorify war forge their weapons and array their regiments. Secondly, when we seek this real collective security for ourselves we offer it most earnestly to all others. Great Britain and France ask for themselves no single guarantee of safety and independence that they are not willing and resolute to extend to the great German people, with whom we all sincerely desire to dwell in peace and goodwill.

Someone asked me: 'If Germany and Russia went to war, would you be in favour of Germany or of Russia?' That is a very easy question to answer. Our feelings and any action we are bound to take under the Covenant of the League of Nations would be against the unprovoked aggressor. It would not be a question of Germany or Russia. It would not be a question of Right or Left. It would be a question of right or wrong. I should like to see, and there are many in Britain who think with me, so tremendous an organisation of nations ready to fall upon the aggressor that no one would dare to break the peace of Europe. If Governments are to band themselves together for collective security, it follows that they must rigorously abstain from organised interference in the internal affairs of their neighbours and fellow members in the League. When we speak of aggression we mean unprovoked aggression. Propaganda carried on by foreign money in any country is a serious form of provocation.

LAWRENCE OF ARABIA

3 October 1936

Memorial unveiling, Oxford High School

Lawrence of Arabia had been a personal friend of Churchill's over many years. Frequently, and often unannounced, he would arrive at Chartwell on his motor cycle for Sunday lunch with Churchill and his family. It had been Lawrence who, dressed in Arab garb, had masterminded and inspired the Arab Revolt against the Ottoman Turks in the First World War.

Although more than a year has passed since Lawrence was taken from us, the impression of his personality remains living and vivid upon the minds of his friends, and the sense of his loss is in no way dimmed among his countrymen. All feel the poorer that he has gone from us. In these days dangers and difficulties gather upon Britain and her Empire, and we are also conscious of a lack of outstanding figures with which to overcome them. Here was a man in whom there existed not only an immense capacity for service, but that touch of genius which every one recognises and no one can define. Whether in his great period of adventure and command or in these later years of self-suppression and self-imposed eclipse, he always reigned over those with whom he came in contact. They felt themselves in the presence of an extraordinary being. They felt that his latent reserves of force and will power were beyond measurement. If he roused himself to action, who should say what crisis he could not surmount or quell? If things were going very badly, how glad one would be to see him come round the corner.

Part of the secret of this stimulating ascendancy lay of course in his disdain for most of the prizes, the pleasures and comforts of life. The world naturally looks with some awe upon a man who appears unconcernedly indifferent to home, money, comfort, rank, or even power and fame. The world feels not without a certain apprehension that here is someone outside its jurisdiction; someone before whom its allurements may be spread in vain; someone strangely enfranchised, untamed, untrammelled by convention, moving independently of the ordinary currents of human action; a being readily capable of violent revolt or supreme sacrifice; a man, solitary, austere, to whom existence is no more than a duty, yet a duty to be faithfully discharged. He was indeed a dweller upon the mountain tops where the air is cold, crisp, and rarefied, and where the view on clear days commands all the kingdoms of the world and the glory of them.

Lawrence was one of those beings whose pace of life was faster and more intense than what is normal. Just as an aeroplane only flies by its speed and pressure against the air, so he flew best and easiest in the hurricane. He was not in complete harmony with the normal. The fury of the Great War raised the pitch of life to the Lawrence standard. The multitudes were swept forward till their pace was the same as his. In this heroic period he found himself in perfect relation both to men and events.

I have often wondered what would have happened to Lawrence if the Great War had continued for several more years. His fame was spreading fast and with the momentum of the fabulous throughout Asia. The earth trembled with the wrath of the warring nations. All the metals were molten. Everything was in motion. No one could say what was impossible. Lawrence might have realised Napoleon's young dream of conquering the East; he might have arrived at Constantinople in 1919 or 1920 with most of the tribes and races of Asia Minor and Arabia at his back. But the storm wind ceased as suddenly as it had arisen. The skies were clear; the bells of Armistice rang out. Mankind returned with indescribable relief to its long interrupted, fondly-cherished ordinary life, and Lawrence was left once more moving alone on a different plane and at a different speed.

In this we find an explanation of the last phase of his all too brief life. It is not the only explanation. The sufferings and stresses he had undergone, both physical and psychic, during the war had left their scars and injuries upon him. These were aggravated by the distress which he felt at which he deemed the ill-usage of his Arab friends and allies to whom he had pledged the word of Britain, and the word of Lawrence. He was capable of suffering mental pain in an exceptional degree. I am sure that the ordeal of watching the helplessness of his Arab friends in the grand confusions of the Peace Conference was the main cause which decided his renunciation of all power, and so far as possible of all interest in great public affairs.

In this premature retirement he had to lay hold of detailed tasks wherewith to fill the days and the hours. The writing of his book *The Seven Pillars* was a powerful solace to him. To all of us it is one of the treasures of English literature. *The Seven Pillars* as a narrative of war and adventure, as a portrayal of all that the Arabs mean in the world, is unsurpassed. It ranks with the greatest books ever written in the English language. It is not, I think, excessive to class it in interest and charm with *Pilgrim's Progress*, *Robinson Crusoe*, and *Gulliver's Travels*. If Lawrence had never done anything except write this book as a mere work of the imagination his fame would last, in Macaulay's familiar phrase, 'as long as the English language is spoken in any quarter of the globe.' But this was a book of fact, not fiction, and the author was also the commander. When most of the vast literature of the Great War has been sifted and superseded by the epitomes, commentaries, and histories of future generations, when the complicated and infinitely costly operations of ponderous armies are the concern only of the military student, when our struggles are viewed in a fading perspective and in truer proportion, Lawrence's tale of the revolt in the desert will gleam with immortal fire.

When this literary masterpiece was written, lost, and written again; when every illustration had been profoundly considered and every incident of typography and paragraphing settled with meticulous care; when Lawrence on his bicycle had carried the precious volumes to the few – the very few – he deemed worthy to read them, happily he found another task to his hands which cheered and comforted his soul. He saw as clearly as anyone the vision of air power and all that it would mean in traffic and war. He found in the life of an aircraftman that balm of peace and equipoise which no great station or command could have bestowed upon him. He felt that in living the life of a private in the Royal Air Force he would dignify that honourable calling and help to attract all that is keenest in our youthful manhood to the sphere where it is most urgently needed. For this service and example, to which he devoted the last 12 years of his life, we owe him a separate debt. It was in itself a princely gift.

If on this occasion I have seemed to dwell upon Lawrence's sorrows and heart-searchings rather than upon his achievements and prowess, it is because the latter are so justly famous. He had a full measure of the versatility of genius. He held one of those master keys which unlock the doors of many kinds of treasure-houses. He was a savant as well as a soldier. He was an archaeologist as well as a man of action. He was an accomplished scholar as well as an Arab partisan. He was a mechanic as well as a philosopher. His background of sombre experience and reflection only seemed to set forth more brightly the charm and gaiety of his companionship, and the generous majesty of his nature. Those who knew him best miss him most; but our country misses him most of all; and misses him most of all now. For this is a time when the great problems upon which his thought and work had so long centred, problems of aerial defence, problems of our relations with the Arab people, fill an ever larger space in our affairs. For all his reiterated renunciations I always felt that he was a man who held himself ready for a Call. While Lawrence lived one always felt – I certainly felt it strongly – that some overpowering need would draw him from the modest path he chose to tread, and set him once again in full action at the centre of memorable events. It was not to be. The summons which reached him, and for which he was equally prepared, was of a different order. It came as he would have wished it, swift and sudden on the wings of Speed. He had reached the last leap in his gallant course through life.

> All is over! Fleet career.
> Dash of greyhound slipping thongs,
> Flight of falcon, bound of deer,
> Mad hoof-thunder in our rear,
> Cold air rushing up our lungs,
> Din of many tongues.

King George the Fifth wrote to Lawrence's brother 'His name will live in history.' Can we doubt that that is true? It will live in English letters; it will live in the traditions of the Royal Air Force; it will live in the annals of war and in the legend of Arabia. It will also live here in his old school, forever proclaimed and honoured by the monument we have today unveiled.

'THE LOCUST YEARS'

12 November 1936

House of Commons

This must be counted one of the most powerful and devastating of Churchill's attacks on the Baldwin Government, that was dithering with Britain's defences.

I have, with some friends, put an Amendment on the Paper. . . . It is the same as the Amendment which I submitted two years ago, and I have put it in exactly the same terms because I thought it would be a good thing to remind the House of what has happened in these two years. Our Amendment in November 1934 was the culmination of a long series of efforts by private Members and by the Conservative party in the country to warn His Majesty's Government of the dangers to Europe and to this country which were coming upon us through the vast process of German rearmament then already in full swing. The speech which I made on that occasion was much censured as being alarmist by leading Conservative newspapers, and I remember that Mr Lloyd George congratulated the Prime Minister, who was then Lord President, on having so satisfactorily demolished my extravagant fears.

What would have been said, I wonder, if I could two years ago have forecast to the House the actual course of events? Suppose we had then been told that Germany would spend for two years £800,000,000 a year upon warlike preparations; that her industries would be organised for war, as the industries of no country have ever been; that by breaking all Treaty engagements she would create a gigantic air force and an army based on universal compulsory service, which by the present time, in 1936, amounts to upwards of thirty-nine divisions of highly equipped troops, including mechanised divisions of almost unmeasured strength, and that behind all this there lay millions of armed and trained men, for whom the formations and equipment are rapidly being prepared to form another eighty divisions in addition to those already perfected. Suppose we had then known that by now two years of compulsory military service would be the rule, with a preliminary year of training in labour camps; that the Rhineland would be occupied by powerful forces and fortified with great skill, and that Germany would be building with our approval, signified by treaty, a large submarine fleet.

Suppose we had also been able to foresee the degeneration of the foreign situation, our quarrel with Italy, the Italo-German association, the Belgian declaration about neutrality – which, if the worst interpretation of it proves to be true, so greatly affects the security of this country – and the disarray of the smaller Powers of Central Europe. Suppose all that had been forecast – why, no one would have believed in the truth of such a nightmare tale. Yet just two years have gone by and we see it all in broad daylight. Where shall we be this time in two years? I hesitate now to predict.

Let me say, however, that I will not accept the mood of panic or of despair. There is another side – a side which deserves our study, and can be studied without derogating in any way from the urgency which ought to animate our military preparations. The British Navy is, and will continue to be, for a good many months to come, at least equal in numbers and superior in maturity to the German Army. The British and French air forces together are a very different proposition from either of those forces considered separately. While no one can prophesy, it seems to me that the Western democracies, provided they are knit closely together, would be tolerably safe for a considerable number of months ahead. No one can say to a month or two, or even a quarter or two, how long this period of comparative equipoise will last. But it seems certain that during the year 1937 the German Army will become more numerous than the French Army, and very much more efficient than it is now. It seems certain that the German air force will continue to improve upon the long lead which it already has over us, particularly in respect of long-distance bombing machines. The year 1937 will certainly be marked by a great increase in the adverse factors which only intense efforts on our part can, to any effective extent, countervail.

The efforts of rearmament which France and Britain are making will not by themselves be sufficient. It will be necessary for the Western democracies, even at some extension of their risks, to gather round them all the elements of collective security or of combined defensive strength against aggression – if you prefer, as I do myself, to call it so – which can be assembled on the basis of the Covenant of the League of Nations. Thus I hope we may succeed in again achieving a position of superior force, and then will be the time, not to repeat the folly which we committed when we were all-powerful and supreme, but to invite Germany to make common cause with us in assuaging the griefs of Europe and opening a new door to peace and disarmament.

I now turn more directly to the issues of this Debate [on the Address]. Let us examine our own position. No one can refuse his sympathy to the Minister for the Co-ordination of Defence [Sir Thomas Inskip]. From time to time my right hon. Friend lets fall phrases or facts which show that he realises, more than anyone else on that bench it seems to me, the danger in which we stand. One such phrase came from his lips the other night. He spoke of 'the years that the locust hath eaten.' Let us see which are these 'years that the locust hath eaten,' even if we do not pry too closely in search of the locusts who have eaten these precious years. For this purpose we must look into the past. From the year 1932, certainly from the beginning of 1933, when Herr Hitler came into power, it was general public knowledge in this country that serious rearmament had begun in Germany. There was a change in the situation. Three years ago, at the Conservative Conference at Birmingham, that vigorous and faithful servant of this country, Lord Lloyd, moved the following resolution:

> That this Conference desires to record its grave anxiety in regard to the inadequacy of the provisions made for Imperial Defence.

That was three years ago, and I see, from *The Times* report of that occasion, that I said:

> During the last four or five years the world had grown gravely darker. . . . We have steadily disarmed, partly with a sincere desire to give a lead to other countries, and partly through the severe financial pressure of the time. But a change must now be made. We must not continue longer on a course in which we alone are growing weaker while every other nation is growing stronger.

The resolution was passed unanimously, with only a rider informing the Chancellor of the Exchequer that all necessary burdens of taxation would be cheerfully borne. There were no locusts there, at any rate.

I am very glad to see the Prime Minister [Mr Baldwin] restored to his vigour, and to learn that he has been recuperated by his rest and also, as we hear, rejuvenated. It has been my fortune to have ups and downs in my political relations with him, the downs on the whole predominating perhaps, but at any rate we have always preserved agreeable personal relations, which, so far as I am concerned, are greatly valued. I am sure he would not wish in his conduct of public affairs that there should be any shrinking from putting the real issues of criticism which arise, and I shall certainly proceed in that sense. My right hon. Friend has had all the power for a good many years, and therefore there rests upon him inevitably the main responsibility for everything that has been done, or not done, and also the responsibility for what is to be done or not done now. So far as the air is concerned, this responsibility was assumed by him in a very direct personal manner even before he became Prime Minister. I must recall the words which he used in the Debate on 8th March, 1934, nearly three years ago. In answer to an appeal which I made to him, both publicly and privately, he said:

Any Government of this country – a National Government more than
any, and this Government – will see to it that in air strength and air
power this country shall no longer be in a position inferior to any
country within striking distance of our shores.

Well, Sir, I accepted that solemn promise, but some of my friends,
like Sir Edward Grigg and Captain Guest, wanted what the Minister
for the Co-ordination of Defence, in another state of being, would
have called 'further and better particulars', and they raised a debate
after dinner, when the Prime Minister, then Lord President, came
down to the House and really showed less than his usual urbanity in
chiding those Members for even venturing to doubt the intention of
the Government to make good in every respect the pledge which he
had so solemnly given in the afternoon. I do not think that
responsibility was ever more directly assumed in a more personal
manner. The Prime Minister was not successful in discharging that
task, and he admitted with manly candour a year later that he had
been led into error upon the important question of the relative
strength of the British and German air power.

No doubt as a whole His Majesty's Government were very slow in
accepting the unwelcome fact of German rearmament. They still
clung to the policy of one-sided disarmament. It was one of those
experiments, we are told, which had to be, to use a vulgarism, 'tried
out', just as the experiments of non-military sanctions against Italy
had to be tried out. Both experiments have now been tried out, and
Ministers are accustomed to plume themselves upon the very clear
results of those experiments. They are held to prove conclusively that
the policies subjected to the experiments were all wrong, utterly
foolish, and should never be used again, and the very same men who
were foremost in urging those experiments are now foremost in
proclaiming and denouncing the fallacies upon which they were
based. They have bought their knowledge, they have bought it dear,
they have bought it at our expense, but at any rate let us be duly
thankful that they now at last possess it.

In July 1935, before the General Election, there was a very strong
movement in this House in favour of the appointment of a Minister
to concert the action of the three fighting Services. Moreover, at that
time the Departments of State were all engaged in drawing up the
large schemes of rearmament in all branches which have been laid
before us in the White Paper and upon which we are now engaged.
One would have thought that that was the time when this new
Minister or Co-ordinator was most necessary. He was not, however,

in fact appointed until nearly nine months later, in March 1936. No explanation has yet been given to us why these nine months were wasted before the taking of what is now an admittedly necessary measure. The Prime Minister dilated the other night, no doubt very properly, on the great advantages which had flowed from the appointment of the Minister for the Co-ordination of Defence. Every argument used to show how useful has been the work which he has done accuses the failure to appoint him nine months earlier, when inestimable benefits would have accrued to us by the saving of this long period.

When at last, in March, after all the delays, the Prime Minister eventually made the appointment, the arrangement of duties was so ill-conceived that no man could possibly discharge them with efficiency or even make a speech about them without embarrassment. I have repeatedly pointed out the obvious mistake in organisation of jumbling together – and practically everyone in the House is agreed upon this – the functions of defence with those of a Minister of Supply. The proper organisation, let me repeat, is four Departments – the Navy, the Army, the Air Force and the Ministry of Supply, with the Minister for the Co-ordination of Defence over the four, exercising a general supervision, concerting their actions, and assigning the high priorities of manufacture in relation to some comprehensive strategic conception. The House is familiar with the many requests and arguments which have been made to the Government to create a Ministry of Supply. These arguments have received powerful reinforcement from another angle in the report of the Royal Commission on Arms Manufacture.

The first work of this new Parliament, and the first work of the Minister for the Co-ordination of Defence if he had known as much about the subject when he was appointed as he does now, would have been to set up a Ministry of Supply which should, step by step, have taken over the whole business of the design and manufacture of all the supplies needed by the Air Force and the Army, and everything needed for the Navy, except warships, heavy ordnance, torpedoes and one or two ancillaries. All the rest of the industries of Britain should have been surveyed from a general integral standpoint, and all existing resources utilised so far as was necessary to execute the programme.

The Minister for the Co-ordination of Defence has argued as usual against a Ministry of Supply. The arguments which he used were weighty, and even ponderous – it would disturb and delay existing programmes; it would do more harm than good; it would upset the life and industry of the country; it would destroy the export trade and demoralise finance at the moment when it was most needed; it would turn this country into one vast munitions camp. Certainly these are massive arguments, if they are true. One would have thought that they would carry conviction to any man who accepted them. But then my right hon. Friend went on somewhat surprisingly to say, 'The decision is not final.' It would be reviewed again in a few weeks. What will you know in a few weeks about this matter that you do not know now, that you ought not to have known a year ago, and have not been told any time in the last six months? What is going to happen in the next few weeks which will invalidate all these magnificent arguments by which you have been overwhelmed, and suddenly make it worth your while to paralyse the export trade, to destroy the finances, and to turn the country into a great munitions camp?

The First Lord of the Admiralty [Sir Samuel Hoare] in his speech the other night went even farther. He said, 'We are always reviewing the position.' Everything, he assured us, is entirely fluid. I am sure that that is true. Anyone can see what the position is. The Government simply cannot make up their minds, or they cannot get the Prime Minister to make up his mind. So they go on in strange paradox, decided only to be undecided, resolved to be irresolute, adamant for drift, solid for fluidity, all-powerful to be impotent. So we go on preparing more months and years – precious, perhaps vital to the greatness of Britain – for the locusts to eat. They will say to me, 'A Minister of Supply is not necessary, for all is going well.' I deny it. 'The position is satisfactory.' It is not true. 'All is proceeding according to plan.' We know what that means.

Let me come to the Territorial Army. In March of this year I stigmatised a sentence in the War Office Memorandum about the Territorial Army, in which it was said the equipment of the Territorials could not be undertaken until that of the Regular Army had been completed. What has been done about all that? It is certain the evils are not yet removed. I agree wholeheartedly with all that was said by Lord Winterton the other day about the Army and the Territorial Force. When I think how these young men who join the Territorials come forward, almost alone in the population, and take on a liability to serve anywhere in any part of the world, not even with a guarantee to serve in their own units; come forward in spite of every conceivable deterrent; come forward – 140,000 of them, although they are still not up to strength – and then find that the Government does not take their effort seriously enough even to equip and arm them properly, I marvel at their patriotism. It is a marvel, it is also a glory, but a glory we have no right to profit by unless we can secure proper and efficient equipment for them.

A friend of mine the other day saw a number of persons engaged in peculiar evolutions, genuflections and gestures in the neighbourhood of London. His curiosity was excited. He wondered whether it was some novel form of gymnastics, or a new religion – there are new religions which are very popular in some countries nowadays – or whether they were a party of lunatics out for an airing. On approaching closer he learned that they were a Searchlight Company of London Territorials who were doing their exercises as well as they could without having the searchlights. Yet we are told there is no need for a Ministry of Supply.

In the manoeuvres of the Regular Army many of the most important new weapons have to be represented by flags and discs. When we remember how small our land forces are – altogether only a few hundred thousand men – it seems incredible that the very flexible industry of Britain, if properly handled, could not supply them with their modest requirements. In Italy, whose industry is so much smaller, whose wealth and credit are a small fraction of this country's, a Dictator is able to boast that he has bayonets and equipment for 8,000,000 men. Halve the figure, if you like, and the moral remains equally cogent.

The Army lacks almost every weapon which is required for the latest form of modern war. Where are the anti-tank guns, where are the short-distance wireless sets, where are the field anti-aircraft guns against low-flying armoured aeroplanes? We want to know how it is that this country, with its enormous motoring and motor-bicycling public, is not able to have strong mechanised divisions, both Regular and Territorial. Surely, when so much of the interest and the taste of our youth is moving in those mechanical channels, and when the horse is receding with the days of chivalry into the past, it ought to be possible to create an army of the size we want fully up to strength and mechanised to the highest degree.

Look at the Tank Corps. The tank was a British invention. This idea, which has revolutionised the conditions of modern war, was a British idea forced on the War Office by outsiders. Let me say they would have just as hard work today to force a new idea on it. I speak from what I know. During the war we had almost a monopoly, let alone the leadership, in tank warfare, and for several years afterwards we held the foremost place. To England all eyes were turned. All that has gone now. Nothing has been done in 'the years that the locust hath eaten' to equip the Tank Corps with new machines. The medium tank which they possess, which in its day was the best in the world, is now long obsolete. Not only in number – for there we have never tried to compete with other countries – but in quality these British weapons are now surpassed by those of Germany, Russia, Italy and the United States. All the shell plants and gun plants in the Army, apart from the very small peace-time services, are in an elementary stage. A very long period must intervene before any effectual flow of munitions can be expected, even for the small forces of which we dispose. Still we are told there is no necessity for a Ministry of Supply, no emergency which should induce us to impinge on the normal course of trade. If we go on like this, and I do not see what power can prevent us from going on like this, some day there may be a terrible reckoning, and those who take the responsibility so entirely upon themselves are either of a hardy disposition or they are incapable of foreseeing the possibilities which may arise.

Now I come to the greatest matter of all, the air. We received on Tuesday night, from the First Lord of the Admiralty [Sir Samuel Hoare], the assurance that there is no foundation whatever for the statement that we are 'vastly behindhand' with our Air Force programme. It is clear from his words that we are behindhand. The only question is, what meaning does the First Lord attach to the word 'vastly'? He also used the expression, about the progress of air expansion, that it was 'not unsatisfactory'. One does not know what his standard is. His standards change from time to time. In that speech of the 11th of September about the League of Nations there was one standard, and in the Hoare–Laval Pact there was clearly another.

In August last some of us went in a deputation to the Prime Minister in order to express the anxieties which we felt about national defence, and to make a number of statements which we preferred not to be forced to make in public. I personally made a statement on the state of the Air Force, to the preparation of which I had devoted several weeks and which, I am sorry to say, took an hour to read. My right hon. Friend the Prime Minister listened with his customary exemplary patience. I think I told him beforehand that he is a good listener, and perhaps he will retort that he learned to be when I was his colleague. At any rate, he listened with patience, and that is always something. During the three months that have passed since then I have checked those facts again in the light of current events and later knowledge, and were it not that foreign ears listen to all that is said here, or if we were in secret Session, I would repeat my statement here. And even if only one half were true I am sure the House would consider that a very grave state of emergency existed, and also, I regret to say, a state of things from which a certain suspicion of mismanagement cannot be excluded. I am not going into any of those details. I make it a rule, as far as I possibly can, to say nothing in this House upon matters which I am not sure are already known to the General Staffs of foreign countries; but there is one statement of very great importance which the Minister for the Co-ordination of Defence made in his speech on Tuesday [10 Nov. 1936]. He said:

> The process of building up squadrons and forming new training units and skeleton squadrons is familiar to everybody connected with the Air Force. The number of squadrons in present circumstances at home today is eighty, and that figure includes sixteen auxiliary squadrons, but excludes the Fleet Air Arm, and, of course, does not include the squadrons abroad.

From that figure, and the reservations by which it was prefaced, it is possible for the House, and also for foreign countries, to deduce pretty accurately the progress of our Air Force expansion. I feel, therefore, at liberty to comment on it.

Parliament was promised a total of seventy-one new squadrons, making a total of 124 squadrons in the home defence force, by 31 March 1937. This was thought to be the minimum compatible with our safety. At the end of the last financial year our strength was fifty-three squadrons, including auxiliary squadrons. Therefore, in the thirty-two weeks which have passed since the financial year began we have added twenty-eight squadrons – that is to say, less than one new squadron each week. In order to make the progress which Parliament was promised, in order to maintain the programme which was put forward as the minimum, we shall have to add forty-three squadrons in the remaining twenty weeks, or over two squadrons a week. The rate at which new squadrons will have to be formed from now till the end of March will have to be nearly three times as fast as hitherto. I do not propose to analyse the composition of the eighty squadrons we now have, but the Minister, in his speech, used a suggestive expression, 'skeleton squadrons' – applying at least to a portion of them – but even if every one of the eighty squadrons had an average strength of twelve aeroplanes, each fitted with war equipment, and the reserves upon which my right hon. Friend dwelt, we should only have a total of 960 first-line home-defence aircraft.

What is the comparable German strength? I am not going to give an estimate and say that the Germans have not got more than a certain number, but I will take it upon myself to say that they most certainly at this moment have not got less than a certain number. Most certainly they have not got less than 1500 first-line aeroplanes, comprised in not less than 130 or 140 squadrons, including auxiliary squadrons. It must also be remembered that Germany has not got in its squadrons any machine the design and construction of which is more than three years old. It must also be remembered that Germany has specialised in long-distance bombing aeroplanes and that her preponderance in that respect is far greater than any of these figures would suggest.

We were promised most solemnly by the Government that air parity with Germany would be maintained by the home defence forces. At the present time, putting everything at the very best, we are, upon the figures given by the Minister for the Co-ordination of Defence, only about two-thirds as strong as the German air force, assuming that I am not very much understating their present strength. How then does the First Lord of the Admiralty [Sir Samuel Hoare] think it right to say:

> On the whole, our forecast of the strength of other Air Forces proves to be accurate; on the other hand, our own estimates have also proved to be accurate.
>
> I am authorised to say that the position is satisfactory.

I simply cannot understand it. Perhaps the Prime Minister will explain the position. I should like to remind the House that I have made no revelation affecting this country and that I have introduced no new fact in our air defence which does not arise from the figures given by the Minister and from the official estimates that have been published.

What ought we to do? I know of only one way in which this matter can be carried further. The House ought to demand a Parliamentary inquiry. It ought to appoint six, seven or eight independent Members, responsible, experienced, discreet Members, who have some acquaintance with these matters and are representative of all parties, to interview Ministers and to find out what are, in fact, the answers to a series of questions; then to make a brief report to the House, whether of reassurance or of suggestion for remedying the shortcomings. That, I think, is what any Parliament worthy of the name would do in these circumstances. Parliaments of the past days in which the greatness of our country was abuilding would never have hesitated. They would have felt they could not discharge their duty to their constituents if they did not satisfy themselves that the safety of the country was being effectively maintained.

The French Parliament, through its committees, has a very wide, deep knowledge of the state of national defence, and I am not aware that their secrets leak out in any exceptional way. There is no reason why our secrets should leak out in any exceptional way. It is because so many members of the French Parliament are associated in one way or another with the progress of the national defence that the French Government were induced to supply, six years ago, upward of £60,000,000 sterling to construct the Maginot Line of fortifications, when our Government was assuring them that wars were over and that France must not lag behind Britain in her disarmament. Even now I hope that Members of the House of Commons will rise above considerations of party discipline, and will insist upon knowing where we stand in a matter which affects our liberties and our lives. I should have thought that the Government, and above all the Prime Minister, whose load is so heavy, would have welcomed such a suggestion.

Owing to past neglect, in the face of the plainest warnings, we have now entered upon a period of danger greater than has befallen Britain since the U-boat campaign was crushed; perhaps, indeed, it is a more grievous period than that, because at that time at least we were possessed of the means of securing ourselves and of defeating that campaign. Now we have no such assurance. The era of procrastination, of half-measures, of soothing and baffling expedients, of delays, is coming to its close. In its place we are entering a period of consequences. We have entered a period in which for more than a year, or a year and a half, the considerable preparations which are now on foot in Britain will not, as the Minister clearly showed, yield results which can be effective in actual fighting strength; while during this very period Germany may well reach the culminating point of her gigantic military preparations, and be forced by financial and economic stringency to contemplate a sharp decline, or perhaps some other exit from her difficulties. It is this lamentable conjunction of events which seems to present the danger of Europe in its most disquieting form. We cannot avoid this period; we are in it now. Surely, if we can abridge it by even a few months, if we can shorten this period when the German Army will begin to be so much larger than the French Army, and before the British Air Force has come to play its complementary part, we may be the architects who build the peace of the world on sure foundations.

Two things, I confess, have staggered me, after a long Parliamentary experience, in these Debates. The first has been the dangers that have so swiftly come upon us in a few years, and have been transforming our position and the whole outlook of the world. Secondly, I have been staggered by the failure of the House of Commons to react effectively against those dangers. That, I am bound to say, I never expected. I never would have believed that we should have been allowed to go on getting into this plight, month by month and year by year, and that even the Government's own confessions of error would have produced no concentration of Parliamentary opinion and force capable of lifting our efforts to the level of emergency. I say that unless the House resolves to find out the truth for itself it will have committed an act of abdication of duty without parallel in its long history.

'EUROPE . . . IS NOW APPROACHING THE MOST DANGEROUS MOMENT IN HISTORY'

25 November 1936

New Commonwealth Society Luncheon, Dorchester Hotel, London

Churchill saw, with greater clarity than any other parliamentarian, the new and cardinal importance of air power, as well as Britain's acute vulnerability to this form of warfare.

Europe, and it might well be the world, is now approaching the most dangerous moment in history. The struggle which is now opening between rival forms of dictatorships threatens to disturb the internal peace of many countries and to range them against each other. That alone would bring us into grave danger. Yet I feel that danger can be surmounted and kept within bounds if it were not that in this self-same, ill-starred epoch men had learned to fly. The aeroplane has put all countries and all parts of every country simultaneously at the mercy of a sudden blasting attack. Already, helpless nations have accepted the bombing of open cities and the indiscriminate slaughter of civilian inhabitants as the inevitable commonplace of the routine of war. What has been planned and was being planned will certainly in time of war be carried into ruthless effect.

Attack from the air, moreover, requires no mobilisation of fleets and slow gathering of armies. It can be launched by mere word or gesture; and, once launched, will be irrevocable in its consequences. It is this conjunction of new air power with the rise of dictatorships that has brought all countries into a peril unknown in barbarous times, or even in the most brutal periods of human history. It seems very unlikely that the world will be able to preserve any semblance of civilisation unless bombing by air power is brought under complete control by international organisation.

It follows that, in present circumstances, we are bound to support all well-considered necessary measures to enable the country to defend itself and to bear its part in a combined defensive system against aggression. We view with the strongest reprehension activities like those of Mr Lansbury and Canon Sheppard, who are ceaselessly trying to dissuade the youth of this country from joining its defensive forces, and seek to impede and discourage the military preparations which the state of the world forces upon us.

If it is true, as the Prime Minister stated last week in a deplorable utterance, that 'democracy is always two years behind the dictator', then democracy will be destroyed. In the Great War it was the Parliamentary nations that conquered, and the autocratic Empires that fell to pieces without exception. If democracy in Great Britain and in other countries is in danger now, as perhaps it might be, it is not democracy that is at fault, but the leadership that it has received.

Who should say that Europe cannot save itself if it tries? If mankind means to have peace, its will can be made effective, but only if it acts upon a plan and obeys the law on which that plan is based. If only the people of Spain six months ago could have foreseen the horror that has overtaken them, how easy it would have been for them to stop it. When I brood on that tragedy, I ask myself whether it is not a portent to warn all Europe of the fate which might lie at no great distance from us all, upon a scale to which the Spanish horror would be but a small working model. I ask all who are concerned with peace to rise to the level of events, and to trifle no more on the edge of the abyss, but to embrace the sacrifices and discipline of mind and body which the cause requires.

'THE ABDICATION OF KING EDWARD VIII'

10 December 1936

House of Commons

Churchill made himself even more unpopular and isolated by stepping forward as a champion of his friend, the new King, who wished to marry an American divorcee, Mrs Wallis Simpson.

Nothing is more certain or more obvious than that recrimination or controversy at this time would be not only useless but harmful and wrong. What is done is done. What has been done or left undone belongs to history, and to history, so far as I am concerned, it shall be left. I will, therefore, make two observations only. The first is this: It is clear from what we have been told this afternoon that there was at no time any constitutional issue between the King and his Ministers or between the King and Parliament. The supremacy of Parliament over the Crown: the duty of the Sovereign to act in accordance with the advice of his Ministers: neither of those was ever at any moment in question. Supporting my right hon. Friend the Leader of the Liberal party, I venture to say that no Sovereign has ever conformed more strictly or more faithfully to the letter and spirit of the Constitution than his present Majesty. In fact, he has voluntarily made a sacrifice for the peace and strength of his Realm which goes far beyond the bounds required by the law and the Constitution. That is my first observation.

My second is this: I have, throughout, pleaded for time; anyone can see how grave would have been the evils of protracted controversy. On the other hand, it was, in my view, our duty to endure these evils even at serious inconvenience, if there was any hope that time would bring a solution. Whether there was any hope or not is a mystery which, at the present time, it is impossible to resolve. Time was also important from another point of view. It was essential that there should be no room for aspersions, after the event, that the King had been hurried in his decision. I believe that, if this decision had been taken last week, it could not have been declared that it was an unhurried decision, so far as the King himself was concerned, but now I accept wholeheartedly what the Prime Minister has proved, namely, that the decision taken this week has been taken by His Majesty freely, voluntarily and spontaneously, in his own time and in his own way. As I have been looking at this matter, as is well known, from an angle different from that of most hon. Members, I thought it my duty to place this fact also upon record.

That is all I have to say upon the disputable part of this matter, but I hope the House will bear with me for a minute or two, because it was my duty as Home Secretary, more than a quarter of a century ago, to stand beside his present Majesty and proclaim his style and titles at his investiture as Prince of Wales amid the sunlit battlements of Carnarvon Castle, and ever since then he has honoured me here, and also in wartime, with his personal kindness and, I may even say, friendship. I should have been ashamed if, in my independent and unofficial position, I had not cast about for every lawful means, even the most forlorn, to keep him on the Throne of his fathers, to which he only recently succeeded amid the hopes and prayers of all. In this Prince there were discerned qualities of courage, of simplicity, of sympathy, and, above all, of sincerity, qualities rare and precious which might have made his reign glorious in the annals of this ancient monarchy. It is the acme of tragedy that these very virtues should, in the private sphere, have led only to this melancholy and bitter conclusion. But, although our hopes today are withered, still I will assert that his personality will not go down uncherished to future ages, that it will be particularly remembered in the homes of his poorer subjects, and that they will ever wish from the bottom of their hearts for his private peace and happiness and for the happiness of those who are dear to him.

I must say one word more, and I say it specially to those here and out of doors – and do not underrate their numbers – who are most poignantly afflicted by what has occurred. Danger gathers upon our path. We cannot afford – we have no right – to look back. We must look forward; we must obey the exhortation of the Prime Minister to look forward. The stronger the advocate of monarchical principle a man may be, the more zealously must he now endeavour to fortify the Throne and to give to His Majesty's successor that strength which can only come from the love of a united nation and Empire.

RUDYARD KIPLING

17 November 1937

Rudyard Kipling Memorial Fund Inaugural Dinner,
Grosvenor House, London

Rudyard Kipling holds one of the foremost places in the last century of English letters. During the long noonday of his activity his literary output, though always distinguished by a sense of rarity, reached impressive dimensions. Behind it lay a volume of knowledge always penetrating, often profound, which was vast and majestic. This knowledge was gathered by ceaseless study, observation, and reflection, and constituted the most wonderful mental possession that can be imagined.

To place these treasures at the service of his country and his age there was needed the magic gift of genius. This supreme reagent he enjoyed in a glorious intensity. The pith, the force, the terse and syncopated vivacity of his style immediately arrested and commanded attention. The immense variety of subjects to which he seemed to hold the master-key is a source of unending amazement to his innumerable readers and admirers throughout the King's Dominions and far beyond them.

There seemed to be no gallery of human activity which he could not enter easily and unchallenged and which, having entered, he could not illuminate with a light unexpected, piercing, enchanting, and all his own. All sorts of conditions of men, all classes and professions, every part of the Empire, the souls of children, the lives of animals, became in turn visible, intelligible, fascinating to that ever-increasing company by whom he was attended in his journey through life. He created a whole series of new values for his fellow-countrymen and made them participate in an unbroken succession of novel experiences and adventures.

There have been in our own time greater poets and sages, more vehement and sentient interpreters of pathos and passion, more fertile stylists than Rudyard Kipling. But in the glittering rank which he took by right Divine there never has been anyone like him. No one has ever written like Kipling before, and his work, with all its characteristics and idiosyncrasies, while it charmed and inspired so many, has been successfully imitated by none. He was unique and irreplaceable.

The light of genius expressed in literature does not fail with the death of the author. His galleries are still displayed for our instruction and enjoyment. But the magic key which could have opened new ones to our eager desire has gone forever. Let us, then, guard the treasures which he has bequeathed.

The structure and pageant of British rule in India gave him his first and main inspiration. To read with faithful eye Kipling's Indian stories, short or long, is to gain a truer knowledge of that great episode, the British contact with India, than will be found in many ponderous Blue-books, or in much of the glib, smooth patter which is now in fashion.

We serve the Queen with 'Soldiers Three'. We see the life of the young officer, of the lonely collector. We satirise the bureaucracy and Viceregal society. We share the domestic troubles of the Anglo-Indian official, we shed bitter tears with 'Wee Willie Winkle'. On the hard Frontier we follow 'The Drums of the Fore and Aft'. We play polo with the Maltese Cat. We fight for dear life in the skin of the mongoose Rikki against the poison cobra. We roam the jungles with Mowgli, and we walk with Kim among the vast multitudes of Hindustan.

Even should the British Empire in India pass from life into history, the works of Rudyard Kipling will remain to prove that while we were there we did our best for all.

AUSTRIA ANNEXED

14 March 1938

House of Commons

On 11 March Germany invaded and, with minimal resistance, annexed Austria.

The gravity of the event of the 11th of March cannot be exaggerated. Europe is confronted with a programme of aggression, nicely calculated and timed, unfolding stage by stage, and there is only one choice open, not only to us, but to other countries who are unfortunately concerned – either to submit, like Austria, or else to take effective measures while time remains to ward off the danger and, if it cannot be warded off, to cope with it. Resistance will be hard, yet I am persuaded – and the Prime Minister's speech confirms me – that it is to this conclusion of resistance to overweening encroachment that His Majesty's Government will come, and the House of Commons will certainly sustain them in playing a great part in the effort to preserve the peace of Europe, and, if it cannot be preserved, to preserve the freedom of the nations of Europe. If we were to delay, if we were to go on waiting upon events for a considerable period, how much should we throw away of resources which are now available for our security and for the maintenance of peace? How many friends would be alienated, how many potential allies should we see go, one by one, down the grisly gulf, how many times would bluff succeed, until behind bluff ever-gathering forces had accumulated reality? Where shall we be two years hence, for instance, when the German Army will certainly be much larger than the French Army, and when all the small nations will have fled from Geneva to pay homage to the ever-waxing power of the Nazi system, and to make the best terms they can for themselves?

We cannot leave the Austrian question where it is. We await the further statement of the Government, but it is quite clear that we cannot accept as a final solution of the problem of Central Europe the event which occurred on March 11. The public mind has been concentrated upon the moral and sentimental aspects of the Nazi conquest of Austria – a small country brutally struck down, its Government scattered to the winds, the oppression of the Nazi party doctrine imposed upon a Catholic population and upon the working-classes of Austria and of Vienna, the hard ill-usage of persecution which indeed will ensue – which is probably in progress at the moment – of those who, this time last week, were exercising their undoubted political rights, discharging their duties faithfully to their own country. All this we see very clearly, but there are some things which I have not seen brought out in the public Press and which do not seem to be present in the public mind, and they are practical considerations of the utmost significance.

Vienna is the centre of all the communication of all the countries which formed the old Austro-Hungarian Empire, and of all the countries lying to the south-east of Europe. A long stretch of the Danube is now in German hands. This mastery of Vienna gives to Nazi Germany military and economic control of the whole of the communications of south-eastern Europe, by road, by river, and by rail. What is the effect of it upon what is called the balance of power, such as it is, and upon what is called the Little Entente? I must say a word about this group of Powers called the Little Entente. Taken singly, the three countries of the Little Entente may be called Powers of the second rank, but they are very vigorous States, and united they are a Great Power. They have hitherto been, and are, still, united by the closest military agreement. Together they make the complement of a Great Power and of the military machinery of a Great Power. Rumania has the oil; Yugoslavia has the minerals and raw materials. Both have large armies; both are mainly supplied with munitions from Czechoslovakia. To English ears, the name of Czechoslovakia sounds outlandish. No doubt they are only a small democratic State, no doubt they have an army only two or three times as large as ours, no doubt they have a munitions supply only three times as great as that of Italy, but still they are a virile people; they have their treaty rights, they have a line of fortresses, and they have a strongly manifested will to live freely.

Czechoslovakia is at this moment isolated, both in the economic and in the military sense. Her trade outlet through Hamburg, which is based upon the Peace Treaty, can, of course, be closed at any moment. Now her communications by rail and river to the south, and after the south to the south-east, are liable to be severed at any moment. Her trade may be subjected to tolls of an absolutely strangling character. Here is a country which was once the greatest manufacturing area in the old Austro-Hungarian Empire. It is now cut off, or may be cut off at once unless, out of these discussions which must follow, arrangements are made securing the communications of Czechoslovakia. You may be cut off at once from the sources of her raw material in Yugoslavia and from the natural markets which she has established there. The economic life of this small State may be practically destroyed as a result of the act of violence which was perpetrated last Friday night. A wedge has been driven into the heart of what is called the Little Entente, this group of countries which have as much right to live in Europe unmolested as any of us have the right to live unmolested in our native land.

It would be too complicated to pursue the economic, military, and material reactions, apart from moral sentiments altogether, into the other countries. It would take too long, but the effects of what has happened now upon Rumania, upon Hungary, upon Bulgaria, upon Turkey, must be the subject of the closest possible study, not only by His Majesty's Government, but by all who aspire to take part in the public discussion of these matters. By what has happened it is not too much to say that Nazi Germany, in its present mood, if matters are left as they are, is in a position to dominate the whole of south-east Europe. Over an area inhabited perhaps by 200,000,000 of people Nazidom and all that it involves is moving on to absolute control. . . .

It seems to me quite clear that we cannot possibly confine ourselves only to a renewed effort at rearmament. I know that some of my hon. Friends on this side of the House will laugh when I offer them this advice. I say, 'Laugh, but listen.' I affirm that the Government should express in the strongest terms our adherence to the Covenant of the League of Nations and our resolve to procure by international action the reign of law in Europe. I agree entirely with what has been said by the Leaders of the two Opposition parties upon that subject; and I was extremely glad to notice that at the beginning and in the very forefront of his speech the Prime Minister referred to the League of Nations and made that one of the bases of our right to intervene and to be consulted upon affairs in Central Europe. The matter has an importance in this country. There must be a moral basis for British rearmament and British foreign policy. We must have that basis if we are to unite and inspire our people and procure their wholehearted action, and if we are to stir the English-speaking people throughout the world.

Our affairs have come to such a pass that there is no escape without running risks. On every ground of prudence as well as of duty I urge His Majesty's Government to proclaim a renewed, revivified, unflinching adherence to the Covenant of the League of Nations. What is there ridiculous about collective security? The only thing that is ridiculous about it is that we have not got it. Let us see whether we cannot do something to procure a strong element of collective security for ourselves and for others. We have been urged to make common cause in self-defence with the French Republic. What is that but the beginning of collective security? I agree with that. Not so lightly will the two great liberal democracies of the West be challenged, and not so easily, if challenged, will they be subjugated. That is the beginning of collective security. But why stop there? Why be edged and pushed farther down the slope in a disorderly expostulating crowd of embarrassed States. Why not make a stand while there is still a good company of united, very powerful countries that share our dangers and aspirations? Why should we delay until we are confronted with a general landslide of those small countries passing over, because they have no other choice, to the overwhelming power of the Nazi régime?

If a number of States were assembled around Great Britain and France in a solemn treaty for mutual defence against aggression; if they had their forces marshalled in what you may call a Grand Alliance; if they had their Staff arrangements concerted; if all this rested, as it can honourably rest, upon the Covenant of the League of Nations, in pursuance of all the purposes and ideals of the League of Nations; if that were sustained, as it would be, by the moral sense of the world; and if it were done in the year 1938 – and, believe me, it may be the last chance there will be for doing it – then I say that you might even now arrest this approaching war. Then perhaps the curse which overhangs Europe would pass away. Then perhaps the ferocious passions which now grip a great people would turn inwards and not outwards in an internal rather than an external explosion, and mankind would be spared the deadly ordeal towards which we have been sagging and sliding month by month. I have ventured to indicate a positive conception, a practical and realistic conception, and one which I am convinced will unite all the forces of this country without whose help your armies cannot be filled or your munitions made. Before we cast away this hope, this cause and this plan, which I do not at all disguise has an element of risk, let those who wish to reject it ponder well and earnestly upon what will happen to us if, when all else has been thrown to the wolves, we are left to face our fate alone.

'I HAVE WATCHED THIS FAMOUS ISLAND DESCENDING . . . THE STAIRWAY . . .'

24 March 1938

House of Commons

Strangely, the final four-paragraph peroration of this speech, including the powerful passage 'I have watched this famous island descending incontinently, fecklessly, the stairway which leads to a dark gulf . . .' is not to be found in Robert Rhodes James's Complete Speeches of Winston Churchill.

The Prime Minister [Neville Chamberlain], in what I think it is not presumptuous for me to describe as a very fine speech, set before us the object which is in all our minds – namely, how to prevent war. A country like ours, possessed of immense territory and wealth, whose defences have been neglected, cannot avoid war by dilating upon its horrors, or even by a continuous display of pacific qualities, or by ignoring the fate of the victims of aggression elsewhere. War will be avoided, in present circumstances, only by the accumulation of deterrents against the aggressor. If our defences are weak, we must seek allies; and, of course, if we seek allies, alliances involve commitments. But the increase of commitments may be justified if it is followed by a still greater increase of deterrents against aggression.

I was very glad to hear the Prime Minister reaffirm in such direct terms our arrangements for mutual defence with the French Republic. Evidently they amount to a defensive alliance. Why not say so? Why not make it effective by a military convention of the most detailed character? Are we, once again, to have all the disadvantages of an alliance without its advantages, and to have commitments without full security? Great Britain and France have to stand together for mutual protection. Why should not the conditions be worked out precisely and the broad facts made public? Everyone knows, for instance, that our Air Force is tripled in deterrent effectiveness if it operates from French bases and, as I pointed out in the House three weeks ago, the fact that an attack upon this country would bring the attacker into conflict with the French Army is another great security to us here. We are obliged in return to go to the aid of France, and hitherto we have always been better than our word.

Here, then, is the great security for the two countries. Do not conceal it. Proclaim it, implement it, work it out in thorough detail. Treat the defensive problems of the two countries as if they were one. Then you will have a real deterrent against unprovoked aggression, and if the deterrent fails to deter, you will have a highly organised method of coping with the aggressor. The present rulers of Germany will hesitate long before they attack the British Empire and the French Republic if those are woven together for defence purposes into one very powerful unit. Having gone so far, there is no safe halting-place short of an open defensive alliance with France, not with loose obligations, but with defined obligations on both sides and complete inter-staff arrangements. Even an isolationist would, I think, go so far as to say, 'If we have to mix ourselves up with the Continent, let us, at any rate, get the maximum of safety from our commitments.' . . .

I must say I do not feel sure even now, after this latest decision, that the problem of rearmament is being dealt with on the right lines.

Is the method of organisation to be employed adapted to a nation-wide effort? Ought there not to be created, however tardily, a Ministry of Supply? Ought there not be created a far more effective Ministry of Defence? Are there not problems pressing for solution which can be handled only by a Minister of Defence? Ought there not to be a Defence of the Realm Act giving the necessary powers to divert industry, as far as may be necessary, from the ordinary channels of commerce so as to fit our rearmament in with the needs of our export trade and yet make sure that rearmament has the supreme priority?

I will venture to echo the question which was posed by Mr Amery last week. Is our system of government adapted to the present fierce, swift movement of events? Twenty-two gentlemen of blameless party character sitting round an overcrowded table, each having a voice – is that a system which can reach decisions from week to week and cope with the problems descending upon us and with the men at the head of dictator States? It broke down hopelessly in the war. But is this peace in which we are living? Is it not war without cannon firing? Is it not war of a decisive character, where victories are gained and territories conquered, and where ascendancy and dominance are established over large populations with extraordinary rapidity? If we are to prevent this bloodless war being turned into bloody war, ought not His Majesty's Government to adopt a system more on a level with the period of crisis in which we live? . . .

Let me give a warning drawn from our recent experiences. Very likely this immediate crisis will pass, will dissipate itself and calm down. After a boa constrictor has devoured its prey it often has a considerable digestive spell. It was so after the revelation of the secret German air force. There was a pause. It was so after German conscription was proclaimed in breach of the Treaty. It was so after the Rhineland was forcibly occupied. The House may recall that we were told how glad we ought to be because there would be no question of fortifying it. Now, after Austria has been struck down, we are all disturbed and alarmed, but in a little while there may be another pause. There may not – we cannot tell. But if there is a pause, then people will be saying, 'See how the alarmists have been confuted; Europe has calmed down, it has all blown over, and the war scare has passed away.' The Prime Minister will perhaps repeat what he said a few weeks ago, that the tension in Europe is greatly relaxed. *The Times* will write a leading article to say how silly those people look who on the morrow of the Austrian incorporation raised a clamour for exceptional action in foreign policy and home defence, and how wise the Government were not to let themselves be carried away by this passing incident.

All this time the vast degeneration of the forces of Parliamentary democracy will be proceeding throughout Europe. Every six weeks another corps will be added to the German army. All this time important countries and great rail and river communications will pass under the control of the German General Staff. All this time populations will be continually reduced to the rigours of Nazi domination and assimilated to that system. All this time the forces of conquest and intimidation will be consolidated, towering up soon in real and not make-believe strength and superiority. Then presently will come another stroke. Upon whom? Our questions with Germany are unsettled and unanswered. We cannot tell. What I dread is that the impulse now given to active effort may pass away when the dangers are not diminishing, but accumulating and gathering as country after country is involved in the Nazi system, and as their vast preparations reach their final perfection.

For five years I have talked to the House on these matters – not with very great success. I have watched this famous island descending incontinently, fecklessly, the stairway which leads to a dark gulf. It is a fine broad stairway at the beginning, but after a bit the carpet ends. A little farther on there are only flagstones, and a little farther on still these break beneath your feet. Look back over the last five years. It is true that great mistakes were made in the years immediately after the war. But at Locarno we laid the foundation from which a great forward movement could have been made. Look back upon the last five years – since, that is to say, Germany began to rearm in earnest and openly to seek revenge. If we study the history of Rome and Carthage, we can understand what happened and why. It is not difficult to form an intelligent view about the three Punic Wars; but if mortal catastrophe should overtake the British Nation and the British Empire, historians a thousand years hence will still be baffled by the mystery of our affairs. They will never understand how it was that a victorious nation, with everything in hand, suffered themselves to be brought low, and to cast away all that they had gained by measureless sacrifice and absolute victory – gone with the wind!

Now the victors are the vanquished, and those who threw down their arms in the field and sued for an armistice are striding on to world mastery. That is the position – that is the terrible transformation that has taken place bit by bit. I rejoice to hear from the Prime Minister that a further supreme effort is to be made to place us in a position of security. Now is the time at last to rouse the nation. Perhaps it is the last time it can be roused with a chance of preventing war, or with a chance of coming through to victory should our efforts to prevent war fail. We should lay aside every hindrance and endeavour by uniting the whole force and spirit of our people to raise again a great British nation standing up before all the world; for such a nation, rising in its ancient vigour, can even at this hour save civilisation.

'THE SENTINEL TOWERS
OF THE WESTERN APPROACHES'

5 May 1938

House of Commons

Churchill denounces the Government's abandonment of the right of the Royal Navy, under the terms of the 1921 Irish Treaty, to use Ireland's three 'Treaty Ports'. Their feckless and gratuitous concessions to the Irish Republic were to cost Britain dear when, within two years, she would be fighting for her life, in the face of the German U-boat menace.

I confess that I was wholly unprepared to read in the newspapers that we have abandoned all our contentions about the repudiation of the Treaty, about the annuities, and, above all – and this is the subject which makes me feel compelled to speak – our contentions about the strategic ports. It is this issue of the strategic ports which makes me undertake the thankless task of bringing some of these matters very respectfully to the attention of the House. The ports in question, Queenstown, Berehaven and Lough Swilly, are to be handed over unconditionally, with no guarantees of any kind, as a gesture of our trust and goodwill, as the Prime Minister said, to the Government of the Irish Republic. When the Irish Treaty was being shaped in 1921 I was instructed by the Cabinet to prepare that part of the Agreement which dealt with strategic reservations. I negotiated with Mr Michael Collins, and I was advised by Admiral Beatty, who had behind him the whole staff of the Admiralty, which had just come out of the successful conduct of the Great War. Therefore, we had high authority in prescribing the indispensable minimum of reservations for strategic security.

The Admiralty of those days assured me that without the use of these ports it would be very difficult, perhaps almost impossible, to feed this Island in time of war. Queenstown and Berehaven shelter the flotillas which keep clear the approaches to the Bristol and English Channels, and Lough Swilly is the base from which the access to the Mersey and the Clyde is covered. In a war against an enemy possessing a numerous and powerful fleet of submarines these are the essential bases from which the whole operation of hunting submarines and protecting incoming convoys is conducted. I am very sorry to have to strike a jarring note this afternoon, but all opinions should be heard and put on record. If we are denied the use of Lough Swilly and have to work from Lamlash, we should strike 200 miles from the effective radius of our flotillas, out and home; and if we are denied Berehaven and Queenstown, and have to work from Pembroke Dock, we should strike 400 miles from their effective radius out and home. These ports are, in fact, the sentinel towers of the western approaches, by which the 45,000,000 people in this Island so enormously depend on foreign food for their daily bread, and by which they can carry on their trade, which is equally important to their existence.

In 1922 the Irish delegates made no difficulty about this. They saw that it was vital to our safety that we should be able to use these ports and, therefore, the matter passed into the structure of the Treaty without any serious controversy. Now we are to give them up, unconditionally, to an Irish Government led by men – I do not want to use hard words – whose rise to power has been proportionate to the animosity with which they have acted against this country, no doubt in pursuance of their own patriotic impulses, and whose present position in power is based upon the violation of solemn Treaty engagements. . . .

I wish it were possible, even at this stage, to postpone the passage of the Bill – I put it to the Prime Minister, if I may, even at this stage – until some further arrangements could be made about the Treaty ports, or some more general arrangement could be made about common action and defence. Would it not be far better to give up the £10,000,000, and acquire the legal right, be it only on a lease granted by treaty, to use these harbours when necessary? Surely, there should be some right retained. The garrisons, of course, are at present only small ones, little more than care and maintainance parties. It would be a serious step for a Dublin Government to attack these forts while they are in our possession and while we have the right to occupy them. It would be an easy step for a Dublin Government to deny their use to us once we have gone. The cannon are there, the mines will be there. But more important for this purpose, the juridical right will be there. We are going away, we are giving up the ports, and giving to this other Government the right as well as the power to forbid our re-entry. You had the rights. You have ceded them. You hope in their place to have goodwill, strong enough to endure tribulation for your sake. Suppose you have it not. It will be no use saying, 'Then we will retake the ports.' You will have no right to do so. To violate Irish neutrality, should it be declared at the moment of a great war, may put you out of court in the opinion of the world, and may vitiate the cause by which you may be involved in war. If ever we have to fight again, we shall be fighting in the name of law, of respect for the rights of small countries – Belgium, for instance – and upon that basis and within the ambit of the Covenant of the League of Nations.

When we are proceeding, as we should be in such unhappy circumstances, upon the basis of law and equity, how could we justify ourselves if we began by violating the neutrality of what the world regard, and what we are teaching the world to regard, as the Independent Irish Republic? At the moment when the goodwill of the United States in matters of blockade and supply might be of the highest possible consequence, you might be forced to take violent action against all law and accepted usage, or alternatively you might be forced to sacrifice Ulster or, in the third place, do without the use of these almost vitally important strategic ports. What is it all being done for? What are the new facts which have led to this sudden departure? To me, it is incomprehensible. To the world, to all the hungry aggressive nations, it will be taken as another sign that Britain has only to be pressed and worried long enough and hard enough for her to give way. If that is so, by that very fact you will bring the possibility of war nearer and you will lessen your resources for dealing with that danger. You are inviting demands from every quarter. You are casting away real and important means of security and survival for vain shadows and for ease.

'SAVE MANKIND FROM MARTYRDOM'

26 September 1938

London

With Hitler threatening to invade the Sudeten (or German-speaking) provinces of Czechoslovakia, the British Prime Minister, Neville Chamberlain, made three journeys in the space of two weeks to visit Hitler in a futile attempt to safeguard peace. Meanwhile, equally vainly, Churchill appeals to the Government and people of the United States to involve themselves in the deepening crisis.

There is still one good chance of preserving peace. A solemn warning should be presented to the German Government in joint or simultaneous Notes by Great Britain, France, and Russia that the invasion of Czechoslovakia at the present juncture would be taken as an act of war against these Powers. The terms of this Note should be communicated to all neutral countries, some of whom may be balancing their actions, and most particularly to the Government of the USA.

If such steps had been taken a month ago it is improbable matters would have reached their present pass. Even at the last moment clear and resolute action may avert the catastrophe into which we are drifting. Not only the German Government but the German people have a right to know where we all stand.

If the Government and people of the USA have a word to speak for the salvation of the world, now is the time and now is the last time when words will be of any use. Afterwards, through years of struggle and torment, deeds alone will serve and deeds will be forthcoming. It will indeed be a tragedy if this last effort is not made in the only way in which it may be effective to save mankind from martyrdom.

'A TOTAL AND UNMITIGATED DEFEAT'

5 October 1938

House of Commons

On 1 October, Chamberlain returned to an ecstatic public reception in London following his meeting with Hitler at Munich, brandishing his now infamous scrap of paper, with Hitler's signature and his own, pledging that Britain and Germany would never again go to war. Churchill's damning speech struck a jarring note that stood in stark contrast to the praise being lavished upon Chamberlain in Parliament, the Press and the nation. At this point Churchill could number his political allies in the House on the fingers of one hand.

If I do not begin this afternoon by paying the usual, and indeed almost invariable, tributes to the Prime Minister for his handling of this crisis, it is certainly not from any lack of personal regard. We have always, over a great many years, had very pleasant relations, and I have deeply understood from personal experiences of my own in a similar crisis the stress and strain he has had to bear; but I am sure it is much better to say exactly what we think about public affairs, and this is certainly not the time when it is worth anyone's while to court political popularity. We had a shining example of firmness of character from the late First Lord of the Admiralty two days ago. He showed that firmness of character which is utterly unmoved by currents of opinion, however swift and violent they may be. My hon. Friend the Member for South-West Hull (Mr Law), to whose compulsive speech the House listened on Monday – which I had not the good fortune to hear, but which I read, and which I am assured by all who heard it revived the memory of his famous father, so cherished in this House, and made us feel that his gifts did not die with him – was quite right in reminding us that the Prime Minister has himself throughout his conduct of these matters shown a robust indifference to cheers or boos and to the alternations of criticism and applause. If that be so, such qualities and elevation of mind should make it possible for the most severe expressions of honest opinion to be interchanged in this House without rupturing personal relations, and for all points of view to receive the fullest possible expression.

Having thus fortified myself by the example of others, I will proceed to emulate them. I will, therefore, begin by saying the most unpopular and most unwelcome thing. I will begin by saying what everybody would like to ignore or forget but which must nevertheless be stated, namely, that we have sustained a total and unmitigated defeat, and that France has suffered even more than we have.

Viscountess Astor: Nonsense.

Mr Churchill: When the Noble Lady cries 'Nonsense', she could not have heard the Chancellor of the Exchequer [Sir John Simon] admit in his illuminating and comprehensive speech just now that Herr Hitler had gained in this particular leap forward in substance all he set out to gain. The utmost my right hon. Friend the Prime Minister has been able to secure by all his immense exertions, by all the great efforts and mobilisations which took place in this country, and by all the anguish and strain through which we have passed in this country, the utmost he has been able to gain – [*Hon. Members*: 'Is peace.'] I thought I might be allowed to make that point in its due place, and I propose to deal with it. The utmost he has been able to gain for Czechoslovakia and in the matters which were in dispute has been that the German dictator, instead of snatching his victuals from the table, has been content to have them served to him course by course.

The Chancellor of the Exchequer said it was the first time Herr Hitler had been made to retract – I think that was the word – in any degree. We really must not waste time, after all this long debate, upon the difference between the positions reached at Berchtesgaden, at Godesberg and at Munich. They can be very simply epitomised, if the House will permit me to vary the metaphor. £1 was demanded at the pistol's point. When it was given, £2 were demanded at the pistol's point. Finally, the dictator consented to take £1 17s. 6d. and the rest in promises of goodwill for the future.

Now I come to the point, which was mentioned to me just now from some quarters of the House, about the saving of peace. No one has been a more resolute and uncompromising struggler for peace than the Prime Minister. Everyone knows that. Never has there been such intense and undaunted determination to maintain and to secure peace. That is quite true. Nevertheless, I am not quite clear why there was so much danger of Great Britain or France being involved in a war with Germany at this juncture if, in fact, they were ready all along to sacrifice Czechoslovakia. The terms which the Prime Minister brought back with him – I quite agree at the last moment; everything had got off the rails and nothing but his intervention could have saved the peace, but I am talking of the events of the summer – could easily have been agreed, I believe, through the ordinary diplomatic channels at any time during the summer. And I will say this, that I believe the Czechs, left to themselves and told they were going to get no help from the Western Powers, would have been able to make better terms than they have got – they could hardly have worse – after all this tremendous perturbation.

There never can be any absolute certainty that there will be a fight if one side is determined that it will give way completely. When one reads the Munich terms, when one sees what is happening in Czechoslovakia from hour to hour, when one is sure, I will not say of Parliamentary approval but of Parliamentary acquiescence, when the Chancellor of the Exchequer makes a speech which at any rate tries to put in a very powerful and persuasive manner the fact that, after all, it was inevitable and indeed righteous – right – when we saw all this, and everyone on this side of the House, including many Members of the Conservative Party who are supposed to be vigilant and careful guardians of the national interest, it is quite clear that nothing vitally affecting us was at stake, it seems to me that one must ask, What was all the trouble and fuss about?

The resolve was taken by the British and the French Governments. Let me say that it is very important to realise that it is by no means a question which the British Government only have had to decide. I very much admire the manner in which, in the House, all references of a recriminatory nature have been repressed, but it must be realised that this resolve did not emanate particularly from one or other of the Governments but was a resolve for which both must share in common the responsibility. When this resolve was taken and the course was followed – you may say it was wise or unwise, prudent or short-sighted – once it had been decided not to make the defence of Czechoslovakia a matter of war, then there was really no reason, if the matter had been handled during the summer in the ordinary way, to call into being all this formidable apparatus of crisis. I think that point should be considered.

We are asked to vote for this Motion ['That this House approves the policy of His Majesty's Government by which war was averted in the recent crisis and supports their efforts to secure a lasting peace'] which has been put upon the Paper, and it is certainly a Motion couched in very uncontroversial terms, as, indeed, is the Amendment moved from the Opposition side. I cannot myself express my agreement with the steps which have been taken and, as the Chancellor of the Exchequer has put his side of the case with so much ability I will attempt, if I may be permitted, to put the case from a different angle. I have always held the view that the maintenance of peace depends upon the accumulation of deterrents against the aggressor, coupled with a sincere effort to redress grievances. Herr Hitler's victory, like so many of the famous struggles that have governed the fate of the world, was won upon the narrowest of margins. After the seizure of Austria in March we faced this problem in our Debates. I ventured to appeal to the Government to go a little further than the Prime Minister went, and to give a pledge that in conjunction with France and other Powers they would guarantee the security of Czechoslovakia while the Sudeten-Deutsch question was being examined either by a League of Nations Commission or some other impartial body, and I still believe that if that course had been followed events would not have fallen into this disastrous state. I agree very much with my right hon. Friend the Member for Sparkbrook (Mr Amery) when he said on that occasion – I cannot remember his actual words – 'Do one thing or the other: either say you will disinterest yourself in the matter altogether or take the step of giving a guarantee which will have the greatest chance of securing protection for that country.'

France and Great Britain together, especially if they had maintained a close contact with Russia, which certainly was not done, would have been able in those days in the summer, when they had the prestige, to influence many of the smaller States of Europe, and I believe they could have determined the attitude of Poland. Such a combination, prepared at a time when the German dictator was not deeply and irrevocably committed to his new adventure, would, I believe, have given strength to all those forces in Germany which resisted this departure, this new design. They were varying forces, those of a military character which declared that Germany was not ready to undertake a world war, and all that mass of moderate opinion and popular opinion which dreaded war, and some elements of which still have some influence upon the German Government. Such action would have given strength to all that intense desire for peace which the helpless German masses share with their British and French fellow men, and which, as we have been reminded, found a passionate and rarely permitted vent in the joyous manifestations with which the Prime Minister was acclaimed in Munich.

All these forces, added to the other deterrents which combinations of Powers, great and small, ready to stand firm upon the front of law and for the ordered remedy of grievances, would have formed, might well have been effective. Of course you cannot say for certain that they would. [*Interruption.*] I try to argue fairly with the House. At the same time I do not think it is fair to charge those who wished to see this course followed, and followed consistently and resolutely, with having wished for an immediate war. Between submission and immediate war there was this third alternative, which gave a hope not only of peace but of justice. It is quite true that such a policy in order to succeed demanded that Britain should declare straight out and a long time beforehand that she would, with others, join to defend Czechoslovakia against an unprovoked aggression. His Majesty's Government refused to give that guarantee when it would have saved the situation, yet in the end they gave it when it was too late, and now, for the future, they renew it when they have not the slightest power to make it good.

All is over. Silent, mournful, abandoned, broken, Czechoslovakia recedes into the darkness. She has suffered in every respect by her association with the Western democracies and with the League of Nations, of which she has always been an obedient servant. She has suffered in particular from her association with France, under whose guidance and policy she has been actuated for so long. The very measures taken by His Majesty's Government in the Anglo-French Agreement to give her the best chance possible, namely, the 50 per cent clean cut in certain districts instead of a plebiscite, have turned to her detriment, because there is to be a plebiscite, too, in wide areas, and those other Powers who had claims have also come down upon the helpless victim. Those municipal elections upon whose voting the basis is taken for the 50 per cent cut were held on issues which had nothing to do with joining Germany. When I saw Herr Henlein over here he assured me that was not the desire of his people. Positive statements were made that it was only a question of home rule, of having a position of their own in the Czechoslovakian State. No one has a right to say that the plebiscite which is to be taken in areas under Saar conditions, and the clean-cut of the 50 per cent areas – that those two operations together amount to the slightest degree to a verdict of self-determination. It is a fraud and a farce to invoke that name.

We in this country, as in other Liberal and democratic countries, have a perfect right to exalt the principle of self-determination, but it comes ill out of the mouths of those in totalitarian States who deny even the smallest element of toleration to every section and creed within their bounds. But, however you put it, this particular block of land, this mass of human beings to be handed over, has never expressed the desire to go into the Nazi rule. I do not believe that even now – if their opinion could be asked – they would exercise such an option.

What is the remaining position of Czechoslovakia? Not only are they politically mutilated, but, economically and financially, they are in complete confusion. Their banking, their railway arrangements, are severed and broken, their industries are curtailed, and the movement of their population is most cruel. The Sudeten miners, who are all Czechs and whose families have lived in that area for centuries, must now flee into an area where there are hardly any mines left for them to work. It is a tragedy which has occurred. I did not like to hear the Minister of Transport yesterday talking about Humpty Dumpty. It was the Minister of Transport who was saying that it was a case of Humpty Dumpty that could never be put together again. There must always be the most profound regret and a sense of vexation in British hearts at the treatment and the misfortunes which have overcome the Czechoslovakian Republic. They have not ended here. At any moment there may be a hitch in the programme. At any moment there may be an order for Herr Goebbels to start again his propaganda of calumny and lies; at any moment an incident may be provoked, and now that the fortress line is given away what is there to stop the will of the conqueror? [*Interruption.*] It is too serious a subject to treat lightly. Obviously, we are not in a position to give them the slightest help at the present time, except what everyone is glad to know has been done, the financial aid which the Government have promptly produced.

I venture to think that in future the Czechoslovak State cannot be maintained as an independent entity. You will find that in a period of time which may be measured by years, but may be measured only by months, Czechoslovakia will be engulfed in the Nazi régime. Perhaps they may join it in despair or in revenge. At any rate, that story is over and told. But we cannot consider the abandonment and ruin of Czechoslovakia in the light only of what happened only last month. It is the most grievous consequence which we have yet experienced of what we have done and of what we have left undone in the last five years – five years of futile good intention, five years of eager search started for the line of least resistance, five years of uninterrupted retreat of British power, five years of neglect of our air defences. Those are the features which I stand here to declare and which marked an improvident stewardship for which Great Britain and France have dearly to pay. We have been reduced in those five years from a position of security so overwhelming and so unchallengeable that we never cared to think about it. We have been reduced from a position where the very word 'war' was considered one which would be used only by persons qualifying for a lunatic asylum. We have been reduced from a position of safety and power – power to do good, power to be generous to a beaten foe, power to make terms with Germany, power to give her proper redress for her grievances, power to stop her arming if we chose, power to take any step in strength or mercy or justice which we thought right – reduced in five years from a position safe and unchallenged to where we stand now.

When I think of the fair hopes of a long peace which still lay before Europe at the beginning of 1933 when Herr Hitler first obtained power, and of all the opportunities of arresting the growth of the Nazi power which have been thrown away, when I think of the immense combinations and resources which have been neglected or squandered, I cannot believe that a parallel exists in the whole course of history. So far as this country is concerned the responsibility must rest with those who have the undisputed control of our political affairs. They neither prevented Germany from rearming, nor did they rearm ourselves in time. They quarrelled with Italy without saving Ethiopia. They exploited and discredited the vast institution of the League of Nations and they neglected to make alliances and combinations which might have repaired previous errors, and thus they left us in the hour of trial without adequate national defence or effective international security.

In my holiday I thought it was a chance to study the reign of King Ethelred the Unready. The House will remember that that was a period of great misfortune, in which, from the strong position which we had gained under the descendants of King Alfred, we fell very swiftly into chaos. It was the period of Danegeld and of foreign pressure. I must say that the rugged words of the Anglo-Saxon Chronicle, written 1,000 years ago, seem to me apposite, at least as apposite as those quotations from Shakespeare with which we have been regaled by the last speaker from the Opposition Bench. Here is what the Anglo-Saxon Chronicle said, and I think the words apply very much to our treatment of Germany and our relations with her:

> All these calamities fell upon us because of evil counsel, because tribute was not offered to them at the right time nor yet were they resisted; but when they had done the most evil, then was peace made with them.

That is the wisdom of the past, for all wisdom is not new wisdom. I have ventured to express those views in justifying myself for not being able to support the Motion which is moved tonight, but I recognise that this great matter of Czechoslovakia, and of British and French duty there, has passed into history. New developments may come along, but we are not here to decide whether any of those steps should be taken or not. They have been taken. They have been taken by those who had a right to take them because they bore the highest executive responsibility under the Crown. Whatever we may think of it, we must regard those steps as belonging to the category of affairs which are settled beyond recall. The past is no more, and one can only draw comfort if one feels that one has done one's best to advise rightly and wisely and in good time. I therefore, turn to the future, and to our situation as it is today. Here, again, I am sure I shall have to say something which will not be at all welcome.

We are in the presence of a disaster of the first magnitude which has befallen Great Britain and France. Do not let us blind ourselves to that. It must now be accepted that all the countries of Central and Eastern Europe will make the best terms they can with the triumphant Nazi Power. The system of alliances in Central Europe upon which France has relied for her safety has been swept away, and I can see no means by which it can be reconstituted. The road down the Danube Valley to the Black Sea, the resources of corn and oil, the road which leads as far as Turkey, has been opened. In fact, if not in form, it seems to me that all those countries of Middle Europe, all those Danubian countries, will, one after another, be drawn into this vast system of power politics – not only power military politics but power economic politics – radiating from Berlin, and I believe this can be achieved quite smoothly and swiftly and will not necessarily entail the firing of a single shot. . . .

You will see, day after day, week after week, entire alienation of those regions. Many of those countries, in fear of the rise of the Nazi Power, have already got politicians, Ministers, Governments, who were pro-German, but there was always an enormous popular movement in Poland, Rumania, Bulgaria and Yugoslavia which looked to the Western democracies and loathed the idea of having this arbitrary rule of the totalitarian system thrust upon them, and hoped that a stand would be made. All that has gone by the board. We are talking about countries which are a long way off and of which, as the Prime Minister might say, we know nothing. [*Interruption.*] The noble Lady says that that very harmless allusion is –

Viscountess Astor: Rude.

Mr Churchill: She must very recently have been receiving her finishing course in manners. What will be the position, I want to know, of France and England this year and the year afterwards? What will be the position of that Western front of which we are in full authority the guarantors? The German army at the present time is more numerous than that of France, though not nearly so matured or perfected. Next year it will grow much larger, and its maturity will be more complete. Relieved from all anxiety in the East, and having secured resources which will greatly diminish, if not entirely remove, the deterrent of a naval blockade, the rulers of Nazi Germany will have a free choice open to them in what direction they will turn their eyes. If the Nazi dictator should choose to look westward, as he may, bitterly will France and England regret the loss of that fine army of ancient Bohemia which was estimated last week to require not fewer than 30 German divisions for its destruction.

Can we blind ourselves to the great change which has taken place in the military situation, and to the dangers we have to meet? We are in process, I believe, of adding, in four years, four battalions to the British Army. No fewer than two have already been completed. Here are at least 30 divisions which must now be taken into consideration upon the French front, besides the 12 that were captured when Austria was engulfed. Many people, no doubt, honestly believe that they are only giving away the interests of Czechoslovakia, whereas I fear we shall find that we have deeply compromised, and perhaps fatally endangered, the safety and even the independence of Great Britain and France. This is not merely a question of giving up the German colonies, as I am sure we shall be asked to do. Nor is it a question only of losing influence in Europe. It goes far deeper than that. You have to consider the character of the Nazi movement and the rule which it implies. The Prime Minister desires to see cordial relations between this country and Germany. There is no difficulty at all in having cordial relations with the German people. Our hearts go out to them. But they have no power. You must have diplomatic and correct relations, but there can never be friendship between the British democracy and the Nazi Power, that Power which spurns Christian ethics, which cheers its onward course by a barbarous paganism, which vaunts the spirit of aggression and conquest, which derives strength and perverted pleasure from persecution, and uses, as we have seen, with pitiless brutality the threat of murderous force. That Power cannot ever be the trusted friend of the British democracy.

What I find unendurable is the sense of our country falling into the power, into the orbit and influence of Nazi Germany, and of our existence becoming dependent upon their goodwill or pleasure. It is to prevent that that I have tried my best to urge the maintenance of every bulwark of defence – first the timely creation of an Air Force superior to anything within striking distance of our shores; secondly, the gathering together of the collective strength of many nations; and thirdly, the making of alliances and military conventions, all within the Covenant, in order to gather together forces at any rate to restrain the onward movement of this Power. It has all been in vain. Every position has been successively undermined and abandoned on specious and plausible excuses. We do not want to be led upon the high road to becoming a satellite of the German Nazi system of European domination. In a very few years, perhaps in a very few months, we shall be confronted with demands with which we shall no doubt be invited to comply. Those demands may affect the surrender of territory or the surrender of liberty. I foresee and foretell that the policy of submission will carry with it restrictions upon the freedom of speech and debate in Parliament, on public platforms, and discussions in the Press, for it will be said – indeed, I hear it said sometimes now – that we cannot allow the Nazi system of dictatorship to be criticised by ordinary, common English politicians. Then, with a Press under control, in part direct but more potently indirect, with every organ of public opinion doped and chloroformed into acquiescence, we shall be conducted along further stages of our journey. . . .

I have been casting about to see how measures can be taken to protect us from this advance of the Nazi Power, and to secure those forms of life which are so dear to us. What is the sole method that is open? The sole method that is open is for us to regain our old island independence by acquiring that supremacy in the air which we were promised, that security in our air defences which we were assured we had, and thus to make ourselves an island once again. That, in all this grim outlook, shines out as the overwhelming fact. An effort at rearmament the like of which has not been seen ought to be made forthwith, and all the resources of this country and all its united strength should be bent to that task. I was very glad to see that Lord Baldwin yesterday in the House of Lords said that he would mobilise industry tomorrow. But I think it would have been much better if Lord Baldwin had said that $2\frac{1}{2}$ years ago, when everyone demanded a Ministry of Supply. I will venture to say to hon. Gentlemen sitting here behind the Government Bench, hon. Friends of mine, whom I thank for the patience with which they have listened to what I have to say, that they have some responsibility for all this too, because, if they had given one tithe of the cheers they have lavished upon this transaction of Czechoslovakia to the small band of Members who were endeavouring to get timely rearmament set in motion, we should not now be in the position in which we are. Hon. Gentlemen opposite, and hon. Members on the Liberal benches, are not entitled to throw these stones. I remember for two years having to face, not only the Government's deprecation, but their stern disapproval. Lord Baldwin has now given the signal, tardy though it may be; let us at least obey it.

After all, there are no secrets now about what happened in the air and in the mobilisation of our anti-aircraft defences. These matters have been, as my hon. and gallant Friend the Member for the Abbey Division said, seen by thousands of people. They can form their own opinions of the character of the statements which have been persistently made to us by Ministers on this subject. Who pretends now that there is air parity with Germany? Who pretends now that our anti-aircraft defences were adequately manned or armed? We know that the German General Staff are well informed upon these subjects, but the House of Commons has hitherto not taken seriously its duty of requiring to assure itself on these matters. The Home Secretary [Sir Samuel Hoare] said the other night that he would welcome investigation. Many things have been done which reflect the greatest credit upon the administration. But the vital matters are what we want to know about. I have asked again and again during these three years for a secret Session where these matters could be thrashed out, or for an investigation by a Select Committee of the House, or for some other method. I ask now that, when we meet again in the autumn, that should be a matter on which the Government should take the House into its confidence, because we have a right to know where we stand and what measures are being taken to secure our position.

I do not grudge our loyal, brave people, who were ready to do their duty no matter what the cost, who never flinched under the strain of last week – I do not grudge them the natural, spontaneous outburst of joy and relief when they learned that the hard ordeal would no longer be required of them at the moment; but they should know the truth. They should know that there has been gross neglect and deficiency in our defences; they should know that we have sustained a defeat without a war, the consequences of which will travel far with us along our road; they should know that we have passed an awful milestone in our history, when the whole equilibrium of Europe has been deranged, and that the terrible words have for the time being been pronounced against the Western democracies:

'Thou art weighed in the balance and found wanting.'

And do not suppose that this is the end. This is only the beginning of the reckoning. This is only the first sip, the first foretaste of a bitter cup which will be proffered to us year by year unless, by a supreme recovery of moral health and martial vigour, we arise again and take our stand for freedom as in the olden time.

'THE LIGHTS ARE GOING OUT'

16 October 1938

Broadcast to the United States, London

Churchill renews his appeal to America.

I avail myself with relief of the opportunity of speaking to the people of the United States. I do not know how long such liberties will be allowed. The stations of uncensored expression are closing down; the lights are going out; but there is still time for those to whom freedom and Parliamentary government mean something, to consult together. Let me, then, speak in truth and earnestness while time remains.

The American people have, it seems to me, formed a true judgment upon the disaster which has befallen Europe. They realise, perhaps more clearly than the French and British publics have yet done, the far-reaching consequences of the abandonment and ruin of the Czechoslovak Republic. I hold to the conviction I expressed some months ago, that if in April, May or June, Great Britain, France and Russia had jointly declared that they would act together upon Nazi Germany if Herr Hitler committed an act of unprovoked aggression against this small state, and if they had told Poland, Yugoslavia and Rumania what they meant to do in good time, and invited them to join the combination of peace-defending Powers, I hold that the German Dictator would have been confronted with such a formidable array that he would have been deterred from his purpose. This would also have been an opportunity for all the peace-loving and moderate forces in Germany, together with the chiefs of the German Army, to make a great effort to re-establish something like sane and civilised conditions in their own country. If the risks of war which were run by France and Britain at the last moment had been boldly faced in good time, and plain declarations made, and meant, how different would our prospects be today! . . .

The culminating question to which I have been leading is whether the world as we have known it – the great and hopeful world of before the war, the world of increasing hope and enjoyment for the common man, the world of honoured tradition and expanding science – should meet this menace by submission or by resistance. Let us see, then, whether the means of resistance remain to us today. We have sustained an immense disaster; the renown of France is dimmed. In spite of her brave, efficient army, her influence is profoundly diminished. No one has a right to say that Britain, for all her blundering, has broken her word – indeed, when it was too late, she was better than her word. Nevertheless, Europe lies at this moment abashed and distracted before the triumphant assertions of a dictatorial power. In the Spanish Peninsula, a purely Spanish quarrel has been carried by the intervention, or shall I say the 'non-intervention' (to quote the current jargon), of Dictators into the region of a world cause. But it is not only in Europe that these oppressions prevail. China is being torn to pieces by a military clique in Japan; the poor, tormented Chinese people there are making a brave and stubborn defence. The ancient empire of Ethiopia has been overrun. The Ethiopians were taught to look to the sanctity of public law, to the tribunal of many nations in majestic union. But all failed; they were deceived, and now they are winning back their right to live by beginning again from the bottom a struggle on primordial lines. Even in South America the Nazi régime begins to undermine the fabric of Brazilian society.

Far away, happily protected by the Atlantic and Pacific Oceans, you, the people of the United States, to whom I now have the chance to speak, are the spectators; and, I may add, the increasingly involved spectators of these tragedies and crimes. We are left in no doubt where American conviction and sympathies lie: but will you wait until British freedom and independence have succumbed, and then take up the cause when it is three-quarters ruined, yourselves alone? I hear that they are saying in the United States that, because England and France have failed to do their duty, therefore the American people can wash their hands of the whole business. This may be the passing mood of many people, but there is no sense in it. If things have got much worse, all the more must we try to cope with them.

For, after all, survey the remaining forces of civilisation; they are overwhelming. If only they were united in a common conception of right and duty, there would be no war. On the contrary, the German people, industrious and faithful, valiant, but alas! lacking in the proper spirit of civic independence, liberated from their present nightmare would take their honoured place in the vanguard of human society. Alexander the Great remarked that the people of Asia were slaves because they had not learned to pronounce the word 'No'. Let that not be the epitaph of the English-speaking peoples or of Parliamentary democracy, or of France, or of the many surviving Liberal states of Europe.

There, in one single word, is the resolve which the forces of freedom and progress, of tolerance and goodwill, should take. It is not in the power of one nation, however formidably armed, still less is it in the power of a small group of men, violent, ruthless men, who have always to cast their eyes back over their shoulders, to cramp and fetter the forward march of human destiny. The preponderant world forces are upon our side; they have but to be combined to be obeyed. We must arm. Britain must arm. America must arm. If, through an earnest desire for peace, we have placed ourselves at a disadvantage, we must make up for it by redoubled exertions, and, if necessary, by fortitude in suffering. We shall, no doubt, arm. Britain, casting away the habits of centuries, will decree national service upon her citizens. The British people will stand erect, and will face whatever may be coming.

But arms – instrumentalities, as President Wilson called them – are not sufficient by themselves. We must add to them the power of ideas. People say we ought not to allow ourselves to be drawn into a theoretical antagonism between Nazidom and democracy; but the antagonism is here now. It is this very conflict of spiritual and moral ideas which gives the free countries a great part of their strength. You see these dictators on their pedestals, surrounded by the bayonets of their soldiers and the truncheons of their police. On all sides they are guarded by masses of armed men, cannons, aeroplanes, fortifications, and the like – they boast and vaunt themselves before the world, yet in their hearts there is unspoken fear. They are afraid of words and thoughts: words spoken abroad, thoughts stirring at home – all the more powerful because forbidden – terrify them. A little mouse of thought appears in the room, and even the mightiest potentates are thrown into panic. They make frantic efforts to bar out thoughts and words; they are afraid of the workings of the human mind. Cannons, aeroplanes, they can manufacture in large quantities; but how are they to quell the natural promptings of human nature, which after all these centuries of trial and progress has inherited a whole armoury of potent and indestructible knowledge?

Dictatorship – the fetish worship of one man – is a passing phase. A state of society where men may not speak their minds, where children denounce their parents to the police, where a businessman or small shopkeeper ruins his competitor by telling tales about his private opinions – such a state of society cannot long endure if brought into contact with the healthy outside world. The light of civilised progress with its tolerances and co-operation, with its dignities and joys, has often in the past been blotted out. But I hold the belief that we have now at last got far enough ahead of barbarism to control it, and to avert if, if only we realise what is afoot and make up our minds in time. We shall do it in the end. But how much harder our toil for every day's delay!

Is this a call to war? Does anyone pretend that preparation for resistance to aggression is unleashing war? I declare it to be the sole guarantee of peace. We need the swift gathering of forces to confront not only military but moral aggression; the resolute and sober acceptance of their duty by the English-speaking peoples and by all the nations, great and small, who wish to walk with them. Their faithful and zealous comradeship would almost between night and morning clear the path of progress and banish from all our lives the fear which already darkens the sunlight to hundreds of millions of men.

'THE BITTER FRUITS OF MUNICH'

14 March 1939

Waltham Abbey

On this very day, with brazen contempt for the Munich Agreement, Germany invaded Czechoslovakia, exposing Chamberlain's much-vaunted agreement for the sham it was. Meanwhile Churchill was fighting for his political life in his Epping constituency, following attempts by Conservative Central Office to have him de-selected as Conservative candidate in the forthcoming General Election.

Complaint has been made in some of the outlying parts of the Constituency of my speech on the Munich Agreement. In this I pointed out that a disaster of the first magnitude had befallen France and England. Is that not so? Why do you suppose we are making all these preparations? Why do you suppose that the French military service has been lengthened, and we have promised to send nineteen divisions to the Continent? It is because in the destruction of Czechoslovakia the entire balance of Europe was changed.

The great and growing German Army is now free to turn in any direction: we do not know in what direction it will turn. . . .

Many people at the time of the September crisis thought they were only giving away the interests of Czechoslovakia, but with every month that passes you will see that they were also giving away the interests of Britain, and the interests of peace and justice. Now I have defended this speech which has been attacked, and I say never did I make a truer statement to Parliament. Practically everything that I said has already proved true. And who are these people who go about saying that even if it were true, why state the facts? I reply, why mislead the nation? What is the use of Parliament if it is not the place where true statements can be brought before the people? What is the use of sending Members to the House of Commons who say just the popular things of the moment, and merely endeavour to give satisfaction to the Government Whips by cheering loudly every Ministerial platitude, and by walking through the Lobbies oblivious of the criticisms they hear? People talk about our Parliamentary institutions and Parliamentary democracy; but if these are to survive, it will not be because the Constituencies return tame, docile, subservient Members, and try to stamp out every form of independent judgment.

'THE SURGE OF UNITY AND OF DUTY'

20 April 1939

Canada Club, London

Some foreigners mock at the British Empire because there are no parchment bonds or hard steel shackles which compel its united action. But there are other forces, far more subtle and far more compulsive to which the whole fabric spontaneously responds. These deep tides are flowing now. They sweep away in their flow differences of class and Party. They override the vast ocean spaces which separate the Dominions of the King. The electric telegraph is an old story; the wireless broadcast is a new one; but we rely on a process far more widespread and equally instantaneous. There are certain things which could happen, which it would not be necessary for us to argue about. No Constitutional issues would arise. Everyone, in the loneliest ranch, or in the most self-centred legislature, would see duty staring him in the face, and all hearts would have the same conviction. And not only the same conviction, but the same resolve to action. . . .

One would underrate altogether the sentiment and repressed passion which unites the British Empire or Commonwealth, as many like to call it, by supposing that outworn Jingoism or grasping Imperialism play an important part. If we in this small island have gradually grown to a considerable estate, and have been able to give our wage-earners some relief from the harder forms of economic pressure, and to build up a decent, tolerant, compassionate, flexible, and infinitely varied society, it is because in all the great crises of our history the interest of Britain has marched with the progress and freedom of mankind. If in these hours of anxiety, but by no means of fear, we feel the surge of unity and of duty thrilling the pulses of the British race, it is because we are bound together by principles, themes and conceptions which make their appeal not only to the British Empire, but to the conscience and to the genius of humanity.

It is refreshing to find that in the great American Republic these same resolves to resist at all costs the new machine-made forms of tyranny and oppression are also instinctive and strong. Canada has a great part to play in the relations of Great Britain and the United States. She spans the Atlantic Ocean with her loyalties; she clasps the

American hand with her faith and goodwill. That long frontier from the Atlantic to the Pacific Oceans, guarded only by neighbourly respect and honourable obligations, is an example to every country and a pattern for the future of the world. . . .

We must not turn from the path of duty. If the British Empire is fated to pass from life into history, we must hope it will not be by the slow processes of dispersion and decay, but in some supreme exertion for freedom, for right and for truth. Why is it that from so many lands men look towards us today? It is certainly not because we have gained advantages in a race of armaments, or have scored a point by some deeply planned diplomatic intrigue, or because we exhibit the blatancy and terrorism of ruthless power. It is because we stand on the side of the general need. In the British Empire we not only look out across the seas towards each other, but backwards to our own history, to Magna Carta, to Habeas Corpus, to the Petition of Right, to Trial by Jury, to the English Common Law and to Parliamentary Democracy. These are the milestones and monuments that mark the path along which the British race has marched to leadership and freedom. And over all this, uniting each Dominion with the other and uniting us all with our majestic past, is the gold circle of the Crown. What is within the circle? Not only the glory of an ancient unconquered people, but the hope, the sure hope, of a broadening life for hundreds of millions of men.

'REPUDIATION OF THE BALFOUR DECLARATION'

23 May 1939

House of Commons

Now I come to the gravamen of the case. I regret very much that the pledge of the Balfour Declaration, endorsed as it has been by successive Governments, and the conditions under which we obtained the Mandate, have both been violated by the Government's proposals. There is much in this White Paper which is alien to the spirit of the Balfour Declaration, but I will not trouble about that. I select the one point upon which there is plainly a breach and repudiation of the Balfour Declaration – the provision that Jewish immigration can be stopped in five years' time by the decision of an

Arab majority. That is a plain breach of a solemn obligation. I am astonished that my right hon. Friend the Prime Minister, of all others, and at this moment above all others, should have lent himself to this new and sudden default.

To whom was the pledge of the Balfour Declaration made? It was not made to the Jews of Palestine, it was not made to those who were actually living in Palestine. It was made to world Jewry and in particular to the Zionist associations. It was in consequence of and on the basis of this pledge that we received important help in the war, and that after the war we received from the Allied and Associated Powers the Mandate for Palestine. This pledge of a home of refuge, or an asylum, was not made to the Jews in Palestine but to the Jews outside Palestine, to that vast, unhappy mass of scattered, persecuted, wandering Jews whose intense, unchanging, unconquerable desire has been for a National Home – to quote the words to which my right hon. Friend the Prime Minister subscribed in the Memorial which he and others sent to us:

> the Jewish people who have through centuries of dispersion and persecution patiently awaited the hour of its restoration to its ancestral home.

Those are the words. They were the people outside, not the people in. It is not with the Jews in Palestine that we have now or at any future time to deal, but with world Jewry, with Jews all over the world. That is the pledge which was given, and that is the pledge which we are now asked to break, for how can this pledge be kept, I want to know, if in five years' time the National Home is to be barred and no more Jews are to be allowed in without the permission of the Arabs?

I entirely accept the distinction between making a Jewish National Home in Palestine and making Palestine a Jewish National Home. I think I was one of the first to draw that distinction. The Government quote me, and they seem to associate me with them on this subject in their White Paper, but what sort of National Home is offered to the Jews of the world when we are asked to declare that in five years' time the door of that home is to be shut and barred in their faces? The idea of home to wanderers is, surely, a place to which they can resort. When grievous and painful words like 'breach of pledge', 'repudiation' and 'default' are used in respect of the public action of men and Ministers who in private life observe a stainless honour – the country must discuss these matters as they present themselves in their public aspect – it is necessary to be precise, and to do them justice His Majesty's Government have been brutally precise. On page 11 of the White Paper, in sub-section (3) of paragraph 14 there is this provision:

> After the period of five years no further Jewish immigration will be permitted unless the Arabs of Palestine are prepared to acquiesce in it.

Now, there is the breach; there is the violation of the pledge; there is the abandonment of the Balfour Declaration; there is the end of the vision, of the hope, of the dream. If you leave out those words this White Paper is no more than one of the several experiments and essays in Palestinian constitution-making which we have had of recent years, but put in those three lines and there is the crux, the peccant point, the breach, and we must have an answer to it. . . .

I cannot feel that we have accorded to the Arab race unfair treatment after the support which they gave us in the late war. The Palestinian Arabs, of course, were for the most part fighting against us, but elsewhere over vast regions inhabited by the Arabs independent Arab Kingdoms and principalities have come into being such as had never been known in Arab history before. Some have been established by Great Britain and others by France. When I wrote this despatch in 1922 I was advised by, among others, Colonel Lawrence, the truest champion of Arab rights whom modern times have known. He has recorded his opinion that the settlement was fair and just – his definite, settled opinion. Together we placed the Emir Abdullah in Transjordania, where he remains faithful and prosperous to this day. Together, under the responsibility of the Prime Minister of those days, King Feisal was placed upon the throne of Iraq, where his descendants now rule. But we also showed ourselves continually resolved to close no door upon the ultimate development of a Jewish National Home, fed by continual Jewish immigration into Palestine. Colonel Lawrence thought this was fair then. Why should it be pretended that it is unfair now? . . .

I end upon the land of Palestine. It is strange indeed that we should turn away from our task in Palestine at the moment when, as the Secretary of State told us yesterday, the local disorders have been largely mastered. It is stranger still that we should turn away when the great experiment and bright dream, the historic dream, has proved its power to succeed. Yesterday the Minister responsible descanted eloquently in glowing passages upon the magnificent work which the Jewish colonists have done. They have made the desert bloom. They have started a score of thriving industries, he said. They have founded a great city on the barren shore. They have harnessed the Jordan and spread its electricity throughout the land. So far from being persecuted, the Arabs have crowded into the country and multiplied till their population has increased more than even all world Jewry could lift up the Jewish population. Now we are asked to decree that all this is to stop and all this is to come to an end. We are now asked to submit – and this is what rankles most with me – to an agitation which is fed with foreign money and ceaselessly inflamed by Nazi and by fascist propaganda.

It is 20 years ago since my right hon. Friend used these stirring words:

> A great responsibility will rest upon the Zionists, who, before long, will be proceeding, with joy in their hearts, to the ancient seat of their people. Theirs will be the task to build up a new prosperity and a new civilisation in old Palestine, so long neglected and mis-ruled.

Well, they have answered his call. They have fulfilled his hopes. How can he find it in his heart to strike them this mortal blow?

'A HUSH OVER EUROPE'

8 August 1939

Broadcast to the US from London

Churchill makes one final effort to arouse the Great Republic from its reveries, barely four weeks before the outbreak of war in Europe.

There is a hush over all Europe, nay, over all the world, broken only by the dull thud of Japanese bombs falling on Chinese cities, on Chinese Universities or near British and American ships. But then, China is a long way off, so why worry? The Chinese are fighting for what the founders of the American Constitution in their stately language called: 'Life, liberty and the pursuit of happiness.' And they seem to be fighting very well. Many good judges think they are going to win. Anyhow, let's wish them luck! Let's give them a wave of encouragement – as your President did last week, when he gave notice about ending the commercial treaty. After all, the suffering

Chinese are fighting our battle – the battle of democracy. They are defending the soil, the good earth, that has been theirs since the dawn of time against cruel and unprovoked aggression. Give them a cheer across the ocean – no one knows whose turn it may be next. If this habit of military dictatorships' breaking into other people's lands with bomb and shell and bullet, stealing the property and killing the proprietors, spreads too widely, we may none of us be able to think of summer holidays for quite a while.

But to come back to the hush I said was hanging over Europe. What kind of a hush is it? Alas! it is the hush of suspense, and in many lands it is the hush of fear. Listen! No, listen carefully; I think I hear something – yes, there it was quite clear. Don't you hear it? It is the tramp of armies crunching the gravel of the parade-grounds, splashing through rain-soaked fields, the tramp of two million German soldiers and more than a million Italians – 'going on manoeuvres' – yes, only on manoeuvres! Of course it's only manoeuvres – just like last year. After all, the Dictators must train their soldiers. They could scarcely do less in common prudence, when the Danes, the Dutch, the Swiss, the Albanians – and of course the Jews – may leap out upon them at any moment and rob them of their living-space, and make them sign another paper to say who began it. Besides, these German and Italian armies may have another work of Liberation to perform. It was only last year they liberated Austria from the horrors of self-government. It was only in March they freed the Czechoslovak Republic from the misery of independent existence. It is only two years ago that Signor Mussolini gave the ancient kingdom of Abyssinia its Magna Carta. It is only two months ago that little Albania got its writ of Habeas Corpus, and Mussolini sent in his Bill of Rights for King Zog to pay. Why, even at this moment, the mountaineers of the Tyrol, a German-speaking population who have dwelt in their beautiful valleys for a thousand years, are being *liberated*, that is to say, uprooted, from the land they love, from the soil which Andreas Hofer died to defend. No wonder the armies are tramping on when there is so much liberation to be done, and no wonder there is a hush among all the neighbours of Germany and Italy while they are wondering which one is going to be 'liberated' next.

The Nazis say that they are being encircled. They have encircled themselves with a ring of neighbours who have to keep on guessing who will be struck down next. This kind of guesswork is a very tiring game. Countries, especially small countries, have long ceased to find it amusing. Can you wonder that the neighbours of Germany, both great and small, have begun to think of stopping the game, by simply saying to the Nazis on the principle of the Covenant of the League of Nations: 'He who attacks any, attacks all. He who attacks the weakest will find he has attacked the strongest'? That is how we are spending our holiday over here, in poor weather, in a lot of clouds. We hope it is better with you.

One thing has struck me as very strange, and that is the resurgence of the one-man power after all these centuries of experience and progress. It is curious how the English-speaking peoples have always had this horror of one-man power. They are quite ready to follow a leader for a time, as long as he is serviceable to them; but the idea of handing themselves over, lock, stock and barrel, body and soul, to one man, and worshipping him as if he were an idol – that has always been odious to the whole theme and nature of our civilisation. The architects of the American Constitution were as careful as those who shaped the British Constitution to guard against the whole life and fortunes, and all the laws and freedom of the nation, being placed in the hands of a tyrant. Checks and counter-checks in the body politic, large devolutions of State government, instruments and processes of free debate, frequent recurrence to first principles, the right of opposition to the most powerful governments, and above all ceaseless vigilance, have preserved, and will preserve, the broad characteristics of British and American institutions. But in Germany, on a mountain peak, there sits one man who in a single day can release the world from the fear which now oppresses it; or in a single day can plunge all that we have and are into a volcano of smoke and flame.

If Herr Hitler does not make war, there will be no war. No one else is going to make war. Britain and France are determined to shed no blood except in self-defence or in defence of their Allies. No one has ever dreamed of attacking Germany. If Germany desires to be reassured against attack by her neighbours, she has only to say the word and we will give her the fullest guarantees in accordance with the principles of the Covenant of the League. We have said repeatedly we ask nothing for ourselves in the way of security that we are not willing freely to share with the German people. Therefore, if war should come there can be no doubt upon whose head the blood-guiltiness will fall. Thus lies the great issue at this moment, and none can tell how it will be settled.

It is not, believe me, my American friends, from any ignoble shrinking from pain and death that the British and French peoples pray for peace. It is not because we have any doubts how a struggle between Nazi Germany and the civilised world would ultimately end that we pray tonight and every night for peace. But whether it be peace or war – peace with its broadening and brightening prosperity, now within our reach, or war with its measureless carnage and destruction – we must strive to frame some system of human relations in the future which will bring to an end this prolonged hideous uncertainty, which will let the working and creative forces of the world get on with their job, and which will no longer leave the whole life of mankind dependent upon the virtues, the caprice, or the wickedness of a single man.

4. The Glory Years 1939–45

On the very day that Britain and France declared war on Nazi Germany, Prime Minister Neville Chamberlain invited Churchill to resume his old post at the Admiralty. Then, after more than six months of so-called 'phoney' war, Hitler launched his *blitzkrieg* against Belgium, France and the Low Countries. In that same hour of peril, the British people turned for salvation to the man whose warnings they had failed to heed.

Churchill saw it as his prime task to keep the flag of Freedom flying until the 'Great Republic across the Seas' (a favourite Churchillian phrase), awoke from her slumbers. Convinced, against all the odds, that Britain could hold out against Hitler in her island fastness, he was sufficient of a realist to know that only the combined strength of the English-speaking world could in the end defeat Nazi Germany and liberate the enslaved nations of Europe. He held to a fond belief that President Roosevelt would seize any opportunity to join the fray, but it was to take the Japanese attack on the American Fleet at Pearl Harbor – more than 18 months later, in December 1941 – before his hopes became reality.

Churchill then played a key role in persuading the United States to give priority to the defeat of Germany, before getting to grips with Japan. Thus, together with President Roosevelt, he led the free world to victory.

WAR

3 September 1939

House of Commons

At dawn on 1 September Hitler's armies invaded Poland. In accordance with the British and French Governments' Guarantee to Poland, on 2 September an Ultimatum was issued demanding Germany's withdrawal and respect of Polish Sovereignty. At 11.15 on 3 September the British Prime Minister, Neville Chamberlain, announced in his melancholy voice that the Ultimatum had expired without any reply being received from Germany and that, consequently, Britain was at war with Germany. After an air-raid warning, which proved false, the House met in early afternoon and Churchill made his last speech from the backbenches.

Following the debate Chamberlain invited Churchill to become First Lord of the Admiralty. At 6 p.m. he took up his post and the signal was flashed to the Fleet: 'Winston is back!' As he later wrote in The Gathering Storm: *'So it was that I came again to the room I had quitted in pain and sorrow almost a quarter of a century before. . . . Once again we must fight for life and honour against all the might and fury of the valiant, disciplined and ruthless German race. Once again! So be it!'*

In this solemn hour it is a consolation to recall and to dwell upon our repeated efforts for peace. All have been ill-starred, but all have been faithful and sincere. This is of the highest moral value – and not only moral value, but practical value – at the present time, because the wholehearted concurrence of scores of millions of men and women, whose co-operation is indispensable and whose comradeship and brotherhood are indispensable, is the only foundation upon which the trial and tribulation of modern war can be endured and surmounted. This moral conviction alone affords that ever-fresh resilience which renews the strength and energy of people in long, doubtful and dark days. Outside, the storms of war may blow and the lands may be lashed with the fury of its gales, but in our own hearts this Sunday morning there is peace. Our hands may be active, but our consciences are at rest.

We must not underrate the gravity of the task which lies before us or the temerity of the ordeal, to which we shall not be found unequal. We must expect many disappointments, and many unpleasant surprises, but we may be sure that the task which we have freely accepted is one not beyond the compass and the strength of the British Empire and the French Republic. The Prime Minister said it was a sad day, and that is indeed true, but at the present time there is another note which may be present, and that is a feeling of thankfulness that, if these great trials were to come upon our Island, there is a generation of Britons here now ready to prove itself not unworthy of the days of yore and not unworthy of those great men, the fathers of our land, who laid the foundations of our laws and shaped the greatness of our country.

This is not a question of fighting for Danzig or fighting for Poland. We are fighting to save the whole world from the pestilence of Nazi tyranny and in defence of all that is most sacred to man. This is no war of domination or imperial aggrandizement or material gain; no war to shut any country out of its sunlight and means of progress. It is a war, viewed in its inherent quality, to establish, on impregnable rocks, the rights of the individual, and it is a war to establish and revive the stature of man. Perhaps it might seem a paradox that a war undertaken in the name of liberty and right should require, as a necessary part of its processes, the surrender for the time being of so many of the dearly valued liberties and rights. In these last few days the House of Commons has been voting dozens of Bills which hand over to the executive our most dearly valued traditional liberties. We are sure that these liberties will be in hands which will not abuse them, which will use them for no class or party interests, which will cherish and guard them, and we look forward to the day, surely and confidently we look forward to the day, when our liberties and rights will be restored to us, and when we shall be able to share them with the peoples to whom such blessings are unknown.

RUSSIA: 'A RIDDLE, WRAPPED IN A MYSTERY, INSIDE AN ENIGMA'

1 October 1939

Broadcast, London

Under the secret clauses of the Nazi-Soviet Pact the German and Russian dictators attacked Poland from East and West to dismember the country.

The British Empire and the French Republic have been at war with Nazi Germany for a month tonight. We have not yet come at all to the severity of fighting which is to be expected; but three important things have happened.

First, Poland has been again overrun by two of the great Powers which held her in bondage for 150 years, but were unable to quench the spirit of the Polish nation. The heroic defence of Warsaw shows that the soul of Poland is indestructible, and that she will rise again like a rock, which may for a spell be submerged by a tidal wave, but which remains a rock.

What is the second event of this first month? It is, of course, the assertion of the power of Russia. Russia has pursued a cold policy of self-interest. We could have wished that the Russian armies should be standing on their present line as the friends and allies of Poland instead of as invaders. But that the Russian armies should stand on this line was clearly necessary for the safety of Russia against the Nazi menace. At any rate, the line is there, and an Eastern Front has been created which Nazi Germany does not dare assail. When Herr von Ribbentrop was summoned to Moscow last week, it was to learn the fact, and to accept the fact, that the Nazi designs upon the Baltic States and upon the Ukraine must come to a dead stop.

I cannot forecast to you the action of Russia. It is a riddle, wrapped in a mystery, inside an enigma; but perhaps there is a key. That key is Russian national interest. It cannot be in accordance with the interest or the safety of Russia that Germany should plant itself upon the shores of the Black Sea, or that it should overrun the Balkan States and subjugate the Slavonic peoples of south-eastern Europe. That would be contrary to the historic life-interest of Russia.

But in this quarter of the world – the south-east of Europe – these interests of Russia fall into the same channel as the interests of Britain and France. None of these three Powers can afford to see Rumania, Yugoslavia, Bulgaria, and above all Turkey, put under the German heel. Through the fog of confusion and uncertainty we may discern quite plainly the community of interests which exists between England, France and Russia – a community of interests to prevent the Nazis carrying the flames of war into the Balkans and Turkey. Thus, my friends, at some risk of being proved wrong by events, I will proclaim tonight my conviction that the second great fact of the first month of the war is that Hitler, and all that Hitler stands for, have been and are being warned off the east and the south-east of Europe.

What is the third event? Here I speak as First Lord of the Admiralty, with especial caution. It would seem that the U-boat attack upon the life of the British Isles has not so far proved successful. It is true that when they sprang out upon us and we were going about our ordinary business, with two thousand ships in constant movement every day upon the seas, they managed to do some serious damage. But the Royal Navy has immediately attacked the U-boats, and is hunting them night and day – I will not say without mercy, because God forbid we should ever part company with that – but at any rate with zeal and not altogether without relish. And it looks tonight very much as if it is the U-boats who are feeling the weather, and not the Royal Navy or the world-wide commerce of Britain. A week has passed since a British ship, alone or in convoy, has been sunk or even molested by a U-boat on the high seas; and during the first month of the war we have captured by our efficient contraband control 150,000 tons more German merchandise – food, oil, minerals and other commodities – for our own benefit than we have lost by all the U-boat sinkings put together. In fact, up to date – please observe I make no promises (we must deal in performance and not in promises) – up to date we have actually got 150,000 tons of very desirable supplies into this Island more than we should have got if war had not been declared, and if no U-boat had ever cast sailormen to their fate upon the stormy seas. This seems to be a very solid, tangible fact which has emerged from the first month of the war against Nazidom.

Of course, we are told that all the U-boats have gone home just to tell their master about their exploits and their experiences. But that is not true, because every day we are attacking them upon the approaches to the British Isles. Some undoubtedly have preferred to go off and sink the unprotected neutral ships of Norway and Sweden. I hope the day will come when the Admiralty will be able to invite the ships of all nations to join the British convoys, and to insure them on their voyages at a reasonable rate. We must, of course, expect that the U-boat attack upon the seaborne commerce of the world will be renewed presently on a greater scale. We hope, however, that by the end of October we shall have three times as many hunting-craft at work as we had at the beginning of the war; and we hope that by the measures we have taken, our means of putting down this pest will grow continually. I can assure you we are taking great care about all that.

Therefore, to sum up the results of the first month, let us say that Poland has been overrun, but will rise again; that Russia has warned Hitler off his Eastern dreams; and that U-boats may be safely left to the care and constant attention of the British Navy.

'THE NAVY'S HERE!'

23 February 1940

Luncheon for crewmen of HMS Exeter *and* Ajax,
The Guildhall, London

Churchill ordered the Navy to intercept the German auxiliary Altmark, *carrying captured British merchant seamen, whose ships had been sunk by the* Graf Spee. *HMS* Cossack *boarded the* Altmark *in Josing Fjord, Norway, with a cry to the prisoners: 'The Navy's here!'*

My colleagues of the Board of Admiralty and of the War Cabinet are grateful to you for inviting us here today to share the hospitality which the City of London has extended to the victors of the River Plate. It is an occasion at once joyous, memorable and unique. It is the highest compliment your ancient Corporation could give to the officers and men of the *Exeter* and *Ajax* and through them to the whole of our Navy, upon whom, under Providence, our lives and State depend from hour to hour.

I do not suppose that the bonds which unite the British Navy to the British nation – and they have taken a long time to form – or those which join the Navy and the Mercantile Marine were ever so strong as they are today. The brunt of the war so far has fallen upon

Welcoming home the crew of HMS *Exeter*, Plymouth, 1940.

the sailormen, and their comrades in the Coastal Air Force, and we have already lost nearly 3,000 lives in a hard, unrelenting struggle which goes on night and day and is going on now without a moment's respite. The brilliant sea fight which Admiral Harwood conceived, and which those who are here executed, takes its place in our naval annals, and I might add that in a dark, cold winter it warmed the cockles of the British heart. But it is not only in those few glittering, deadly hours of action, which rivet all eyes, that the strain falls upon the Navy. Far more does it fall in the weeks and months of ceaseless trial and vigilance on cold, dark, stormy seas from whose waves at any moment death and destruction may leap with sullen roar. There is the task which these men were discharging and which their comrades are discharging. There was the task from which, in a sense, the fierce action was almost a relief.

Here let me say a word for the naval members of the Board of Admiralty and especially for the First Sea Lord, Sir Dudley Pound, and his Deputy-Chief of Naval Staff [the newly promoted Vice-Admiral Phillips] for the skilful combination for which they have been responsible. You must remember that for one stroke that goes home, for one clutch that grips the raider, there are many that miss their mark on the broad oceans; for every success there are many disappointments. You must never forget that the dangers that are seen are only a small part of those that are warded off by care and foresight, and therefore pass unnoticed. The Admiralty and the Fleet are learning together the special conditions of this hard and novel war; and, although mistakes and accidents will certainly occur, and sorrow will fall from time to time upon us, we hope that from Whitehall the sense of resolution and design at the centre will impart itself to all afloat, and will lighten the burden of their task and concert the vigour of their action. It is not, for instance, a mere coincidence that has brought the *Achilles* out of the vast Pacific Ocean to the shores of far-off New Zealand, in order to receive in the Antipodes the same warm-hearted welcome as her sisters the *Ajax* and the *Exeter* are receiving now in dear old London.

The spirit of all our forces serving on salt water has never been more strong and high than now. The warrior heroes of the past may look down, as Nelson's monument looks down upon us now, without any feeling that the island race has lost its daring or that the examples they set in bygone centuries have faded as the generations have succeeded one another. It was not for nothing that Admiral Harwood, as he instantly at full speed attacked an enemy which might have sunk any one of his ships by a single successful salvo from its far heavier guns, flew Nelson's immortal signal, of which neither the new occasion, nor the conduct of all ranks and ratings, nor the final result were found unworthy.

To the glorious tale of the action off the Plate there has recently been added an epilogue – the rescue last week by the *Cossack* and her flotilla, under the nose of the enemy and amid the tangles of one-sided neutrality, of the British captives taken from the sunken German raider. Their rescue at the very moment when these unhappy men were about to be delivered over to German bondage proves that the long arm of British sea power can be stretched out, not only for foes but also for faithful friends. And to Nelson's signal of 135 years ago, 'England expects that every man will do his duty,' there may now be added last week's no less proud reply: 'The Navy is here!'

'BLOOD, TOIL, TEARS AND SWEAT'

13 May 1940

House of Commons

With mounting criticism in the House and in the country of his ineffectual leadership, Neville Chamberlain was forced to step down as Prime Minister. He and a majority of the Conservative Party favoured Lord Halifax as his successor, as did King George VI. But Halifax declined, realising that, as a member of the House of Lords, his acceptance would give rise to enormous practical and constitutional difficulties.

Thus it was that, on 10 May 1940, Winston Churchill – already 65 years of age – accepted the King's commission to form a government. That same day Hitler launched his devastating blitzkrieg *against Belgium, France and Holland. In* The Gathering Storm *Churchill recorded his thoughts as he went to bed that night: 'I felt as if I were walking with destiny and that all my past life had been but a preparation for this hour and for this trial.'*

On 13 May Churchill invited the House of Commons to affirm its support for the new Administration. It was a crucial moment in the life of Great Britain. In the country people were confused and alarmed. In the House, and especially in the ranks of his own Conservative Party, he had many enemies, who viewed him with dislike and distrust. With this speech, which was subsequently broadcast to the world, Churchill electrified the House and the nation. The message was stark: Britain would fight to the death! In the House as he sat down, there was a moment of stunned silence, followed by a wholly exceptional standing ovation.

I beg to move,

> That this House welcomes the formation of a Government represent-
> ing the united and inflexible resolve of the nation to prosecute the war
> with Germany to a victorious conclusion.

On Friday evening last I received His Majesty's Commission to form a new Administration. It was the evident wish and will of Parliament and the nation that this should be conceived on the broadest possible basis and that it should include all parties, both those who supported the late Government and also the parties of the Opposition. I have completed the most important part of this task. A War Cabinet has been formed of five Members, representing, with the Opposition Liberals, the unity of the nation. The three party Leaders have agreed to serve, either in the War Cabinet or in high executive office. The three Fighting Services have been filled. It was necessary that this should be done in one single day, on account of the extreme urgency and rigour of events. A number of other positions, key positions, were filled yesterday, and I am submitting a further list to His Majesty tonight. I hope to complete the appointment of the principal Ministers during tomorrow. The appointment of the other Ministers usually takes a little longer, but I trust that, when Parliament meets again, this part of my task will be completed, and that the administration will be complete in all respects.

I considered it in the public interest to suggest that the House should be summoned to meet today. Mr Speaker agreed, and took the necessary steps, in accordance with the powers conferred upon him by the Resolution of the House. At the end of the proceedings today, the Adjournment of the House will be proposed until Tuesday, 21st May, with, of course, provision for earlier meeting, if need be. The business to be considered during that week will be notified to Members at the earliest opportunity. I now invite the House, by the Motion which stands in my name, to record its approval of the steps taken and to declare its confidence in the new Government.

To form an Administration of this scale and complexity is a serious undertaking in itself, but it must be remembered that we are in the preliminary stage of one of the greatest battles in history, that we are in action at many other points in Norway and in Holland, that we have to be prepared in the Mediterranean, that the air battle is continuous and that many preparations, such as have been indicated by my hon. Friend below the Gangway, have to be made here at home. In this crisis I hope I may be pardoned if I do not address the House at any length today. I hope that any of my friends and colleagues, or former colleagues, who are affected by the political reconstruction, will make allowance, all allowance, for any lack of ceremony with which it has been necessary to act. I would say to the House, as I said to those who have joined this Government: 'I have nothing to offer but blood, toil, tears and sweat.'

We have before us an ordeal of the most grievous kind. We have before us many, many long months of struggle and of suffering. You ask, what is our policy? I can say: It is to wage war, by sea, land and air, with all our might and with all the strength that God can give us; to wage war against a monstrous tyranny, never surpassed in the dark, lamentable catalogue of human crime. That is our policy. You ask, what is our aim? I can answer in one word: It is victory, victory at all costs, victory in spite of all terror, victory, however long and hard the road may be; for without victory, there is no survival. Let that be realised; no survival for the British Empire, no survival for all that the British Empire has stood for, no survival for the urge and impulse of the ages, that mankind will move forward towards its goal. But I take up my task with buoyancy and hope. I feel sure that our cause will not be suffered to fail among men. At this time I feel entitled to claim the aid of all, and I say, 'Come then, let us go forward together with our united strength.'

'ARM YOURSELVES, AND BE YE MEN OF VALOUR!'

19 May 1940

Broadcast, London

On 15 May Holland had fallen, meanwhile the French Armies, in the face of overwhelming German attack by Land and Air, were in full retreat. In Paris the Government was talking of surrender. Mean-while in London the Cabinet was informed that Lord Gort, who commanded the British Expeditionary Force in Northern France and Belgium, comprising almost all Britain's professional army, was 'examining a possible withdrawal towards Dunkirk'. It was in these dire circumstances that Churchill made his first broadcast as Prime Minister to the British people.

I speak to you for the first time as Prime Minister in a solemn hour for the life of our country, of our Empire, of our Allies, and, above all, of the cause of Freedom. A tremendous battle is raging in France and Flanders. The Germans, by a remarkable combination of air bombing and heavily armoured tanks, have broken through the French defences north of the Maginot Line, and strong columns of their armoured vehicles are ravaging the open country, which for the first day or two was without defenders. They have penetrated deeply and spread alarm and confusion in their track. Behind them there are now appearing infantry in lorries, and behind them, again, the large masses are moving forward. The re-groupment of the French armies to make head against, and also to strike at, this intruding wedge has been proceeding for several days, largely assisted by the magnificent efforts of the Royal Air Force.

We must not allow ourselves to be intimidated by the presence of these armoured vehicles in unexpected places behind our lines. If they are behind our Front, the French are also at many points fighting actively behind theirs. Both sides are therefore in an extremely dangerous position. And if the French Army, and our own Army, are well handled, as I believe they will be; if the French retain that genius for recovery and counter-attack for which they have so long been famous; and if the British Army shows the dogged endurance and solid fighting power of which there have been so many examples in the past – then a sudden transformation of the scene might spring into being.

It would be foolish, however, to disguise the gravity of the hour. It would be still more foolish to lose heart and courage or to suppose that well-trained, well-equipped armies numbering three or four millions of men can be overcome in the space of a few weeks, or even months, by a scoop, or raid of mechanised vehicles, however formidable. We may look with confidence to the stabilisation of the Front in France, and to the general engagement of the masses, which will enable the qualities of the French and British soldiers to be matched squarely against those of their adversaries. For myself, I have invincible confidence in the French Army and its leaders. Only a very small part of that splendid Army has yet been heavily engaged; and only a very small part of France has yet been invaded. There is good evidence to show that practically the whole of the specialised and mechanised forces of the enemy have been already thrown into the battle; and we know that very heavy losses have been inflicted upon them. No officer or man, no brigade or division, which grapples at close quarters with the enemy, wherever encountered, can fail to make a worthy contribution to the general result. The Armies must cast away the idea of resisting behind concrete lines or natural obstacles, and must realise that mastery can only be regained by furious and unrelenting assault. And this spirit must not only animate the High Command, but must inspire every fighting man.

In the air – often at serious odds, often at odds hitherto thought overwhelming – we have been clawing down three or four to one of our enemies; and the relative balance of the British and German Air Forces is now considerably more favourable to us than at the beginning of the battle. In cutting down the German bombers we are fighting our own battle as well as that of France. My confidence in our ability to fight it out to the finish with the German Air Force has been strengthened by the fierce encounters which have taken place and are taking place. At the same time, our heavy bombers are striking nightly at the tap-root of German mechanised power, and have already inflicted serious damage upon the oil refineries on which the Nazi effort to dominate the world directly depends.

We must expect that as soon as stability is reached on the Western Front, the bulk of that hideous apparatus of aggression which gashed Holland into ruin and slavery in a few days will be turned upon us. I am sure I speak for all when I say we are ready to face it; to endure it; and to retaliate against it – to any extent that the unwritten laws of war permit. There will be many men and many women in this Island who when the ordeal comes upon them, as come it will, will feel comfort, and even a pride, that they are sharing the perils of our lads at the Front – soldiers, sailors and airmen, God bless them – and are drawing away from them a part at least of the onslaught they have to bear. Is not this the appointed time for all to make the utmost exertions in their power? If the battle is to be won, we must provide our men with ever-increasing quantities of the weapons and ammunition they need. We must have, and have quickly, more aeroplanes, more tanks, more shells, more guns. There is imperious need for these vital munitions. They increase our strength against the powerfully armed enemy. They replace the wastage of the obstinate struggle; and the knowledge that wastage will speedily be replaced enables us to draw more readily upon our reserves and throw them in now that everything counts so much.

Our task is not only to win the battle – but to win the war. After this battle in France abates its force, there will come the battle for our Island – for all that Britain is, and all that Britain means. That will be the struggle. In that supreme emergency we shall not hesitate to take every step, even the most drastic, to call forth from our people the last ounce and the last inch of effort of which they are capable. The interests of property, the hours of labour, are nothing compared with the struggle of life and honour, for right and freedom, to which we have vowed ourselves.

I have received from the Chiefs of the French Republic, and in particular from its indomitable Prime Minister, M. Reynaud, the most sacred pledges that whatever happens they will fight to the end, be it bitter or be it glorious. Nay, if we fight to the end, it can only be glorious.

Having received His Majesty's commission, I have formed an Administration of men and women of every Party and of almost every point of view. We have differed and quarrelled in the past; but now one bond unites us all – to wage war until victory is won, and never to surrender ourselves to servitude and shame, whatever the cost and the agony may be. This is one of the most awe-striking periods in the long history of France and Britain. It is also beyond doubt the most sublime. Side by side, unaided except by their kith and kin in the great Dominions and by the wide Empires which rest beneath their shield – side by side, the British and French peoples have advanced to rescue not only Europe but mankind from the foulest and most soul-destroying tyranny which has ever darkened and stained the pages of history. Behind them – behind us – behind the Armies and Fleets of Britain and France – gather a group of shattered States and bludgeoned races: the Czechs, the Poles, the Norwegians, the Danes, the Dutch, the Belgians – upon all of whom the long night of barbarism will descend, unbroken even by a star of hope, unless we conquer, as conquer we must; as conquer we shall.

Today is Trinity Sunday. Centuries ago words were written to be a call and a spur to the faithful servants of Truth and Justice: 'Arm yourselves, and be ye men of valour, and be in readiness for the conflict; for it is better for us to perish in battle than to look upon the outrage of our nation and our altar. As the Will of God is in Heaven, even so let it be.'

'WARS ARE NOT WON BY EVACUATIONS'

4 June 1940

House of Commons

With the Belgian front broken, the only escape for the British Expeditionary Force was to fight its way to Dunkirk on the Channel coast. On 26 May Operation 'Dynamo' – the evacuation from Dunkirk – was launched. Very heavy casualties and the loss of three-quarters of Britain's professional army was feared. To cover the evacuation, the Prime Minister ordered that Calais be held to the last man. On 27 May King Leopold announced the surrender of Belgium. Thanks to the valiant efforts of the Royal Air Force, and the combined efforts of the Royal Navy and an armada of civilian 'small ships', 338,000 Allied troops were evacuated from beneath the guns of the enemy. National rejoicing verged on euphoria, which Churchill was anxious to dampen down.

From the moment that the French defences at Sedan and on the Meuse were broken at the end of the second week of May, only a rapid retreat to Amiens and the south could have saved the British and French Armies who had entered Belgium at the appeal of the Belgian King; but this strategic fact was not immediately realised. The French High Command hoped they would be able to close the gap, and the Armies of the north were under their orders. Moreover, a retirement of this kind would have involved almost certainly the destruction of the fine Belgian Army of over 20 divisions and the abandonment of the whole of Belgium. Therefore, when the force and scope of the German penetration were realised and when a new French Generalissimo, General Weygand, assumed command in place of General Gamelin, an effort was made by the French and British Armies in Belgium to keep on holding the right hand of the Belgians and to give their own right hand to a newly created French Army which was to have advanced across the Somme in great strength to grasp it.

However, the German eruption swept like a sharp scythe around the right and rear of the Armies of the north. Eight or nine armoured divisions, each of about four hundred armoured vehicles of different kinds, but carefully assorted to be complementary and divisible into small self-contained units, cut off all communications between us and the main French Armies. It severed our own communications for food and ammunition, which ran first to Amiens and afterwards through Abbeville, and it shore its way up the coast to Boulogne and Calais, and almost to Dunkirk. Behind this armoured and mechanised onslaught came a number of German divisions in lorries, and behind them again there plodded comparatively slowly the dull brute mass of the ordinary German Army and German people, always so ready to be led to the trampling down in other lands of liberties and comforts which they have never known in their own.

I have said this armoured scythe-stroke almost reached Dunkirk – almost but not quite. Boulogne and Calais were the scenes of desperate fighting. The Guards defended Boulogne for a while and were then withdrawn by orders from this country. The Rifle Brigade, the 60th Rifles, and the Queen Victoria's Rifles, with a battalion of British tanks and 1,000 Frenchmen, in all about four thousand strong, defended Calais to the last. The British Brigadier was given an hour to surrender. He spurned the offer, and four days of intense street fighting passed before silence reigned over Calais, which marked the end of a memorable resistance. Only 30 unwounded survivors were brought off by the Navy, and we do not know the fate of their comrades. Their sacrifice, however, was not in vain. At least two armoured divisions, which otherwise would have been turned against the British Expeditionary Force, had to be sent to overcome them. They have added another page to the glories of the light division, and the time gained enabled the Gravelines waterlines to be flooded and to be held by the French troops.

Thus it was that the port of Dunkirk was kept open. When it was found impossible for the Armies of the north to reopen their communications to Amiens with the main French Armies, only one choice remained. It seemed, indeed, forlorn. The Belgian, British and French Armies were almost surrounded. Their sole line of retreat was to a single port and to its neighbouring beaches. They were pressed on every side by heavy attacks and far outnumbered in the air.

When, a week ago today, I asked the House to fix this afternoon as the occasion for a statement, I feared it would be my hard lot to announce the greatest military disaster in our long history. I thought – and some good judges agreed with me – that perhaps 20,000 or 30,000 men might be re-embarked. But it certainly seemed that the whole of the French First Army and the whole of the British

Expeditionary Force north of the Amiens-Abbeville gap would be broken up in the open field or else would have to capitulate for lack of food and ammunition. These were the hard and heavy tidings for which I called upon the House and the nation to prepare themselves a week ago. The whole root and core and brain of the British Army, on which and around which we were to build, and are to build, the great British Armies in the later years of the war, seemed about to perish upon the field or to be led into an ignominious and starving captivity.

That was the prospect a week ago. But another blow which might well have proved final was yet to fall upon us. The King of the Belgians had called upon us to come to his aid. Had not this Ruler and his Government severed themselves from the Allies, who rescued their country from extinction in the late war, and had they not sought refuge in what was proved to be a fatal neutrality, the French and British Armies might well at the outset have saved not only Belgium but perhaps even Poland. Yet at the last moment, when Belgium was already invaded, King Leopold called upon us to come to his aid, and even at the last moment we came. He and his brave, efficient Army, nearly half a million strong, guarded our left flank and thus kept open our only line of retreat to the sea. Suddenly, without prior consultation, with the least possible notice, without the advice of his Ministers and upon his own personal act, he sent a plenipotentiary to the German Command, surrendered his Army, and exposed our whole flank and means of retreat.

I asked the House a week ago to suspend its judgment because the facts were not clear, but I do not feel that any reason now exists why we should not form our own opinions upon this pitiful episode. The surrender of the Belgian Army compelled the British at the shortest notice to cover a flank to the sea more than 30 miles in length. Otherwise all would have been cut off, and all would have shared the fate to which King Leopold had condemned the finest Army his country had ever formed. So in doing this and in exposing this flank, as anyone who followed the operations on the map will see, contact was lost between the British and two out of the three corps forming the First French Army, who were still farther from the coast than we were, and it seemed impossible that any large number of Allied troops could reach the coast.

The enemy attacked on all sides with great strength and fierceness, and their main power, the power of their far more numerous Air Force, was thrown into the battle or else concentrated upon Dunkirk and the beaches. Pressing in upon the narrow exit, both from the east and from the west, the enemy began to fire with cannon upon the beaches by which alone the shipping could approach or depart. They sowed magnetic mines in the channels and seas; they sent repeated waves of hostile aircraft, sometimes more than a hundred strong in one formation, to cast their bombs upon the single pier that remained, and upon the sand dunes upon which the troops had their eyes for shelter. Their U-boats, one of which was sunk, and their motor launches took their toll of the vast traffic which now began. For four or five days an intense struggle reigned. All their armoured divisions – or what was left of them – together with great masses of infantry and artillery, hurled themselves in vain upon the ever-narrowing, ever-contracting appendix within which the British and French Armies fought.

Meanwhile, the Royal Navy, with the willing help of countless merchant seamen, strained every nerve to embark the British and Allied troops; 220 light warships and 650 other vessels were engaged. They had to operate upon the difficult coast, often in adverse weather, under an almost ceaseless hail of bombs and an increasing concentration of artillery fire. Nor were the seas, as I have said, themselves free from mines and torpedoes. It was in conditions such as these that our men carried on, with little or no rest, for days and nights on end, making trip after trip across the dangerous waters, bringing with them always men whom they had rescued. The numbers they have brought back are the measure of their devotion and their courage. The hospital ships, which brought off many thousands of British and French wounded, being so plainly marked were a special target for Nazi bombs; but the men and women on board them never faltered in their duty.

Meanwhile, the Royal Air Force, which had already been intervening in the battle, so far as its range would allow, from home bases, now used part of its main metropolitan fighter strength, and struck at the German bombers and at the fighters which in large numbers protected them. This struggle was protracted and fierce. Suddenly the scene has cleared, the crash and thunder has for the moment – but only for the moment – died away. A miracle of deliverance, achieved by valour, by perseverance, by perfect discipline, by faultless service, by resource, by skill, by unconquerable fidelity, is manifest to us all. The enemy was hurled back by the retreating British and French troops. He was so roughly handled that he did not harry their departure seriously. The Royal Air Force engaged the main strength of the German Air Force, and inflicted upon them losses of at least four to one; and the Navy, using nearly 1,100 ships of all kinds, carried over 335,000 men, French and British, out of the jaws of death and shame, to their native land and to the tasks which lie immediately ahead. We must be very careful not to assign to this deliverance the attributes of a victory. Wars are not won by evacuations. But there was a victory inside this deliverance, which should be noted. It was gained by the Air Force. Many of our soldiers coming back have not seen the Air Force at work; they saw only the bombers which escaped its protective attack. They underrate its achievements. I have heard much talk of this; that is why I go out of my way to say this. I will tell you about it.

This was a great trial of strength between the British and German Air Forces. Can you conceive a greater objective for the Germans in the air than to make evacuation from these beaches impossible, and to sink all these ships which were displayed, almost to the extent of thousands? Could there have been an objective of greater military importance and significance for the whole purpose of the war than this? They tried hard, and they were beaten back; they were frustrated in their task. We got the Army away; and they have paid fourfold for any losses which they have inflicted. Very large formations of German aeroplanes – and we know that they are a very brave race – have turned on several occasions from the attack of one-quarter of their number of the Royal Air Force, and have dispersed in different directions. Twelve aeroplanes have been hunted by two. One aeroplane was driven into the water and cast away by the mere charge of a British aeroplane, which had no more ammunition. All of our types – the Hurricane, the Spitfire and the new Defiant – and all our pilots have been vindicated as superior to what they have at present to face.

When we consider how much greater would be our advantage in defending the air above this Island against an overseas attack, I must say that I find in these facts a sure basis upon which practical and reassuring thoughts may rest. I will pay my tribute to these young airmen. The great French Army was very largely, for the time being, cast back and disturbed by the onrush of a few thousands of armoured vehicles. May it not also be that the cause of civilisation itself will be defended by the skill and devotion of a few thousand airmen? There never has been, I suppose, in all the world, in all the history of war, such an opportunity for youth. The Knights of the Round Table, the Crusaders, all fall back into the past – not only distant but prosaic; these young men, going forth every morn to guard their native land and all that we stand for, holding in their hands these instruments of colossal and shattering power, of whom it may be said that

> Every morn brought forth a noble chance
> And every chance brought forth a noble knight,

deserve our gratitude, as do all the brave men who, in so many ways and on so many occasions, are ready, and continue ready to give life and all for their native land.

I return to the Army. In the long series of very fierce battles, now on this front, now on that, fighting on three fronts at once, battles fought by two or three divisions against an unequal or somewhat larger number of the enemy, and fought fiercely on some of the old grounds that so many of us knew so well – in these battles our losses in men have exceeded 30,000 killed, wounded and missing. I take occasion to express the sympathy of the House to all who have suffered bereavement or who are still anxious. The President of the Board of Trade [Sir Andrew Duncan] is not here today. His son has been killed, and many in the House have felt the pangs of affliction in the sharpest form. But I will say this about the missing: We have had a large number of wounded come home safely to this country, but I would say about the missing that there may be very many reported missing who will come back home, some day, in one way or another. In the confusion of this fight it is inevitable that many have been left in positions where honour required no further resistance from them.

Against the loss of over 30,000 men, we can set a far heavier loss certainly inflicted upon the enemy. But our losses in material are enormous. We have perhaps lost one-third of the men we lost in the opening days of the battle of 21st March, 1918, but we have lost nearly as many guns – nearly one thousand – and all our transport, all the armoured vehicles that were with the Army in the north. This loss will impose a further delay on the expansion of our military strength. That expansion had not been proceeding as far as we had hoped. The best of all we had to give had gone to the British Expeditionary Force, and although they had not the numbers of tanks and some articles of equipment which were desirable, they were a very well and finely equipped Army. They had the first fruits of all that our industry had to give, and that is gone. And now here is this further delay. How long it will be, how long it will last, depends upon the exertions which we make in this Island. An effort the like of which has never been seen in our records is now being made. Work is proceeding everywhere, night and day, Sundays and week days. Capital and Labour have cast aside their interests, rights, and customs and put them into the common stock. Already the flow of munitions has leaped forward. There is no reason why we should not in a few months overtake the sudden and serious loss that has come upon us, without retarding the development of our general programme.

Nevertheless, our thankfulness at the escape of our Army and so many men, whose loved ones have passed through an agonising week, must not blind us to the fact that what has happened in France and Belgium is a colossal military disaster. The French Army has been weakened, the Belgian Army has been lost, a large part of those fortified lines upon which so much faith had been reposed is gone, many valuable mining districts and factories have passed into the enemy's possession, the whole of the Channel ports are in his hands, with all the tragic consequences that follow from that, and we must expect another blow to be struck almost immediately at us or at France. We are told that Herr Hitler has a plan for invading the British Isles. This has often been thought of before. When Napoleon lay at Boulogne for a year with his flat-bottomed boats and his Grand Army, he was told by someone. 'There are bitter weeds in England.' There are certainly a great many more of them since the British Expeditionary Force returned.

The whole question of home defence against invasion is, of course, powerfully affected by the fact that we have for the time being in this Island incomparably more powerful military forces than we have ever had at any moment in this war or the last. But this will not continue. We shall not be content with a defensive war. We have our duty to our Ally. We have to reconstitute and build up the British Expeditionary Force once again, under its gallant Commander-in-Chief, Lord Gort. All this is in train; but in the interval we must put our defences in this Island into such a high state of organisation that the fewest possible numbers will be required to give effective security and that the largest possible potential of offensive effort may be realised. On this we are now engaged. It will be very convenient, if it be the desire of the House, to enter upon this subject in a secret Session. Not that the government would necessarily be able to reveal in very great detail military secrets, but we like to have our discussions free, without the restraint imposed by the fact that they will be read the next day by the enemy; and the Government would benefit by views freely expressed in all parts of the House by Members with their knowledge of so many different parts of the country. I understand that some request is to be made upon this subject, which will be readily acceded to by His Majesty's Government.

We have found it necessary to take measures of increasing stringency, not only against enemy aliens and suspicious characters of other nationalities, but also against British subjects who may become a danger or a nuisance should the war be transported to the United Kingdom. I know there are a great many people affected by the orders which we have made who are the passionate enemies of Nazi Germany. I am very sorry for them, but we cannot, at the present time and under the present stress, draw all the distinctions which we should like to do. If parachute landings were attempted and fierce fighting attendant upon them followed, these unfortunate people would be far better out of the way, for their own sakes as well as for ours. There is, however, another class, for which I feel not the slightest sympathy. Parliament has given us the powers to put down Fifth Column activities with a strong hand, and we shall use those powers subject to the supervision and correction of the House, without the slightest hesitation until we are satisfied, and more than satisfied, that this malignancy in our midst has been effectively stamped out.

Turning once again, and this time more generally, to the question of invasion, I would observe that there has never been a period in all these long centuries of which we boast when an absolute guarantee against invasion, still less against serious raids, could have been given to our people. In the days of Napoleon the same wind which would have carried his transports across the Channel might have driven away the blockading fleet. There was always the chance, and it is that chance which has excited and befooled the imaginations of many Continental tyrants. Many are the tales that are told. We are assured that novel methods will be adopted, and when we see the originality of malice, the ingenuity of aggression, which our enemy displays, we may certainly prepare ourselves for every kind of novel stratagem and every kind of brutal and treacherous manoeuvre. I think that no idea is so outlandish that it should not be considered and viewed with a searching, but at the same time, I hope, with a steady eye. We must never forget the solid assurances of sea power and those which belong to air power if it can be locally exercised.

I have, myself, full confidence that if all do their duty, if nothing is neglected, and if the best arrangements are made, as they are being made, we shall prove ourselves once again able to defend our Island home, to ride out the storm of war, and to outlive the menace of tyranny, if necessary for years, if necessary alone. At any rate, that is what we are going to try to do. That is the resolve of His Majesty's Government – every man of them. That is the will of Parliament and the nation. The British Empire and the French Republic, linked together in their cause and in their need, will defend to the death their native soil, aiding each other like good comrades to the utmost of their strength. Even though large tracts of Europe and many old and famous States have fallen or may fall into the grip of the Gestapo and all the odious apparatus of Nazi rule, we shall not flag or fail. We shall go on to the end, we shall fight in France, we shall fight on the seas and oceans, we shall fight with growing confidence and growing strength in the air, we shall defend our Island, whatever the cost may be, we shall fight on the beaches, we shall fight on the landing grounds, we shall fight in the fields and in the streets, we shall fight in the hills; we shall never surrender, and even if, which I do not for a moment believe, this Island or a large part of it were subjugated and starving, then our Empire beyond the seas, armed and guarded by the British Fleet, would carry on the struggle, until, in God's good time, the New World, with all its power and might, steps forth to the rescue and the liberation of the old.

'THE NEWS FROM FRANCE IS VERY BAD'

17 June 1940

Broadcast, London

Despite all Churchill's efforts to persuade the French to fight on, the French Government, reconstituted the day before under the World War I hero, Marshal Pétain, surrendered on 17 June, after less than six weeks of struggle.

The news from France is very bad and I grieve for the gallant French people who have fallen into this terrible misfortune. Nothing will alter our feelings towards them or our faith that the genius of France will rise again. What has happened in France makes no difference to our actions and purpose. We have become the sole champions now in arms to defend the world cause. We shall do our best to be worthy of this high honour. We shall defend our Island home, and with the British Empire we shall fight on unconquerable until the curse of Hitler is lifted from the brows of mankind. We are sure that in the end all will come right.

'THIS WAS THEIR FINEST HOUR'

18 June 1940

House of Commons

Determined to quell suggestions – especially abroad – that Britain might soon succumb to the German onslaught like France, Churchill delivered this immortal speech to a packed House of Commons.

I spoke the other day of the colossal military disaster which occurred when the French High Command failed to withdraw the northern Armies from Belgium at the moment when they knew that the French front was decisively broken at Sedan and on the Meuse. This delay entailed the loss of fifteen or sixteen French divisions and threw out of action for the critical period the whole of the British Expeditionary Force. Our Army and 120,000 French troops were indeed rescued by the British Navy from Dunkirk but only with the loss of their cannon, vehicles and modern equipment. This loss inevitably took some weeks to repair, and in the first two of those weeks the battle in France has been lost. When we consider the heroic resistance made by the French Army against heavy odds in this battle, the enormous losses inflicted upon the enemy and the evident exhaustion of the enemy, it may well be the thought that these 25 divisions of the best-trained and best-equipped troops might have turned the scale. However, General Weygand had to fight without them. Only three British divisions or their equivalent were able to stand in the line with their French comrades. They have suffered severely, but they have fought well. We sent every man we could to France as fast as we could re-equip and transport their formations.

Upon this battle depends the
survival of Christian civilization.

Upon it depends our own British life
and the long continuity of our
institutions, and our Empire.

The whole fury and might of the enemy
must very soon be turned on us.

Hitler knows that we will hv to break
us in this Island, or lose the war.

If we can stand up to him,
all Europe may be freed,
and the life of the world
may move forward into the
broad and sunlit uplands.

But if we fail,
then the whole world,
including the United States,
and all that we have known and
cared for,
will sink into the abyss of a
new Dark Age
made more sinister and
perhaps more prolonged by
the lights of perverted
Science.

Let us therefore brace ourselves to
our duty, and so bear ourselves that
if the British Empire and
Commonwealth lasts for a
thousand years, men will still
say,

'This was their finest hour'.

'Their Finest Hour', House of Commons, 18 June 1940.

I am not reciting these facts for the purpose of recrimination. That I judge to be utterly futile and even harmful. We cannot afford it. I recite them in order to explain why it was we did not have, as we could have had, between twelve and fourteen British divisions fighting in the line in this great battle instead of only three. Now I put all this aside. I put it on the shelf, from which the historians, when they have time, will select their documents to tell their stories. We have to think of the future and not of the past. This also applies in a small way to our own affairs at home. There are many who would hold an inquest in the House of Commons on the conduct of the Governments – and of Parliaments, for they are in it, too – during the years which led up to this catastrophe. They seek to indict those who were responsible for the guidance of our affairs. This also would be a foolish and pernicious process. There are too many in it. Let each man search his conscience and search his speeches. I frequently search mine.

Of this I am quite sure, that if we open a quarrel between the past and the present, we shall find that we have lost the future. Therefore, I cannot accept the drawing of any distinctions between Members of the present Government. It was formed at a moment of crisis in order to unite all the Parties and all sections of opinion. It has received the almost unanimous support of both Houses of Parliament. Its Members are going to stand together, and, subject to the authority of the House of Commons, we are going to govern the country and fight the war. It is absolutely necessary at a time like this that every Minister who tries each day to do his duty shall be respected; and their subordinates must know that their chiefs are not threatened men, men who are here today and gone tomorrow, but that their directions must be punctually and faithfully obeyed. Without this concentrated power we cannot face what lies before us. I should not think it would be very advantageous for the House to prolong this Debate this afternoon under conditions of public stress. Many facts are not clear that will be clear in a short time. We are to have a secret Session on Thursday, and I should think that would be a better oportunity for the many earnest expressions of opinion which Members will desire to make and for the House to discuss vital matters without having everything read the next morning by our dangerous foes.

The disastrous military events which have happened during the past fortnight have not come to me with any sense of surprise. Indeed, I indicated a fortnight ago as clearly as I could to the House that the worst possibilities were open; and I made it perfectly clear then that whatever happened in France would make no difference to the resolve of Britain and the British Empire to fight on, 'if necessary for years, if necessary alone.' During the last few days we have successfully brought off the great majority of the troops we had on the line of communication in France; and seven-eighths of the troops we have sent to France since the beginning of the war – that is to say, about 350,000 out of 400,000 men – are safely back in this country. Others are still fighting with the French, and fighting with consider-able success in their local encounters with the enemy. We have also brought back a great mass of stores, rifles and munitions of all kinds which had been accumulated in France during the last nine months.

We have, therefore, in this Island today a very large and powerful military force. This force comprises all our best-trained and our finest troops, including scores of thousands of those who have already measured their quality against the Germans and found themselves at no disadvantage. We have under arms at the present time in this Island over a million and a quarter men. Behind these we have the Local Defence Volunteers, numbering half a million, only a portion of whom, however, are yet armed with rifles or other firearms. We have incorporated into our Defence Forces every man for whom we have a weapon. We expect very large additions to our weapons in the near future, and in preparation for this we intend forthwith to call up, drill and train further large numbers. Those who are not called up, or else are employed during the vast business of munitions production in all its branches – and their ramifications are innumer-able – will serve their country best by remaining at their ordinary work until they receive their summons. We have also over here Dominions armies. The Canadians had actually landed in France, but have now been safely withdrawn, much disappointed, but in perfect order, with all their artillery and equipment. And these very high-class forces from the Dominions will now take part in the defence of the Mother Country.

Lest the account which I have given of these large forces should raise the question: Why did they not take part in the great battle in France? I must make it clear that, apart from the divisions training and organising at home, only 12 divisions were equipped to fight upon a scale which justified their being sent abroad. And this was fully up to the number which the French had been led to expect would be available in France at the ninth month of the war. The rest of our forces at home have a fighting value for home defence which will, of course, steadily increase every week that passes. Thus, the invasion of Great Britain would at this time require the transportation across the sea of hostile armies on a very large scale, and after they had been so transported they would have to be continually maintained with all the masses of munitions and supplies which are required for continuous battle – as continuous battle it will surely be.

Here is where we come to the Navy – and, after all, we have a Navy. Some people seem to forget that we have a Navy. We must remind them. For the last thirty years I have been concerned in discussions about the possibilities of oversea invasion, and I took the responsibility on behalf of the Admiralty, at the beginning of the last war, of allowing all regular troops to be sent out of the country. That was a very serious step to take, because our Territorials had only just been called up and were quite untrained. Therefore, this Island was for several months particularly denuded of fighting troops. The Admiralty had confidence at that time in their ability to prevent a mass invasion even though at that time the Germans had a magnificent battle fleet in the proportion of 10 to 16, even though they were capable of fighting a general engagement every day and any day, whereas now they have only a couple of heavy ships worth speaking of – the *Scharnhorst* and the *Gneisenau*. We are also told that the Italian Navy is to come out and gain sea superiority in these waters. If they seriously intend it, I shall only say that we shall be delighted to offer Signor Mussolini a free and safeguarded passage through the Strait of Gibraltar in order that he may play the part to which he aspires. There is a general curiosity in the British Fleet to find out whether the Italians are up to the level they were at in the last war or whether they have fallen off at all.

Therefore, it seems to me that as far as seaborne invasion on a great scale is concerned, we are far more capable of meeting it today than we were at many periods in the last war and during the early months of this war, before our other troops were trained, and while the BEF had proceeded abroad. Now, the Navy have never pretended to be able to prevent raids by bodies of 5,000 or 10,000 men flung suddenly across and thrown ashore at several points on the coast some dark night or foggy morning. The efficacy of sea power, especially under modern conditions, depends upon the invading force being of large size. It has to be of large size, in view of our military strength, to be of any use. If it is of large size, then the Navy have something they can find and meet and, as it were, bite on. Now, we must remember that even five divisions, however lightly equipped, would require 200 to 250 ships, and with modern air reconnaissance and photography it would not be easy to collect such an armada, marshal it, and conduct it across the sea without any powerful naval forces to escort it; and there would be very great possibilities, to put it mildly, that this armada would be intercepted long before it reached the coast, and all the men drowned in the sea or, at the worst, blown to pieces with their equipment while they were trying to land. We also have a great system of minefields, recently strongly reinforced, through which we alone know the channels. If the enemy tries to sweep passages through these minefields, it will be the task of the Navy to destroy the minesweepers and any other forces employed to protect them. There should be no difficulty in this, owing to our great superiority at sea.

Those are the regular, well-tested, well-proved arguments on which we have relied during many years in peace and war. But the question is whether there are any new methods by which those solid assurances can be circumvented. Odd as it may seem, some attention has been given to this by the Admiralty, whose prime duty and responsibility is to destroy any large seaborne expedition before it reaches, or at the moment when it reaches, these shores. It would not be a good thing for me to go into details of this. It might suggest ideas to other people which they have not thought of, and they would not be likely to give us any of their ideas in exchange. All I will say is that untiring vigilance and mind-searching must be devoted to the subject, because the enemy is crafty and cunning and full of novel treacheries and stratagems. The House may be assured that the utmost ingenuity is being displayed and imagination is being evoked from large numbers of competent officers, well-trained in tactics and thoroughly up to date, to measure and counterwork novel possibilities. Untiring vigilance and untiring searching of the mind is being, and must be, devoted to the subject, because, remember, the enemy is crafty and there is no dirty trick he will not do.

Some people will ask why, then, was it that the British Navy was not able to prevent the movement of a large army from Germany into Norway across the Skagerrak? But the conditions in the Channel and in the North Sea are in no way like those which prevail in the Skagerrak. In the Skagerrak, because of the distance, we could give no air support to our surface ships, and consequently, lying as we did close to the enemy's main air power, we were compelled to use only our submarines. We could not enforce the decisive blockade or interruption which is possible from surface vessels. Our submarines took a heavy toll but could not, by themselves, prevent the invasion of Norway. In the Channel and in the North Sea, on the other hand, our superior naval surface forces, aided by our submarines, will operate with close and effective air assistance.

This brings me, naturally, to the great question of invasion from the air, and of the impending struggle between the British and German Air Forces. It seems quite clear that no invasion on a scale beyond the capacity of our land forces to crush speedily is likely to take place from the air until our Air Force has been definitely overpowered. In the meantime, there may be raids by parachute troops and attempted descents of airborne soldiers. We should be able to give those gentry a warm reception both in the air and on the ground, if they reach it in any condition to continue the dispute. But the great question is: Can we break Hitler's air weapon? Now, of course, it is a very great pity that we have not got an Air Force at least equal to that of the most powerful enemy within striking distance of these shores. But we have a very powerful Air Force which has proved itself far superior in quality, both in men and in many types of machine, to what we have met so far in the numerous and fierce air battles which have been fought with the Germans. In France, where we were at a considerable disadvantage and lost many machines on the ground when they were standing round the aerodromes, we were accustomed to inflict in the air losses of as much as two and two-and-a-half to one. In the fighting over Dunkirk, which was a sort of no-man's-land, we undoubtedly beat the German Air Force, and gained the mastery of the local air, inflicting here a loss of three or four to one day after day. Anyone who looks at the photographs which were published a week or so ago of the re-embarkation, showing the masses of troops assembled on the beach and forming an ideal target for hours at a time, must realise that this re-embarkation would not have been possible unless the enemy had resigned all hope of recovering air superiority at that time and at that place.

In the defence of this Island the advantages to the defenders will be much greater than they were in the fighting around Dunkirk. We hope to improve on the rate of three or four to one which was realised at Dunkirk; and in addition all our injured machines and their crews which get down safely – and, surprisingly, a very great many injured machines and men do get down safely in modern air fighting – all of these will fall, in an attack upon these Islands, on friendly soil and live to fight another day; whereas all the injured enemy machines and their complements will be total losses as far as the war is concerned.

During the great battle in France, we gave very powerful and continuous aid to the French Army, both by fighters and bombers; but in spite of every kind of pressure we never would allow the entire metropolitan fighter strength of the Air Force to be consumed. This decision was painful, but it was also right, because the fortunes of the battle of France could not have been decisively affected even if we had thrown in our entire fighter force. That battle was lost by the unfortunate strategical opening, by the extraordinary and unforeseen power of the armoured columns, and by the great preponderance of the German Army in numbers. Our fighter Air Force might easily have been exhausted as a mere accident in that great struggle, and then we should have found ourselves at the present time in a very serious plight. But as it is, I am happy to inform the House that our fighter strength is stronger at the present time relatively to the Germans, who have suffered terrible losses, than it has ever been; and consequently we believe ourselves possessed of the capacity to continue the war in the air under better conditions than we have ever experienced before. I look forward confidently to the exploits of our fighter pilots – these splendid men, this brilliant youth – who will have the glory of saving their native land, their island home, and all they love, from the most deadly of all attacks.

There remains, of course, the danger of bombing attacks, which will certainly be made very soon upon us by the bomber forces of the enemy. It is true that the German bomber force is superior in numbers to ours; but we have a very large bomber force also, which we shall use to strike at military targets in Germany without intermission. I do not at all underrate the severity of the ordeal which lies before us; but I believe our countrymen will show themselves capable of standing up to it, like the brave men of Barcelona, and will be able to stand up to it, and carry on in spite of it, at least as well as any other people in the world. Much will depend upon this; every man and every woman will have the chance to show the finest qualities of their race, and render the highest service to their cause. For all of us, at this time, whatever our sphere, our station, our occupation or our duties, it will be a help to remember the famous lines:

> He nothing common did or mean,
> Upon that memorable scene.

I have thought it right upon this occasion to give the House and the country some indication of the solid, practical grounds upon which we base our inflexible resolve to continue the war. There are a good many people who say, 'Never mind. Win or lose, sink or swim, better die than submit to tyranny – and such a tyranny.' And I do not dissociate myself from them. But I can assure them that our professional advisers of the three Services unitedly advise that we should carry on the war, and that there are good and reasonable hopes of final victory. We have fully informed and consulted all the self-governing Dominions, these great communities far beyond the oceans who have been built up on our laws and on our civilisation, and who are absolutely free to choose their course, but are absolutely devoted to the ancient Motherland, and who feel themselves inspired by the same emotions which lead me to stake our all upon duty and honour. We have fully consulted them, and I have received from their Prime Ministers, Mr Mackenzie King of Canada, Mr Menzies of Australia, Mr Fraser of New Zealand, and General Smuts of South Africa – that wonderful man, with his immense profound mind, and his eye watching from a distance the whole panorama of European affairs – I have received from all these eminent men, who all have Governments behind them elected on wide franchises, who are all there because they represent the will of their people, messages couched in the most moving terms in which they endorse our decision to fight on, and declare themselves ready to share our fortunes and to persevere to the end. That is what we are going to do.

We may now ask ourselves: In what way has our position worsened since the beginning of the war? It has worsened by the fact that the Germans have conquered a large part of the coastline of Western Europe, and many small countries have been overrun by them. This aggravates the possibilities of air attack and adds to our naval preoccupations. It in no way diminishes, but on the contrary definitely increases, the power of our long-distance blockade. Similarly, the entrance of Italy into the war increases the power of our long-distance blockade. We have stopped the worst leak by that. We do not know whether military resistance will come to an end in France or not, but should it do so, then of course the Germans will be able to concentrate their forces, both military and industrial, upon us. But for the reasons I have given to the House these will not be found so easy to apply. If invasion has become more imminent, as no doubt it has, we, being relieved from the task of maintaining a large army in France, have far larger and more efficient forces to meet it.

If Hitler can bring under his despotic control the industries of the countries he has conquered, this will add greatly to his already vast armament output. On the other hand, this will not happen immediately, and we are now assured of immense, continuous and increasing support in supplies and munitions of all kinds from the United States; and especially of aeroplanes and pilots from the

Dominions and across the oceans coming from regions which are beyond the reach of enemy bombers.

I do not see how any of these factors can operate to our detriment on balance before the winter comes; and the winter will impose a strain upon the Nazi régime, with almost all Europe writhing and starving under its cruel heel, which, for all their ruthlessness, will run them very hard. We must not forget that from the moment when we declared war on the 3rd September it was always possible for Germany to turn all her Air Force upon this country, together with any other devices of invasion she might conceive, and that France could have done little or nothing to prevent her doing so. We have, therefore, lived under the danger, in principle and in a slightly modified form, during all these months. In the meanwhile, however, we have enormously improved our methods of defence, and we have learned what we had no right to assume at the beginning, namely, that the individual aircraft and the individual British pilot have a sure and definite superiority. Therefore, in casting up this dread balance-sheet and contemplating our dangers with a disillusioned eye, I see great reason for intense vigilance and exertion, but none whatever for panic or despair.

During the first four years of the last war the Allies experienced nothing but disaster and disappointment. That was our constant fear: one blow after another, terrible losses, frightful dangers. Everything miscarried. And yet at the end of those four years the morale of the Allies was higher than that of the Germans, who had moved from one aggressive triumph to another, who stood everywhere triumphant invaders of the lands into which they had broken. During that war we repeatedly asked ourselves the question: How are we going to win? and no one was able ever to answer it with much precision, until at the end, quite suddenly, quite unexpectedly, our terrible foe collapsed before us, and we were so glutted with victory that in our folly we threw it away.

We do not yet know what will happen in France or whether the French resistance will be prolonged, both in France and in the French Empire overseas. The French Government will be throwing away great opportunities and casting adrift their future if they do not continue the war in accordance with their Treaty obligations, from which we have not felt able to release them. The House will have read the historic declaration in which, at the desire of many Frenchmen – and of our own hearts – we have proclaimed our willingness at the darkest hour in French history to conclude a union of common citizenship in this struggle. However matters may go in

France or with the French Government, or other French Governments, we in this Island and in the British Empire will never lose our
sense of comradeship with the French people. If we are now called
upon to endure what they have been suffering, we shall emulate their
courage, and if final victory rewards our toils they shall share the
gains, aye, and freedom shall be restored to all. We abate nothing of
our just demands; not one jot or tittle do we recede. Czechs, Poles,
Norwegians, Dutch, Belgians have joined their causes to our own. All
these shall be restored.

What General Weygand called the Battle of France is over. I expect
that the Battle of Britain is about to begin. Upon this battle depends
the survival of Christian civilisation. Upon it depends our own
British life, and the long continuity of our institutions and our
Empire. The whole fury and might of the enemy must very soon be
turned on us. Hitler knows that he will have to break us in this Island
or lose the war. If we can stand up to him, all Europe may be free
and the life of the world may move forward into broad, sunlit
uplands. But if we fail, then the whole world, including the United
States, including all that we have known and cared for, will sink into
the abyss of a new Dark Age made more sinister, and perhaps more
protracted, by the lights of perverted science. Let us therefore brace
ourselves to our duties, and so bear ourselves that, if the British
Empire and its Commonwealth last for a thousand years, men will
still say, '*This* was their finest hour.'

DESTRUCTION OF THE FRENCH FLEET

4 July 1940

House of Commons

*Churchill decided that the French Fleet in North Africa could not be
allowed to fall into enemy hands. Accordingly the Royal Navy's
Gibraltar Squadron was ordered to take decisive action. When, on 3
July, the French ships failed to surrender, they were destroyed by
naval gunfire in the port of Oran with heavy loss of life. Churchill
later wrote in* Their Finest Hour: *'This was a hateful decision, the
most unnatural and painful in which I have ever been concerned'.
But the message this action sent to the world – at a time when a*

German invasion of Britain was expected at any moment – was clear:
Britain was fighting for her life and would take all measures, even the
most extreme, in her battle for survival. The effect abroad, especially
in the United States, was profound and gave the lie to the unhelpful
reports being sent to President Roosevelt by the American Ambassa-
dor to Britain, Joseph P. Kennedy, suggesting that Britain was done
for and not worth supporting.

It is with sincere sorrow that I must now announce to the House the
measures which we have felt bound to take in order to prevent the
French Fleet from falling into German hands. When two nations are
fighting together under long and solemn alliance against a common
foe, one of them may be stricken down and overwhelmed, and may
be forced to ask its ally to release it from its obligations. But the least
that could be expected was that the French Government, in
abandoning the conflict and leaving its whole weight to fall upon
Great Britain and the British Empire, would have been careful not to
inflict needless injury upon their faithful comrade, in whose final
victory the sole chance of French freedom lay, and lies. . . .

Two of the finest vessels of the French Fleet, the *Dunkerque* and
the *Strasbourg*, modern battle-cruisers much superior to *Scharnhorst*
and *Gneisenau* – and built for the purpose of being superior to them
– lay with two battleships, several light cruisers, and a number of
destroyers and submarines and other vessels at Oran and at its
adjacent military port of Mers-el-Kebir on the northern African
shore of Morocco. Yesterday morning, a carefully chosen British
officer, Captain Holland, late Naval Attaché in Paris, was sent on in
a destroyer and waited upon the French Admiral Gensoul. After
being refused an interview, he presented the following document,
which I will read to the House. The first two paragraphs of the
document deal with the general question of the Armistice, which I
have already explained in my own words. The fourth paragraph
begins as follows – this is the operative paragraph:

> It is impossible for us, your comrades up to now, to allow your fine
> ships to fall into the power of the German or Italian enemy. We are
> determined to fight on to the end, and if we win, as we think we shall,
> we shall never forget that France was our Ally, that our interests are
> the same as hers, and that our common enemy is Germany. Should we
> conquer, we solemnly declare that we shall restore the greatness and
> territory of France. For this purpose, we must make sure that the best
> ships of the French Navy are not used against us by the common foe.

In these circumstances, His Majesty's Government have instructed me [that is, the British Admiral] to demand that the French Fleet now at Mers-el-Kebir and Oran shall act in accordance with one of the following alternatives:

(*a*) Sail with us and continue to fight for victory against the Germans and Italians.

(*b*) Sail with reduced crews under our control to a British port. The reduced crews will be repatriated at the earliest moment.

If either of these courses is adopted by you, we will restore your ships to France at the conclusion of the war or pay full compensation, if they are damaged meanwhile.

(*c*) Alternatively, if you feel bound to stipulate that your ships should not be used against the Germans or Italians unless these break the Armistice, then sail them with us, with reduced crews, to some French port in the West Indies – Martinique, for instance – where they can be demilitarised to our satisfaction or be perhaps entrusted to the United States and remain safe until the end of the war, the crews being repatriated.

If you refuse these fair offers, I must, with profound regret, require you to sink your ships within six hours.

Finally, failing the above, I have the orders of His Majesty's Government to use whatever force may be necessary to prevent your ships from falling into German or Italian hands.

We had hoped that one or other of the alternatives which we presented would have been accepted, without the necessity of using the terrible force of a British battle squadron. Such a squadron arrived before Oran two hours after Captain Holland and his destroyer. This battle squadron was commanded by Vice-Admiral Somerville, an officer who distinguished himself lately in the bringing off of over 100,000 Frenchmen during the evacuation from Dunkirk. Admiral Somerville was further provided, besides his battleships, with a cruiser force and strong flotillas. All day the parleys continued, and we hoped until the afternoon that our terms would be accepted without bloodshed. However, no doubt in obedience to the orders dictated by the Germans from Wiesbaden, where the Franco-German Armistice Commission is in session, Admiral Gensoul refused to comply and announced his intention of fighting. Admiral Somerville was, therefore, ordered to complete his mission before darkness fell, and at 5.53 p.m. he opened fire upon this powerful French Fleet, which was also protected by its shore batteries. At 6 p.m. he reported that he was heavily engaged. The action lasted for some ten minutes and was followed by heavy attacks from our naval aircraft, carried in the *Ark Royal*. At 7.20 p.m. Admiral Somerville forwarded a further report, which stated that a battle-cruiser of the *Strasbourg* class was damaged and ashore; that a battleship of the *Bretagne* class had been sunk, that another of the same class had been heavily damaged, and that two French destroyers and a seaplane carrier, *Commandant Teste*, were also sunk or burned.

While this melancholy action was being fought, either the battle-cruiser *Strasbourg* or the *Dunkerque*, one or the other, managed to slip out of harbour in a gallant effort to reach Toulon or a North African port and place herself under German control, in accordance with the Armistice terms of the Bordeaux Government – though all this her crew and captain may not have realised. She was pursued by aircraft of the Fleet Air Arm and hit by at least one torpedo. She may have been joined by other French vessels from Algiers, which were well placed to do so and to reach Toulon before we would overtake them. She will, at any rate, be out of action for many months to come.

I need hardly say that the French ships fought, albeit in this unnatural cause, with the characteristic courage of the French Navy, and every allowance must be made for Admiral Gensoul and his officers, who felt themselves obliged to obey the orders they received from their Government and could not look behind that Government to see the German dictation. I fear the loss of life among the French and in the harbour must have been very heavy, as we were compelled to use a severe measure of force and several immense explosions were heard. None of the British ships taking part in the action was in any way affected in gun-power or mobility by the heavy fire directed upon them. I have not yet received any reports of our casualties, but Admiral Somerville's Fleet is, in all military respects, intact and ready for further action. The Italian Navy, for whose reception we had also made arrangements and which is, of course, considerably stronger numerically than the Fleet we used at Oran, kept prudently out of the way. However, we trust that their turn will come during the operations which we shall pursue to secure the effectual command of the Mediterranean.

A large proportion of the French Fleet has, therefore, passed into our hands or has been put out of action or otherwise withheld from Germany by yesterday's events. The House will not expect me to say anything about other French ships which are at large except that it is our inflexible resolve to do everything that is possible in order to prevent them falling into the German grip. I leave the judgment of our action, with confidence, to Parliament. I leave it to the nation, and I leave it to the United States. I leave it to the world and history.

Now I turn to the immediate future. We must, of course, expect to be attacked, or even invaded, if that proves to be possible – it has not been proved yet – in our own Island before very long. We are making every preparation in our power to repel the assaults of the enemy, whether they be directed upon Great Britain, or upon Ireland, which all Irishmen, without distinction of creed or party, should realise is in imminent danger. These again are matters upon which we have clear views. These preparations are constantly occupying our toil from morn till night, and far into the night. But, although we have clear views, it would not, I think, be profitable for us to discuss them in public, or even, so far as the Government are concerned, except under very considerable reserve in a private Session. I call upon all subjects of His Majesty, and upon our Allies, and well-wishers – and they are not a few – all over the world, on both sides of the Atlantic, to give us their utmost aid. In the fullest harmony with our Dominions, we are moving through a period of extreme danger and of splendid hope, when every virtue of our race will be tested, and all that we have and are will be freely staked. This is no time for doubt or weakness. It is the supreme hour to which we have been called.

I will venture to read to the House a message which I have caused to be sent to all who are serving in positions of importance under the Crown, and if the House should view it with sympathy, I should be very glad to send a copy of it to every Member for his own use – not that such exhortations are needed. This is the message:

On what may be the eve of an attempted invasion or battle for our native land, the Prime Minister desires to impress upon all persons holding responsible positions in the Government, in the fighting Services, or in the Civil Departments, their duty to maintain a spirit of alert and confident energy. While every precaution must be taken that time and means afford, there are no grounds for supposing that more German troops can be landed in this country, either from the air or across the sea, than can be destroyed or captured by the strong forces at present under arms. The Royal Air Force is in excellent order and at the highest strength it has yet attained. The German Navy was never so weak, nor the British Army at home so strong as now. The Prime Minister expects all His Majesty's servants in high places to set an example of steadiness and resolution. They should check and rebuke expressions of loose and ill-digested opinion in their circle, or by their subordinates. They should not hesitate to report, or if necessary remove, any officers or officials who are found to be consciously exercising a disturbing or depressing influence, and whose talk is calculated to spread alarm and despondency. Thus alone will they be worthy of the fighting men, who, in the air, on the sea, and on land, have already met the enemy without any sense of being outmatched in martial qualities.

In conclusion, I feel that we are entitled to the confidence of the House and that we shall not fail in our duty, however painful. The action we have already taken should be, in itself, sufficient to dispose once and for all of the lies and rumours which have been so industriously spread by German propaganda and through Fifth Column activities that we have the slightest intention of entering into negotiations in any form and through any channel with the German and Italian Governments. We shall, on the contrary, prosecute the war with the utmost vigour by all the means that are open to us until the righteous purposes for which we entered upon it have been fulfilled.

'THE WAR OF THE UNKNOWN WARRIORS'

14 July 1940

Broadcast, London

To prepare for the launching of Operation 'Sealion' – code-name for the planned invasion of Britain – Hitler ordered a massive air bombardment of Britain, with the aim of destroying the Royal Air Force. What came to be known as the 'Battle of Britain' began on 10 July.

Today is the fourteenth of July, the national festival of France. A year ago in Paris I watched the stately parade down the Champs Elysées of the French Army and the French Empire. Who can foresee what the course of other years will bring? Faith is given to us to help and comfort us when we stand in awe before the unfurling scroll of human destiny. And I proclaim my faith that some of us will live to see a fourteenth of July when a liberated France will once again rejoice in her greatness and in her glory, and once again stand forward as the champion of the freedom and the rights of man. When the day dawns, as dawn it will, the soul of France will turn with comprehension and with kindness to those Frenchmen and Frenchwomen, wherever they may be, who in the darkest hour did not despair of the Republic. . . .

And now it has come to us to stand alone in the breach, and face the worst that the tyrant's might and enmity can do. Bearing ourselves humbly before God, but conscious that we serve an unfolding purpose, we are ready to defend our native land against the invasion by which it is threatened. We are fighting *by* ourselves alone; but we are not fighting *for* ourselves alone. Here in this strong City of Refuge which enshrines the title-deeds of human progress and is of deep consequence to Christian civilisation; here, girt about by the seas and oceans where the Navy reigns; shielded from above by the prowess and devotion of our airmen – we await undismayed the impending assault. Perhaps it will come tonight. Perhaps it will come next week. Perhaps it will never come. We must show ourselves equally capable of meeting a sudden violent shock or – what is perhaps a harder test – a prolonged vigil. But be the ordeal sharp or long, or both, we shall seek no terms, we shall tolerate no parley; we may show mercy – we shall ask for none.

I can easily understand how sympathetic onlookers across the Atlantic, or anxious friends in the yet unravished countries of Europe, who cannot measure our resources or our resolve, may have feared for our survival when they saw so many States and kingdoms torn to pieces in a few weeks or even days by the monstrous force of the Nazi war machine. But Hitler has not yet been withstood by a great nation with a will power the equal of his own. Many of these countries have been poisoned by intrigue before they were struck down by violence. They have been rotted from within before they were smitten from without. How else can you explain what has happened to France? – to the French Army, to the French people, to the leaders of the French people? . . .

We have a million and a half men in the British Army under arms tonight, and every week of June and July has seen their organisation, their defences and their striking power advance by leaps and bounds. No praise is too high for the officers and men – aye, and civilians – who have made this immense transformation in so short a time. Behind these soldiers of the regular Army, as a means of destruction for parachutists, airborne invaders, and any traitors that may be found in our midst (but I do not believe there are many – woe betide them, they will get short shrift) – behind the regular Army we have more than a million of the Local Defence Volunteers, or, as they are much better called, the 'Home Guard'. These officers and men, a large proportion of whom have been through the last war, have the strongest desire to attack and come to close quarters with the enemy wherever he may appear. Should the invader come to Britain, there will be no placid lying down of the people in submission before him, as we have seen, alas, in other countries. We shall defend every village, every town, and every city. The vast mass of London itself, fought street by street, could easily devour an entire hostile army; and we would rather see London laid in ruins and ashes than that it should be tamely and abjectly enslaved. I am bound to state these facts, because it is necessary to inform our people of our intentions, and thus to reassure them. . . .

I stand at the head of a Government representing all Parties in the State – all creeds, all causes, every recognisable section of opinion. We are ranged beneath the Crown of our ancient monarchy. We are supported by a free Parliament and a free Press; but there is one bond which unites us all and sustains us in the public regard – namely (as is increasingly becoming known), that we are prepared to proceed to all extremities, to endure them and to enforce them; *that* is our bond of union in His Majesty's Government tonight. Thus only, in times like these, can nations preserve their freedom; and thus only can they uphold the cause entrusted to their care.

But all depends now upon the whole life-strength of the British race in every part of the world and of all our associated peoples and of all our well-wishers in every land, doing their utmost night and day, giving all, daring all, enduring all – to the utmost – to the end. This is no war of chieftains or of princes, of dynasties or national ambition; it is a war of peoples and of causes. There are vast numbers, not only in this Island but in every land, who will render faithful service in this war, but whose names will never be known, whose deeds will never be recorded. This is a War of the Unknown Warriors; but let all strive without failing in faith or in duty, and the dark curse of Hitler will be lifted from our age.

'THE FEW'

20 August 1940

House of Commons

As the Battle of Britain reached its climax in the skies over southern Britain, Churchill paid this immortal tribute to the handful of young men, on whose skill and courage the nation's and the cause of Freedom's survival depended.

Almost a year has passed since the war began, and it is natural for us, I think, to pause on our journey at this milestone and survey the dark, wide field. It is also useful to compare the first year of this second war against German aggression with its forerunner a quarter of a century ago. Although this war is in fact only a continuation of the last, very great differences in its character are apparent. In the last war millions of men fought by hurling enormous masses of steel at one another. 'Men and shells' was the cry, and prodigious slaughter was the consequence. In this war nothing of this kind has yet appeared. It is a conflict of strategy, of organisation, of technical apparatus, of science, mechanics and morale. The British casualties in the first 12 months of the Great War amounted to 365,000. In this war, I am thankful to say, British killed, wounded, prisoners and missing, including civilians, do not exceed 92,000, and of these a large proportion are alive as prisoners of war. Looking more widely around, one may say that throughout all Europe, for one man killed or wounded in the first year perhaps five were killed or wounded in 1914–15.

The slaughter is only a small fraction, but the consequences to the belligerents have been even more deadly. We have seen great countries with powerful armies dashed out of coherent existence in a few weeks. We have seen the French Republic and the renowned French Army beaten into complete and total submission with less than the casualties which they suffered in any one of half a dozen of the battles of 1914–18. The entire body – it might almost seem at times the soul – of France has succumbed to physical effects incomparably less terrible than those which were sustained with fortitude and undaunted willpower 25 years ago. Although up to the present the loss of life has been mercifully diminished, the decisions

The gratitude of every home in our Island,
  in our Empire, and indeed throughout
   the world, except in the abodes of
            the guilty,

    goes out to the British airmen who,
     undaunted by odds,
       unwearied in their constant
          challenge and of mortal danger,

   are turning the tide of world war
    by their prowess and by their
                              devotion.

Never in the field of human conflict
  was so much owed by so many to so few.

All hearts go out to the Fighter pilots,
  whose brilliant actions we see with
      our own eyes day after day,

   but we must never forget that all the
                              time,
      night after night,
        month after month,

    our Bomber Squadrons travel far into
                        Germany,
      find their targets in the darkness
       by the highest navigational skill,
          aim their attacks,
            often under the heaviest fire
             often with heavy loss,
                    at times

  with deliberate careful precision,
   and inflict shattering blows upon
    the whole of the technical and
       war-making structure of the
          Nazi power.

'The Few', House of Commons, 20 August 1940.

reached in the course of the struggle are even more profound upon the fate of nations than anything that has ever happened since barbaric times. Moves are made upon the scientific and strategic boards, advantages are gained by mechanical means, as a result of which scores of millions of men become incapable of further resistance, or judge themselves incapable of further resistance, and a fearful game of chess proceeds from check to mate by which the unhappy players seem to be inexorably bound.

There is another more obvious difference from 1914. The whole of the warring nations are engaged, not only soldiers, but the entire population, men, women and children. The fronts are everywhere. The trenches are dug in the towns and streets. Every village is fortified. Every road is barred. The front line runs through the factories. The workmen are soldiers with different weapons but the same courage. These are great and distinctive changes from what many of us saw in the struggle of a quarter of a century ago. There seems to be every reason to believe that this new kind of war is well suited to the genius and the resources of the British nation and the British Empire; and that, once we get properly equipped and properly started, a war of this kind will be more favourable to us than the sombre mass slaughters of the Somme and Passchendaele. If it is a case of the whole nation fighting and suffering together, that ought to suit us, because we are the most united of all the nations, because we entered the war upon the national will and with our eyes open, and because we have been nurtured in freedom and individual responsibility and are the products, not of totalitarian uniformity, but of tolerance and variety. If all these qualities are turned, as they are being turned, to the arts of war, we may be able to show the enemy quite a lot of things that they have not thought of yet. Since the Germans drove the Jews out and lowered their technical standards, our science is definitely ahead of theirs. Our geographical position, the command of the sea, and the friendship of the United States enable us to draw resources from the whole world and to manufacture weapons of war of every kind, but especially of the superfine kinds, on a scale hitherto practised only by Nazi Germany.

Hitler is now sprawled over Europe. Our offensive springs are being slowly compressed, and we must resolutely and methodically prepare ourselves for the campaigns of 1941 and 1942. Two or three years are not a long time, even in our short, precarious lives. They are nothing in the history of the nation, and when we are doing the finest thing in the world, and have the honour to be the sole champion of the liberties of all Europe, we must not grudge these years or weary as we toil and struggle through them. It does not follow that our energies in future years will be exclusively confined to defending ourselves and our possessions. Many opportunities may lie open to amphibious power, and we must be ready to take advantage of them. One of the ways to bring this war to a speedy end is to convince the enemy, not by words, but by deeds, that we have both the will and the means, not only to go on indefinitely, but to strike heavy and unexpected blows. The road to victory may not be so long as we expect. But we have no right to count upon this. Be it long or short, rough or smooth, we mean to reach our journey's end.

It is our intention to maintain and enforce a strict blockade, not only of Germany, but of Italy, France, and all the other countries that have fallen into the German power. I read in the papers that Herr Hitler has also proclaimed a strict blockade of the British Islands. No one can complain of that. I remember the Kaiser doing it in the last war. What indeed would be a matter of general complaint would be if we were to prolong the agony of all Europe by allowing food to come in to nourish the Nazis and aid their war effort, or to allow food to go in to the subjugated peoples, which certainly would be pillaged off them by their Nazi conquerors.

There have been many proposals, founded on the highest motives, that food should be allowed to pass the blockade for the relief of these populations. I regret that we must refuse these requests. The Nazis declare that they have created a new unified economy in Europe. They have repeatedly stated that they possess ample reserves of food and that they can feed their captive peoples. In a German broadcast of 27th June it was said that while Mr Hoover's plan for relieving France, Belgium and Holland deserved commendation, the German forces had already taken the necessary steps. We know that in Norway when the German troops went in, there were food supplies to last for a year. We know that Poland, though not a rich country, usually produces sufficient food for her people. Moreover, the other countries which Herr Hitler has invaded all held consider-able stocks when the Germans entered and are themselves, in many cases, very substantial food producers. If all this food is not available now, it can only be because it has been removed to feed the people of Germany and to give them increased rations – for a change – during the last few months. At this season of the year and for some months to come, there is the least chance of scarcity as the harvest has just been gathered in. The only agencies which can create famine in any part of Europe, now and during the coming winter, will be German exactions or German failure to distribute the supplies which they command.

There is another aspect. Many of the most valuable foods are essential to the manufacture of vital war material. Fats are used to make explosives. Potatoes make the alcohol for motor spirit. The plastic materials now so largely used in the construction of aircraft are made of milk. If the Germans use these commodities to help them to bomb our women and children, rather than to feed the populations who produce them, we may be sure that imported foods would go the same way, directly or indirectly, or be employed to relieve the enemy of the responsibilities he has so wantonly assumed. Let Hitler bear his responsibilities to the full, and let the peoples of Europe who groan beneath his yoke aid in every way the coming of the day when that yoke will be broken. Meanwhile, we can and we will arrange in advance for the speedy entry of food into any part of the enslaved area, when this part has been wholly cleared of German forces, and has genuinely regained its freedom. We shall do our best to encourage the building up of reserves of food all over the world, so that there will always be held up before the eyes of the peoples of Europe, including – I say deliberately – the German and Austrian peoples, the certainty that the shattering of the Nazi power will bring to them all immediate food, freedom and peace.

Rather more than a quarter of a year has passed since the new Government came into power in this country. What a cataract of disaster has poured out upon us since then! The trustful Dutch overwhelmed; their beloved and respected Sovereign driven into exile; the peaceful city of Rotterdam the scene of a massacre as hideous and brutal as anything in the Thirty Years' War; Belgium invaded and beaten down; our own fine Expeditionary Force, which King Leopold called to his rescue, cut off and almost captured, escaping as it seemed only by a miracle and with the loss of all its equipment; our Ally, France, out; Italy in against us; all France in the power of the enemy, all its arsenals and vast masses of military material converted or convertible to the enemy's use; a puppet Government set up at Vichy which may at any moment be forced to become our foe; the whole western seaboard of Europe from the North Cape to the Spanish frontier in German hands; all the ports, all the airfields on this immense front employed against us as potential springboards of invasion. Moreover, the German air power, numerically so far outstripping ours, has been brought so close to our Island that what we used to dread greatly has come to pass and the hostile bombers not only reach our shores in a few minutes and from many directions, but can be escorted by their fighter aircraft. Why, Sir, if we had been confronted at the beginning of May with such a prospect, it would have seemed incredible that at the end of a period of horror and disaster, or at this point in a period of horror and disaster, we should stand erect, sure of ourselves, masters of our fate and with the conviction of final victory burning unquenchable in our hearts. Few would have believed we could survive; none would have believed that we should today not only feel stronger but should actually be stronger than we have ever been before.

Let us see what has happened on the other side of the scales. The British nation and the British Empire, finding themselves alone, stood undismayed against disaster. No one flinched or wavered; nay, some who formerly thought of peace, now think only of war. Our people are united and resolved, as they have never been before. Death and ruin have become small things compared with the shame of defeat or failure in duty. We cannot tell what lies ahead. It may be that even greater ordeals lie before us. We shall face whatever is coming to us. We are sure of ourselves and of our cause, and that is the supreme fact which has emerged in these months of trial.

Meanwhile, we have not only fortified our hearts but our Island. We have rearmed and rebuilt our armies in a degree which would have been deemed impossible a few months ago. We have ferried across the Atlantic, in the month of July, thanks to our friends over there, an immense mass of munitions of all kinds: cannon, rifles, machine guns, cartridges and shell, all safely landed without the loss of a gun or a round. The output of our own factories, working as they have never worked before, has poured forth to the troops. The whole British Army is at home. More than 2,000,000 determined men have rifles and bayonets in their hands tonight, and three-quarters of them are in regular military formations. We have never had armies like this in our Island in time of war. The whole Island bristles against invaders, from the sea or from the air. As I explained to the House in the middle of June, the stronger our Army at home, the larger must the invading expedition be, and the larger the invading expedition, the less difficult will be the task of the Navy in detecting its assembly and in intercepting and destroying it in passage; and the greater also would be the difficulty of feeding and supplying the invaders if ever they landed, in the teeth of continuous naval and air attack on their communications. All this is classical and venerable doctrine. As in Nelson's day, the maxim holds, 'Our first line of defence is the enemy's ports.' Now air reconnaissance and photography have brought to an old principle a new and potent aid.

Our Navy is far stronger than it was at the begining of the war. The great flow of new construction set on foot at the outbreak is now beginning to come in. We hope our friends across the ocean will send us a timely reinforcement to bridge the gap between the peace flotillas of 1939 and the war flotillas of 1941. There is no difficulty in sending such aid. The seas and oceans are open. The U-boats are contained. The magnetic mine is, up to the present time, effectively mastered. The merchant tonnage under the British flag, after a year of unlimited U-boat war, after eight months of intensive mining attack, is larger than when we began. We have, in addition, under our control at least 4,000,000 tons of shipping from the captive countries which has taken refuge here or in the harbours of the Empire. Our stocks of food of all kinds are far more abundant than in the days of peace, and a large and growing programme of food production is on foot.

Why do I say all this? Not, assuredly, to boast; not, assuredly, to give the slightest countenance to complacency. The dangers we face are still enormous, but so are our advantages and resources. I recount them because the people have a right to know that there are solid grounds for the confidence which we feel, and that we have good reason to believe ourselves capable, as I said in a very dark hour two months ago, of continuing the war 'if necessary alone, if necessary for years'. I say it also because the fact that the British Empire stands invincible, and that Nazidom is still being resisted, will kindle again the spark of hope in the breasts of hundreds of millions of downtrodden or despairing men and women throughout Europe, and far beyond its bounds, and that from these sparks there will presently come cleansing and devouring flame.

The great air battle which has been in progress over this Island for the last few weeks has recently attained a high intensity. It is too soon to attempt to assign limits either to its scale or to its duration. We must certainly expect that greater efforts will be made by the enemy than any he has so far put forth. Hostile airfields are still being developed in France and the Low Countries, and the movement of squadrons and material for attacking us is still proceeding. It is quite plain that Herr Hitler could not admit defeat in his air attack on Great Britain without sustaining most serious injury. If after all his boastings and bloodcurdling threats and lurid accounts trumpeted round the world of the damage he has inflicted, of the vast numbers of our Air Force he has shot down, so he says, with so little loss to himself; if after tales of the panic-stricken British crushed in their holes cursing the plutocratic Parliament which has led them to such a plight – if after all this his whole air onslaught were forced after a while tamely to peter out, the Führer's reputation for veracity of statement might be seriously impugned. We may be sure, therefore, that he will continue as long as he has the strength to do so, and as long as any preoccupations he may have in respect of the Russian Air Force allow him to do so.

On the other hand, the conditions and course of the fighting have so far been favourable to us. I told the House two months ago that, whereas in France our fighter aircraft were wont to inflict a loss of two or three to one upon the Germans, and in the fighting at Dunkirk, which was a kind of no-man's-land, a loss of about three or four to one, we expected that in an attack on this Island we should achieve a larger ratio. This has certainly come true. It must also be remembered that all the enemy machines and pilots which are shot down over our Island, or over the seas which surround it, are either destroyed or captured; whereas a considerable proportion of our machines, and also of our pilots, are saved, and soon again in many cases come into action.

A vast and admirable system of salvage, directed by the Ministry of Aircraft Production, ensures the speediest return to the fighting line of damaged machines, and the most provident and speedy use of all the spare parts and material. At the same time the splendid – nay, astounding – increase in the output and repair of British aircraft and engines which Lord Beaverbrook has achieved by a genius of organisation and drive, which looks like magic, has given us overflowing reserves of every type of aircraft, and an ever-mounting stream of production both in quantity and quality. The enemy is, of course, far more numerous than we are. But our new production already, as I am advised, largely exceeds his, and the American production is only just beginning to flow in. It is a fact, as I see from my daily returns, that our bomber and fighter strength now, after all this fighting, are larger than they have ever been. We believe that we shall be able to continue the air struggle indefinitely and as long as the enemy pleases, and the longer it continues the more rapid will be our approach, first towards that parity, and then into that superiority, in the air upon which in a large measure the decision of the war depends.

The gratitude of every home in our Island, in our Empire, and indeed throughout the world, except in the abodes of the guilty, goes out to the British airmen who, undaunted by odds, unwearied in their constant challenge and mortal danger, are turning the tide of the World War by their prowess and by their devotion. Never in the field of human conflict was so much owed by so many to so few. All hearts go out to the fighter pilots, whose brilliant actions we see with our own eyes day after day; but we must never forget that all the time, night after night, month after month, our bomber squadrons travel far into Germany, find their targets in the darkness by the highest navigational skill, aim their attacks, often under the heaviest fire, often with serious loss, with deliberate careful discrimination, and inflict shattering blows upon the whole of the technical and war-making structure of the Nazi power. On no part of the Royal Air Force does the weight of the war fall more heavily than on the daylight bombers, who will play an invaluable part in the case of invasion and whose unflinching zeal it has been necessary in the meanwhile on numerous occasions to restrain.

We are able to verify the results of bombing military targets in Germany, not only by reports which reach us through many sources, but also, of course, by photography. I have no hesitation in saying that this process of bombing the military industries and communications of Germany and the air bases and storage depots from which we are attacked, which process will continue upon an ever-increasing scale until the end of the war, and may in another year attain dimensions hitherto undreamed of, affords one at least of the most certain, if not the shortest, of all the roads to victory. Even if the Nazi legions stood triumphant on the Black Sea, or indeed upon the Caspian, even if Hitler was at the gates of India, it would profit him nothing if at the same time the entire economic and scientific apparatus of German war power lay shattered and pulverised at home.

The fact that the invasion of this Island upon a large scale has become a far more difficult operation with every week that has passed since we saved our Army at Dunkirk, and our very great preponderance of sea power enable us to turn our eyes and to turn our strength increasingly towards the Mediterranean and against that other enemy who, without the slightest provocation, coldly and deliberately, for greed and gain, stabbed France in the back in the moment of her agony, and is now marching against us in Africa. The defection of France has, of course, been deeply damaging to our position in what is called, somewhat oddly, the Middle East. In the defence of Somaliland, for instance, we had counted upon strong French forces attacking the Italians from Jibuti. We had counted also upon the use of the French naval and air bases in the Mediterranean, and particularly upon the North African shore. We had counted upon the French Fleet. Even though metropolitan France was temporarily overrun, there was no reason why the French Navy, substantial parts of the French Army, the French Air Force and the French Empire overseas should not have continued the struggle at our side.

Shielded by overwhelming sea power, possessed of invaluable strategic bases and of ample funds, France might have remained one of the great combatants in the struggle. By so doing, France would have preserved the continuity of her life, and the French Empire might have advanced with the British Empire to the rescue of the independence and integrity of the French Motherland. In our own case, if we had been put in the terrible position of France, a contingency now happily impossible, although, of course, it would have been the duty of all war leaders to fight on here to the end, it would also have been their duty, as I indicated in my speech of 4th June, to provide as far as possible for the Naval security of Canada and our Dominions and to make sure they had the means to carry on the struggle from beyond the oceans. Most of the other countries that have been overrun by Germany for the time being have persevered valiantly and faithfully. The Czechs, the Poles, the Norwegians, the Dutch, the Belgians are still in the field, sword in hand, recognised by Great Britain and the United States as the sole representative authorities and lawful Governments of their respective States.

That France alone should lie prostrate at this moment is the crime, not of a great and noble nation, but of what are called 'the men of Vichy'. We have profound sympathy with the French people. Our old comradeship with France is not dead. In General de Gaulle and his gallant band, that comradeship takes an effective form. These free Frenchmen have been condemned to death by Vichy, but the day will come, as surely as the sun will rise tomorrow, when their names will be held in honour, and their names will be graven in stone in the streets and villages of a France restored in a liberated Europe to its full freedom and its ancient fame. But this conviction which I feel of the future cannot affect the immediate problems which confront us in the Mediterranean and in Africa. It had been decided some time before the beginning of the war not to defend the Protectorate of Somaliland. That policy was changed in the early months of the war. When the French gave in, and when our small forces there, a few battalions, a few guns, were attacked by all the Italian troops, nearly two divisions, which had formerly faced the French at Jibuti, it was right to withdraw our detachments, virtually intact, for action elsewhere. Far larger operations no doubt impend in the Middle East theatre, and I shall certainly not attempt to discuss or prophesy about their probable course. We have large armies and many means of reinforcing them. We have the complete sea command of the eastern Mediterranean. We intend to do our best to give a good account of ourselves, and to discharge faithfully and resolutely all our obligations and duties in that quarter of the world. More than that I do not think the House would wish me to say at the present time.

A good many people have written to me to ask me to make on this occasion a fuller statement of our war aims, and of the kind of peace we wish to make after the war, than is contained in the very considerable declaration which was made early in the autumn. Since then we have made common cause with Norway, Holland and Belgium. We have recognised the Czech Government of Dr Beneš, and we have told General de Gaulle that our success will carry with it the restoration of France. I do not think it would be wise at this moment, while the battle rages and the war is still perhaps only in its earlier stage, to embark upon elaborate speculations about the future shape which should be given to Europe or the new securities which must be arranged to spare mankind the miseries of a third World War. The ground is not new, it has been frequently traversed and explored, and many ideas are held about it in common by all good men, and all free men. But before we can undertake the task of rebuilding we have not only to be convinced ourselves, but we have to convince all other countries that the Nazi tyranny is going to be finally broken. The right to guide the course of world history is the noblest prize of victory. We are still toiling up the hill; we have not yet reached the crest-line of it; we cannot survey the landscape or even imagine what its condition will be when that longed-for morning comes. The task which lies before us immediately is at once more practical, more simple and more stern. I hope – indeed, I pray – that we shall not be found unworthy of our victory if after toil and tribulation it is granted to us. For the rest, we have to gain the victory. That is our task.

There is, however, one direction in which we can see a little more clearly ahead. We have to think not only for ourselves but for the lasting security of the cause and principle for which we are fighting and of the long future of the British Commonwealth of Nations. Some months ago we came to the conclusion that the interests of the United States and of the British Empire both required that the United States should have facilities for the naval and air defence of the

Western Hemisphere against the attack of a Nazi power which might have acquired temporary but lengthy control of a large part of Western Europe and its formidable resources. We had therefore decided spontaneously, and without being asked or offered any inducement, to inform the Government of the United States that we would be glad to place such defence facilities at their disposal by leasing suitable sites in our Transatlantic possessions for their greater security against the unmeasured dangers of the future. The principle of association of interests for common purposes between Great Britain and the United States had developed even before the war. Various agreements had been reached about certain small islands in the Pacific Ocean which had become important as air fuelling points. In all this line of thought we found ourselves in very close harmony with the Government of Canada.

Presently we learned that anxiety was also felt in the United States about the air and naval defence of their Atlantic seaboard, and President Roosevelt has recently made it clear that he would like to discuss with us, and with the Dominion of Canada and with Newfoundland, the development of American naval and air facilities in Newfoundland and in the West Indies. There is, of course, no question of any transference of sovereignty – that has never been suggested – or of any action being taken without the consent or against the wishes of the various Colonies concerned; but for our part, His Majesty's Government are entirely willing to accord defence facilities to the United States on a 99 years' leasehold basis, and we feel sure that our interests no less than theirs, and the interests of the Colonies themselves and of Canada and Newfoundland, will be served thereby. These are important steps. Undoubtedly this process means that these two great organisations of the English-speaking democracies, the British Empire and the United States, will have to be somewhat mixed up together in some of their affairs for mutual and general advantage. For my own part, looking out upon the future, I do not view the process with any misgivings. I could not stop it if I wished; no one can stop it. Like the Mississippi, it just keeps rolling along. Let it roll. Let it roll on full flood, inexorable, irresistible, benignant, to broader lands and better days.

FIFTY AMERICAN DESTROYERS

5 September 1940

House of Commons

On 3 September the US Government agreed to exchange 50 of their older destroyers for a 99-year lease of certain British bases in the North and South Atlantic. These proved to be of vital assistance in the developing Battle of the Atlantic against the German U-boats.

The memorable transactions between Great Britain and the United States, which were foreshadowed when I last addressed the House, have now been completed. As far as I can make out, they have been completed to the general satisfaction of the British and American peoples and to the encouragement of our friends all over the world. It would be a mistake to try to read into the official notes which have passed more than the documents bear on their face. The exchanges which have taken place are simply measures of mutual assistance rendered to one another by two friendly nations, in a spirit of confidence, sympathy and goodwill. These measures are linked together in a formal agreement. They must be accepted exactly as they stand. Only very ignorant persons would suggest that the transfer of American destroyers to the British flag constitutes the slightest violation of international law or affects in the smallest degree the non-belligerency of the United States.

I have no doubt that Herr Hitler will not like this transference of destroyers, and I have no doubt that he will pay the United States out, if ever he gets the chance. That is why I am very glad that the army, air and naval frontiers of the United States have been advanced along a wide arc into the Atlantic Ocean, and that will enable them to take danger by the throat while it is still hundreds of miles away from their homeland. The Admiralty tell us also that they are very glad to have these 50 destroyers, and that they will come in most conveniently to bridge the gap which, as I have previously explained to the House, inevitably intervenes before our considerable wartime programme of new construction comes into service.

I suppose the House realises that we shall be a good deal stronger next year on the sea than we are now, although that is quite strong enough for the immediate work in hand. There will be no delay in bringing the American destroyers into active service; in fact, British crews are already meeting them at the various ports where they are being delivered.

'THESE CRUEL, WANTON, INDISCRIMINATE BOMBINGS OF LONDON ...'

11 September 1940

Broadcast, London

On 5 September the Luftwaffe switched tactics. Suddenly the weight of enemy attack was concentrated no longer against the bases of the Royal Air Force, but against the civilian population of London and other major cities. Churchill here gives full rein to his outrage and reavows his determination to secure victory. Following the 11 September 2001 terrorist outrages which destroyed the World Trade Center's Twin Towers in New York, this speech was much quoted by Mayor Rudolph Giuliani and others. By an amazing coincidence the dates are the same.

When I said in the House of Commons the other day that I thought it improbable that the enemy's air attack in September could be more than three times as great as it was in August, I was not, of course, referring to barbarous attacks upon the civil population, but to the great air battle which is being fought out between our fighters and the German Air Force.

You will understand that whenever the weather is favourable, waves of German bombers, protected by fighters, often three or four hundred at a time, surge over this Island, especially the promontory of Kent, in the hope of attacking military and other objectives by daylight. However, they are met by our fighter squadrons and nearly always broken up; and their losses average three to one in machines and six to one in pilots.

This effort of the Germans to secure daylight mastery of the air over England is, of course, the crux of the whole war. So far it has failed conspicuously. It has cost them very dear, and we have felt stronger, and actually are relatively a good deal stronger, than when the hard fighting began in July. There is no doubt that Herr Hitler is using up his fighter force at a very high rate, and that if he goes on for many more weeks he will wear down and ruin this vital part of his Air Force. That will give us a very great advantage.

On the other hand, for him to try to invade this country without having secured mastery in the air would be a very hazardous undertaking. Nevertheless, all his preparations for invasion on a great scale are steadily going forward. Several hundreds of self-propelled barges are moving down the coasts of Europe, from the German and Dutch harbours to the ports of northern France; from Dunkirk to Brest; and beyond Brest to the French harbours in the Bay of Biscay.

Besides this, convoys of merchant ships in tens of dozens are being moved through the Straits of Dover into the Channel, dodging along from port to port under the protection of the new batteries which the Germans have built on the French shore. There are now considerable gatherings of shipping in the German, Dutch, Belgian and French harbours – all the way from Hamburg to Brest. Finally, there are some preparations made of ships to carry an invading force from the Norwegian harbours.

Behind these clusters of ships or barges, there stand very large numbers of German troops, awaiting the order to go on board and set out on their very dangerous and uncertain voyage across the seas. We cannot tell when they will try to come; we cannot be sure that in fact they will try at all; but no one should blind himself to the fact that a heavy, full-scale invasion of this Island is being prepared with all the usual German thoroughness and method, and that it may be launched now – upon England, upon Scotland, or upon Ireland, or upon all three.

If this invasion is going to be tried at all, it does not seem that it can be long delayed. The weather may break at any time. Besides this, it is difficult for the enemy to keep these gatherings of ships waiting about indefinitely, while they are bombed every night by our bombers, and very often shelled by our warships which are waiting for them outside.

Therefore, we must regard the next week or so as a very important period in our history. It ranks with the days when the Spanish Armada was approaching the Channel, and Drake was finishing his game of bowls; or when Nelson stood between us and Napoleon's Grand Army at Boulogne. We have read all about this in the history books; but what is happening now is on a far greater scale and of far more consequence to the life and future of the world and its civilisation than these brave old days of the past.

Every man and woman will therefore prepare himself to do his duty, whatever it may be, with special pride and care. Our fleets and flotillas are very powerful and numerous; our Air Force is at the highest strength it has ever reached, and it is conscious of its proved superiority, not indeed in numbers, but in men and machines. Our shores are well fortified and strongly manned, and behind them, ready to attack the invaders, we have a far larger and better equipped mobile Army than we have ever had before.

Besides this, we have more than a million and a half men of the Home Guard, who are just as much soldiers of the Regular Army as the Grenadier Guards, and who are determined to fight for every inch of the ground in every village and in every street.

It is with devout but sure confidence that I say: Let God defend the Right.

These cruel, wanton, indiscriminate bombings of London are, of course, a part of Hitler's invasion plans. He hopes, by killing large numbers of civilians, and women and children, that he will terrorise and cow the people of this mighty imperial city, and make them a burden and an anxiety to the Government and thus distract our attention unduly from the ferocious onslaught he is preparing. Little does he know the spirit of the British nation, or the tough fibre of the Londoners, whose forebears played a leading part in the establishment of Parliamentary institutions and who have been bred to value freedom far above their lives. This wicked man, the repository and embodiment of many forms of soul-destroying hatred, this monstrous product of former wrongs and shame, has now resolved to try to break our famous Island race by a process of indiscriminate slaughter and destruction. What he has done is to kindle a fire in British hearts, here and all over the world, which will glow long after all traces of the conflagration he has caused in London have been removed. He has lighted a fire which will burn with a steady and consuming flame until the last vestiges of Nazi tyranny have been burnt out of Europe, and until the Old World – and the New – can join hands to rebuild the temples of man's freedom and man's honour, upon foundations which will not soon or easily be overthrown.

This is a time for everyone to stand together, and hold firm, as they are doing. I express my admiration for the exemplary manner in which all the Air Raid Precautions services of London are being discharged, especially the Fire Brigade, whose work has been so heavy and also dangerous. All the world that is still free marvels at the composure and fortitude with which the citizens of London are facing and surmounting the great ordeal to which they are subjected, the end of which or the severity of which cannot yet be foreseen.

It is a message of good cheer to our fighting Forces on the seas, in the air, and in our waiting Armies in all their posts and stations, that we send them from this capital city. They know that they have behind them a people who will not flinch or weary of the struggle – hard and protracted though it will be; but that we shall rather draw from the heart of suffering itself the means of inspiration and survival, and of a victory won not only for ourselves but for all – a victory won not only for our own time, but for the long and better days that are to come.

SECRET SESSION: 'WE WILL ALL GO DOWN FIGHTING TO THE END'

17 September 1940

Secret Session, House of Commons

Two days before, on 15 September, the Battle of Britain reached its climax. On that day all the British reserves had been thrown into the life-or-death struggle with the enemy, but the back of the German air attack had been broken. On 17 September – though this was not known at the time – Hitler took the decision to postpone Operation 'Sealion', as it turned out, indefinitely.

The reason why I asked the House to go into Secret Session was not because I had anything particularly secret or momentous to say. It was only because there are some things which it is better for us to talk over among ourselves than when we are overheard by the Germans. I wish to speak about the sittings of the House and how we are to discharge our Parliamentary duties. . . .

We ought not to flatter ourselves by imagining that we are irreplaceable, but at the same time it cannot be denied that two or three hundred by-elections would be a quite needless complication of our affairs at this particular juncture. Moreover, I suppose that if Hitler made a clean sweep of the Houses of Parliament it would give widespread and unwholesome satisfaction throughout Germany, and be vaunted as another triumph for the Nazi system of government.

We must exercise reasonable prudence and a certain amount of guile in combating the malice of the enemy. It is no part of good sense to proclaim the hour and dates of our meetings long beforehand. . . .

These next few weeks are grave and anxious. I said just now in the Public Session that the deployment of the enemy's invasion preparations and the assembly of his ships and barges are steadily proceeding, and that any moment a major assault may be launched upon this island. I now say in secret that upwards of seventeen hundred self-propelled barges and more than two hundred seagoing ships, some very large ships, are already gathering at the many invasion ports in German occupation. If this is all a pretence and stratagem to pin us down here, it has been executed with surprising thoroughness and on a gigantic scale. Some of these ships and barges, when struck by our bombing counterattack and preventive attack, have blown up with tremendous explosions, showing that they are fully loaded with all the munitions needed for the invading armies and to beat us down and subjugate us utterly. The shipping available and now assembled is sufficient to carry in one voyage nearly *half* a million men. We should, of course, expect to drown a great many on the way over, and to destroy a large proportion of their vessels. But when you reflect upon the many points from which they could start, and upon the fact that even the most likely sector of invasion, i.e., the sector in which enemy fighter support is available for their bombers and dive bombers, extending from the Wash to the Isle of Wight, is nearly as long as the whole front in France from the Alps to the sea, and also upon the dangers of fog or artificial fog, one must expect many lodgments or attempted lodgments to be made on our island simultaneously. These we shall hope to deal with as they occur, and also to cut off the supply across the sea by which the enemy will seek to nourish his lodgments.

The difficulties of the invader are not ended when he sets foot on shore. A new chapter of perils opens upon him. I am confident that we shall succeed in defeating and largely destroying this most tremendous onslaught by which we are now threatened, and anyhow, whatever happens, we will all go down fighting to the end. I feel as sure as the sun will rise tomorrow that we shall be victorious.

'WE CAN TAKE IT!'

8 October 1940

House of Commons

A month has passed since Herr Hitler turned his rage and malice on to the civil population of our great cities and particularly of London. He declared in his speech of 4th September that he would raze our cities to the ground, and since then he has been trying to carry out his fell purpose. Naturally, the first question we should ask is to what extent the full strength of the German bombing force has been deployed. I will give the House the best opinion I have been able to form on what is necessarily to some extent a matter of speculation. After their very severe mauling on 15th August, the German short-range dive bombers, of which there are several hundred, have been kept carefully out of the air fighting. This may be, of course, because they are being held in reserve so that they may play their part in a general plan of invasion or re-appear in some other theatre of war. We have, therefore, had to deal with the long-range German bombers alone.

It would seem that, taking day and night together, nearly 400 of these machines have, on the average, visited our shores every 24 hours. We are doubtful whether this rate of sustained attack could be greatly exceeded. . . .

Neither by material damage nor by slaughter will the people of the British Empire be turned from their solemn and inexorable purpose. It is the practice and in some cases the duty of many of my colleagues and many Members of the House to visit the scenes of destruction as promptly as possible, and I go myself from time to time. In all my life, I have never been treated with so much kindness as by the people who have suffered most. One would think one had brought some great benefit to them, instead of the blood and tears, the toil and sweat which is all I have ever promised. On every side, there is the cry, 'We can take it,' but with it, there is also the cry, 'Give it 'em back.' . . .

Meanwhile, what has happened to the invasion which we have been promised every month and almost every week since the beginning of July? Do not let us be lured into supposing that the danger is past. On the contrary, unwearying vigilance and the swift and steady strengthening of our Force by land, sea and air which is in progress must be at all costs maintained. Now that we are in October, however, the weather becomes very uncertain, and there are not many lucid intervals of two or three days together in which river barges can cross the narrow seas and land upon our beaches. Still, those intervals may occur. Fogs may aid the foe. Our Armies, which are growing continually in numbers, equipment, mobility and training, must be maintained all through the winter, not only along the beaches but in reserve, as the majority are, like leopards crouching to spring at the invader's throat. The enemy has certainly got prepared enough shipping and barges to throw half a million men in a single night on to salt water – or into it. The Home Guard, which now amounts to 1,700,000 men, must nurse their weapons and sharpen their bayonets. . . .

Because we feel easier in ourselves and see our way more clearly through our difficulties and dangers than we did some months ago, because foreign countries, friends or foes, recognise the giant, enduring, resilient strength of Britain and the British Empire, do not let us dull for one moment the sense of the awful hazards in which we stand. Do not let us lose the conviction that it is only by supreme and superb exertions, unwearying and indomitable, that we shall save our souls alive. No one can predict, no one can even imagine, how this terrible war against German and Nazi aggression will run its course or how far it will spread or how long it will last. Long, dark months of trials and tribulations lie before us. Not only great dangers, but many more misfortunes, many shortcomings, many mistakes, many disappointments will surely be our lot. Death and sorrow will be the companions of our journey; hardship our garment; constancy and valour our only shield. We must be united, we must be undaunted, we must be inflexible. Our qualities and deeds must burn and glow through the gloom of Europe until they become the veritable beacon of its salvation.

'DIEU PROTÈGE LA FRANCE'

21 October 1940

Broadcast, London

The power and majesty of his words, broadcast by the BBC, reaching its crescendo in the final paragraph, gave courage and hope to all patriots, not only in France, but throughout Occupied Europe.

Frenchmen! For more than thirty years in peace and war I have marched with you, and I am marching still along the same road. Tonight I speak to you at your firesides wherever you may be, or whatever your fortunes are: I repeat the prayer around the *louis d'or*, '*Dieu protège la France*'. Here at home in England, under the fire of the Boche, we do not forget the ties and links that unite us to France, and we are persevering steadfastly and in good heart in the cause of European freedom and fair dealing for the common people of all countries, for which, with you, we drew the sword. When good people get into trouble because they are attacked and heavily smitten by the vile and wicked, they must be very careful not to get at loggerheads with one another. The common enemy is always trying to bring this about, and, of course, in bad luck a lot of things happen which play into the enemy's hands. We must just make the best of things as they come along.

Here in London, which Herr Hitler says he will reduce to ashes, and which his aeroplanes are now bombarding, our people are bearing up unflinchingly. Our Air Force has more than held its own. We are waiting for the long-promised invasion. So are the fishes. But, of course, this for us is only the beginning. Now in 1940, in spite of occasional losses, we have, as ever, command of the seas. In 1941 we shall have the command of the air. Remember what that means. Herr Hitler with his tanks and other mechanical weapons, and also by Fifth Column intrigue with traitors, has managed to subjugate for the time being most of the finest races in Europe, and his little Italian accomplice is trotting along hopefully and hungrily, but rather wearily and very timidly, at his side. They both wish to carve up France and her Empire as if it were a fowl; to one a leg, to another a wing or perhaps part of the breast. Not only the French Empire will be devoured by these two ugly customers, but Alsace-Lorraine will

go once again under the German yoke, and Nice, Savoy and Corsica
– Napoleon's Corsica – will be torn from the fair realm of France.
But Herr Hitler is not thinking only of stealing other people's
territories, or flinging gobbets of them to his little confederate. I tell
you truly what you must believe when I say this evil man, this
monstrous abortion of hatred and defeat, is resolved on nothing less
than the complete wiping out of the French nation, and the
disintegration of its whole life and future. By all kinds of sly and
savage means, he is plotting and working to quench for ever the
fountain of characteristic French culture and of French inspiration to
the world. All Europe, if he has his way, will be reduced to one
uniform Boche-land, to be exploited, pillaged, and bullied by his
Nazi gangsters. You will excuse my speaking frankly because this is
not a time to mince words. It is not defeat that France will now be
made to suffer at German hands, but the doom of complete
obliteration. Army, Navy, Air Force, religion, law, language, culture,
institutions, literature, history, tradition – all are to be effaced by the
brute strength of a triumphant Army and the scientific low cunning
of a ruthless Police Force.

Frenchmen – rearm your spirits before it is too late. Remember
how Napoleon said before one of his battles: 'These same Prussians
who are so boastful today were three to one at Jena, and six to one at
Montmirail.' Never will I believe that the soul of France is dead.
Never will I believe that her place amongst the greatest nations of the
world has been lost for ever! All these schemes and crimes of Herr
Hitler's are bringing upon him and upon all who belong to his
system a retribution which many of us will live to see. The story is
not yet finished, but it will not be so long. We are on his track, and so
are our friends across the Atlantic Ocean, and your friends across the
Atlantic Ocean. If he cannot destroy us, we will surely destroy him
and all his gang, and all their works. Therefore, have hope and faith,
for all will come right.

Now, what is it we British ask of you in this present hard and
bitter time? What we ask at this moment in our struggle to win the
victory which we will share with you, is that if you cannot help us, at
least you will not hinder us. Presently you will be able to weight the
arm that strikes for you, and you ought to do so. But even now we
believe that Frenchmen, wherever they may be, feel their hearts warm
and a proud blood tingle in their veins when we have some success in
the air or on the sea, or presently – for that will come – upon the
land.

Remember we shall never stop, never weary, and never give in, and that our whole people and Empire have vowed themselves to the task of cleansing Europe from the Nazi pestilence and saving the world from the new Dark Ages. Do not imagine, as the German-controlled wireless tells you, that we English seek to take your ships and colonies. We seek to beat the life and soul out of Hitler and Hitlerism. That alone, that all the time, that to the end. We do not covet anything from any nation except their respect. Those French who are in the French Empire, and those who are in so-called unoccupied France, may see their way from time to time to useful action. I will not go into details. Hostile ears are listening. As for those to whom English hearts go out in full, because they see them under the sharp discipline, oppression, and spying of the Hun – as to those Frenchmen in the occupied regions – to them I say, when they think of the future let them remember the words which Thiers, that great Frenchman, uttered after 1870 about the future of France and what was to come: 'Think of it always: speak of it never.'

Good night, then: sleep to gather strength for the morning. For the morning will come. Brightly will it shine on the brave and true, kindly upon all who suffer for the cause, glorious upon the tombs of heroes. Thus will shine the dawn. *Vive la France!*

'GIVE US THE TOOLS'

9 February 1941

Broadcast, London

Wendell Willkie, the Republican candidate in the previous November's presidential elections, arrived in Britain in late January. He carried with him a letter of introduction to Churchill from his erstwhile opponent, President Roosevelt. The message included the celebrated lines from Longfellow, which moved Churchill greatly.

Five months have passed since I spoke to the British nation and the Empire on the broadcast. In wartime there is a lot to be said for the motto: 'Deeds, not words.' All the same, it is a good thing to look around from time to time and take stock, and certainly our affairs have prospered in several directions during these last four or five months, far better than most of us would have ventured to hope.

We stood our ground and faced the two Dictators in the hour of what seemed their overwhelming triumph, and we have shown ourselves capable, so far, of standing up against them alone. After the heavy defeats of the German air force by our fighters in August and September, Herr Hitler did not dare attempt the invasion of this Island, although he had every need to do so and although he had made vast preparations. Baffled in this mighty project, he sought to break the spirit of the British nation by the bombing, first of London, and afterwards of our great cities. It has now been proved, to the admiration of the world, and of our friends in the United States, that this form of blackmail by murder and terrorism, so far from weakening the spirit of the British nation, has only roused it to a more intense and universal flame than was ever seen before in any modern community.

The whole British Empire has been proud of the Mother Country, and they long to be with us over here in even larger numbers. We have been deeply conscious of the love for us which has flowed from the Dominions of the Crown across the broad ocean spaces. *There* is the first of our war aims: to be worthy of that love, and to preserve it.

All through these dark winter months the enemy has had the power to drop three or four tons of bombs upon us for every ton we could send to Germany in return. We are arranging so that presently this will be rather the other way round; but, meanwhile, London and our big cities have had to stand their pounding. They remind me of the British squares at Waterloo. They are not squares of soldiers; they do not wear scarlet coats. They are just ordinary English, Scottish and Welsh folk – men, women and children – standing steadfastly together. But their spirit is the same, their glory is the same; and, in the end, their victory will be greater than far-famed Waterloo. . . .

It is just exactly two months ago, to a day, that I was waiting anxiously, but also eagerly, for the news of the great counter-stroke which had been planned against the Italian invaders of Egypt. The secret had been well kept. The preparations had been well made. But to leap across those seventy miles of desert, and attack an army of ten or eleven divisions, equipped with all the appliances of modern war, who had been fortifying themselves for three months – that was a most hazardous adventure.

When the brilliant decisive victory at Sidi Barrani, with its tens of thousands of prisoners, proved that we had quality, manoeuvring power and weapons superior to the enemy, who had boasted so much of his virility and his military virtues, it was evident that all the other Italian forces in eastern Libya were in great danger. They could not easily beat a retreat along the coastal road without running the risk of being caught in the open by our armoured divisions and brigades, ranging far out into the desert in tremendous swoops and scoops. They had to expose themselves to being attacked piecemeal.

General Wavell – nay, all our leaders, and all their lithe, active, ardent men, British, Australian, Indian, in the Imperial Army – saw their opportunity. At that time I ventured to draw General Wavell's attention to the seventh chapter of the Gospel of St Matthew, at the seventh verse, where, as you all know – or ought to know – it is written: 'Ask, and it shall be given; seek, and ye shall find; knock, and it shall be opened unto you.' The Army of the Nile has asked, and it was given; they sought, and they have found; they knocked, and it has been opened unto them. In barely eight weeks, by a campaign which will long be studied as a model of the military art, an advance of over 400 miles has been made. The whole Italian Army in the east of Libya, which was reputed to exceed 150,000 men, has been captured or destroyed. The entire province of Cyrenaica – nearly as big as England and Wales – has been conquered. The unhappy Arab tribes, who have for thirty years suffered from the cruelty of Italian rule, carried in some cases to the point of methodical extermination, these Bedouin survivors have at last seen their oppressors in disorderly flight, or led off in endless droves as prisoners of war.

Egypt and the Suez Canal are safe, and the port, the base and the airfields of Benghazi constitute a strategic point of high consequence to the whole of the war in the Eastern Mediterranean.

In order to win the war Hitler must destroy Great Britain. He may carry havoc into the Balkan States; he may tear great provinces out of Russia, he may march to the Caspian; he may march to the gates of India. All this will avail him nothing. It may spend his curse more widely throughout Europe and Asia, but it will not avert his doom. With every month that passes the many proud and once happy countries he is now holding down by brute force and vile intrigue are learning to hate the Prussian yoke and the Nazi name as nothing has ever been hated so fiercely and so widely among men before. And all the time, masters of the sea and air, the British Empire – nay, in a certain sense, the whole English-speaking world – will be on is track, bearing with them the swords of justice.

The other day, President Roosevelt gave his opponent in the late Presidential Election [Mr Wendell Willkie] a letter of introduction to me, and in it he wrote out a verse, in his own handwriting, from

Longfellow, which he said, 'applies to you people as it does to us.'
Here is the verse:

> ... Sail on, O Ship of State!
> Sail on, O Union, strong and great!
> Humanity with all its fears,
> With all the hopes of future years,
> Is hanging breathless on thy fate!

What is the answer that I shall give, in your name, to this great man,
the thrice-chosen head of a nation of a hundred and thirty millions?
Here is the answer which I will give to President Roosevelt: Put your
confidence in us. Give us your faith and your blessing, and, under
Providence, all will be well.

We shall not fail or falter; we shall not weaken or tire. Neither the
sudden shock of battle, nor the long-drawn trials of vigilance and
exertion will wear us down. Give us the tools, and we will finish the
job.

'THIS BATTLE OF THE ATLANTIC'

18 March 1941

Pilgrims' Society Luncheon, London

*The Battle of the Atlantic was at its height with German U-boats,
long-range aircraft and surface raiders, taking a toll of more than
500,000 tons of Allied shipping during each of the months of March,
April and May. Churchill was delighted when Roosevelt recalled the
defeatist Joseph P. Kennedy and replaced him as Ambassador to
Britain by John G. Winant. His welcome was heart-felt and
unstinted.*

We are met here today under the strong impression and impact of the
historic declaration made on Saturday last by the President of the
United States, and where could there be a more fitting opportunity
than at this gathering of the Pilgrims to greet the new American
Ambassador for me to express on behalf of the British nation and
Empire the sense of encouragement and fortification in our resolve
which has come to us from across the ocean in those stirring, august,

and fateful presidential words? You have come here, Mr Winant, to a community which is being tried and proved before mankind and history, and tried and proved to a degree and on a scale and under conditions which have not previously been known to human experience.

We have here a free society, governed through a Parliament which rests upon universal suffrage and upon the public opinion of the whole nation. We are being subjected to daily assaults which, if not effectively resisted and repelled, would soon prove mortal. We have to call upon our whole people – men, women, and children alike – to stand up with composure and fortitude to the fire of the enemy, and to accept increasing privations while making increasing efforts. Nothing like this has ever been seen before.

We have our faults, and our social system has its faults, but we hope that, with God's help, we shall be able to prove for all time, or at any rate, for a long time, that a State or Commonwealth of Nations, founded on long-enjoyed freedom and steadily-evolving democracy, possesses amid the sharpest shocks the faculty of survival in a high and honourable and, indeed, in a glorious degree. At such a moment, and under such an ordeal, the words and the acts of the President and people of the United States come to us like a draught of life, and they tell us by an ocean-borne trumpet call that we are no longer alone.

We know that other hearts in millions and scores of millions beat with ours; that other voices proclaim the cause for which we strive; other strong hands wield the hammers and shape the weapons we need; other clear and gleaming eyes are fixed in hard conviction upon the tyrannies that must and shall be destroyed. We welcome you here, Mr Winant, at the moment when a great battle in which your Government and nation are deeply interested is developing its full scope and severity. The Battle of the Atlantic must be won in a decisive manner. It must be won beyond all doubt if the declared policies of the Government and people of the United States are not to be forcibly frustrated. Not only German U-boats, but German battle cruisers have crossed to the American side of the Atlantic and have already sunk some of our independently-routed ships not sailing in convoy. They have sunk these ships as far west as the 42nd meridian of longitude.

Over here upon the approaches to our island an intense and unrelenting struggle is being waged to bring in the endless stream of munitions and food without which our war effort here and in the Middle East – for that shall not be relaxed – cannot be maintained.

Our losses have risen for the time being, and we are applying our fullest strength and resource, and all the skill and science we can command, in order to meet this potentially mortal challenge. And not only, I must remind you, does our shipping suffer by the attacks of the enemy, but also the fertility of its importing power is reduced by many of the precautions and measures which we must take to master and dominate the attacks which are made upon us.

But our strength is growing every week. The American destroyers which reached us in the autumn and winter are increasingly coming into action. Our flotillas are growing in number. Our air power over the island and over the seas is growing fast. We are striking back with increasing effect. Only yesterday I received the news of the certain destruction of three German U-boats. Not since October 13, 1939, had I been cheered by such delectable tidings of a triple event.

It is my rule, as you know, not to conceal the gravity of the danger from our people, and therefore I have a right to be believed when I also proclaim our confidence that we shall overcome them. But anyone can see how bitter is the need of Hitler and his gang to cut the sea roads between Great Britain and the United States, and, having divided these mighty Powers, to destroy them one by one. Therefore we must regard this Battle of the Atlantic as one of the most momentous ever fought in all the annals of war. Therefore, Mr Winant, you come to us at a grand turning-point in the world's history. We rejoice to have you with us in these days of storm and trial, because we know we have a friend and a faithful comrade who will 'report us and our cause aright'. But no one who has met you can doubt that you hold, and embody in a strong and intense degree, the convictions and ideals which in the name of American democracy President Roosevelt has proclaimed.

In the last few months we have had a succession of eminent American citizens visiting these storm-beaten shores and finding them unconquered and unconquerable – Mr Hopkins, Mr Willkie, Colonel Donovan, and now today we have here Mr Harriman and yourself. I have dwelt with all these men in mind and spirit, and there is one thing I have discerned in them all – they would be ready to give their lives, nay, be proud to give their lives, rather than that the good cause should be trampled down and the darkness of barbarism again engulf mankind. Mr Ambassador, you share our purpose, you will share our dangers, you will share our anxieties, you shall share our secrets, and the day will come when the British Empire and the United States will share together the solemn but splendid duties which are the crown of victory.

YUGOSLAVIA INVADED

9 April 1941

House of Commons

On 6 April Germany invaded Yugoslavia and Greece. By 24 April Greece had surrendered, but Yugoslavia struggled on defiant.

I therefore turn to the story of Yugoslavia. This valiant, steadfast people whose history for centuries has been a struggle for life, and who owe their survival to their mountains and to their fighting qualities, made every endeavour to placate the Nazi monster. If they had made common cause with the Greeks when the Greeks, having been attacked by Italy, hurled back the invaders, the complete destruction of the Italian armies in Albania could certainly and swiftly have been achieved long before the German forces could have reached the theatre of war. And even in January and February of this year, this extraordinary military opportunity was still open. But the Government of Prince Paul, untaught by the fate of so many of the smaller countries of Europe, not only observed the strictest neutrality and refused even to enter into effective Staff conversations with Greece or with Turkey or with us, but hugged the delusion that they could preserve their independence by patching up some sort of pact or compromise with Hitler. Once again we saw the odious German poisoning technique employed. In this case, however, it was to the Government rather than to the nation that the doses and the inoculations were administered. The process was not hurried. Why should it have been? All the time the German armies and air force were massing in Bulgaria. From a few handfuls of tourists, admiring the beauty of the Bulgarian landscape in the wintry weather, the German forces grew to 7, 12, 20, and finally to 25 divisions. Presently, the weak and unfortunate Prince, and afterwards his Ministers, were summoned, like others before them, to Herr Hitler's footstool, and a pact was signed which would have given Germany complete control not only over the body but over the soul of the Slav nation. Then at last the people of Yugoslavia saw their peril, and with a universal spasm of revolt and national resurgence very similar to that which in 1808 convulsed and glorified the people of Spain, they swept from power those who were leading them into a shameful tutelage, and resolved at the eleventh hour to guard their freedom and their honour with their lives. All this happened only a fortnight ago.

A boa constrictor who had already covered his prey with his foul saliva and then had it suddenly wrested from his coils, would be in an amiable mood compared with Hitler, Goering, Ribbentrop and the rest of the Nazi gang when they experienced this bitter disappointment. A frightful vengeance was vowed against the Southern Slavs. Rapid, perhaps hurried, redispositions were made of the German forces and German diplomacy. Hungary was offered large territorial gains to become the accomplice in the assault upon a friendly neighbour with whom she had just signed a solemn pact of friendship and non-aggression. Count Teleki preferred to take his own life rather than join in such a deed of shame. A heavy forward movement of the German armies already gathered in and dominating Austria was set in motion through Hungary to the northern frontier of Yugoslavia. A ferocious howl of hatred from the supreme miscreant was the signal for the actual invasion. The open city of Belgrade was laid in ashes, and at the same time a tremendous drive by the German armoured forces, which had been so improvidently allowed to gather in Bulgaria, was launched westward into southern Serbia. And as it was no longer worthwhile to keep up the farce of love for Greece, other powerful forces rolled forward into Greece, where they were at once unflinchingly encountered, and have alrady sustained more than one bloody repulse at the hands of that heroic Army. The British and Imperial troops have not up to the present been engaged. Further than this I cannot, at the moment, go.

'WESTWARD LOOK, THE LAND IS BRIGHT'

27 April 1941

Broadcast, London

As Britain fought on alone against the might of Nazi Germany, American military supplies and the Atlantic sea-lanes played a vital role in Britain's survival. In reply to Roosevelt's verse from Longfellow, Churchill ends this broadcast with the emotive lines of Arthur Hugh Clough from 'Say Not the Struggle Naught Availeth'.

I was asked last week whether I was aware of some uneasiness which it was said existed in the country on account of the gravity, as it was described, of the war situation. So I thought it would be a good thing to go and see for myself what this 'uneasiness' amounted to, and I went to some of our great cities and seaports which had been most heavily bombed, and to some of the places where the poorest people had got it worst. I have come back not only reassured, but refreshed. To leave the offices of Whitehall with their ceaseless hum of activity and stress, and to go out to the front, by which I mean the streets and wharves of London or Liverpool, Manchester, Cardiff, Swansea or Bristol, is like going out of a hothouse on to the bridge of a fighting ship. It is a tonic which I should recommend any who are suffering from fretfulness to take in strong doses when they have need of it.

It is quite true that I have seen many painful scenes of havoc, and of fine buildings and acres of cottage homes blasted into rubble-heaps of ruin. But it is just in those very places where the malice of the savage enemy has done its worst, and where the ordeal of the men, women and children has been most severe, that I found their morale most high and splendid. Indeed, I felt encompassed by an exaltation of spirit in the people which seemed to lift mankind and its troubles above the level of material facts into that joyous serenity we think belongs to a better world than this.

Of their kindness to me I cannot speak, because I have never sought it or dreamed of it, and can never deserve it. I can only assure you that I and my colleagues, or comrades rather – for that is what they are – will toil with every scrap of life and strength, according to the lights that are granted to us, not to fail these people or be wholly unworthy of their faithful and generous regard. The British nation is stirred and moved as it has never been at any time in its long, eventful, famous history, and it is no hackneyed trope of speech to say that they mean to conquer or to die.

What a triumph the life of these battered cities is, over the worst that fire and bomb can do. What a vindication of the civilised and decent way of living we have been trying to work for and work towards in our Island. What a proof of the virtues of free institutions. What a test of the quality of our local authorities, and of institutions and customs and societies so steadily built. This ordeal by fire has even in a certain sense exhilarated the manhood and womanhood of Britain. The sublime but also terrible and sombre experiences and emotions of the battlefield which for centuries had been reserved for the soldiers and sailors, are now shared, for good or ill, by the entire population. All are proud to be under the fire of the enemy. Old men, little children, the crippled veterans of former wars, aged women, the ordinary hard-pressed citizen or subject of the King, as he likes to call himself, the sturdy workmen who swing the hammers or load the ships; skilful craftsmen; the members of every kind of ARP service, are proud to feel that they stand in the line together with our fighting men, when one of the greatest of causes is being fought out, as fought out it will be, to the end. This is indeed the grand heroic period of our history, and the light of glory shines on all.

You may imagine how deeply I feel my own responsibility to all these people; my responsibility to bear my part in bringing them safely out of this long, stern, scowling valley through which we are marching, and not to demand from them their sacrifices and exertions in vain.

I have thought in this difficult period, when so much fighting and so many critical and complicated manoeuvres are going on, that it is above all things important that our policy and conduct should be upon the highest level, and that honour should be our guide. Very few people realise how small were the forces with which General Wavell, that fine Commander whom we cheered in good days and will back through bad – how small were the forces which took the bulk of the Italian masses in Libya prisoners. In none of his successive victories could General Wavell maintain in the desert or bring into action more than two divisions, or about 30,000 men. When we reached Benghazi, and what was left of Mussolini's legions scurried back along the dusty road to Tripoli, a call was made upon us which we could not resist. Let me tell you about that call.

You will remember how in November the Italian Dictator fell upon the unoffending Greeks, and without reason and without warning invaded their country, and how the Greek nation, reviving their classic fame, hurled his armies back at the double-quick. Meanwhile Hitler, who had been creeping and worming his way steadily forward, doping and poisoning and pinioning, one after the other, Hungary, Rumania and Bulgaria, suddenly made it clear that he would come to the rescue of his fellow-criminal. The lack of unity among the Balkan States had enabled him to build up a mighty army in their midst. While nearly all the Greek troops were busy beating the Italians, the tremendous German military machine suddenly towered up on their other frontier. In their mortal peril the Greeks turned to us for succour. Strained as were our own resources, we could not say them nay. By solemn guarantee given before the war, Great Britain had promised them her help. They declared they would fight for their native soil even if neither of their neighbours made common cause with them, and even if we left them to their fate. But we could not do that. There are rules against that kind of thing; and to break those rules would be fatal to the honour of the British Empire, without which we could neither hope nor deserve to win this hard war. Military defeat or miscalculation can be redeemed. The fortunes of war are fickle and changing. But an act of shame would deprive us of the respect which we now enjoy throughout the world, and this would sap the vitals of our strength.

During the last year we have gained by our bearing and conduct a potent hold upon the sentiments of the people of the United States. Never, never in our history, have we been held in such admiration and regard across the Atlantic Ocean. In that great Republic, now in much travail and stress of soul, it is customary to use all the many valid, solid arguments about American interests and American safety, which depend upon the destruction of Hitler and his foul gang and even fouler doctrines. But in the long run – believe me, for I know – the action of the United States will be dictated, not by methodical calculations of profit and loss, but by moral sentiment, and by that gleaming flash of resolve which lifts the hearts of men and nations, and springs from the spiritual foundations of human life itself.

We, for our part, were of course bound to hearken to the Greek appeal to the utmost limit of our strength. We put the case to the Dominions of Australia and New Zealand, and their Governments, without in any way ignoring the hazards, told us that they felt the same as we did. So an important part of the mobile portion of the Army of the Nile was sent to Greece in fulfilment of our pledge. It happened that the divisions available and best suited to this task were from New Zealand and Australia, and that only about half the troops who took part in this dangerous expedition came from the Mother Country. I see the German propaganda is trying to make bad blood between us and Australia by making out that we have used them to do what we would not have asked of the British Army. I shall leave it to Australia to deal with that taunt.

Let us see what has happened. We knew, of course, that the forces we could send to Greece would not by themselves alone be sufficient to stem the German tide of invasion. But there was a very real hope that the neighbours of Greece would by our intervention be drawn to stand in the line together with her while time remained. How nearly that came off will be known some day. The tragedy of Yugoslavia has been that these brave people had a government who hoped to purchase an ignoble immunity by submission to the Nazi will. Thus when at last the people of Yugoslavia found out where they were being taken, and rose in one spontaneous surge of revolt, they saved the soul and future of their country: but it was already too late to save its territory. They had no time to mobilise their armies. They were struck down by the ruthless and highly-mechanised Hun before they could even bring their armies into the field. Great disasters have occurred in the Balkans. Yugoslavia has been beaten down. Only in the mountains can she continue her resistance. The Greeks have been overwhelmed. Their victorious Albanian army has been cut off and forced to surrender, and it has been left to the Anzacs and their British comrades to fight their way back to the sea, leaving their mark on all who hindered them.

I turn aside from the stony path we have to tread, to indulge a moment of lighter relief. I daresay you have read in the newspapers that, by a special proclamation, the Italian Dictator has congratulated the Italian army in Albania on the glorious laurels they have gained by their victory over the Greeks. Here surely is the world's record in the domain of the ridiculous and the contemptible. This whipped jackal, Mussolini, who to save his own skin has made all Italy a vassal state of Hitler's Empire comes frisking up at the side of the German tiger with yelpings not only of appetite – that can be understood – but even of triumph. Different things strike different people in different ways. But I am sure there are a great many millions in the British Empire and in the United States, who will find a new object in life in making sure that when we come to the final reckoning this absurd impostor will be abandoned to public justice and universal scorn.

While these grievous events were taking place in the Balkan Peninsula and in Greece, our forces in Libya have sustained a vexatious and damaging defeat. The Germans advanced sooner and in greater strength than we or our Generals expected. The bulk of our armoured troops, which had played such a decisive part in beating the Italians, had to be refitted, and the single armoured brigade which had been judged sufficient to hold the frontier till about the middle of May was worsted and its vehicles largely destroyed by a somewhat stronger German armoured force. Our Infantry, which had not exceeded one division, had to fall back upon the very large Imperial armies that have been assembled and can be nourished and maintained in the fertile delta of the Nile.

Tobruk – the fortress of Tobruk – which flanks any German advance on Egypt, we hold strongly. There we have repulsed many attacks, causing the enemy heavy losses and taking many prisoners. That is how the matter stands in Egypt and on the Libyan front.

We must now expect the war in the Mediterranean on the sea, in the desert, and above all in the air, to become very fierce, varied and widespread. We had cleaned the Italians out of Cyrenaica, and it now lies with us to purge that province of the Germans. That will be a harder task, and we cannot expect to do it at once. You know I never try to make out that defeats are victories. I have never underrated the German as a warrior. Indeed I told you a month ago that the swift, unbroken course of victories which we had gained over the Italians could not possibly continue, and that misfortunes must be expected. There is only one thing certain about war, that it is full of disappointments and also full of mistakes. It remains to be seen, however, whether it is the Germans who have made the mistake in trampling down the Balkan States and in making a river of blood and hate between themselves and the Greek and Yugoslav peoples. It remains also to be seen whether they have made a mistake in their attempt to invade Egypt with the forces and means of supply which they have now got. Taught by experience, I make it a rule not to prophesy about battles which have yet to be fought out. This, however, I will venture to say, that I should be very sorry to see the tasks of the combatants in the Middle East exchanged, and that General Wavell's armies should be in the position of the German invaders. That is only a personal opinion, and I can well understand you may take a different view. It is certain that fresh dangers besides those which threaten Egypt may come upon us in the Mediterranean. The war may spread to Spain and Morocco. It may spread eastward to Turkey and Russia. The Huns may lay their hands for a time upon the granaries of the Ukraine and the oil-wells of the Caucasus. They may dominate the Black Sea. They may dominate the Caspian. Who can tell? We shall do our best to meet them and fight them wherever they go. But there is one thing which is certain. There is one thing which rises out of the vast welter which is sure and solid, and which no one in his senses can mistake. Hitler cannot find safety from avenging justice in the East, in the Middle East, or in the Far East. In order to win this war, he must either conquer this Island by invasion, or he must cut the ocean lifeline which joins us to the United States.

Let us look into these alternatives, if you will bear with me for a few minutes longer. When I spoke to you last, early in February, many people believed the Nazi boastings that the invasion of Britain was about to begin. It has not begun yet, and with every week that passes we grow stronger on the sea, in the air, and in the numbers, quality, training and equipment of the great Armies that now guard our Island. When I compare the position at home as it is today with what it was in the summer of last year, even after making allowance for a much more elaborate mechanical preparation on the part of the enemy, I feel that we have very much to be thankful for, and I believe that, provided our exertions and our vigilance are not relaxed even for a moment, we may be confident that we shall give a very good account of ourselves. More than that it would be boastful to say. Less than that it would be foolish to believe.

But how about our lifeline across the Atlantic? What is to happen if so many of our merchant ships are sunk that we cannot bring in the food we need to nourish our brave people? What if the supplies of war materials and war weapons which the United States are seeking to send us in such enormous quantities should in large part be sunk on the way? What is to happen then? In February, as you may remember, that bad man in one of his raving outbursts threatened us with a terrifying increase in the numbers and activities of his U-boats and in his air attack – not only on our Island but, thanks to his use of French and Norwegian harbours, and thanks to the denial to us of the Irish bases – upon our shipping far out into the Atlantic. We have taken and are taking all possible measures to meet this deadly attack, and we are now fighting against it with might and main. That is what is called the Battle of the Atlantic, which in order to survive we have got to win on salt water just as decisively as we had to win the Battle of Britain last August and September in the air.

Wonderful exertions have been made by our Navy and Air Force; by the hundreds of mine-sweeping vessels which with their marvellous appliances keep our ports clear in spite of all the enemy can do; by the men who build and repair our immense fleets of merchant ships; by the men who load and unload them; and need I say by the officers and men of the Merchant Navy who go out in all weathers and in the teeth of all dangers to fight for the life of their native land and for a cause they comprehend and serve. Still, when you think how easy it is to sink ships at sea and how hard it is to build them and protect them, and when you remember that we have never less than two thousand ships afloat and three or four hundred in the danger zone; when you think of the great armies we are maintaining and reinforcing in the East, and of the world-wide traffic we have to carry on – when you remember all this, can you wonder that it is the Battle of the Atlantic which holds the first place in the thoughts of those upon whom rests the responsibility for procuring the victory?

It was therefore with indescribable relief that I learned of the tremendous decisions lately taken by the President and people of the United States. The American Fleet and flying boats have been ordered to patrol the wide waters of the Western Hemisphere, and to warn the peaceful shipping of all nations outside the combat zone of the presence of lurking U-boats or raiding cruisers belonging to the two aggressor nations. We British shall therefore be able to concentrate our protecting forces far more upon the routes nearer home, and to take a far heavier toll of the U-boats there. I have felt for some time that something like this was bound to happen. The President and Congress of the United States, having newly fortified themselves by contact with their electors, have solemnly pledged their aid to Britain in this war because they deem our cause just, and because they know their own interests and safety would be endangered if we were destroyed. They are taxing themselves heavily. They have passed great legislation. They have turned a large part of their gigantic industry to making the munitions which we need. They have even given us or lent us valuable weapons of their own. I could not believe that they would allow the high purposes to which they have set themselves to be frustrated and the products of their skill and labour sunk to the bottom of the sea. U-boat warfare as conducted by Germany is entirely contrary to international agreements freely subscribed to by Germany only a few years ago. There is no effective blockade, but only a merciless murder and marauding over wide, indiscriminate areas utterly beyond the control of the German seapower. When I said ten weeks ago: 'Give us the tools and we will finish the job,' I meant, *give* them to us: put them within our reach – and that is what it now seems the Americans are going to do. And that is why I feel a very strong conviction that though the Battle of the Atlantic will be long and hard, and its issue is by no means yet determined, it has entered upon a more grim but at the same time a far more favourable phase. When you come to think of it, the United States are very closely bound up with us now, and have engaged themselves deeply in giving us moral, material, and, within the limits I have mentioned, naval support.

It is worth while therefore to take a look on both sides of the ocean at the forces which are facing each other in this awful struggle, from which there can be no drawing back. No prudent and far-seeing man can doubt that the eventual and total defeat of Hitler and Mussolini is certain, in view of the respective declared resolves of the British and American democracies. There are less than seventy million malignant Huns – some of whom are curable and others killable – many of whom are already engaged in holding down Austrians, Czechs, Poles, French, and the many other ancient races they now bully and pillage. The peoples of the British Empire and of the United

States number nearly two hundred millions in their homelands and in the British Dominions alone. They possess the unchallengeable command of the oceans, and will soon obtain decisive superiority in the air. They have more wealth, more technical resources, and they make more steel, than the whole of the rest of the world put together. They are determined that the cause of freedom shall not be trampled down, nor the tide of world progress turned backwards, by the criminal Dictators.

While therefore we naturally view with sorrow and anxiety much that is happening in Europe and in Africa, and may happen in Asia, we must not lose our sense of proportion and thus become discouraged or alarmed. When we face with a steady eye the difficulties which lie before us, we may derive new confidence from remembering those we have already overcome. Nothing that is happening now is comparable in gravity with the dangers through which we passed last year. Nothing that can happen in the East is comparable with what is happening in the West.

Last time I spoke to you I quoted the lines of Longfellow which President Roosevelt had written out for me in his own hand. I have some other lines which are less well known but which seem apt and appropriate to our fortunes tonight, and I believe they will be so judged wherever the English language is spoken or the flag of freedom flies:

> For while the tired waves, vainly breaking,
> Seem here no painful inch to gain,
> Far back, through creeks and inlets making,
> Comes silent, flooding in, the main.
> And not by eastern windows only,
> When daylight comes, comes in the light;
> In front the sun climbs slow, how slowly!
> But westward, look, the land is bright.

VOTE OF CONFIDENCE

7 May 1941

House of Commons

The arrival in North Africa, on 12 February, of Field Marshal Erwin Rommel with strong German reinforcements, drastically altered the balance of power in the Libyan desert. On 31 March the Germans launched their first offensive and the British, whose forces had been weakened in a vain effort to support Greece, suffered a severe reverse. With a terrible toll being taken in the Battle of the Atlantic, voices of criticism were raised and the Prime Minister determined to bring his critics, who included the former Prime Minister, Lloyd George, into the open by demanding a Vote of Confidence. The vote was won by 447 votes to 3, but it was to be Churchill's last speech in the old House of Commons: three days later the Chamber was destroyed by an enemy bomb.

This Debate, as I think will be agreed on all hands, has been marked by a high sense of discretion and a high degree of responsibility in all who have taken part in it. If there were any speech I could single out especially for praise, it would, I think, be the last, to which we have just listened. The Member for Derby [Mr Noel-Baker] is a great devotee of the Greek cause, and all that he has said has shown how deeply he has studied the articulation of their defences and, of course, their fortunes. If there were any speech which I felt was not particularly exhilarating, it was the speech of the Member for Carnarvon Boroughs [Mr Lloyd George], who honoured us by one of his always deeply important and much valued appearances in the House. . . .

I must, however, say that I did not think Mr Lloyd George's speech was particularly helpful at a period of what he himself called discouragement and disheartenment. It was not the sort of speech which one would have expected from the great war leader of former days, who was accustomed to brush aside despondency and alarm, and push on irresistibly towards the final goal. It was the sort of speech with which, I imagine, the illustrious and venerable Marshal Pétain might well have enlivened the closing days of M. Reynaud's Cabinet. But in one respect I am grateful to my right hon. Friend for the note which he struck, because if anything could make it clearer that we ought to close our Debate by a Vote of Confidence, it is the kind of speech which he delivered, and the kind of speeches we have heard from some of the ablest and most eminent Members of the House. I think the Government were right to put down a Motion of Confidence, because after our reverses and disappointments in the field, His Majesty's Government have a right to know where they stand with the House of Commons, and where the House of Commons stands with the country. Still more is this knowledge important for the sake of foreign nations, especially nations which are balancing their policy at the present time, and who ought to be left in no doubt about the stability or otherwise of this resolved and obstinate war Government. Questions are asked, conversations take place in the Lobbies, paragraphs are written in the political columns of the newspapers, and before you know where you are, you hear in all the Embassies with which we are in relation queries, 'Will the Government last? – Are they going to break up? – Will there be a change of administration and a change of policy?'

I think it is essential, considering the tremendous issues which are at stake, and, not to exaggerate, the frightful risks we are all going to run, and are running, that we should have certitude on these matters. In enemy countries they take a lively interest in our proceedings, and I flatter myself that high hopes are entertained that all will not go well with His Majesty's present advisers. The only way in which these doubts can be removed and these expectations disappointed is by a full Debate followed by a Division, and the Government are entitled to ask that such a Vote shall express itself in unmistakable terms. I see that one of the newspapers, which is described as a supporter of the Government, and which supports us by being the most active in keeping us up to the mark – like the Noble Lord the Member for Horsham [Earl Winterton], now relieved from all necessity of keeping himself up to the mark – has deplored the fact of this Motion of Confidence being proposed, because such a procedure might lead some Members to make speeches in favour of the Government, whereas it would be much more useful if the Debate consisted entirely of informative criticism. I am not one, and I should be the last, unduly to resent unfair criticism, or even fair criticism, which is so much more searching. I have been a critic myself – I cannot at all see how I should have stood the test of being a mere spectator in the drama which is now passing. But there is a kind of criticism which is a little irritating. It is like that of a bystander who, when he sees a team of horses dragging a heavy wagon painfully up a hill, cuts a switch from the fence, and there are many switches, and belabours them lustily. He may well be animated by a benevolent purpose, and who shall say the horses may not benefit from his efforts, and the wagon get quicker to the top of the hill?

I think that it would be a pity if this important and critical Debate at this moment which my right hon. Friend describes as disheartening and discouraging, consisted solely of critical and condemnatory speeches, because, apart from the inartistic monotony, it would tend to give a distorted impression to many important and interested foreign observers who are not very well acquainted with our Parliamentary or political affairs. Therefore I ask the House for a Vote of Confidence. I hope that those, if such there be, who sincerely in their hearts believe that we are not doing our best and that they could do much better, I hope that they will carry their opinion to its logical and ultimate conclusion in the Lobby. Here I must point out, only for the benefit of foreign countries, that they would run no risk in doing so. They are answerable only to their consciences and to their constituents. It is a free Parliament in a free country. We have succeeded in maintaining, under difficulties which are unprecedented, and in dangers which, in some cases, might well be mortal, the whole process and reality of Parliamentary institutions. I am proud of this. It is one of the things for which we are fighting. Moreover, I cannot imagine that any man would want to bear, or consent to bear, the kind of burden which falls upon the principal Ministers in the Government, or upon the head of the Government in this terrible war, unless he were sustained, and continually sustained, by strong convinced support, not only of the House of Commons, but of the nation to which the House of Commons is itself responsible.

It is very natural that the House should not be entirely satisfied with the recent turn of events in the Middle East, and that some Members should be acutely disappointed that we have not been able to defend Greece successfully against the Italian or German armies, and that we should have been unable to keep or extend our conquests in Libya. This sudden darkening of the landscape, after we had been cheered by a long succession of victories over the Italians, is particularly painful. For myself, I must confess that I watched the fate of Greece, after her repulse of the Italian invader, with agony. The only relief I feel is that everything in human power was done by us and that our honour as a nation is clear. If anything could add a pang to this emotion, it would be the knowledge we had of the approaching and impending outrage, with so little power to avert from this heroic and famous people a fate so hideous and so undeserved. . . .

My right hon. Friend the Member of Devonport [Mr Hore-Belisha], who is so far-seeing now that we have lost his services and who told us at the end of November, 1939, that we were comfortably winning the war, had the temerity yesterday to raise the subject of our admitted shortage of tanks. There is one very simple point about tanks, which I think he might have mentioned to us, in the years preceding the war when he was at the head of the War Office and had the opportunity of the highest technical advice. In the last war, tanks were built to go three or four miles an hour and to stand up to rifle or machine-gun bullets. In the interval the process of mechanical science had advanced so much that it became possible to make a tank which could go 15, 20 or 25 miles an hour and stand up to cannon fire. That was a great revolution, by which Hitler has profited. That is a simple fact which was perfectly well known to the military and technical services three or four years before the war. It did not spring from German brains. It sprang from British brains, and from brains like those of General de Gaulle in France, and it has been exploited and turned to our grievous injury by the uninventive but highly competent and imitative Germans. The British Tank Corps knew all about it and wrote it down, but apparently my right hon. Friend did not take it in – at any rate, he did not mention it to us in those simple terms, and, indeed, it may be that the point may not have struck him until now. It would have been a very valuable contribution to our pre-war preparations. My right hon. Friend played a worthy part in bringing in compulsory service. I should not have referred to this matter if he had not endeavoured to give the House a sort of idea of his super-prevision and super-efficiency and shown himself so aggressive when, I think, with all goodwill, he sometimes stands in need of some humility in regard to the past.

Let me tell him that we are now making every month as many heavy tanks as there existed in the whole British Army at the time he left the War Office – and that we shall very soon, before the end of this year, be producing nearly double that number. This takes no account of the immense productive efforts in the United States. I only say this to him by way of reassuring him that the good work which he did, the foundations which he laid, have not been left to stand where they were when he went out of office. He must learn to 'forgive us our trespasses as we forgive them that trespass against us.'

My right hon. Friend the Member for Carnarvon Boroughs [Mr Lloyd George] made his usual criticisms about the composition and character of the Government, of the war control and of the War Cabinet, and the House is entitled to know, has a right to know, who are responsible for the conduct of the war. The War Cabinet consists of eight members, five of whom have no regular Department, and three of whom represent the main organisms of the State, to wit, Foreign Affairs, Finance and Labour, which in their different ways come into every great question that has to be settled. That is the body which gives its broad sanction to the main policy and conduct of the war. Under their authority, the Chiefs of Staff of the three Services sit each day together, and I, as Prime Minister and Minister of Defence, convene them and preside over them when I think it necessary, inviting, when business requires it, the three Service Ministers. All large issues of military policy are brought before the Defence Committee, which has for several months consisted of the three Chiefs of Staff, the three Service Ministers, and four members of the War Cabinet, namely, myself, the Lord Privy Seal, who has no Department, the Foreign Secretary, and Lord Beaverbrook. This is the body, this is the machine; it works easily and flexibly at the present time, and I do not propose to make any changes in it until further advised.

My right hon. Friend spoke of the great importance of my being surrounded by people who would stand up to me and say, 'No, No, No.' Why, good gracious, has he no idea how strong the negative principle is in the constitution and working of the British war-making machine? The difficulty is not, I assure him, to have more brakes put on the wheels; the difficulty is to get more impetus and speed behind it. At one moment we are asked to emulate the Germans in their audacity and vigour, and the next moment the Prime Minister is to be assisted by being surrounded by a number of 'No-men' to resist me at every point and prevent me from making anything in the nature of a speedy, rapid and, above all, positive constructive decision.

However, I must say that, in this whole business of Libya and Greece, I can assure the House that no violence has been done to expert military opinion, either in the Chiefs of Staff Committee at home or in the generals commanding in the field. All decisions have been taken unitedly and freely and in good will, in response to the hard pressure of events. I would make it clear, however, that, in certain circumstances or emergencies, the responsible political Minister representing the Government of the country would not hesitate to assume responsibility for decisions which might have to be taken, and I, personally, as head of the Government, obviously assume that responsibility in the most direct personal form. It follows, therefore, when all is said and done, that I am the one whose head should be cut off if we do not win the war. I am very ready that this should be so, because, as my hon. Friend the Member for Seaham [Mr Shinwell] feelingly reminded us yesterday, most of the Members of the House would probably experience an even more unpleasant fate at the hands of the triumphant Hun.

I notice a tendency in some quarters, especially abroad, to talk about the Middle East as if we could afford to lose our position there and yet carry on the war to victory on the oceans and in the air. Stated as an academic and strategic fact, that may be true, but do not let anyone underrate the gravity of the issues which are being fought for in the Nile Valley. The loss of the Nile Valley and the Suez Canal and the loss of our position in the Mediterranean, as well as the loss of Malta, would be among the heaviest blows which we could sustain. We are determined to fight for them with all the resources of the British Empire, and we have every reason to believe that we shall be successful. General Wavell has under his orders at the present moment nearly 500,000 men. . . .

I ask you to witness, Mr Speaker, that I have never promised anything or offered anything but blood, tears, toil and sweat, to which I will now add our fair share of mistakes, shortcomings and disappointments, and also that this may go on for a very long time, at the end of which I firmly believe – though it is not a promise or a guarantee, only a profession of faith – that there will be complete, absolute and final victory. . . .

In some quarters of the House, or at any rate among some Members, there is a very acute realisation of the gravity of our problems and of our dangers. I have never underrated them. I feel we are fighting for life and survival from day to day and from hour to hour. But, believe me, Herr Hitler has his problems, too, and if we only remain united and strive our utmost to increase our exertions, and work like one great family, standing together and helping each other, as 5,000,000 families in Britain are doing today under the fire of the enemy, I cannot conceive how anyone can doubt that victory will crown the good cause we serve. Government and Parliament alike have to be worthy of the undaunted and unconquerable people who give us their trust and who give their country their all.

It is a year almost to a day since, in the crash of the disastrous Battle of France, His Majesty's present Administration was formed. Men of all parties, duly authorised by their parties, joined hands together to fight this business to the end. That was a dark hour, and little did we know what storms and perils lay before us, and little did Herr Hitler know, when in June, 1940, he received the total capitulation of France and when he expected to be master of all Europe in a few weeks and the world in a few years, that ten months later, in May, 1941, he would be appealing to the much-tried German people to prepare themselves for the war of 1942. When I look back on the perils which have been overcome, upon the great mountain waves through which the gallant ship has driven, when I remember all that has gone wrong, and remember also all that has gone right, I feel sure we have no need to fear the tempest. Let it roar, and let it rage. We shall come through.

'THE *BISMARCK* IS SUNK!'

27 May 1941

House of Commons

At this critical juncture in the war – with British armour in retreat in North Africa and superior German air power compelling the evacuation of British forces from Crete – the German battleship Bismarck, *accompanied by the cruiser* Prinz Eugen, *sailed from Bergen in Norway, intercepting and sinking in the Denmark Strait the British battle-cruiser* Hood, *the fastest capital ship in the world. All the resources of the Home Fleet were deployed to counter this new peril and, just after Churchill sat down, he was handed a note to say that the* Bismarck *had been sunk after being crippled by attacks by aircraft from the carrier* Ark Royal.

On Wednesday of last week, 21st May, the new German battleship, the *Bismarck*, accompanied by the new 8-in. gun cruiser *Prince Eugen*, was discovered by our air reconnaissance at Bergen, and on Thursday, 22nd May, it was known that they had left. Many arrangements were made to intercept them should they attempt, as seemed probable, to break out into the Atlantic Ocean with a view to striking at our convoys from the United States. During the night of 23rd to 24th our cruisers got into visual contact with them as they were passing through the Denmark Strait between Iceland and Greenland. At dawn on Saturday morning the *Prince of Wales* and the *Hood* intercepted the two enemy vessels. I have no detailed account of the action, because events have been moving so rapidly, but the *Hood* was struck at about 23,000 yards by a shell which penetrated into one of her magazines, and blew up, leaving only very few survivors. This splendid vessel, designed 23 years ago, is a serious loss to the Royal Navy, and even more so are the men and officers who manned her.

During the whole of Saturday our ships remained in touch with the *Bismarck* and her consort. In the night aircraft of the Fleet Air Arm from the *Victorious* struck the *Bismarck* with a torpedo, and arrangements were made for effective battle at dawn yesterday morning; but as the night wore on the weather deteriorated, the visibility decreased, and the *Bismarck*, by making a sharp turn, shook off the pursuit. I do not know what has happened to the *Prince Eugen*, but measures are being taken in respect of her. Yesterday, shortly before midday, a Catalina aircraft – one of the considerable number of these very far-ranging scouting aeroplanes which have been sent to us by the United States – picked up the *Bismarck*, and it was seen that she was apparently making for the French ports – Brest or Saint Nazaire. On this, further rapid dispositions were made by the Admiralty and by the Commander-in-Chief, and, of course, I may say that the moment the *Bismarck* was known to be at sea the whole apparatus of our ocean control came into play, very far-reaching combinations began to work, and from yesterday afternoon – I have not had time to prepare a detailed statement – Fleet Air Arm torpedo-carrying seaplanes from the *Ark Royal* made a succession of attacks upon the *Bismarck*, which now appears to be alone and without her consort. About midnight we learned that the *Bismarck* had been struck by two torpedoes, one amidships and the other astern. This second torpedo apparently affected the steering of the ship, for not only was she reduced to a very slow speed, but she continued making uncontrollable circles in the sea. While in this condition she was attacked by one of our flotillas, and hit by two more torpedoes, which brought her virtually to a standstill, far from help and far outside the range at which the enemy bomber aircraft from the French coast could have come upon the scene. This morning, at daylight or shortly after daylight, the *Bismarck* was attacked by the British pursuing battleships. I do not know what were the results of the bombardment; it appears, however, that the *Bismarck* was not sunk by gunfire, and she will now be dispatched by torpedo. It is thought that this is now proceeding, and it is also thought that there cannot be any lengthy delay in disposing of this vessel.

Great as is our loss in the *Hood*, the *Bismarck* must be regarded as the most powerful, as she is the newest, battleship in the world; and this striking of her from the German Navy is a very definite simplification of the task of maintaining the effective mastery of the Northern seas and the maintenance of the Northern blockade. I daresay that in a few days it will be possible to give a much more detailed account, but the essentials are before the House, and although there is shade as well as light in this picture, I feel that we have every reason to be satisfied with the outcome of this fierce and memorable naval encounter.

[*Later.*] I do not know whether I might venture, with great respect, to intervene for one moment. I have just received news that the *Bismarck* is sunk.

'OUR SOLID, STUBBORN STRENGTH'

12 June 1941

Dominion High Commissioners and Allied Countries' Ministers Conference, London

In the twenty-second month of the war against Nazism we meet here in this old Palace of St James's, itself not unscarred by the fire of the enemy, in order to proclaim the high purposes and resolves of the lawful constitutional Governments of Europe whose countries have been overrun; and we meet here also to cheer the hopes of free men and free peoples throughout the world. Here before us on the table lie the title-deeds of ten nations or States whose soil has been invaded and polluted, and whose men, women, and children lie prostrate or writhing under the Hitler yoke. But here also, duly authorised by the Parliament and democracy of Britain, are gathered the servants of the ancient British Monarchy and the accredited representatives of the British Dominions beyond the seas, of Canada, Australia, New Zealand, and South Africa, of the Empire of India, of Burma, and of our Colonies in every quarter of the globe. They have drawn their swords in this cause. They will never let them fall till life is gone or victory is won. Here we meet, while from across the Atlantic Ocean the hammers and lathes of the United States signal in a rising hum their message of encouragement and their promise of swift and ever-growing aid.

What tragedies, what horrors, what crimes have Hitler and all that Hitler stands for brought upon Europe and the world! The ruins of Warsaw, of Rotterdam, of Belgrade are monuments which will long recall to future generations the outrage of the unopposed air-bombing applied with calculated scientific cruelty to helpless populations. Here in London and throughout the cities of our Island, and in Ireland, there may also be seen the marks of devastation. They are being repaid, and presently they will be more than repaid.

But far worse than these visible injuries is the misery of the conquered peoples. We see them hounded, terrorised, exploited. Their manhood by the million is forced to work under conditions indistinguishable in many cases from actual slavery. Their goods and chattels are pillaged, or filched for worthless money. Their homes, their daily life are pried into and spied upon by the all-pervading system of secret political police which, having reduced the Germans themselves to abject docility, now stalk the streets and byways of a dozen lands. Their religious faiths are affronted, persecuted, or oppressed in the interests of a fantastic paganism devised to perpetuate the worship and sustain the tyranny of one abominable creature. Their traditions, their culture, their laws, their institutions, social and political alike, are suppressed by force or undermined by subtle, coldly-planned intrigue.

The prisons of the Continent no longer suffice. The concentration camps are overcrowded. Every dawn the German volleys crack. Czechs, Poles, Dutchmen, Norwegians, Yugoslavs and Greeks, Frenchmen, Belgians, Luxembourgers, make the great sacrifice for faith and country. A vile race of quislings – to use the new word which will carry the scorn of mankind down the centuries – is hired to fawn upon the conqueror, to collaborate in his designs, and to enforce his rule upon their fellow-countrymen, while grovelling low themselves. Such is the plight of once glorious Europe, and such are the atrocities against which we are in arms.

It is upon this foundation that Hitler, with his tattered lackey Mussolini at his tail and Admiral Darlan frisking by his side, pretends to build out of hatred, appetite, and racial assertion a new order for Europe. Never did so mocking a fantasy obsess the mind of mortal man. We cannot tell what the course of this fell war will be as it spreads remorselessly through ever-wider regions. We know it will be hard, we expect it will be long; we cannot predict or measure its episodes or its tribulations. But one thing is certain, one thing is sure, one thing stands out stark and undeniable, massive and unassailable, for all the world to see.

It will not be by German hands that the structure of Europe will be rebuilt or the union of the European family achieved. In every country into which the German armies and the Nazi police have broken there has sprung up from the soil a hatred of the German name and a contempt for the Nazi creed which the passage of hundreds of years will not efface from human memory. We cannot yet see how deliverance will come, or when it will come, but nothing is more certain than that every trace of Hitler's footsteps, every stain of his infected and corroding fingers will be sponged and purged and, if need be, blasted from the surface of the earth.

We are here to affirm and fortify our union in that ceaseless and unwearying effort which must be made if the captive peoples are to be set free. A year ago His Majesty's Government was left alone to face the storm, and to many of our friends and enemies alike it may have seemed that our days too were numbered, and that Britain and its institutions would sink for ever beneath the verge. But I may with some pride remind your Excellencies that, even in that dark hour when our Army was disorganised and almost weaponless, when scarcely a gun or a tank remained in Britain, when almost all our stores and ammunitions had been lost in France, never for one moment did the British people dream of making peace with the conqueror, and never for a moment did they despair of the common cause. On the contrary, we proclaimed at that very time to all men, not only to ourselves, our determination not to make peace until every one of the ravaged and enslaved countries was liberated and until the Nazi domination was broken and destroyed.

See how far we have travelled since those breathless days of June a year ago. Our solid, stubborn strength has stood the awful test. We are masters of our own air, and now reach out in ever-growing retribution upon the enemy. The Royal Navy holds the seas. The Italian fleet cowers diminished in harbour, the German Navy is largely crippled or sunk. The murderous raids upon our ports, cities, and factories have been powerless to quench the spirit of the British nation, to stop our national life, or check the immense expansion of our war industry. The food and arms from across the oceans are coming safely in. Full provision to replace all sunken tonnage is being made here, and still more by our friends in the United States. We are becoming an armed community. Our land forces are being perfected in equipment and training.

Hitler may turn and trample this way and that through tortured Europe. He may spread his course far and wide, and carry his curse with him: he may break into Africa or into Asia. But it is here, in this island fortress, that he will have to reckon in the end. We shall strive to resist by land and sea. We shall be on his track wherever he goes. Our air power will continue to teach the German homeland that war is not all loot and triumph.

We shall aid and stir the people of every conquered country to resistance and revolt. We shall break up and derange every effort which Hitler makes to systematise and consolidate his subjugation. He will find no peace, no rest, no halting-place, no parley. And if, driven to desperate hazards, he attempts the invasion of the British Isles, as well he may, we shall not flinch from the supreme trial. With the help of God, of which we must all feel daily conscious, we shall continue steadfast in faith and duty till our task is done.

This, then, is the message which we send forth today to all the States and nations, bond or free, to all the men in all the lands who care for freedom's cause, to our allies and well-wishers in Europe, to our American friends and helpers drawing ever closer in their might across the ocean: this is the message – Lift up your hearts. All will come right. Out of the depths of sorrow and sacrifice will be born again the glory of mankind.

'THE OLD LION'

16 June 1941

*Broadcast, London to the United States
on Receiving an Honorary Degree*

Invoking his American blood, Churchill in his final sentence, 'United we can save the world', appeals to America to join the fray.

I am grateful, President Valentine, for the honour which you have conferred upon me in making me a Doctor of Laws of Rochester University in the State of New York. I am extremely complimented by the expressions of praise and commendation in which you have addressed me, not because I am or ever can be worthy of them, but because they are an expression of American confidence and affection which I shall ever strive to deserve.

But what touches me most in this ceremony is that sense of kinship and of unity which I feel exists between us this afternoon. As I speak from Downing Street to Rochester University and through you to the people of the United States, I almost feel I have the right to do so, because my mother, as you have stated, was born in your city, and here my grandfather, Leonard Jerome, lived for so many years, conducting as a prominent and rising citizen a newspaper with the excellent eighteenth-century title of the *Plain Dealer*.

The great Burke has truly said, 'People will not look forward to posterity who never look backward to their ancestors,' and I feel it most agreeable to recall to you that the Jeromes were rooted for many generations in American soil, and fought in Washington's armies for the independence of the American Colonies and the foundation of the United States. I expect I was on both sides then. And I must say I feel on both sides of the Atlantic Ocean now.

At intervals during the last forty years I have addressed scores of great American audiences in almost every part of the Union. I have learnt to admire the courtesy of these audiences; their sense of fair play; their sovereign sense of humour, never minding the joke that is turned against themselves; their earnest, voracious desire to come to the root of the matter and to be well and truly informed on Old World affairs.

And now, in this time of world storm, when I have been called upon by King and Parliament and with the support of all parties in the State to bear the chief responsibility in Great Britain, and when I have had the supreme honour of speaking for the British nation in its most deadly danger and in its finest hour, it has given me comfort and inspiration to feel that I think as you do, that our hands are joined across the oceans, and that our pulses throb and beat as one. Indeed I will make so bold as to say that here at least, in my mother's birth city of Rochester, I hold a latchkey to American hearts.

Strong tides of emotion, fierce surges of passion, sweep the broad expanses of the Union in this year of fate. In that prodigious travail there are many elemental forces, there is much heart-searching and self-questioning; some pangs, some sorrow, some conflict of voices, but no fear. The world is witnessing the birth throes of a sublime resolve. I shall presume to confess to you that I have no doubts what that resolve will be.

The destiny of mankind is not decided by material computation. When great causes are on the move in the world, stirring all men's souls, drawing them from their firesides, casting aside comfort, wealth and the pursuit of happiness in response to impulses at once awe-striking and irresistible, we learn that we are spirits, not animals, and that something is going on in space and time, and beyond space and time, which, whether we like it or not, spells duty.

A wonderful story is unfolding before our eyes. How it will end we are not allowed to know. But on both sides of the Atlantic we all feel, I repeat, all, that we are a part of it, that our future and that of many generations is at stake. We are sure that the character of human society will be shaped by the resolves we take and the deeds we do. We need not bewail the fact that we have been called upon to face such solemn responsibilities. We may be proud, and even rejoice amid our tribulations, that we have been born at this cardinal time for so great an age and so splendid an opportunity of service here below.

Wickedness, enormous, panoplied, embattled, seemingly triumphant, casts its shadow over Europe and Asia. Laws, customs and traditions are broken up. Justice is cast from her seat. The rights of the weak are trampled down. The grand freedoms of which the President of the United States has spoken so movingly are spurned and chained. The whole stature of man, his genius, his initiative and his nobility, is ground down under systems of mechanical barbarism and of organised and scheduled terror.

For more than a year we British have stood alone, uplifted by your sympathy and respect and sustained by our own unconquerable will-power and by the increasing growth and hopes of your massive aid. In these British Islands that look so small upon the map we stand, the faithful guardians of the rights and dearest hopes of a dozen States and nations now gripped and tormented in a base and cruel servitude. Whatever happens we shall endure to the end.

But what is the explanation of the enslavement of Europe by the German Nazi régime? How did they do it? It is but a few years ago since one united gesture by the peoples, great and small, who are now broken in the dust, would have warded off from mankind the fearful ordeal it has had to undergo. But there was no unity. There was no vision. The nations were pulled down one by one while the others gaped and chattered. One by one, each in his turn, they let themselves be caught. One after another they were felled by brutal violence or poisoned from within by subtle intrigue.

And now the old lion with her lion cubs at her side stands alone against hunters who are armed with deadly weapons and impelled by desperate and destructive rage. Is the tragedy to repeat itself once more? Ah no! This is not the end of the tale. The stars in their courses proclaim the deliverance of mankind. Not so easily shall the onward progress of the peoples be barred. Not so easily shall the lights of freedom die.

But time is short. Every month that passes adds to the length and to the perils of the journey that will have to be made. United we stand. Divided we fall. Divided, the dark age returns. United, we can save and guide the world.

ALLIANCE WITH RUSSIA

22 June 1941

Broadcast, London

On 22 June, in defiance of the Nazi–Soviet Pact, Germany invaded Russia, rapidly overwhelming the Russian armies. Instantly Churchill proclaimed Britain's Alliance with Russia. When, shortly before this speech was delivered, his private secretary, J.R. Colville, remarked on the irony of Churchill allying himself with that same Bolshevism that he had sought to 'strangle in its cradle', Churchill retorted: 'If Hitler invaded Hell, I would make at least a favourable reference to the Devil in the House of Commons!'

I have taken occasion to speak to you tonight because we have reached one of the climacterics of the war. The first of these intense turning-points was a year ago when France fell prostrate under the German hammer, and when we had to face the storm alone. The second was when the Royal Air Force beat the Hun raiders out of the daylight air, and thus warded off the Nazi invasion of our island while we were still ill-armed and ill-prepared. The third turning-point was when the President and Congress of the United States passed the Lease-and-Lend enactment, devoting nearly 2,000 millions sterling of wealth of the New World to help us to defend our liberties and their own. Those were the three climacterics. The fourth is now upon us.

At four o'clock this morning Hitler attacked and invaded Russia. All his usual formalities of perfidy were observed with scrupulous technique. A non-aggression treaty had been solemnly signed and was in force between the two countries. No complaint had been made by Germany of its non-fulfilment. Under its cloak of false confidence, the German armies drew up in immense strength along a line which stretches from the White Sea to the Black Sea; and their air fleets and armoured divisions slowly and methodically took their stations. Then, suddenly, without declaration of war, without even an ultimatum, German bombs rained down from the air upon the Russian cities, the German troops violated the frontiers; and an hour later the German Ambassador, who till the night before was lavishing his assurances of friendship, almost of alliance, upon the Russians, called upon the Russian Foreign Minister to tell him that a state of war existed between Germany and Russia.

Thus was repeated on a far larger scale the same kind of outrage against every form of signed compact and international faith which we have witnessed in Norway, Denmark, Holland and Belgium, and which Hitler's accomplice, the jackal Mussolini, so faithfully imitated in the case of Greece.

All this was no surprise to me. In fact I gave clear and precise warnings to Stalin of what was coming. I gave him warning as I have given warning to others before. I can only hope that this warning did not fall unheeded. All we know at present is that the Russian people are defending their native soil and that their leaders have called upon them to resist to the utmost.

Hitler is a monster of wickedness, insatiable in his lust for blood and plunder. Not content with having all Europe under his heel, or else terrorised into various forms of abject submission, he must now carry his work of butchery and desolation among the vast multitudes of Russia and of Asia. The terrible military machine, which we and the rest of the civilised world so foolishly, so supinely, so insensately allowed the Nazi gangsters to build up year by year from almost nothing, cannot stand idle lest it rust or fall to pieces. It must be in continual motion, grinding up human lives and trampling down the homes and the rights of hundreds of millions of men. Moreover it must be fed, not only with flesh but with oil.

So now this bloodthirsty guttersnipe must launch his mechanised armies upon new fields of slaughter, pillage and devastation. Poor as are the Russian peasants, workmen and soldiers, he must steal from them their daily bread; he must devour their harvests; he must rob them of the oil which drives their ploughs; and thus produce a famine without example in human history. And even the carnage and ruin which his victory, should he gain it – he has not gained it yet – will bring upon the Russian people, will itself be only a stepping-stone to the attempt to plunge the four or five hundred millions who live in China, and the three hundred and fifty millions who live in India, into that bottomless pit of human degradation over which the diabolic emblem of the Swastika flaunts itself. It is not too much to say here this summer evening that the lives and happiness of a thousand million additional people are now menaced with brutal Nazi violence. That is enough to make us hold our breath. But presently I shall show you something else that lies behind, and something that touches very nearly the life of Britain and of the United States.

The Nazi régime is indistinguishable from the worst features of Communism. It is devoid of all theme and principle except appetite and racial domination. It excels all forms of human wickedness in the efficiency of its cruelty and ferocious aggression. No one has been a more consistent opponent of Communism than I have for the last twenty-five years. I will unsay no word that I have spoken about it. But all this fades away before the spectacle which is now unfolding. The past with its crimes, its follies and its tragedies, flashes away. I see the Russian soldiers standing on the threshold of their native land, guarding the fields which their fathers have tilled from time immemorial. I see them guarding their homes where mothers and wives pray – ah yes, for there are times when all pray – for the safety of their loved ones, the return of the breadwinner, of their champion, of their protector. I see the ten thousand villages of Russia, where the means of existence was wrung so hardly from the soil, but where there are still primordial human joys, where maidens laugh and children play. I see advancing upon all this in hideous onslaught the Nazi war machine, with its clanking, heel-clicking, dandified Prussian officers, its crafty expert agents fresh from the cowing and tying-down of a dozen countries. I see also the dull, drilled, docile, brutish masses of the Hun soldiery plodding on like a swarm of crawling locusts. I see the German bombers and fighters in the sky, still smarting from many a British whipping, delighted to find what they believe is an easier and a safer prey.

Behind all this glare, behind all this storm, I see that small group of villainous men who plan, organise and launch this cataract of horrors upon mankind. And then my mind goes back across the years to the days when the Russian armies were our allies against the same deadly foe; when they fought with so much valour and constancy, and helped to gain a victory from all share in which, alas, they were – through no fault of ours – utterly cut off. I have lived through all this, and you will pardon me if I express my feelings and the stir of old memories.

But now I have to declare the decision of His Majesty's Government – and I feel sure it is a decision in which the great Dominions will, in due course, concur – for we must speak out now at once, without a day's delay. I have to make the declaration, but can you doubt what our policy will be? We have but one aim and one single, irrevocable purpose. We are resolved to destroy Hitler and every vestige of the Nazi régime. From this nothing will turn us – nothing. We will never parley, we will never negotiate with Hitler or any of his gang. We shall fight him by land, we shall fight him by sea, we shall fight him in the air, until with God's help we have rid the earth of his shadow and liberated its peoples from his yoke. Any man or state who fights on against Nazidom will have our aid. Any man or state who marches with Hitler is our foe. This applies not only to organised states but to all representatives of that vile race of quislings who make themselves the tools and agents of the Nazi régime against their fellow-countrymen and the lands of their birth. They – these quislings – like the Nazi leaders themselves, if not disposed of by their fellow-countrymen, which would save trouble, will be delivered by us on the morrow of victory to the justice of the Allied tribunals. That is our policy and that is our declaration. It follows, therefore, that we shall give whatever help we can to Russia and the Russian people. We shall appeal to all our friends and allies in every part of the world to take the same course and pursue it, as we shall, faithfully and steadfastly to the end.

We have offered the Government of Soviet Russia any technical or economic assistance which is in our power, and which is likely to be of service to them. We shall bomb Germany by day as well as by night in ever-increasing measure, casting upon them month by month a heavier discharge of bombs, and making the German people taste and gulp each month a sharper dose of the miseries they have showered upon mankind. It is noteworthy that only yesterday the Royal Air Force, fighting inland over French territory, cut down with very small loss to themselves 28 of the Hun fighting machines in the air above the French soil they have invaded, defiled and profess to hold. But this is only a beginning. From now forward the main expansion of our Air Force proceeds with gathering speed. In another six months the weight of the help we are receiving from the United States in war materials of all kinds, and especially in heavy bombers, will begin to tell.

This is no class war, but a war in which the whole British Empire and Commonwealth of Nations is engaged without distinction of race, creed or party. It is not for me to speak of the action of the United States, but this I will say: if Hitler imagines that his attack on Soviet Russia will cause the slightest division of aims or slackening of effort in the great Democracies who are resolved upon his doom, he is woefully mistaken. On the contrary, we shall be fortified and encouraged in our efforts to rescue mankind from his tyranny. We shall be strengthened and not weakened in determination and in resources.

This is no time to moralise on the follies of countries and governments which have allowed themselves to be struck down one by one, when by united action they could have saved themselves and saved the world from this catastrophe. But when I spoke a few minutes ago of Hitler's blood-lust and the hateful appetites which have impelled or lured him on his Russian adventure, I said there was one deeper motive behind his outrage. He wishes to destroy the Russian power because he hopes that if he succeeds in this, he will be able to bring back the main strength of his army and air force from the East and hurl it upon this Island, which he knows he must conquer or suffer the penalty of his crimes. His invasion of Russia is no more than a prelude to an attempted invasion of the British Isles. He hopes, no doubt, that all this may be accomplished before the winter comes, and that he can overwhelm Great Britain before the fleet and air power of the United States may intervene. He hopes that he may once again repeat, upon a greater scale than ever before, that process of destroying his enemies one by one, by which he has so long thrived and prospered, and that then the scene will be clear for the final act, without which all his conquests would be in vain – namely, the subjugation of the Western Hemisphere to his will and to his system.

The Russian danger is therefore our danger, and the danger of the United States, just as the cause of any Russian fighting for his hearth and home is the cause of free men and free peoples in every quarter of the globe. Let us learn the lessons already taught by such cruel experience. Let us redouble our exertions, and strike with united strength while life and power remain.

'THE GRIT AND STAMINA OF LONDONERS'

14 July 1941

County Hall, London

In September last, having been defeated in his invasion plans by the RAF, Hitler declared his intention to raze the cities of Britain to the ground, and in the early days of that month he set the whole fury of the Hun upon London.

None of us quite knew what would be the result of a concentrated and prolonged bombardment of this vast centre of population. Here in the Thames Valley, over 8,000,000 people are maintained at a very high level of modern civilisation. They are dependent from day to day upon light, heat, power, water, sewerage, and communications on the most complicated scale.

The administration of London in all its branches was confronted with problems hitherto unknown and unmeasured in all the history of the past. Public order, public health, the maintenance of all the essential services, the handling of the millions of people who came in and out of London every day; the shelter – not indeed from the enemy's bombs, for that was beyond us, but from their blast and splinters – the shelter of millions of men and women, and the removal of the dead and wounded from the shattered buildings; the care of the wounded when hospitals were being ruthlessly bombed, and the provision for the homeless – sometimes amounting to many thousands in a single day, and accumulating to many more after three or four days of successive attacks – all these things, with the welfare and the education amid these scenes of our great numbers of children here – all these presented tasks which, viewed in cold blood beforehand, might well have seemed overwhelming.

Indeed, before the war, when the imagination painted pictures of what might happen in the great air raids on our cities, plans were made to move the Government, to move all the great controlling services which are centred in London, and disperse them about the countryside, and also it was always considered a very great danger that a sudden wave of panic might send millions of people crowding out into the countryside along all the roads.

Well, when you are doing your duty and you are sure of that, you need not worry too much about the dangers or the consequences. We have not been moved in this war except by the promptings of duty and conscience, and therefore we do not need to be deterred from action by pictures which our imagination or careful forethought painted of what the consequences would be.

I must, however, admit that when the storm broke in September, I was for several weeks very anxious about the result. We were then not prepared as we are now. Our defences had not the advantages they have since attained, and again I must admit that I greatly feared injury to our public services, I feared the ravages of fire, I feared the dislocation of life and the stoppage of work, I feared epidemics of serious disease or even pestilence among the crowds who took refuge in our by no means completely constructed or well-equipped shelters.

I remember one winter evening travelling to a railway station – which still worked – on my way north to visit troops. It was cold and raining. Darkness had almost fallen on the blacked-out streets. I saw everywhere long queues of people, among them hundreds of young girls in their silk stockings and high-heeled shoes, who had worked hard all day and were waiting for bus after bus, which came by already overcrowded, in the hope of reaching their homes for the night. When at that moment the doleful wail of the siren betokened the approach of the German bombers, I confess to you that my heart bled for London and the Londoners.

All this sort of thing went on for more than four months with hardly any intermission. I used to hold meetings of my Ministerial colleagues and members of the authorities concerned every week in Downing Street in order to check up and see how we stood. Sometimes the gas had failed over large areas – the only means of cooking for great numbers of people; sometimes the electricity. There were grievous complaints about the shelters and about conditions in them. Water was cut off, railways were cut or broken, large districts were destroyed by fire, 20,000 people were killed, and many more thousands were wounded.

But there was one thing about which there was never any doubt. The courage, the unconquerable grit and stamina of the Londoners showed itself from the very outset. Without that all would have failed. Upon that rock, all stood unshakeable. All the public services were carried on, and all the intricate arrangements, far-reaching details, involving the daily lives of so many millions, were carried out, improvised, elaborated, and perfected in the very teeth of the cruel and devastating storm. . . .

If the storm is to renew itself, London will be ready, London will not flinch, London can take it again.

Thanking the ship's company of HMS *Prince of Wales* on his return from the Atlantic Charter meeting, 19 August 1941.

We ask no favours of the enemy. We seek from them no compunction. On the contrary, if tonight the people of London were asked to cast their vote whether a convention should be entered into to stop the bombing of all cities, the overwhelming majority would cry, 'No, we will mete out to the Germans the measure, and more than the measure, that they have meted out to us.' The people of London with one voice would say to Hitler: 'You have committed every crime under the sun. Where you have been the least resisted there you have been the most brutal. It was you who began the indiscriminate bombing. We remember Warsaw in the very first few days of the war. We remember Rotterdam. We have been newly reminded of your habits by the hideous massacre of Belgrade. We know too well the bestial assault you are making upon the Russian people, to whom our hearts go out in their valiant struggle. We will have no truce or parley with you, or the grisly gang who work your wicked will. You do your worst – and we will do our best.'

THE ATLANTIC CHARTER

24 August 1941

Broadcast, London

Churchill arranged to meet President Roosevelt – it was to be their first meeting – in Placentia Bay on the barren shores of Newfoundland. He made the journey across the Atlantic aboard Britain's newest battleship HMS Prince of Wales, *travelling at high speed with frequent alterations of course to evade German U-boats. On 12 August the Prime Minister and President put their signatures to what has come to be known as the 'Atlantic Charter'.*

I thought you would like me to tell you something about the voyage which I made across the ocean to meet our great friend, the President of the United States. Exactly where we met is a secret, but I don't think I shall be indiscreet if I go so far as to say that it was 'somewhere in the Atlantic'.

In a spacious, landlocked bay which reminded me of the West Coast of Scotland, powerful American warships protected by strong flotillas and far-ranging aircraft awaited our arrival, and, as it were, stretched out a hand to help us in. Our party arrived in the newest, or almost the newest, British battleship, the *Prince of Wales*, with a modern escort of British and Canadian destroyers, and there for three days I spent my time in company, and I think I may say in comradeship, with Mr Roosevelt; while all the time the chiefs of the staff and the naval and military commanders both of the British Empire and of the United States sat together in continual council.

President Roosevelt is the thrice-chosen head of the most powerful state and community in the world. I am the servant of King and Parliament at present charged with the principal direction of our affairs in these fateful times, and it is my duty also to make sure, as I have made sure, that anything I say or do in the exercise of my office is approved and sustained by the whole British Commonwealth of Nations. Therefore this meeting was bound to be important, because of the enormous forces at present only partially mobilised but steadily mobilising which are at the disposal of these two major groupings of the human family: the British Empire and the United States, who, fortunately for the progress of mankind, happen to speak the same language, and very largely think the same thoughts, or anyhow think a lot of the same thoughts.

The meeting was therefore symbolic. That is its prime importance. It symbolises, in a form and manner which everyone can understand in every land and in every clime, the deep underlying unities which stir and at decisive moments rule the English-speaking peoples throughout the world. Would it be presumptuous for me to say that it symbolises something even more majestic – namely, the marshalling of the good forces of the world against the evil forces which are now so formidable and triumphant and which have cast their cruel spell over the whole of Europe and a large part of Asia?

This was a meeting which marks for ever in the pages of history the taking-up by the English-speaking nations, amid all this peril, tumult and confusion, of the guidance of the fortunes of the broad toiling masses in all the continents; and our loyal effort without any clog of selfish interest to lead them forward out of the miseries into which they have been plunged back to the broad highroad of freedom and justice. This is the highest honour and the most glorious opportunity which could ever have come to any branch of the human race.

When one beholds how many currents of extraordinary and terrible events have flowed together to make this harmony, even the most sceptical person must have the feeling that we all have the chance to play our part and do our duty in some great design, the end of which no mortal can foresee. Awful and horrible things are happening in these days. The whole of Europe has been wrecked and trampled down by the mechanical weapons and barbaric fury of the Nazis; the most deadly instruments of war-science have been joined to the extreme refinements of treachery and the most brutal exhibitions of ruthlessness, and thus have formed a combine of aggression the like of which has never been known, before which the rights, the traditions, the characteristics and the structure of many ancient honoured states and peoples have been laid prostrate and are now ground down under the heel and terror of a monster. The Austrians, the Czechs, the Poles, the Norwegians, the Danes, the Belgians, the Dutch, the Greeks, the Croats and the Serbs, above all the great French nation, have been stunned and pinioned. Italy, Hungary, Rumania, Bulgaria have bought a shameful respite by becoming the jackals of the tiger, but their situation is very little different and will presently be indistinguishable from that of his victims. Sweden, Spain and Turkey stand appalled, wondering which will be struck down next.

Here, then, is the vast pit into which all the most famous states and races of Europe have been flung and from which unaided they can never climb. But all this did not satiate Adolf Hitler; he made a treaty of non-aggression with Soviet Russia, just as he made one with Turkey, in order to keep them quiet till he was ready to attack them, and then, nine weeks ago today, without a vestige of provocation, he hurled millions of soldiers, with all their apparatus, upon the neighbour he had called his friend, with the avowed object of destroying Russia and tearing her in pieces. This frightful business is now unfolding day by day before our eyes. Here is a devil who, in a mere spasm of his pride and lust for domination, can condemn two or three millions, perhaps it may be many more, of human beings, to speedy and violent death. 'Let Russia be blotted out – Let Russia be destroyed. Order the armies to advance.' Such were his decrees. Accordingly from the Arctic Ocean to the Black Sea, six or seven millions of soldiers are locked in mortal struggle. Ah, but this time it was not so easy.

This time it was not all one way. The Russian armies and all the peoples of the Russian Republic have rallied to the defence of their hearths and homes. For the first time Nazi blood has flowed in a fearful torrent. Certainly 1,500,000, perhaps 2,000,000 of Nazi cannon-fodder have bit the dust of the endless plains of Russia. The tremendous battle rages along nearly 2,000 miles of front. The Russians fight with magnificent devotion; not only that, our generals who have visited the Russian front line report with admiration the efficiency of their military organisation and the excellence of their equipment. The aggressor is surprised, startled, staggered. For the first time in his experience mass murder has become unprofitable. He retaliates by the most frightful cruelties. As his armies advance, whole districts are being exterminated. Scores of thousands – literally scores of thousands – of executions in cold blood are being perpetrated by the German police-troops upon the Russian patriots who defend their native soil. Since the Mongol invasions of Europe in the sixteenth century, there has never been methodical, merciless butchery on such a scale, or approaching such a scale. And this is but the beginning. Famine and pestilence have yet to follow in the bloody ruts of Hitler's tanks. We are in the presence of a crime without a name.

But Europe is not the only continent to be tormented and devastated by aggressions. For five long years the Japanese military factions, seeking to emulate the style of Hitler and Mussolini, taking all their posturing as if it were a new European revelation, have been invading and harrying the 500,000,000 inhabitants of China. Japanese armies have been wandering about that vast land in futile excursions, carrying with them carnage, ruin and corruption and calling it the 'Chinese Incident'. Now they stretch a grasping hand into the southern seas of China; they snatch Indo-China from the wretched Vichy French; they menace by their movements Siam; menace Singapore, the British link with Australia; and menace the Philippine Islands under the protection of the United States. It is certain that this has got to stop. Every effort will be made to secure a peaceful settlement. The United States are labouring with infinite patience to arrive at a fair and amicable settlement which will give Japan the utmost reassurance for her legitimate interests. We earnestly hope these negotiations will succeed. But this I must say: that if these hopes should fail we shall of course range ourselves unhesitatingly at the side of the United States.

And thus we come back to the quiet bay somewhere in the Atlantic where misty sunshine plays on great ships which carry the White Ensign, or the Stars and Stripes. We had the idea, when we met there – the President and I – that without attempting to draw up final and formal peace aims, or war aims, it was necessary to give all peoples, especially the oppressed and conquered peoples, a simple, rough-and-ready wartime statement of the goal towards which the British Commonwealth and the United States mean to make their way, and thus make a way for others to march with them upon a road which will certainly be painful, and may be long!

There are, however, two distinct and marked differences in this joint declaration from the attitude adopted by the Allies during the latter part of the last war; and no one should overlook them. The United States and Great Britain do not now assume that there will never be any more war again. On the contrary, we intend to take ample precautions to prevent its renewal in any period we can foresee by effectively disarming the guilty nations while remaining suitably protected ourselves.

The second difference is this: that instead of trying to ruin German trade by all kinds of additional trade barriers and hindrances as was the mood of 1917, we have definitely adopted the view that it is not in the interests of the world and of our two countries that any large nation should be unprosperous or shut out from the means of making a decent living for itself and its people by its industry and enterprise. These are far-reaching changes of principle upon which all countries should ponder. Above all, it was necessary to give hope and the assurance of final victory to those many scores of millions of men and women who are battling for life and freedom, or who are already bent down under the Nazi yoke. Hitler and his confederates have for some time past been adjuring, bullying and beseeching the populations whom they have wronged and injured, to bow to their fate, to resign themselves to their servitude, and for the sake of some mitigations and indulgences, to 'collaborate' – that is the word – in what is called the New Order in Europe.

What is this New Order which they seek to fasten first upon Europe and if possible – for their ambitions are boundless – upon all the continents of the globe? It is the rule of the *Herrenvolk* – the master-race – who are to put an end to democracy, to parliaments, to the fundamental freedoms and decencies of ordinary men and women, to the historic rights of nations; and give them in exchange the iron rule of Prussia, the universal goose-step, and a strict, efficient discipline enforced upon the working class by the political police, with the German concentration camps and firing parties, now so busy in a dozen lands, always handy in the background. There is the New Order.

Napoleon in his glory and his genius spread his Empire far and wide. There was a time when only the snows of Russia and the white cliffs of Dover with their guardian fleets stood between him and the dominion of the world. Napoleon's armies had a theme: they carried with them the surges of the French Revolution. Liberty, Equality and

Fraternity – that was the cry. There was a sweeping away of outworn medieval systems and aristocratic privilege. There was the land for the people, a new code of law. Nevertheless, Napoleon's Empire vanished like a dream. But Hitler, Hitler has no theme, naught but mania, appetite and exploitation. He has, however, weapons and machinery for grinding down and for holding down conquered countries which are the product, the sadly perverted product, of modern science.

The ordeals, therefore, of the conquered peoples will be hard. We must give them hope; we must give them the conviction that their sufferings and their resistances will not be in vain. The tunnel may be dark and long, but at the end there is light. That is the symbolism and that is the message of the Atlantic meeting. Do not despair, brave Norwegians: your land shall be cleansed not only from the invader but from the filthy quislings who are his tools. Be sure of yourselves, Czechs: your independence shall be restored. Poles, the heroism of your people standing up to cruel oppressors, the courage of your soldiers, sailors and airmen, shall not be forgotten: your country shall live again and resume its rightful part in the new organisation of Europe. Lift up your heads, gallant Frenchmen: not all the infamies of Darlan and of Laval shall stand between you and the restoration of your birthright. Tough, stout-hearted Dutch, Belgians, Luxembourgers, tormented, mishandled, shamefully castaway peoples of Yugoslavia, glorious Greece, now subjected to the crowning insult of the rule of the Italian jackanapes; yield not an inch! Keep your souls clean from all contact with the Nazis; make them feel even in their fleeting hour of brutish triumph that they are the moral outcasts of mankind. Help is coming; mighty forces are arming on your behalf. Have faith. Have hope. Deliverance is sure.

There is the signal which we have flashed across the water; and if it reaches the hearts of those to whom it is sent, they will endure with fortitude and tenacity their present misfortunes in the sure faith that they, too, are still serving the common cause, and that their efforts will not be in vain.

You will perhaps have noticed that the President of the United States and the British representative, in what is aptly called the 'Atlantic Charter', have jointly pledged their countries to the final destruction of the Nazi tyranny. That is a solemn and grave undertaking. It must be made good; it will be made good. And, of course, many practical arrangements to fulfil that purpose have been and are being organised and set in motion.

The question has been asked: how near is the United States to war?

There is certainly one man who knows the answer to that question. If Hitler has not yet declared war upon the United States, it is surely not out of his love for American institutions; it is certainly not because he could not find a pretext. He has murdered half a dozen countries for far less. Fear of immediately redoubling the tremendous energies now being employed against him is no doubt a restraining influence. But the real reason is, I am sure, to be found in the method to which he has so faithfully adhered and by which he has gained so much.

What is that method? It is a very simple method. One by one: that is his plan; that is his guiding rule; that is the trick by which he has enslaved so large a portion of the world. Three and a half years ago I appealed to my fellow-countrymen to take the lead in weaving together a strong defensive union within the principles of the League of Nations, a union of all the countries who felt themselves in ever-growing danger. But none would listen; all stood idle while Germany rearmed. Czechoslovakia was subjugated; a French Government deserted their faithful ally and broke a plighted word in that ally's hour of need. Russia was cajoled and deceived into a kind of neutrality or partnership, while the French Army was being annihilated. The Low Countries and the Scandinavian countries, acting with France and Great Britain in good time, even after the war had begun, might have altered its course, and would have had, at any rate, a fighting chance. The Balkan States had only to stand together to save themselves from the ruin by which they are now engulfed. But one by one they were undermined and overwhelmed. Never was the career of crime made more smooth.

Now Hitler is striking at Russia with all his might, well knowing the difficulties of geography which stand between Russia and the aid which the Western Democracies are trying to bring. We shall strive our utmost to overcome all obstacles and to bring this aid. We have arranged for a conference in Moscow between the United States, British and Russian authorities to settle the whole plan. No barrier must stand in the way. But why is Hitler striking at Russia, and inflicting and suffering himself or, rather, making his soldiers suffer, this frightful slaughter? It is with the declared object of turning his whole force upon the British Islands, and if he could succeed in beating the life and the strength out of us, which is not so easy, then is the moment when he will settle his account, and it is already a long one, with the people of the United States and generally with the Western Hemisphere. One by one, there is the process; there is the simple, dismal plan which has served Hitler so well. It needs but one final successful application to make him the master of the world. I am devoutly thankful that some eyes at least are fully opened to it while time remains. I rejoiced to find that the President saw in their true light and proportion the extreme dangers by which the American people as well as the British people are now beset. It was indeed by the mercy of God that he began eight years ago that revival of the strength of the American Navy without which the New World today would have to take its orders from the European dictators, but with which the United States still retains the power to marshal her gigantic strength, and in saving herself to render an incomparable service to mankind.

We had a church parade on the Sunday in our Atlantic bay. The President came on to the quarter-deck of the *Prince of Wales*, where there were mingled together many hundreds of American and British sailors and marines. The sun shone bright and warm while we all sang the old hymns which are our common inheritance and which we learned as children in our homes. We sang the hymn founded on the psalms which John Hampden's soldiers sang when they bore his body to the grave, and in which the brief, precarious span of human life is contrasted with the immutability of Him to Whom a thousand ages are but as yesterday, and as a watch in the night. We sang the sailors' hymn 'For those in peril' – and there are very many – 'on the sea'. We sang 'Onward Christian Soldiers'. And indeed I felt that this was no vain presumption, but that we had the right to feel that we were serving a cause for the sake of which a trumpet has sounded from on high.

When I looked upon that densely-packed congregation of fighting men of the same language, of the same faith, of the same fundamental laws and the same ideals, and now to a large extent of the same interests, and certainly in different degrees facing the same dangers, it swept across me that here was the only hope, but also the sure hope, of saving the world from measureless degradation.

And so we came back across the ocean waves, uplifted in spirit, fortified in resolve. Some American destroyers which were carrying mails to the United States marines in Iceland happened to be going the same way, too, so we made a goodly company at sea together.

And when we were right out in mid-passage one afternoon a noble sight broke on the view. We overtook one of the convoys which carry the munitions and supplies of the New World to sustain the champions of freedom in the Old. The whole broad horizon seemed filled with ships; seventy or eighty ships of all kinds and sizes, arrayed in fourteen lines, each of which could have been drawn with a ruler, hardly a wisp of smoke, not a straggler, but all bristling with cannons and other precautions on which I will not dwell, and all surrounded by their British escorting vessels, while overhead the far-ranging Catalina air-boats soared – vigilant, protecting eagles in the sky. Then I felt that – hard and terrible and long drawn-out as this struggle may be – we shall not be denied the strength to do our duty to the end.

'WE ARE STILL CAPTAIN OF OUR SOULS'

9 September 1941

House of Commons

The magnificent resistance of the Russian Armies and the skilful manner in which their vast front is being withdrawn in the teeth of Nazi invasion make it certain that Hitler's hopes of a short war with Russia will be dispelled. Already in three months he has lost more German blood than was shed in any single year of the last war. Already he faces the certainty of having to maintain his armies on the whole front from the Arctic to the Black Sea, at the end of long, inadequate, assailed and precarious lines of communication, through all the severity of a Russian winter, with the vigorous counter-strokes which may be expected from the Russian Armies. From the moment, now nearly 80 days ago, when Russia was attacked, we have cast about for every means of giving the most speedy and effective help to our new Ally. I am not prepared to discuss the military projects which have been examined. Such a discussion would be harmful to our interests, both by what was said and by what was not said. Nor will it be possible for anyone representing the Government to enter upon any argument on such questions. In the field of supply more can be said. I agreed with President Roosevelt upon the message which was sent to Premier Stalin, the terms of which have already been made public. The need is urgent, and the scale heavy. A considerable part of the munition industry and the iron and steel production of Russia has fallen into the hands of the enemy. On the other hand, the Soviet Union disposes of anything from ten to fifteen million soldiers, for nearly all of whom they have equipment and arms. To aid in the supply of these masses, to enable them to realise their long-continuing force, and to organise the operation of their supply, will be the task of the Anglo-American-Russian Conference. . . .

Thus far then have we travelled along the terrible road we chose at the call of duty. The mood of Britain is wisely and rightly averse from every form of shallow or premature exultation. This is no time for boasts or glowing prophecies, but there is this – a year ago our position looked forlorn and well nigh desperate to all eyes but our own. Today we may say aloud before an awe-struck world, 'We are still masters of our fate. We are still captain of our souls.'

'NEVER GIVE IN!'

29 October 1941

Harrow School

For the second time as Prime Minister Churchill visited his alma mater. *For the traditional School Songs an additional verse had been added in his honour to the song* 'Stet Fortuna Domus':

> 'Nor less we praise in darker days
>   The leader of our nation,
> And Churchill's name shall win acclaim
>   From each new generation.
> For you have power in danger's hour
>   Our freedom to defend, Sir!
> Though long the fight we know that right
>   Will triumph in the end, Sir!'

To the Headmaster's dismay, Churchill upbraided him for the reference to 'darker' days, proclaiming: 'These are not dark days, these are *great* days – *the greatest our nation has ever lived!'* *Thereupon he substituted 'sterner days' for 'darker days'.*

Almost a year has passed since I came down here at your Head Master's kind invitation in order to cheer myself and cheer the hearts of a few of my friends by singing some of our own songs. The ten months that have passed have seen very terrible catastrophic events in the world – ups and downs, misfortunes – but can anyone sitting here this afternoon, this October afternoon, not feel deeply thankful for what has happened in the time that has passed and for the very great improvement in the position of our country and of our home? Why, when I was here last time we were quite alone, desperately alone, and we had been so for five or six months. We were poorly armed. We are not so poorly armed today; but then we were very poorly armed. We had the unmeasured menace of the enemy and their air attack still beating upon us, and you yourselves had had experience of this attack; and I expect you are beginning to feel impatient that there has been this long lull with nothing particular turning up!

But we must learn to be equally good at what is short and sharp and what is long and tough. It is generally said that the British are often better at the last. They do not expect to move from crisis to crisis; they do not always expect that each day will bring up some noble chance of war; but when they very slowly make up their minds that the thing has to be done and the job put through and finished, then, even if it takes months – if it takes years – they do it.

Another lesson I think we may take, just throwing our minds back to our meeting here ten months ago and now, is that appearances are often very deceptive, and as Kipling well says, we must

> ... meet with Triumph and Disaster
> And treat those two impostors just the same.

You cannot tell from appearances how things will go. Sometimes imagination makes things out far worse than they are; yet without imagination not much can be done. Those people who are imaginative see many more dangers than perhaps exist, certainly many more than will happen; but then they must also pray to be given that extra courage to carry this far-reaching imagination. But for everyone, surely, what we have gone through in this period – I am addressing myself to the School – surely from this period of ten months this is the lesson: never give in, never give in, *never, never, never, never* – in nothing, great or small, large or petty – never give in except to convictions of honour and good sense. Never yield to force; never yield to the apparently overwhelming might of the enemy. We stood all alone a year ago, and to many countries it seemed that our account was closed, we were finished. All this tradition of ours, our songs, our School history, this part of the history of this country, were gone and finished and liquidated.

Very different is the mood today. Britain, other nations thought, had drawn a sponge across her slate. But instead our country stood in the gap. There was no flinching and no thought of giving in; and by what seemed almost a miracle to those outside these Islands, though we ourselves never doubted it, we now find ourselves in a position where I say that we can be sure that we have only to persevere to conquer.

You sang here a verse of a School Song; you sang that extra verse written in my honour, which I was very greatly complimented by and which you have repeated today. But there is one word in it I want to alter – I wanted to do so last year, but I did not venture to. It is the line –

Nor less we praise in darker days.

I have obtained the Head Master's permission to alter 'darker' to 'sterner':

Nor less we praise in sterner days.

Do not let us speak of darker days; let us speak rather of sterner days. These are not dark days: these are great days – the greatest days our country has ever lived; and we must all thank God that we have been allowed, each of us according to our stations, to play a part in making these days memorable in the history of our race.

THE LEND-LEASE BILL

10 November 1941

Mansion House, London

This year our ancient Guildhall lies in ruins, our foreign affairs are shrunken, and almost the whole of Europe is prostrate under the Nazi tyranny. The war which Hitler began by invading Poland and which now engulfs the European continent has broken into the north-east of Africa; may well involve the greater part of Asia; nay, it may soon spread to the remaining portions of the globe. Nevertheless, in the same spirit in which you, my Lord Mayor, have celebrated your assumption of office with the time-honoured pageant of Lord Mayor's Day, so I, who have the honour to be your guest, will endeavour to play, though very briefly – for in wartime speeches should be short – the traditional part assigned to those who hold my office.

The condition of Europe is terrible in the last degree. Hitler's firing parties are busy every day in a dozen countries. Norwegians, Belgians, Frenchmen, Dutch, Poles, Czechs, Serbs, Croats, Slovenes, Greeks, and above all in scale Russians, are being butchered by thousands and by tens of thousands after they have surrendered, while individual and mass executions in all the countries I have mentioned have become a part of the regular German routine. The world has been intensely stirred by the massacre of the French hostages. The whole of France, with the exception of the small clique whose public careers depend upon a German victory, has been united in horror and indignation against this slaughter of perfectly innocent people. Admiral Darlan's tributes to German generosity fall unseasonably at this moment on French ears, and his plans for loving collaboration with the conquerors and the murderers of Frenchmen are quite appreciably embarrassed. Nay, even the arch-criminal himself, the Nazi ogre Hitler, has been frightened by the volume and passion of world indignation which his spectacular atrocity has excited. It is he and not the French people who have been intimidated. He has not dared to go forward with his further programme of killing hostages.

This, as you will have little doubt, is not due to mercy, to compassion, to compunction, but to fear, and to a dawning consciousness of personal insecurity rising in a wicked heart.

I would say generally that we must regard all these victims of the Nazi executioners in so many lands, who are labelled Communists and Jews – we must regard them just as if they were brave soldiers who die for their country on the field of battle. Nay, in a way their sacrifice may be more fruitful than that of the soldier who falls with his arms in his hands. A river of blood has flowed and is flowing between the German race and the peoples of nearly all Europe. It is not the hot blood of battle where good blows are given and returned. It is the cold blood of the execution yard and the scaffold, which leaves a stain indelible for generations and for centuries.

Here then are the foundations upon which the New Order of Europe is to be inaugurated. Here then is the house-warming festival of the *Herrenvolk*. Here then is the system of terrorism by which the Nazi criminals and their quisling accomplices seek to rule a dozen ancient famous States of Europe and if possible all the free nations of the world. In no more effective manner could they have frustrated the accomplishment of their own designs. The future and its mysteries are inscrutable. But one thing is plain. Never to those blood-stained accursed hands will the future of Europe be confided.

Since Lord Mayor's Day last year some great changes have taken place in our situation. Then we were alone, the sole champion of freedom. Then we were ill-armed and far outnumbered even in the Air. Now a large part of the United States Navy, as Colonel Knox has told us, is constantly in action against the common foe. Now the valiant resistance of the Russian nation has inflicted most frightful injuries upon the German military power, and at the present moment the German invading armies, after all their losses, lie on the barren steppes exposed to the approaching severities of the Russian winter. Now we have an Air Force which is at last at least equal in size and numbers, not to speak of quality, to the German Air Power.

Rather more than a year ago I announced to Parliament that we were sending a battle fleet back into the Mediterranean. The destruction of the German and Italian convoys – and the Admiralty brings today the news of the destruction of another Italian destroyer – the passage of our own supplies in many directions through that sea, the broken morale of the Italian navy, all these show that we are still the masters there.

Today I am able to go further. Owing to the effective help we are getting in the Atlantic from the United States, owing to the sinking of the *Bismarck*, owing to the completion of our splendid new battleships and aircraft carriers of the largest size, as well as to the cowing of the Italian navy already mentioned, I am able to go further and announce to you here at the Lord Mayor's annual celebration that we now feel ourselves strong enough to provide a powerful naval force of heavy ships, with its necessary ancillary vessels, for service if needed in the Indian and Pacific Oceans. Thus we stretch out the long arm of brotherhood and motherhood to the Australian and New Zealand peoples and to the peoples of India, whose armies and troops have already been fighting with so much distinction in the Mediterranean theatre. And this movement of our naval forces, in conjunction with the United States Main Fleet, may give a practical proof to all who have eyes to see that the forces of freedom and democracy have not by any means reached the limits of their power.

I must admit that, having voted for the Japanese alliance nearly 40 years ago, in 1902, and having always done my very best to promote good relations with the Island Empire of Japan, and always having been a sentimental well-wisher to the Japanese and an admirer of their many gifts and qualities, I should view with keen sorrow the opening of a conflict between Japan and the English-speaking world.

The United States' time-honoured interests in the Far East are well known. They are doing their utmost to find ways of preserving peace in the Pacific. We do not know whether their efforts will be successful, but should they fail I take this occasion to say, and it is my duty to say, that, should the United States become involved in war with Japan, the British declaration will follow within the hour.

Viewing the vast sombre scene as dispassionately as possible, it would seem a very hazardous adventure for the Japanese people to plunge quite needlessly into a world struggle in which they may well find themselves opposed in the Pacific by States whose populations comprise nearly three-quarters of the human race. If steel is the basic foundation of modern war, it would be rather dangerous for a power like Japan, whose steel production is only about 7 million tons a year, to provoke quite gratuitously a struggle with the United States, whose steel production is now about 90 millions; and this would take no account of the powerful contribution which the British Empire can make. I hope therefore that the peace of the Pacific will be preserved in accordance with the known wishes of Japan's wisest statesmen. But every preparation to defend British interests in the Far East, and to defend the common cause now at stake, has been and is being made.

Meanwhile how can we watch without emotion the wonderful defence of their native soil and of their freedom and independence which has been maintained single-handed, all alone, for five long years by the Chinese people under the leadership of that great Asiatic hero and Commander, General Chiang Kai-shek? It would be a disaster of first magnitude to world civilisation if the noble resistance to invasion and exploitation which has been made by the whole Chinese race were not to result in the liberation of their hearths and homes. That, I feel is a sentiment which is deep in all our hearts.

To return for a moment before I sit down to the contrast between our position now and a year ago, I must remind you, I do not need to remind you here in the City, that this time last year we did not know where to turn for a dollar across the American exchange. By very severe measures we had been able to gather and spend in America about £500,000,000 sterling, but the end of our financial resources was in sight – nay, had actually been reached. All we could do at that time a year ago was to place orders in the United States without being able to see our way through, but on a tide of hope and not without important encouragement.

Then came the majestic policy of the President and Congress of the United States in passing the Lend and Lease Bill, under which in two successive enactments about £3,000,000,000 sterling were dedicated to the cause of world freedom without – mark this, for it is unique – the setting up of any account in money. Never again let us hear the taunt that money is the ruling thought or power in the hearts of the American democracy. The Lend and Lease Bill must be regarded without question as the most unsordid act in the whole of recorded history.

We for our part have not been found unworthy of the increasing aid we are receiving. We have made unparalleled financial and economic sacrifices ourselves, and now that the Government and people of the United States have declared their resolve that the aid they are giving shall reach the fighting lines, we shall be able to strike with all our might and main.

Thus we may, without exposing ourselves to any charge of complacency, without in the slightest degree relaxing the intensity of our war effort, give thanks to Almighty God for the many wonders which have been wrought in so brief a space of time, and we may derive fresh confidence from all that has happened and bend ourselves to our task with all the force that is in our souls and with every drop of blood that is in our bodies.

We are told from many quarters that we must soon expect what is called a 'peace offensive' from Berlin. All the usual signs and symptoms are already manifest, as the Foreign Secretary will confirm, in neutral countries, and all these signs point in one direction. They all show that the guilty men who have let Hell loose upon the world are hoping to escape, with their fleeting triumphs and ill-gotten plunders, from the closing net of doom.

We owe it to ourselves, we owe it to our Russian Ally, and to the Government and people of the United States, to make it absolutely clear that whether we are supported or alone, however long and hard the toil may be, the British nation and His Majesty's Government in intimate concert with the Governments of the great Dominions will never enter into any negotiations with Hitler or any party in Germany which represents the Nazi régime. In that resolve, we are sure that the ancient City of London will be with us to the hilt and to the end.

WAR WITH JAPAN

8 December 1941

House of Commons

Churchill was at the Prime Minister's country residence of Chequers with the American Ambassador, John Winant, and the President's personal representative, Averell Harriman, when news came over the radio of the Japanese attack on the American Fleet at Pearl Harbor. Churchill immediately called the President to seek confirmation and, on 8 December, Britain declared war on Japan. Three days later, Germany declared war on the United States.

As soon as I heard, last night, that Japan had attacked the United States, I felt it necessary that Parliament should be immediately summoned. It is indispensable to our system of government that Parliament should play its full part in all the important acts of State and at all the crucial moments of the war; and I am glad to see that so many Members have been able to be in their places, despite the shortness of the notice. With the full approval of the nation, and of the Empire, I pledged the word of Great Britain, about a month ago, that should the United States be involved in war with Japan, a British declaration of war would follow within the hour. I therefore spoke to President Roosevelt on the Atlantic telephone last night, with a view to arranging the timing of our respective declarations. The President told me that he would this morning send a Message to Congress, which, of course, as is well known, can alone make a declaration of war on behalf of the United States, and I then assured him that we would follow immediately.

However, it soon appeared that British territory in Malaya had also been the object of Japanese attack, and later on it was announced from Tokyo that the Japanese High Command – a curious form; not the Imperial Japanese Government – had declared that a state of war existed with Great Britain and the United States. That being so, there was no need to wait for the declaration by Congress. American time is very nearly six hours behind ours. The Cabinet, therefore, which met at 12.30 today, authorised an immediate declaration of war upon Japan. Instructions were sent to His Majesty's Ambassador at Tokyo, and a communication was dispatched to the Japanese Chargé d'Affaires at 1 o'clock today to this effect:

Foreign Office, December 8th

Sir,

On the evening of December 7th His Majesty's Goverment in the United Kingdom learned that Japanese forces, without previous warning, either in the form of a declaration of war or of an ultimatum with a conditional declaration of war, had attempted a landing on the coast of Malaya and bombed Singapore and Hong Kong.

In view of these wanton acts of unprovoked aggression, committed in flagrant violation of International Law, and particularly of Article I of the Third Hague Convention, relative to the opening of hostilities, to which both Japan and the United Kingdom are parties, His Majesty's Ambassador at Tokyo has been instructed to inform the Imperial Japanese Government, in the name of His Majesty's Government in the United Kingdom, that a state of war exists between the two countries.

I have the honour to be, with high consideration,

Sir,

Your obedient servant,

Winston S. Churchill . . .

The Japanese onslaught brought upon the United States and Great Britain very serious injuries to our naval power. In my whole experience I do not remember any naval blow so heavy or so painful as the sinking of the *Prince of Wales* and the *Repulse* on Monday last. These two vast, powerful ships constituted an essential feature in our plans for meeting the new Japanese danger as it loomed against us in the last few months. These ships had reached the right point at the right moment, and were in every respect suited to the task assigned to them. In moving to attack the Japanese transports and landing-craft which were disembarking the invaders of Siam and Malaya at the Kra Isthmus or thereabouts, Admiral Phillips was undertaking a thoroughly sound, well-considered offensive operation, not indeed free from risk, but not different in principle from many similar operations we have repeatedly carried out in the North Sea and in the Mediterranean. Both ships were sunk in repeated air attacks by bombers and by torpedo-aircraft. These attacks were delivered with skill and determination. There were two high-level attacks, both of which scored hits, and three waves of torpedo-aircraft of nine in each wave which struck each of our ships with several torpedoes. There is no reason to suppose that any new weapons or explosives were employed, or any bombs or torpedoes of exceptional size. The continued waves of attack achieved their purpose, and both ships capsized and sank, having destroyed seven of the attacking aircraft.

The escorting destroyers came immediately to the rescue, and have now arrived at Singapore crowded with survivors.

ADDRESS TO A JOINT SESSION OF CONGRESS

26 December 1941

Washington, DC

Churchill wasted no time in heading for Washington aboard the battleship Duke of York, *sister ship of the* Prince of Wales *and* Repulse *that had been sunk by Japanese air attack off Singapore, the day after the attack on Pearl Harbor. He arrived in Washington on 22 December and spent the greater part of the next three weeks as the guest of the President at the White House. Churchill's principal objective was to persuade the American Government to give primacy to the defeat of Nazi Germany and the Liberation of Europe, over action against Japan in the Pacific. On the day after Christmas, he was invited to address a Joint Session of the United States Congress.*

I feel greatly honoured that you should have invited me to enter the United States Senate Chamber and address the representatives of both branches of Congress. The fact that my American forebears have for so many generations played their part in the life of the United States, and that here I am, an Englishman, welcomed in your midst, makes this experience one of the most moving and thrilling in my life, which is already long and has not been entirely uneventful. I wish indeed that my mother, whose memory I cherish across the vale of years, could have been here to see. By the way, I cannot help reflecting that if my father had been American and my mother British, instead of the other way round, I might have got here on my own. In that case, this would not have been the first time you would have heard my voice. In that case I should not have needed any

Address to a Joint Session of Congress, 26 December 1941.

invitation, but if I had, it is hardly likely it would have been unanimous. So perhaps things are better as they are. I may confess, however, that I do not feel quite like a fish out of water in a legislative assembly where English is spoken.

I am a child of the House of Commons. I was brought up in my father's house to believe in democracy. 'Trust the people' – that was his message. I used to see him cheered at meetings and in the streets by crowds of working men way back in those aristocratic Victorian days when, as Disraeli said, the world was for the few, and for the very few. Therefore I have been in full harmony all my life with the tides which have flowed on both sides of the Atlantic against privilege and monopoly, and I have steered confidently towards the Gettysburg ideal of 'government of the people by the people for the people.' I owe my advancement entirely to the House of Commons, whose servant I am. In my country, as in yours, public men are proud to be the servants of the State and would be ashamed to be its masters. On any day, if they thought the people wanted it, the House of Commons could by a simple vote remove me from my office. But I am not worrying about it at all. As a matter of fact, I am sure they will approve very highly of my journey here, for which I obtained the King's permission, in order to meet the President of the United States and to arrange with him all that mapping-out of our military plans, and for all those intimate meetings of the high officers of the armed services of both countries, which are indispensable to the successful prosecution of the war.

I should like to say first of all how much I have been impressed and encouraged by the breadth of view and sense of proportion which I have found in all quarters over here to which I have had access. Anyone who did not understand the size and solidarity of the foundations of the United States might easily have expected to find an excited, disturbed, self-centred atmosphere, with all minds fixed upon the novel, startling, and painful episodes of sudden war as they hit America. After all, the United States have been attacked and set upon by three most powerfully-armed dictator States. The greatest military power in Europe, the greatest military power in Asia, Germany and Japan, Italy, too, have all declared, and are making, war upon you, and a quarrel is opened, which can only end in their overthrow or yours. But here in Washington, in these memorable days, I have found an Olympian fortitude which, far from being based upon complacency, is only the mask of an inflexible purpose and the proof of a sure and well-grounded confidence in the final outcome. We in Britain had the same feeling in our darkest days. We, too, were sure in the end all would be well. You do not, I am certain, underrate the severity of the ordeal to which you and we have still to be subjected. The forces ranged against us are enormous. They are bitter, they are ruthless. The wicked men and their factions who have launched their peoples on the path of war and conquest know that they will be called to terrible account if they cannot beat down by force of arms the peoples they have assailed. They will stop at nothing. They have a vast accumulation of war weapons of all kinds. They have highly-trained, disciplined armies, navies, and air services. They have plans and designs which have long been tried and matured. They will stop at nothing that violence or treachery can suggest.

It is quite true that, on our side, our resources in manpower and materials are far greater than theirs. But only a portion of your resources is as yet mobilised and developed, and we both of us have much to learn in the cruel art of war. We have therefore, without doubt, a time of tribulation before us. In this time some ground will be lost which it will be hard and costly to regain. Many disappointments and unpleasant surprises await us. Many of them will afflict us before the full marshalling of our latent and total power can be accomplished. For the best part of twenty years the youth of Britain and America have been taught that war is evil, which is true, and that it would never come again, which has been proved false. For the best part of twenty years the youth of Germany, Japan and Italy have been taught that aggressive war is the noblest duty of the citizen, and that it should be begun as soon as the necessary weapons and organisation had been made. We have performed the duties and tasks of peace. They have plotted and planned for war. This, naturally, has placed us in Britain and now places you in the United States at a disadvantage which only time, courage, and strenuous, untiring exertions can correct.

We have indeed to be thankful that so much time has been granted to us. If Germany had tried to invade the British Isles after the French collapse in June, 1940, and if Japan had declared war on the British Empire and the United States at about the same date, no one could say what disasters and agonies might not have been our lot. But now, at the end of December, 1941, our transformation from easy-going peace to total war efficiency has made very great progress. The broad flow of munitions in Great Britain has already begun. Immense strides have been made in the conversion of American industry to military purposes, and now that the United States are at war it is possible for orders to be given every day which a year or eighteen months hence will produce results in war power beyond anything that has yet been seen or foreseen in the dictator States. Provided that every effort is made, that nothing is kept back, that the whole man-power, brain-power, virility, valour, and civic virtue of the English-speaking world with all its galaxy of loyal, friendly, associated communities and States – provided all that is bent unremittingly to the simple and supreme task, I think it would be reasonable to hope that the end of 1942 will see us quite definitely in a better position than we are now, and that the year 1943 will enable us to assume the initiative upon an ample scale.

Some people may be startled or momentarily depressed when, like your President, I speak of a long and hard war. But our peoples would rather know the truth, sombre though it be. And after all, when we are doing the noblest work in the world, not only defending our hearths and homes but the cause of freedom in other lands, the question of whether deliverance comes in 1942, 1943, or 1944 falls into its proper place in the grand proportions of human history. Sure I am that this day – now – we are the masters of our fate; that the task which has been set us is not above our strength; that its pangs and toils are not beyond our endurance. As long as we have faith in our cause and an unconquerable willpower, salvation will not be denied us. In the words of the Psalmist, 'He shall not be afraid of evil tidings; his heart is fixed, trusting in the Lord.' Not all the tidings will be evil.

On the contrary, mighty strokes of war have already been dealt against the enemy; the glorious defence of their native soil by the Russian armies and people have inflicted wounds upon the Nazi tyranny and system which have bitten deep, and will fester and inflame not only in the Nazi body but in the Nazi mind. The boastful Mussolini has crumbled already. He is now but a lackey and serf, the merest utensil of his master's will. He has inflicted great suffering and wrong upon his own industrious people. He has been stripped of his African empire, Abyssinia has been liberated. Our armies in the East, which were so weak and ill-equipped at the moment of French desertion, now control all the regions from Teheran to Benghazi, and from Aleppo and Cyprus to the sources of the Nile.

For many months we devoted ourselves to preparing to take the offensive in Libya. The very considerable battle, which has been proceeding for the last six weeks in the desert, has been most fiercely fought on both sides. Owing to the difficulties of supply on the desert flanks, we were never able to bring numerically equal forces to bear upon the enemy. Therefore we had to rely upon a superiority in the numbers and quality of tanks and aircraft, British and American. Aided by these, for the first time, we have fought the enemy with equal weapons. For the first time we have made the Hun feel the sharp edge of those tools with which he has enslaved Europe. The armed forces of the enemy in Cyrenaica amounted to about 150,000, of whom about one-third were Germans. General Auchinleck set out to destroy totally that armed force. I have every reason to believe that his aim will be fully accomplished. I am glad to be able to place before you, members of the Senate and of the House of Representatives, at this moment when you are entering the war, proof that with proper weapons and proper organisation we are able to beat the life out of the savage Nazi. What Hitler is suffering in Libya is only a sample and foretaste of what we must give him and his accomplices, wherever this war shall lead us, in every quarter of the globe.

There are good tidings also from blue water. The lifeline of supplies which joins our two nations across the ocean, without which all might fail, is flowing steadily and freely in spite of all the enemy can do. It is a fact that the British Empire, which many thought eighteen months ago was broken and ruined, is now incomparably stronger, and is growing stronger with every month. Lastly, if you will forgive me for saying it, to me the best tidings of all is that the United States, united as never before, have drawn the sword for freedom and cast away the scabbard.

All these tremendous facts have led the subjugated peoples of Europe to lift up their heads again in hope. They have put aside for ever the shameful temptation of resigning themselves to the conqueror's will. Hope has returned to the hearts of scores of millions of men and women, and with that hope there burns the flame of anger against the brutal, corrupt invader, and still more fiercely burn the fires of hatred and contempt for the squalid quislings whom he has suborned. In a dozen famous ancient States now prostrate under the Nazi yoke, the masses of the people of all classes and creeds await the hour of liberation, when they too will be able once again to play their part and strike their blows like men. That hour will strike, and its solemn peal will proclaim that the night is past and that the dawn has come.

The onslaught upon us so long and so secretly planned by Japan has presented both our countries with grievous problems for which we could not be fully prepared. If people ask me – as they have a right to ask me in England – why is it that you have not got ample equipment of modern aircraft and Army weapons of all kinds in Malaya and in the East Indies, I can only point to the victories

General Auchinleck has gained in the Libyan campaign. Had we diverted and dispersed our gradually growing resources between Libya and Malaya, we should have been found wanting in both theatres. If the United States have been found at a disadvantage at various points in the Pacific Ocean, we know well that it is to no small extent because of the aid you have been giving us in munitions for the defence of the British Isles and for the Libyan campaign, and, above all, because of your help in the battle of the Atlantic, upon which all depends, and which has in consequence been successfully and prosperously maintained. Of course it would have been much better, I freely admit, if we had had enough resources of all kinds to be at full strength at all threatened points; but considering how slowly and reluctantly we brought ourselves to large-scale preparations, and how long such preparations take, we had no right to expect to be in such a fortunate position.

The choice of how to dispose of our hitherto limited resources had to be made by Britain in time of war and by the United States in time of peace; and I believe that history will pronounce that upon the whole – and it is upon the whole that these matters must be judged – the choice made was right. Now that we are together, now that we are linked in a righteous comradeship of arms, now that our two considerable nations, each in perfect unity, have joined all their life energies in a common resolve, a new scene opens upon which a steady light will glow and brighten.

Many people have been astonished that Japan should in a single day have plunged into war against the United States and the British Empire. We all wonder why, if this dark design, with all its laborious and intricate preparations, had been so long filling their secret minds, they did not choose our moment of weakness eighteen months ago. Viewed quite dispassionately, in spite of the losses we have suffered and the further punishment we shall have to take, it certainly appears to be an irrational act. It is, of course, only prudent to assume that they have made very careful calculations and think they see their way through. Nevertheless, there may be another explanation. We know that for many years past the policy of Japan has been dominated by secret societies of subalterns and junior officers of the Army and Navy, who have enforced their will upon successive Japanese Cabinets and Parliaments by the assassination of any Japanese statesman who opposed, or who did not sufficiently further, their aggressive policy. It may be that those societies, dazzled and dizzy with their own schemes of aggression and the prospect of early victories, have forced their country against its better judgment into war. They have certainly embarked upon a very considerable undertaking. For after the outrages they have committed upon us at Pearl Harbor, in the Pacific Islands, in the Philippines, in Malaya, and in the Dutch East Indies, they must now know that the stakes for which they have decided to play are mortal.

When we consider the resources of the United States and the British Empire compared to those of Japan, when we remember those of China, which has so long and valiantly withstood invasion and when also we observe the Russian menace which hangs over Japan, it becomes still more difficult to reconcile Japanese action with prudence or even with sanity. What kind of a people do they think we are? Is it possible they do not realise that we shall never cease to persevere against them until they have been taught a lesson which they and the world will never forget?

Members of the Senate and members of the House of Representatives, I turn for one moment more from the turmoil and convulsions of the present to the broader basis of the future. Here we are together facing a group of mighty foes who seek our ruin; here we are together defending all that to free men is dear. Twice in a single generation the catastrophe of world war has fallen upon us; twice in our lifetime has the long arm of fate reached across the ocean to bring the United States into the forefront of the battle. If we had kept together after the last war, if we had taken common measures for our safety, this renewal of the curse need never have fallen upon us.

Do we not owe it to ourselves, to our children, to mankind tormented, to make sure that these catastrophes shall not engulf us for the third time? It has been proved that pestilences may break out in the Old World, which carry their destructive ravages into the New World, from which, once they are afoot, the New World cannot by any means escape. Duty and prudence alike command first that the germ-centres of hatred and revenge should be constantly and vigilantly surveyed and treated in good time, and, secondly, that an adequate organisation should be set up to make sure that the pestilence can be controlled at its earliest beginnings before it spreads and rages throughout the entire earth.

Five or six years ago it would have been easy, without shedding a drop of blood, for the United States and Great Britain to have insisted on fulfilment of the disarmament clauses of the treaties which Germany signed after the Great War; that also would have been the opportunity for assuring to Germany those raw materials which we declared in the Atlantic Charter should not be denied to any nation, victor or vanquished. That chance has passed. It is gone. Prodigious hammer-strokes have been needed to bring us together again, or if you will allow me to use other language, I will say that he must indeed have a blind soul who cannot see that some great purpose and design is being worked out here below, of which we have the honour to be the faithful servants. It is not given to us to peer into the mysteries of the future. Still, I avow my hope and faith, sure and inviolate, that in the days to come the British and American peoples will for their own safety and for the good of all walk together side by side in majesty, in justice, and in peace.

'SOME CHICKEN! SOME NECK!'

30 December 1941

Joint Session of the Canadian Parliament, Ottawa

Churchill made a brief trip by train to Canada to attend a meeting of the Canadian War Cabinet on 29 December and the next day he addressed the Canadian Parliament.

I should like to point out to you that we have not at any time asked for any mitigation in the fury or malice of the enemy. The peoples of the British Empire may love peace. They do not seek the lands or wealth of any country, but they are a tough and hardy lot. We have not journeyed all this way across the centuries, across the oceans, across the mountains, across the prairies, because we are made of sugar candy.

Look at the Londoners, the Cockneys; look at what they have stood up to. Grim and gay with their cry 'We can take it,' and their wartime mood of 'What is good enough for anybody is good enough for us.' We have not asked that the rules of the game should be modified. We shall never descend to the German and Japanese level, but if anybody likes to play rough we can play rough too. Hitler and his Nazi gang have sown the wind; let them reap the whirlwind. Neither the length of the struggle nor any form of severity which it may assume shall make us weary or shall make us quit. . . .

Let us then look back. We plunged into this war all unprepared because we had pledged our word to stand by the side of Poland, which Hitler had feloniously invaded, and in spite of a gallant resistance had soon struck down. There followed those astonishing seven months which were called on this side of the Atlantic the 'phoney' war. Suddenly the explosion of pent-up German strength and preparation burst upon Norway, Denmark, Holland, and Belgium. All these absolutely blameless neutrals, to most of whom Germany up to the last moment was giving every kind of guarantee and assurance, were overrun and trampled down. The hideous massacre of Rotterdam, where 30,000 people perished, showed the ferocious barbarism in which the German Air Force revels when, as in Warsaw and later Belgrade, it is able to bomb practically undefended cities.

On top of all this came the great French catastrophe. The French Army collapsed, and the French nation was dashed into utter and, as it has so far proved, irretrievable confusion. The French Government had at their own suggestion solemnly bound themselves with us not to make a separate peace. It was their duty and it was also their interest to go to North Africa, where they would have been at the head of the French Empire. In Africa, with our aid, they would have had overwhelming sea power. They would have had the recognition of the United States, and the use of all the gold they had lodged beyond the seas. If they had done this Italy might have been driven out of the war before the end of 1940, and France would have held her place as a nation in the counsels of the Allies and at the conference table of the victors. But their generals misled them. When I warned them that Britain would fight on alone whatever they did, their generals told their Prime Minister and his divided Cabinet, 'In three weeks England will have her neck wrung like a chicken.' Some chicken! Some neck!

'I DEMAND A VOTE OF CONFIDENCE'

27 January 1942

House of Commons

With the war situation deteriorating on all fronts, Churchill hurried back to England by flying-boat via Bermuda. In North Africa Rommel's army was advancing eastwards towards Cairo and the Suez Canal, while in the Far East Hong Kong had fallen to the

Japanese on 25 December and British forces were surrounded in Singapore. Churchill wrote in The Hinge of Fate: *'I resolved to yield nothing to any quarter, to take the prime and direct responsibility upon myself, and to demand a Vote of Confidence from the House of Commons.' This was triumphantly carried, after a three-day debate, by a vote of 464–1.*

From time to time in the life of any Government there come occasions which must be clarified. No one who has read the newspapers of the last few weeks about our affairs at home and abroad can doubt that such an occasion is at hand.

Since my return to this country, I have come to the conclusion that I must ask to be sustained by a Vote of Confidence from the House of Commons. This is a thoroughly normal, constitutional, democratic procedure. A Debate on the war has been asked for. I have arranged it in the fullest and freest manner for three whole days. Any Member will be free to say anything he thinks fit about or against the Administration or against the composition or personalities of the Government, to his heart's content, subject only to the reservation which the House is always so careful to observe about military secrets. Could you have anything freer than that? Could you have any higher expression of democracy than that? Very few other countries have institutions strong enough to sustain such a thing while they are fighting for their lives.

I owe it to the House to explain to them what has led me to ask for their exceptional support at this time. It has been suggested that we should have a three days' Debate of this kind in which the Government would no doubt be lustily belaboured by some of those who have lighter burdens to carry, and that at the end we should separate without a Division. In this case sections of the Press which are hostile – and there are some whose hostility is pronounced – could declare that the Government's credit was broken, and it might even be hinted, after all that has passed and all the discussion there has been, that it had been privately intimated to me that I should be very reckless if I asked for a Vote of Confidence from Parliament.

And the matter does not stop there. It must be remembered that these reports can then be flashed all over the world, and that they are repeated in enemy broadcasts night after night in order to show that the Prime Minister has no right to speak for the nation and that the Government in Britain is about to collapse. Anyone who listens to the fulminations which come from across the water knows that that is no exaggeration. Of course, these statements from foreign sources would not be true, but neither would it be helpful to anyone that there should be any doubt about our position.

There is another aspect. We in this Island for a long time were alone, holding aloft the torch. We are no longer alone now. We are now at the centre and among those at the summit of 26 United Nations, comprising more than three-quarters of the population of the globe. Whoever speaks for Britain at this moment must be known to speak, not only in the name of the people – and that I feel pretty sure I may – but in the name of Parliament and, above all, of the House of Commons. It is a genuine public interest that requires that these facts should be made manifest afresh in a formal way.

We have had a great deal of bad news lately from the Far East, and I think it highly probable, for reasons which I shall presently explain, that we shall have a great deal more. Wrapped up in this bad news will be many tales of blunders and shortcomings, both in foresight and action. No one will pretend for a moment that disasters like these occur without there having been faults and shortcomings. I see all this rolling towards us like the waves in a storm, and that is another reason why I require a formal, solemn Vote of Confidence from the House of Commons, which hitherto in this struggle has never flinched. The House would fail in its duty if it did not insist upon two things, first, freedom of debate, and, secondly, a clear, honest, blunt vote thereafter. Then we shall all know where we are, and all those with whom we have to deal, at home and abroad, friend or foe, will know where we are and where they are. It is because we are to have a free debate, in which perhaps 20 to 30 Members can take part, that I demand an expression of opinion from the 300 or 400 Members who will have to sit silent.

It is because things have gone badly and worse is to come that I demand a Vote of Confidence. This will be placed on the Paper today, to be moved at a later stage. I do not see why this should hamper anyone. If a Member has helpful criticisms to make, or even severe corrections to administer, that may be perfectly consistent with thinking that in respect of the Administration, such as it is, he might go farther and fare worse. But if an hon. Gentleman dislikes the Government very much and feels it in the public interest that it should be broken up, he ought to have the manhood to testify his convictions in the Lobby. There is no need to be mealy-mouthed in debate. There is no objection to anything being said, plain, or even plainer, and the Government will do their utmost to conform to any standard which may be set in the course of the debate. But no one need be mealy-mouthed in debate, and no one should be chicken-hearted in voting. I have voted against Governments I have been elected to support, and, looking back, I have sometimes felt very glad that I did so. Everyone in these rough times must do what he thinks is his duty.

The House of Commons, which is at present the most powerful representative Assembly in the world, must also – I am sure, will also – bear in mind the effect produced abroad by all its proceedings. We have also to remember how oddly foreigners view our country and its way of doing things. When Rudolf Hess flew over here some months ago he firmly believed that he had only to gain access to certain circles in this country for what he described as 'the Churchill clique' to be thrown out of power and for the Government to be set up with which Hitler could negotiate a magnanimous peace. The only importance attaching to the opinions of Hess is the fact that he was fresh from the atmosphere of Hitler's intimate table. But, I can assure you that since I have been back in this country I have had anxious inquiries from a dozen countries, and reports of enemy propaganda in a score of countries, all turning upon the point whether His Majesty's present Government is to be dismissed from power or not. This may seem silly to us, but in those mouths abroad it is hurtful and mischievous to the common effort. I am not asking for any special, personal favours in these circumstances, but I am sure the House would wish to make its position clear; therefore I stand by the ancient, constitutional, Parliamentary doctrine of free debate and faithful voting. . . .

There never has been a moment, there never could have been a moment, when Great Britain or the British Empire, single-handed, could fight Germany and Italy, could wage the Battle of Britain, the Battle of the Atlantic and the Battle of the Middle East – and at the same time stand thoroughly prepared in Burma, the Malay Peninsula, and generally in the Far East against the impact of a vast military Empire like Japan, with more than 70 mobile divisions, the third navy in the world, a great air force, and the thrust of 80 or 90 millions of hardy, warlike Asiatics. If we had started to scatter our forces over these immense areas in the Far East, we should have been ruined. If we had moved large armies of troops urgently needed on the war fronts to regions which were not at war and might never be at war, we should have been altogether wrong. We should have cast away the chance, which has now become something more than a chance, of all of us emerging safely from the terrible plight in which we have been plunged. . . .

The outstanding question upon which the House should form its judgment for the purposes of the impending Division is whether His Majesty's Government were right in giving a marked priority in the distribution of the forces and equipment we could send overseas, to Russia, to Libya, and, to a lesser extent, to the Levant–Caspian danger front, and whether we were right in accepting, for the time being, a far lower standard of forces and equipment for the Far East than for these other theatres. . . .

Let me, in conclusion, return to the terrific changes which have occurred in our affairs during the last few months and particularly in the last few weeks. We have to consider the prospects of the war in 1942 and also in 1943, and, as I said just now, it is not useful to look farther ahead than that. The moment that the United States was set upon and attacked by Japan, Germany and Italy – that is to say, within a few days of December 7, 1941 – I was sure it was my duty to cross the Atlantic and establish the closest possible relationship with the President and Government of the United States, and also to develop the closest contacts, personal and professional, between the British Chiefs of Staff and their transatlantic deputies, and with the American Chiefs of Staff who were there to meet them.

Having crossed the Atlantic, it was plainly my duty to visit the great Dominion of Canada. The House will have read with admiration and deep interest the speech made by the Prime Minister of Canada yesterday on Canada's great and growing contribution to the common cause in men, in money, and in materials. A notable part of that contribution is the financial offer which the Canadian Government have made to this country. The sum involved is one billion Canadian dollars, about £225,000,000. I know the House will wish me to convey to the Government of Canada our lively appreciation of their timely and most generous offer. It is unequalled in its scale in the whole history of the British Empire, and it is a convincing proof of the determination of Canada to make her maximum contribution towards the successful prosecution of the war.

During those three weeks which I spent in Mr Roosevelt's home and family, I established with him relations not only of comradeship, but, I think I may say, of friendship. We can say anything to each other, however painful. When we parted he wrung my hand, saying, 'We will fight this through to the bitter end, whatever the cost may be.' Behind him rises the gigantic and hitherto unmobilised power of the people of the United States, carrying with them in their life and death struggle the entire, or almost the entire, Western hemisphere. . . .

Although I feel the broadening swell of victory and liberation bearing us and all the tortured peoples onwards safely to the final goal, I must confess to feeling the weight of the war upon me even more than in the tremendous summer days of 1940. There are so many fronts which are open, so many vulnerable points to defend, so many inevitable misfortunes, so many shrill voices raised to take advantage, now that we can breathe more freely, of all the turns and twists of war. Therefore, I feel entitled to come to the House of Commons, whose servant I am, and ask them not to press me to act against my conscience and better judgment and make scapegoats in order to improve my own position, not to press me to do the things which may be clamoured for at the moment but which will not help in our war effort, but, on the contrary, to give me their encouragement and to give me their aid. I have never ventured to predict the future. I stand by my original programme, blood, toil, tears and sweat, which is all I have ever offered, to which I added, five months later, 'many shortcomings, mistakes and disappointments'. But it is because I see the light gleaming behind the clouds and broadening on our path, that I make so bold now as to demand a declaration of confidence of the House of Commons as an additional weapon in the armoury of the United Nations.

'SINGAPORE HAS FALLEN'

15 February 1942

Broadcast, London

On 15 February, General Percival, Commander-in-Chief of British and Dominion troops in Singapore, surrendered unconditionally to the Japanese.

Tonight I speak to you at home; I speak to you in Australia and New Zealand, for whose safety we will strain every nerve; to our loyal friends in India and Burma; to our gallant Allies, the Dutch and Chinese; and to our kith and kin in the United States. I speak to you all under the shadow of a heavy and far-reaching military defeat. It is a British and Imperial defeat. Singapore has fallen. All the Malay Peninsula has been overrun. Other dangers gather about us out there, and none of the dangers which we have hitherto successfully withstood at home and in the East are in any way diminished. This, therefore, is one of those moments when the British race and nation can show their quality and their genius. This is one of those moments when it can draw from the heart of misfortune the vital impulses of victory. Here is the moment to display that calm and poise combined with grim determination which not so long ago brought us out of the very jaws of death. Here is another occasion to show – as so often in our long story – that we can meet reverses with dignity and with renewed accessions of strength. We must remember that we are no longer alone. We are in the midst of a great company. Three-quarters of the human race are now moving with us. The whole future of mankind may depend upon our action and upon our conduct. So far we have not failed. We shall not fail now. Let us move forward steadfastly together into the storm and through the storm.

PRIME MINISTER FOR TWO YEARS

10 May 1942

Broadcast, London

Amid all the storms and reverses, Churchill takes stock of his first two years as Prime Minister.

I have now served for two years exactly to a day as the King's First Minister. Therefore I thought it would be a good thing if I had a talk to you on the broadcast, to look back a little on what we have come through, to consider how we stand now, and to peer cautiously, but at the same time resolutely, into the future.

The tremendous period through which we have passed has certainly been full of anxieties and exertions; it has been marked by many misfortunes and disappointments. This time two years ago the Germans were beating down Holland and Belgium by unprovoked brutal, merciless invasion, and very soon there came upon us the total defeat of France and the fatal surrender at Bordeaux. Mussolini, the Italian miscalculator, thought he saw his chance of a cheap and easy triumph, and rich plunder for no fighting. He struck at the back of a dying France, and at what he believed was a doomed Britain. We were left alone – our quarter of a million Dunkirk troops saved, only disarmed; ourselves, as yet unarmed – to face the might of victorious Germany, to face also the carefully saved-up strength of an Italy which then still ranked as a first-class Power.

Here at home in this island, invasion was near; the Mediterranean was closed to us; the long route round the Cape, where General Smuts stands on guard, alone was open; our small, ill-equipped forces in Egypt and the Sudan seemed to await destruction. All the world, even our best friends, thought that our end had come. Accordingly, we prepared ourselves to conquer or to perish. We were united in that solemn, majestic hour; we were all equally resolved at least to go down fighting. We cast calculation to the winds; no wavering voice was heard; we hurled defiance at our foes; we faced our duty, and, by the mercy of God, we were preserved.

It fell to me in those days to express the sentiments and resolves of the British nation in that supreme crisis of its life. That was to me an honour far beyond any dreams or ambitions I had ever nursed, and it is one that cannot be taken away. For a whole year after the fall of France we stood alone, keeping the flag of freedom flying, and the hopes of the world alive. We conquered the Italian Empire, we destroyed or captured almost all Mussolini's African army; we liberated Abyssinia; we have so far successfully protected Palestine, Syria, Persia and Iraq from German designs. We have suffered grievous reverses in going to the aid of the heroic Greeks; we bore unflinching many a heavy blow abroad, and still more in our cities here at home; and all this time, cheered and helped by President Roosevelt and the United States, we stood alone, neither faltering nor flagging.

Where are we now? Can anyone doubt that if we are worthy of it, as we shall be, we have in our hands our own future? As in the last war, so in this, we are moving through many reverses and defeats to complete and final victory. We have only to endure and to persevere, to conquer. Now we are no longer unarmed; we are well armed. Now we are not alone; we have mighty allies, bound irrevocably by solemn faith and common interests to stand with us in the ranks of the United Nations. There can only be one end. When it will come, or how it will come, I cannot tell. But, when we survey the overwhelming resources which are at our disposal, once they are fully marshalled and developed – as they can be, as they will be – we may stride forward into the unknown with growing confidence.

During the time that we were all alone, we were steadily growing stronger. He would have been a bold man, however, who in those days would have put down in black and white exactly how we were going to win. But, as has happened before in our island history, by remaining steadfast and unyielding – stubborn, if you will – against a Continental tyrant, we reached the moment when that tyrant made a fatal blunder. Dictators, as well as democracies and parliamentary governments, make mistakes sometimes. Indeed, when the whole story is told, I believe it will be found that the Dictators, for all their preparations and prolonged scheming, have made greater mistakes than the Democracies they have assailed. Even Hitler makes mistakes sometimes. In June last, without the slightest provocation, and in breach of a pact of non-aggression, he invaded the lands of the Russian people. At that time he had the strongest army in the world, trained in war, flushed with incredible unbroken success, and equipped with limitless munitions and the most modern weapons. He had also secured for himself the advantages of surprise and treachery. Thus he drove the youth and manhood of the German nation forward into Russia.

The Russians, under their warrior chief, Stalin, sustained losses which no other country or government has ever borne in so short a time and lived. But they, like us, were resolved never to give in. They poured out their own blood upon their native soil. They kept their faces to the foe. From the very first day to the end of the year, and on till tonight, they fought with unflinching valour. And, from the very first day when they were attacked, when no one could tell how things would go, we made a brotherhood with them, and a solemn compact to destroy Nazidom and all its works. Then Hitler made his second grand blunder. He forgot about the winter. There is a winter, you know, in Russia. For a good many months the temperature is apt to fall very low. There is snow, there is frost, and all that. Hitler forgot about this Russian winter. He must have been very loosely educated. We all heard about it at school; but he forgot it. I have never made such a bad mistake as that. So winter came, and fell upon his ill-clad armies, and with the winter came the valiant Russian counter-attacks. No one can say with certainty how many millions of Germans have already perished in Russia and its snows. Certainly more have perished than were killed in the whole four and a quarter years of the last war. That is probably an understatement. So besotted is this man in his lust for blood and conquest, so blasting is the power he wields over the lives of Germans, that he even blurted out the other day that his armies would be better clothed and his locomotives better prepared for their second winter in Russia than they were for their first.

There was an admission about the length of the war that struck a chill into German hearts as cold as the icy winds of Russia. What will be the sufferings of the German manhood in this new bloodbath? What is there in front of Hitler now? Certain it is that the Russian armies are stronger than they were last year, that they have learnt by hard experience to fight the Germans in the field, that they are well-equipped, and that their constancy and courage are unquenched. That is what is in front of Hitler. What is he leaving behind him? He leaves behind him a Europe starving and in chains; a Europe in which his execution squads are busy in a dozen countries every day; a Europe which has learned to hate the Nazi name as no name has ever been hated in the recorded history of mankind; a Europe burning for revolt whenever the opportunity comes.

But this is not all he has left behind. We are on his tracks, and so is the great Republic of the United States. Already the Royal Air Force has set about it; the British, and presently the American, bombing offensive against Germany will be one of the principal features in this year's world war. Now is the time to use our increasingly superior air strength, to strike hard and continually at the home front in Germany, from which so much evil has leaked out upon the world, and which is the foundation of the whole enormous German invasion of Russia. Now, while the German armies will be bleeding and burning up their strength against the two-thousand-mile Russian line, and when the news of casualties by hundreds of thousands is streaming back to the German Reich, now is the time to bring home to the German people the wickedness of their rulers, by destroying under their very eyes the factories and seaports on which their war effort depends.

German propaganda has been constantly appealing of late to British public opinion to put a stop to these severe forms of warfare, which, according to the German view, should be the strict monopoly of the *Herrenvolk*. Herr Hitler himself has not taken at all kindly to this treatment, and he has been good enough to mingle terrible threats with his whinings. He warns us, solemnly, that if we go on smashing up the German cities, his war factories and his bases, he will retaliate against our cathedrals and historic monuments – if they are not too far inland. We have heard his threats before. Eighteen months ago, in September, 1940, when he thought he had an overwhelming Air Force at his command, he declared that he would rub out – that was the actual expression, rub out – our towns and cities. And he certainly had a good try. Now the boot is on the other leg. Herr Hitler has even called in question the humanity of these grim developments of war. What a pity this conversation did not take place in his heart before he bombed Warsaw, or massacred twenty thousand Dutch folk in defenceless Rotterdam, or wreaked his cruel vengeance upon the open city of Belgrade! In those days, he used to boast that for every ton of bombs we dropped on Germany, he would drop ten times, or even a hundred times as many on Britain. Those were his words, and that was his belief. Indeed, for a time we had to suffer very severely from his vastly superior strength and utter ruthlessness.

But now it is the other way round. We are in a position to carry into Germany many times the tonnage of high explosives which he can send here, and this proportion will increase all the summer, all the autumn, all the winter, all the spring, all the summer, and so on, till the end! The accuracy of our bombing has nearly doubled, and, with continued practice, I expect it will improve still more. Moreover, at the same time, our methods of dealing with his raiders over here have more than repaid the immense care and science bestowed upon them, and the very large scale upon which they are applied. During the month of April we have destroyed one-tenth of all the raiding aircraft which have assailed our island; whereas, acting on a scale several times as big, the losses which we have suffered have been proportionately far smaller. We have waited long for this turning of the tables, and have taken whatever came to us meanwhile.

You will remember how the German propaganda films, seeking to terrorise neutral countries and glorying in devastating violence, were wont to show rows of great German bombers being loaded up with bombs, then flying in the air in battle array, then casting down showers of bombs upon the defenceless towns and villages below, choking them in smoke and flame. All this was represented from the beginning of the war to neutral countries as the German way of making war. All this was intended to make the world believe that resistance to the German will was impossible, and that subjugation and slavery were the safest and easiest road. Those days are gone. Though the mills of God grind slowly, yet they grind exceedingly small. And for my part, I hail it as an example of sublime and poetic justice that those who have loosed these horrors upon mankind will now in their homes and persons feel the shattering strokes of just retribution.

We have a long list of German cities in which all the vital industries of the German war machine are established. All these it will be our stern duty to deal with, as we have already dealt with Lübeck, and Rostock, and half-a-dozen important places. The civil population of Germany have, however, an easy way to escape from these severities. All they have to do is to leave the cities where munitions work is being carried on – abandon their work, and go into the fields, and watch their home fires burning from a distance. In this way they may find time for meditation and repentance; there they may remember the millions of Russian women and children they have driven out to perish in the snows, and the mass executions of peasantry and prisoners-of-war which in varying scales they are inflicting upon so many of the ancient and famous peoples of Europe. There they may remember that it is the villainous Hitlerite régime which is responsible for dragging Germany through misery and slaughter to ultimate ruin, and learn that the tyrant's overthrow is the first step to world liberation.

We now wait in what is a stormy lull, but still a lull, before the hurricane bursts again in full fury on the Russian front. We cannot tell when it will begin; we have not so far seen any evidences of those great concentrations of German masses which usually precede their large-scale offensives. They may have been successfully concealed, or may not yet have been launched eastward. But it is now the tenth of May, and the days are passing. We send our salutations to the Russian armies, and we hope that the thousands of tanks and aeroplanes which have been carried to their aid from Britain and America will be a useful contribution to their own magnificently developed and reorganised munitions resources.

There is, however, one serious matter which I must mention to you. The Soviet Government have expressed to us the view that the Germans in the desperation of their assault may make use of poison gas against the armies and people of Russia. We are ourselves firmly resolved not to use this odious weapon unless it is used first by the Germans. Knowing our Hun, however, we have not neglected to make preparations on a formidable scale. I wish now to make it plain that we shall treat the unprovoked use of poison gas against our Russian ally exactly as if it were used against ourselves, and if we are satisfied that this new outrage has been committed by Hitler, we shall use our great and growing air superiority in the West to carry gas warfare on the largest possible scale far and wide against military objectives in Germany. It is thus for Hitler to choose whether he wishes to add this additional horror to aerial warfare. We have for some time past been bringing our defensive and precautionary arrangements up to date, and I now give public warning, so that there may be no carelessness or neglect. Of one thing I am sure: that the British people, who have entered into the full comradeship of war with our Russian ally, will not shrink from any sacrifice or trial which that comradeship may require.

Meanwhile, our deliveries of tanks, aircraft and munitions to Russia from Britain and from the United States continue upon the full scale. We have the duty of escorting the northern convoys to their destination. Our sailors and merchant seamen face the fearful storms of the Arctic Circle, the lurking U-boats and shore-based aircraft, as well as attacks by German destroyers and surface craft, with their customary steadfastness and faithful courage. So far, though not without some loss both to the supply ships and their escorts, every convoy has successfully fought its way through, and we intend to persevere and fight it out on this northern route to the utmost of our strength.

Is there anything else we can do to take the weight off Russia? We are urged from many quarters to invade the Continent of Europe and so form a second front. Naturally, I shall not disclose what our intentions are, but there is one thing I will say: I welcome the militant, aggressive spirit of the British nation so strongly shared across the Atlantic Ocean. Is it not far better that in the thirty-second month of this hard war we should find this general desire to come to the closest grips with the enemy, than that there should be any signs of war-weariness? Is it not far better that demonstrations of thousands of people should gather in Trafalgar Square demanding the most vehement and audacious attacks, than that there should be the weepings and wailings and peace agitations which in other lands and other wars have often hampered the action and vigour of governments? It is encouraging and inspiring to feel the strong heartbeats of a free nation, surging forward, stern and undaunted, in a righteous cause. We must not fail them, either in daring or in wisdom.

This week, two islands have been in our minds – one is very large, the other very small – Madagascar and Malta. We have found it necessary to take precautions to prevent Madagascar falling into enemy hands, by some dishonourable and feeble drifting or conniv-ance by Vichy, like that which injured us so much in Indo-China. It is three months since the decision was taken, and more than two months since the expedition left these shores. Its first task was to secure the splendid harbour of Diego Suarez, in the northern part of Madagascar, which, if it had fallen into Japanese hands, might have paralysed all our communications with India and the Middle East. While the troops were on the sea, I must tell you I felt a shiver every time I saw the word 'Madagascar' in the newspapers. All those articles with diagrams and measured maps, showing how very important it was for us to take Madagascar and forestall the Japanese, and be there 'first for once', as they said, filled me with apprehension. There was no question of leakage, or breach of confidence. As they say, great minds think alike. But shrewd surmise may be as dangerous as leakage. And it was with considerable relief that I learned the difficulties of our soldiers and their losses had been exaggerated, and that the operation had been swiftly and effectually carried out.

We hold this island in trust; we hold it in trust for that gallant France which we have known and marched with, and whose restoration to her place among the great Powers of the world is indispensable to the future of Europe. Madagascar rests under the safeguard of the United Nations. Vichy, in the grip of the Germans, has been made to bluster and protest. The France that rose at St Nazaire, and will one day rise in indescribable fury against the Nazis, understands what we have done and gives us its trust.

The smaller island is Malta, a tiny rock of history and romance. Today we welcomed back to our shores General Dobbie, for nearly two years the heroic defender of Malta. The burden which he has borne so honourably and for so long entitles him to release and repose. In Lord Gort we have a new impulse. His work at Gibraltar has been of the highest order. It was not his fault that our armies did not have their chance in France. He is a grand fighter. For the moment the terrific air attack on Malta has slackened. It looks as if a lot of enemy aircraft had moved eastward. I wonder why? If so, another intense air battle for Malta, upon which the enemy have concentrated such an immense preponderance of strength, and for which they have sacrificed so many of those aircraft which they now have to count more carefully every day – another intense air battle will have been definitely won. But other perils remain, and I know of no man in the British Empire to whom I would sooner entrust the combating and beating-down of those perils than Lord Gort.

If we look back today over the course of the war as it has so far unfolded, we can see that it seems to divide itself into four very clearly defined chapters. The first ended with the overrunning by the

Nazis of Western Europe and with the fall of France. The second chapter, Britain alone, ended with Hitler's attack upon Russia. I will call the third chapter which then began, 'the Russian glory'. May it long continue! The fourth chapter opened at Pearl Harbor, when the military party in Japan treacherously attacked the United States and Great Britain in the Far East. That is where we are now.

The aggression of Italy in 1940 had carried the war from Europe to Africa. The aggression of Japan has involved all Asia, including unconquerable China, and in one way or another has drawn in, or will draw in, the whole of the American Continent. Thus the struggle has become world-wide, and the fate of all states and nations and their future is at stake. This latest chapter – universal war – confronts us with many difficulties and immense complications. But is there any thoughtful sensible person who cannot see how vastly and decisively the awful balances have turned to the advantage of the cause of freedom? It is true that the Japanese, taking advantage of our preoccupations elsewhere, and of the fact that the United States had striven for so long to keep the peace, have seized more easily and more quickly than they expected their lands of booty and desire in the East Indian Archipelago. Henceforward they will find resistance stiffening on all their widely-spread fronts. They can ill afford losses such as those they have sustained in the naval action of the Coral Sea; so far we have no detailed accounts, but it is obvious, if only from the lies the Japanese have felt compelled to tell about the sinking of a battleship of the *Warspite* class, that a most vigorous and successful battle has been fought by the United States and Australian naval forces.

The Japanese warlords cannot be indifferent to the losses of aircraft inflicted upon them at so many points, and particularly off the northern coasts of Australia, and in their repulse at Colombo and Trincomalee. At the start the pent-up, saved-up resources of Japan were bound to prevail in the Far Eastern theatre; but the strength of the United States, expressed in units of modern war power, actual and potential, is alone many times greater than the power of Japan. And we also shall make our contribution to the final defeat and punishment of this ambitious and greedy nation. Time will, however, be needed before the true strengths on either side of the Eastern war become manifest. I am not prone to make predictions, but I have no doubt tonight that the British and American sea power will grip and hold the Japanese, and that overwhelming air power, covering vigorous military operations, will lay them low. This would come to pass, of course, very much sooner, should anything happen to Hitler in Europe.

Therefore tonight I give you a message of good cheer. You deserve it, and the facts endorse it. But be it good cheer or be it bad cheer will make no difference to us; we shall drive on to the end, and do our duty, win or die. God helping us, we can do no other.

MOTION OF CENSURE

2 July 1942

House of Commons

This was the nadir of Britain's military fortunes. A long succession of British defeats culminated in the fall of Tobruk in North Africa, bringing the German–Italian army under Field Marshal Rommel within a hundred miles of Cairo. Churchill's critics tabled a motion expressing 'No confidence in the central direction of the war'. Hore-Belisha, Secretary of State for War under Neville Chamberlain, launched a fierce attack on the Prime Minister, declaring: 'In a hundred days we have lost our Empire in the Far East. What will happen in the next hundred days?' Following the Prime Minister's speech, the motion was rejected by 475 to 25 votes.

This long Debate has now reached its final stage. What a remarkable example it has been of the unbridled freedom of our Parliamentary institutions in time of war! Everything that could be thought of or raked up has been used to weaken confidence in the Government, has been used to prove that Ministers are incompetent and to weaken their confidence in themselves, to make the Army distrust the backing it is getting from the civil power, to make the workmen lose confidence in the weapons they are striving so hard to make, to represent the Government as a set of nonentities over whom the Prime Minister towers, and then to undermine him in his own heart and, if possible, before the eyes of the nation. All this poured out by cable and radio to all parts of the world, to the distress of all our friends and to the delight of all our foes. I am in favour of this freedom, which no other country would use, or dare to use, in times of mortal peril such as those through which we are passing. But the story must not end there, and I make now my appeal to the House of Commons to make sure that it does not end there.

Although I have done my best, my utmost, to prepare a full and considered statement for the House, I must confess that I have found it very difficult, even during the bitter animosity of the diatribe of the hon. Member for Ebbw Vale [Mr Bevan], with all its carefully aimed and calculated hostility, to concentrate my thoughts upon this Debate and to withdraw them from the tremendous and most critical battle now raging in Egypt. . . .

The mover of this Vote of Censure has proposed that I should be stripped of my responsibilities for Defence in order that some military figure or some other unnamed personage should assume the general conduct of the war, that he should have complete control of the Armed Forces of the Crown, that he should be the Chief of the Chiefs of the Staff, that he should nominate or dismiss the generals or the admirals, that he should always be ready to resign, that is to say, to match himself against his political colleagues, if colleagues they could be considered, if he did not get all he wanted, that he should have under him a Royal Duke as Commander-in-Chief of the Army, and finally, I presume, though this was not mentioned, that this unnamed personage should find an appendage in the Prime Minister to make the necessary explanations, excuses and apologies to Parliament when things go wrong, as they often do and often will. That is at any rate a policy. It is a system very different from the Parliamentary system under which we live. It might easily amount to or be converted into a dictatorship. I wish to make it perfectly clear that as far as I am concerned I shall take no part in such a system.

Sir J. Wardlaw-Milne: I hope that my right hon. Friend has not forgotten the original sentence, which was 'subject to the War Cabinet'?

Mr Churchill: Subject to the War Cabinet, against which this all-powerful potentate is not to hesitate to resign on every occasion if he could not get his way. It is a plan, but it is not a plan in which I should personally be interested to take part, and I do not think that it is one which would commend itself to this House. The setting down of this Vote of Censure by Members of all parties is a considerable event. Do not, I beg you, let the House underrate the gravity of what has been done. It has been trumpeted all round the world to our disparagement, and when every nation, friend and foe, is waiting to see what is the true resolve and conviction of the House of Commons, it must go forward to the end. All over the world, throughout the United States, as I can testify, in Russia, far away in China, and throughout every subjugated country, all our friends are waiting to know whether there is a strong, solid Government in Britain and whether its national leadership is to be challenged or not. Every vote counts. If those who have assailed us are reduced to contemptible proportions and their Vote of Censure on the National Government is converted to a vote of censure upon its authors, make no mistake, a cheer will go up from every friend of Britain and every faithful servant of our cause, and the knell of disappointment will ring in the ears of the tyrants we are striving to overthrow.

'THE BRIGHT GLEAM OF VICTORY'

10 November 1942

The Lord Mayor's Luncheon, Mansion House, London

The Battle of El Alamein commenced on 28 October and by 4 November it was clear that Britain's Desert Army under Field Marshal Montgomery had won a resounding victory. Meanwhile, on 7 November Operation 'Torch', the Anglo-American invasion of French North Africa at the Western end of the Mediterranean, was launched and carried all before it. The Allies at last had their first taste of victory.

I have never promised anything but blood, tears, toil, and sweat. Now, however, we have a new experience. We have victory – a remarkable and definite victory. The bright gleam has caught the helmets of our soldiers, and warmed and cheered all our hearts.

The late M. Venizelos observed that in all her wars England – he should have said Britain, of course – always wins one battle – the last. It would seem to have begun rather earlier this time. General Alexander, with his brilliant comrade and lieutenant, General Montgomery, has gained a glorious and decisive victory in what I think should be called the Battle of Egypt. Rommel's army has been defeated. It has been routed. It has been very largely destroyed as a fighting force.

This battle was not fought for the sake of gaining positions or so many square miles of desert territory. General Alexander and General Montgomery fought it with one single idea. They meant to destroy the armed force of the enemy, and to destroy it at the place where the disaster would be most far-reaching and irrecoverable.

All the various elements in our line of battle played their parts – Indian troops, Fighting French, the Greeks, the representatives of Czechoslovakia and the others who took part. The Americans rendered powerful and invaluable service in the air. But as it happened – as the course of the battle turned – it has been fought throughout almost entirely by men of British blood from home and from the Dominions on the one hand, and by Germans on the other. The Italians were left to perish in the waterless desert or surrender as they are doing.

The fight between the British and the Germans was intense and fierce in the extreme. It was a deadly grapple. The Germans have been outmatched and outfought with the very kind of weapons with which they had beaten down so many small peoples, and also large unprepared peoples. They have been beaten by the very technical apparatus on which they counted to gain them the domination of the world. Especially is this true of the air and of the tanks and of the artillery, which has come back into its own on the battlefield. The Germans have received back again that measure of fire and steel which they have so often meted out to others.

Now this is not the end. It is not even the begining of the end. But it is, perhaps, the end of the beginning. Henceforth Hitler's Nazis will meet equally well armed, and perhaps better-armed troops. Henceforth they will have to face in many theatres of war that superiority in the air which they have so often used without mercy against others, of which they boasted all round the world, and which they intended to use as an instrument for convincing all other peoples that all resistance to them was hopeless. When I read of the coastal road crammed with fleeing German vehicles under the blasting attacks of the Royal Air Force, I could not but remember those roads of France and Flanders, crowded, not with fighting men, but with helpless refugees – women and children – fleeing with their pitiful barrows and household goods, upon whom such merciless havoc was wreaked. I have, I trust, a humane disposition, but I must say I could not help feeling that what was happening, however grievous, was only justice grimly reclaiming her rights.

It will be my duty in the near future to give to Parliament a full and particular account of these operations. All I will say of them at present is that the victory which has already been gained gives good prospect of becoming decisive and final so far as the defence of Egypt is concerned.

But this Battle of Egypt, in itself so important, was designed and timed as a prelude and counterpart of the momentous enterprise undertaken by the United States at the western end of the Mediterranean – an enterprise under United States command in which our Army, Air Force, and, above all, our Navy, are bearing an honourable and important share. Very full accounts have been published of all that is happening in Morocco, Algeria, and Tunis. The President of the United States, who is Commander-in-Chief of the armed forces of America, is the author of this mighty undertaking, and in all of it I have been his active and ardent lieutenant. . . .

At this time our thoughts turn towards France, groaning in bondage under the German heel. Many ask themselves the question: Is France finished? Is that long and famous history, adorned by so many manifestations of genius and valour, bearing with it so much that is precious to culture and civilisation, and above all to the liberties of mankind – is all that now to sink for ever into the ocean of the past, or will France rise again and resume her rightful place in the structure of what may one day be again the family of Europe? I declare to you here, on this considerable occasion, even now when misguided or suborned Frenchmen are firing upon their rescuers, I declare to you my faith that France will rise again. While there are men like General de Gaulle and all those who follow him – and they are legion throughout France – and men like General Giraud, that gallant warrior whom no prison can hold, while there are men like those to stand forward in the name and in the cause of France, my confidence in the future of France is sure.

For ourselves we have no wish but to see France free and strong, with her Empire gathered round her and with Alsace-Lorraine restored. We covet no French possession; we have no acquisitive appetites or ambitions in North Africa or any other part of the world. We have not entered this war for profit or expansion, but only for honour and to do our duty in defending the right.

Let me, however, make this clear, in case there should be any mistake about it in any quarter. We mean to hold our own. I have not become the King's First Minister in order to preside over the liquidation of the British Empire. For that task, if ever it were prescribed, someone else would have to be found, and, under democracy, I suppose the nation would have to be consulted. I am proud to be a member of that vast commonwealth and society of nations and communities gathered in and around the ancient British monarchy, without which the good cause might well have perished from the face of the earth. Here we are, and here we stand, a veritable rock of salvation in this drifting world.

'THE FRONTIERS OF DELIVERANCE'

29 November 1942

World Broadcast, London

Two Sundays ago all the bells rang to celebrate the victory of our desert Army at Alamein. Here was a martial episode in British history which deserved a special recognition. But the bells also carried with their clashing joyous peals our thanksgiving that, in spite of all our errors and shortcomings, we have been brought nearer to the frontiers of deliverance. . . .

Since we rang the bells for Alamein, the good cause has prospered. The Eighth Army has advanced nearly four hundred miles, driving before them in rout and ruin the powerful forces, or the remnants of the powerful forces, which Rommel boasted and Hitler and Mussolini believed would conquer Egypt. Another serious battle may be impending at the entrance to Tripolitania. I make it a rule not to prophesy about battles before they are fought. Everyone must try to realise the immense distances over which the North African war ranges, and the enormous labours and self-denial of the troops who press forward relentlessly, twenty, thirty, forty and sometimes fifty miles in a single day. I will say no more than that we may have the greatest confidence in Generals Alexander and Montgomery, and in our soldiers and airmen who have at last begun to come into their own.

At the other side of Africa, a thousand miles or more to the westward, the tremendous joint undertaking of the United States and Britain which was fraught with so many hazards has also been crowned with astonishing success. To transport these large armies of several hundred thousand men, with all their intricate elaborate modern apparatus, secretly across the seas and oceans, and to strike to the hour, and almost to the minute, simultaneously at a dozen points, in spite of all the U-boats and all the chances of weather, was a feat of organisation which will long be studied with respect. It was rendered possible only by one sovereign fact – namely the perfect comradeship and understanding prevailing between the British and American staffs and troops. This majestic enterprise is under the direction and responsibility of the President of the United States, and our First British Army is serving under the orders of the American Commander-in-Chief, General Eisenhower, in whose military skill and burning energy we put our faith, and whose orders to attack we shall punctually and unflinchingly obey. Behind all lies the power of the Royal Navy, to which is joined a powerful American Fleet; the whole under the command of Admiral Cunningham, and all subordinated to the Allied Commander-in-Chief. . . .

The ceaseless flow of good news from every theatre of war, which has filled the whole month of November, confronts the British people with a new test. They have proved that they can stand defeat; they have proved that they can bear with fortitude and confidence long periods of unsatisfactory and unexplained inaction. I see no reason at all why we should not show ourselves equally resolute and active in the face of victory. I promise nothing. I predict nothing. I cannot even guarantee that more successes are not on the way. I commend to all the immortal lines of Kipling:

> If you can dream – and not make dreams your master;
> If you can think – and not make thoughts your aim;
> If you can meet with Triumph and Disaster
> And treat those two impostors just the same –

there is my text for this Sunday's sermon, though I have no licence to preach one. Do not let us be led away by any fair-seeming appearances of fortune; let us rather put our trust in those deep, slow-moving tides that have borne us thus far already, and will surely bear us forward, if we know how to use them, until we reach the harbour where we would be.

'THE DESERT ARMY'

3 February 1943

Tripoli

By 2 February all German resistance had ceased in the Battle for Stalingrad. Field Marshal von Paulus, together with 90,000 German soldiers, had been captured. The smashing by the Russian Army of

Address to men of Britain's victorious Desert Army
in the Roman amphitheatre of Carthage, 1 June 1943.

21 German divisions brought to an end Hitler's hopes of conquering Russia. Meanwhile Britain's Desert Army was advancing victoriously through Libya and Tripolitania. Churchill travelled to Tripoli where he addressed some 2,000 officers and men of the army that was proud to call itself the 'Desert Rats'.

The last time I saw this army was in the closing days of August on those sandy and rocky bluffs near Alamein and the Ruweisat ridge, when it was apparent from all the signs that Rommel was about to make his final thrust on Alexandria and Cairo. Then all was to be won or lost. Now I come to you a long way from Alamein, and I find this army and its famous commander with a record of victory behind it which has undoubtedly played a decisive part in altering the whole character of the war.

The fierce and well-fought battle of Alamein, the blasting through of the enemy's seaward flank, and the thunderbolt of the armoured attack, irretrievably broke the army which Rommel had boasted would conquer Egypt, and upon which the German and Italian peoples had set their hopes. Thereafter and ever since, in these remorseless three months, you have chased this hostile army and driven it from pillar to post over a distance of more than 1,400 miles – in fact, as far as from London to Moscow. You have altered the face of the war in a most remarkable way.

What it has meant in the skill and organisation of movement and manoeuvres, what it has meant in the tireless endurance and self-denial of the troops and in the fearless leadership displayed in action, can be appreciated only by those who were actually on the spot. But I must tell you that the fame of the Desert Army has spread throughout the world.

After the surrender of Tobruk, there was a dark period when many people, not knowing us, not knowing the British and the nations of the British Empire, were ready to take a disparaging view. But now everywhere your work is spoken of with respect and admiration. When I was with the Chief of the Imperial General Staff at Casablanca and with the President of the United States, the arrival of the Desert Army in Tripoli was a new factor which influenced the course of our discussions and opened up hopeful vistas for the future. You are entitled to know these things, and to dwell upon them with that satisfaction which men in all modesty feel when a great work has been finally done. You have rendered a high service to your country and the common cause.

It must have been a tremendous experience driving forward day after day over this desert which it has taken me this morning more than six hours to fly at 200 miles an hour. You were pursuing a broken enemy, dragging on behind you this ever-lengthening line of communications, carrying the whole art of desert warfare to perfection. In the words of the old hymn, you have 'nightly pitched your moving tents a day's march nearer home.' Yes, not only in the march of the army but in the progress of the war you have brought home nearer. I am here to thank you on behalf of His Majesty's Government of the British Isles and of all our friends the world over.

Hard struggles lie ahead. Rommel, the fugitive of Egypt, Cyrenaica, and Tripolitania, in a non-stop race of 1,400 miles, is now trying to present himself as the deliverer of Tunisia. Along the eastern coast of Tunisia are large numbers of German and Italian troops, not yet equipped to their previous standard, but growing stronger. On the other side, another great operation, planned in conjunction with your advance, has carried the First British Army, our American comrades, and the French armies to within 30 or 40 miles of Bizerta and Tunis. Therefrom a military situation arises which everyone can understand.

The days of your victories are by no means at an end, and with forces which march from different quarters we may hope to achieve the final destruction or expulsion from the shores of Africa of every armed German or Italian. You must have felt relief when, after those many a hundred miles of desert, you came once more into a green land with trees and grass, and I do not think you will lose that advantage. As you go forward on further missions that will fall to your lot, you will fight in countries which will present undoubtedly serious tactical difficulties, but which none the less will not have that grim character of desert war which you have known how to endure and how to overcome.

Let me then assure you, soldiers and airmen, that your fellow-countrymen regard your joint work with admiration and gratitude, and that after the war when a man is asked what he did it will be quite sufficient for him to say, 'I marched and fought with the Desert Army.' And when history is written and all the facts are known, your feats will gleam and glow and will be a source of song and story long after we who are gathered here have passed away.

TRIBUTE TO MONTGOMERY AND ALEXANDER

11 February 1943

House of Commons

Let me also pay my tribute to this vehement and formidable General Montgomery, a Cromwellian figure, austere, severe, accomplished, tireless, his life given to the study of war, who has attracted to himself in an extraordinary measure the confidence and the devotion of his Army. Let me also pay, in the name of the House, my tribute to General Alexander, on whom the overriding responsibility lay. I read to the House on 11th November the directive which in those critical days I gave to General Alexander. I may perhaps refresh the memory of hon. Members by reading it again:

1. Your prime and main duty will be to take or destroy at the earliest opportunity the German-Italian army commanded by Field-Marshal Rommel, together with all its supplies and establishments in Egypt and Libya.
2. You will discharge, or cause to be discharged, such other duties as pertain to your Command without prejudice to the task described in paragraph 1, which must be considered paramount in His Majesty's interests.

I have now received, when, as it chanced, I visited the Army again, the following official communication from General Alexander, in which General Montgomery took great pleasure, and to which it will be necessary for us to send a reply:

Sir, The Orders you gave me on August 15, 1942, have been fulfilled. His Majesty's enemies, together with their impedimenta, have been completely eliminated from Egypt, Cyrenaica, Libya and Tripolitania. I now await your further instructions.

Well, obviously, we shall have to think of something else, and, indeed, this was one of the more detailed matters which we discussed in the Conference at Casablanca. I did not publish the original instructions to General Alexander until some months afterwards, when the Battle of Egypt had been won, and the House will naturally grant me a similar delay before I make public the reply to him which is now required.

'HEAVIER WORK LIES AHEAD'

19 May 1943

Joint Session of Congress, Washington, DC

On 13 May Allied Forces completed their North African campaigns, achieving total victory. Churchill commented in The Hinge of Fate: *'The sense of victory was in the air. The whole of North Africa was cleared of the enemy. A quarter of a million prisoners were cooped in our cages. Everyone was very proud and delighted. There is no doubt that people like winning very much.' On 16 May the Royal Air Force, in a brilliant raid deep into Germany, destroyed the Möhne and Eder dams, causing widespread flooding and destruction in the Ruhr Valley. It was under these auspicious circumstances that Churchill addressed the US Congress for the second time.*

Seventeen months have passed since I last had the honour to address the Congress of the United States. For more than 500 days, every day a day, we have toiled and suffered and dared shoulder to shoulder against the cruel and mighty enemy. We have acted in close combination or concert in many parts of the world, on land, on sea, and in the air. The fact that you have invited me to come to Congress again a second time, now that we have settled down to the job, and that you should welcome me in so generous a fashion, is certainly a high mark in my life, and it also shows that our partnership has not done so badly.

I am proud that you should have found us good allies, striving forward in comradeship to the accomplishment of our task without grudging or stinting either life or treasure, or, indeed, anything that we have to give. Last time I came at a moment when the United States was aflame with wrath at the treacherous attack upon Pearl Harbor by Japan, and at the subsequent declarations of war upon the United States made by Germany and Italy. For my part I say quite frankly that in those days, after our long – and for a whole year lonely – struggle, I could not repress in my heart a sense of relief and comfort that we were all bound together by common peril, by solemn faith and high purpose, to see this fearful quarrel through, at all costs, to the end.

That was the hour of passionate emotion, an hour most memorable in human records, an hour, I believe, full of hope and glory for the future. The experiences of a long life and the promptings of my blood have wrought in me the conviction that there is nothing more important for the future of the world than the fraternal association of our two peoples in righteous work both in war and peace. . . .

I am free to admit that in North Africa we builded better than we knew. The unexpected came to the aid of the design and multiplied the results. For this we have to thank the military intuition of Corporal Hitler. We may notice, as I predicted in the House of Commons three months ago, the touch of the master hand. The same insensate obstinacy which condemned Field-Marshal von Paulus and his army to destruction at Stalingrad has brought this new catastrophe upon our enemies in Tunisia.

We have destroyed or captured considerably more than a quarter of a million of the enemy's best troops, together with vast masses of material, all of which had been ferried across to Africa after paying a heavy toll to British submarines and British and United States aircraft. No one could count on such follies. They gave us, if I may use the language of finance, a handsome bonus after the full dividend had been earned and paid.

At the time when we planned this great joint African operation, we hoped to be masters of Tunisia even before the end of last year; but the injury we have now inflicted upon the enemies, physical and psychological, and the training our troops have obtained in the hard school of war, and the welding together of the Anglo-American Staff machine – these are advantages which far exceed anything which it was in our power to plan. The German lie factory is volubly explaining how valuable is the time which they bought by the loss of their great armies. Let them not delude themselves. Other operations which will unfold in due course, depending as they do upon the special instruction of large numbers of troops and upon the provision of a vast mass of technical apparatus, these other operations have not been in any way delayed by the obstinate fighting in northern Tunisia.

Mr President, the African war is over. Mussolini's African Empire and Corporal Hitler's strategy are alike exploded. It is interesting to compute what these performances have cost these two wicked men and those who have been their tools or their dupes. The Emperor of

Abyssinia sits again upon the throne from which he was driven by Mussolini's poison gas. All the vast territories from Madagascar to Morocco, from Cairo to Casablanca, from Aden to Dakar, are under British, American, or French control. One continent at least has been cleansed and purged for ever from Fascist or Nazi tyranny.

The African excursions of the two Dictators have cost their countries in killed and captured 950,000 soldiers. In addition nearly 2,400,000 gross tons of shipping have been sunk and nearly 8,000 aircraft destroyed, both of these figures being exclusive of large numbers of ships and aircraft damaged. There have also been lost to the enemy 6,200 guns, 2,550 tanks and 70,000 trucks, which is the American name for lorries, and which, I understand, has been adopted by the combined staffs in North-West Africa in exchange for the use of the word petrol in place of gasolene.

These are the losses of the enemy in the three years of war, and at the end of it all what is it that they have to show? The proud German Army has by its sudden collapse, sudden crumbling and breaking up, unexpected to all of us, the proud German Army has once again proved the truth of the saying, 'The Hun is always either at your throat or at your feet'; and that is a point which may have its bearing upon the future. But for us, arrived at this milestone in the war: we can say 'One Continent redeemed'.

The North-West African campaign, and particularly its Tunisian climax, is the finest example of the co-operation of the troops of three different countries and of the combination under one supreme commander of the sea, land, and air forces which has yet been seen: in particular the British and American Staff work, as I have said, has matched the comradeship of the soldiers of our two countries striding forward side by side under the fire of the enemy.

It was a marvel of efficient organisation which enabled the Second American Corps, or rather Army, for that was its size, to be moved 300 miles from the Southern sector, which had become obsolete through the retreat of the enemy, to the Northern coast, from which, beating down all opposition, they advanced and took the fortress and harbour of Bizerta. In order to accomplish this march of 300 miles, which was covered in twelve days, it was necessary for this very considerable Army, with its immense modern equipment, to traverse at right angles all the communications of the British First Army, which was already engaged or about to be engaged in heavy battle; and this was achieved without in any way disturbing the hour-to-hour supply upon which that Army depended. I am told that these British and American officers worked together without the slightest question of what country they belonged to, each doing his part in the military organisation which must henceforward be regarded as a most powerful and efficient instrument of war.

There is honour, Mr President, for all; and I shall at the proper time and place pay my tribute to the British and American commanders by land and sea who conducted or who were engaged in the battle. This only will I say now: I do not think you could have chosen any man more capable than General Eisenhower of keeping his very large, heterogeneous force together, through bad times as well as good, and of creating the conditions of harmony and energy which were the indispensable elements of victory.

I have dwelt in some detail, but I trust not at undue length, upon these famous events; and I shall now return for a few minutes to the general war, in which they have their setting and proportion. It is a poor heart that never rejoices; but our thanksgiving, however fervent, must be brief.

Heavier work lies ahead, not only in the European, but, as I have indicated, in the Pacific and Indian spheres; and the President and I, and the combined Staffs, are gathered here in order that this work may be, so far as lies within us, well conceived, and thrust forward without losing a day.

Not for one moment must we forget that the main burden of the war on land is still being borne by the Russian armies. They are holding at the present time no fewer than 190 German divisions and 28 satellite divisions on their front. It is always wise, while doing justice to one's own achievements, to preserve a proper sense of proportion; and I therefore mention that the figures of the German forces opposite Russia compare with the equivalent of about 15 divisions which we have destroyed in Tunisia, after a campaign which has cost us about 50,000 casualties. That gives some measure of the Russian effort, and of the debt which we owe to her.

It may well be that a further trial of strength between the German and Russian armies is impending. Russia has already inflicted injuries upon the German military organism which will, I believe, prove ultimately mortal; but there is little doubt that Hitler is reserving his supreme gambler's throw for a third attempt to break the heart and spirit and destroy the armed forces of the mighty nation which he has already twice assaulted in vain.

He will not succeed. But we must do everything in our power that is sensible and practicable to take more of the weight off Russia in 1943. I do not intend to be responsible for any suggestion that the war is won, or that it will soon be over. That it will be won by us I am sure. But how and when cannot be foreseen, still less foretold.

I was driving the other day not far from the field of Gettysburg, which I know well, like most of your battlefields. It was the decisive battle of the American Civil War. No one after Gettysburg doubted which way the dread balance of war would incline, yet far more blood was shed after the Union victory at Gettysburg than in all the fighting which went before. It behoves us, therefore, to search our hearts and brace our sinews and take the most earnest counsel, one with another, in order that the favourable position which has already been reached both against Japan and against Hitler and Mussolini in Europe shall not be let slip.

If we wish to abridge the slaughter and ruin which this war is spreading to so many lands and to which we must ourselves contribute so grievous a measure of suffering and sacrifice, we cannot afford to relax a single fibre of our being or to tolerate the slightest abatement of our efforts. The enemy is still proud and powerful. He is hard to get at. He still possesses enormous armies, vast resources, and invaluable strategic territories. War is full of mysteries and surprises. A false step, a wrong direction, an error in strategy, discord or lassitude among the Allies, might soon give the common enemy power to confront us with new and hideous facts. We have surmounted many serious dangers, but there is one grave danger which will go along with us till the end; that danger is the undue prolongation of the war. No one can tell what new complications and perils might arise in four or five more years of war. And it is in the dragging-out of the war at enormous expense, until the democracies are tired or bored or split, that the main hopes of Germany and Japan must now reside. We must destroy this hope, as we have destroyed so many others, and for that purpose we must beware of every topic however attractive and every tendency however natural which turns our minds and energies from this supreme objective of the general victory of the United Nations. By singleness of purpose, by steadfastness of conduct, by tenacity and endurance such as we have so far displayed – by these, and only by these, can we discharge our duty to the future of the world and to the destiny of man.

'WE EXPECT NO REWARD AND WE WILL ACCEPT NO COMPROMISE'

30 June 1943

Receiving the Freedom of the City of London,
The Guildhall, London

Of all the wars that we have ever waged in the long continuity of our history, there has never been one which more truly united the entire British nation and British race throughout the world than this present fearful struggle for the freedom and progress of mankind.

We entered it of our own free will, without being ourselves directly assaulted. We entered it upon a conviction of purpose which was clearly comprehended by all classes and parties and by the whole mass of the people, and we have persevered together through good and evil fortune without the slightest weakening of our willpower or division of our strength. We entered it ill-prepared and almost unarmed. We entered it without counting the cost, and upon a single spontaneous impulse at the call of honour.

We strove long, too long, for peace, and suffered thereby; but from the moment when we gave our guarantee that we would not stand by idly and see Poland trampled down by Nazi violence, we have never looked back, never flagged, never doubted, never flinched. We were sure of our duty, and we have discharged it and will discharge it, without swerving or slackening, to the end.

We seek no profit, we covet no territory or aggrandisement. We expect no reward and we will accept no compromise. It is on that footing that we wish to be judged, first in our own consciences and afterwards by posterity.

It is even more remarkable that the unity which has existed and endured in this small, densely-populated island should have extended with equal alacrity and steadfastness to all parts of our worldwide Commonwealth and Empire. . . .

Alone in history, the British people, taught by the lessons they had learned in the past, have found the means to attach to the Motherland vast self-governing Dominions upon whom there rests no obligation, other than that of sentiment and tradition, to plunge into war at the side of the Motherland.

None of these Dominions, except Southern Ireland, which does not under its present dispensation fully accept Dominion status, has ever failed to respond, with all the vigour of democratic institutions, to the trumpet-call of a supreme crisis, to the overpowering influences and impulses that make Canada, that make Australia ... New Zealand and South Africa send their manhood across the ocean to fight and die. . . .

But now I must speak of the great Republic of the United States, whose power arouses no fear and whose pre-eminence excites no jealousy in British bosoms. Upon the fraternal association and intimate alignment of policy of the United States and the British Commonwealth and Empire depends, more than on any other factor, the immediate future of the world. If they walk, or if need be march, together in harmony and in accordance with the moral and political conceptions to which the English-speaking peoples have given birth, and which are frequently referred to in the Atlantic Charter, all will be well. If they fall apart and wander astray from the commanding beacon-light of their destiny, there is no end or measure to the miseries and confusion which await modern civilisation.

'THE GIFT OF A COMMON TONGUE'

6 September 1943

Harvard University, Boston

On 21 July, following the successful Allied invasion of Italy, Mussolini resigned. On 1 September Churchill visited the United States to discuss terms of an Italian surrender. On 6 September in Boston he received an Honorary Degree.

Twice in my lifetime the long arm of destiny has searched across the oceans and involved the entire life and manhood of the United States in a deadly struggle. There was no use in saying 'We don't want it; we won't have it; our forebears left Europe to avoid these quarrels; we have founded a new world which has no contact with the old.' There was no use in that. The long arm reaches out remorselessly, and everyone's existence, environment, and outlook undergo a swift and irresistible change. What is the explanation, Mr President, of these strange facts, and what are the deep laws to which they respond? I will offer you one explanation – there are others, but one will suffice. The price of greatness is responsibility. If the people of the United States had continued in a mediocre station, struggling with the wilderness, absorbed in their own affairs, and a factor of no consequence in the movement of the world, they might have remained forgotten and undisturbed beyond their protecting oceans: but one cannot rise to be in many ways the leading community in the civilised world without being involved in its problems, without being convulsed by its agonies and inspired by its causes.

If this has been proved in the past, as it has been, it will become indisputable in the future. The people of the United States cannot escape world responsibility. Although we live in a period so tumultuous that little can be predicted we may be quite sure that this process will be intensified with every forward step the United States make in wealth and in power. . . .

But to the youth of America, as to the youth of Britain, I say 'You cannot stop.' There is no halting-place at this point. We have now reached a stage in the journey where there can be no pause. We must go on. It must be world anarchy or world order. Throughout all this ordeal and struggle which is characteristic of our age, you will find in the British Commonwealth and Empire good comrades to whom you are united by other ties besides those of State policy and public need. To a large extent, they are the ties of blood and history. Naturally, I, a child of both worlds, am conscious of these.

Law, language, literature – these are considerable factors. Common conceptions of what is right and decent, a marked regard for fair play, especially to the weak and poor, a stern sentiment of impartial justice, and above all the love of personal freedom, or as Kipling put it; 'Leave to live by no man's leave underneath the law' – these are common conceptions on both sides of the ocean among the English-speaking peoples. We hold to these conceptions as strongly as you do.

We do not war primarily with races as such. Tyranny is our foe, whatever trappings or disguise it wears, whatever language it speaks, be it external or internal, we must for ever be on our guard, ever mobilised, ever vigilant, always ready to spring at its throat. In all this, we march together. Not only do we march and strive shoulder to shoulder at this moment under the fire of the enemy on the fields of war or in the air, but also in those realms of thought which are consecrated to the rights and the dignity of man. . . .

The great Bismarck – for there were once great men in Germany – is said to have observed towards the close of his life that the most potent factor in human society at the end of the nineteenth century was the fact that the British and American peoples spoke the same language. That was a pregnant saying. Certainly it has enabled us to wage war together with an intimacy and harmony never before achieved among allies.

The gift of a common tongue is a priceless inheritance and it may well some day become the foundation of a common citizenship. I like to think of British and Americans moving about freely over each other's wide estates with hardly a sense of being foreigners to one another. But I do not see why we should not try to spread our common language even more widely throughout the globe and, without seeking selfish advantage over any, possess ourselves of this invaluable amenity and birthright.

'A SENSE OF CROWD AND URGENCY'

28 October 1943

House of Commons

Here Churchill sets out his trenchant view on the very characteristics of the House of Commons and on the planned rebuilding of the Chamber, destroyed by an enemy bomb on the night of 10 May 1941.

I beg to move,

> That a Select Committee be appointed to consider and report upon plans for the rebuilding of the House of Commons, and upon such alterations as may be considered desirable while preserving all its essential features.

On the night of 10th May, 1941, with one of the last bombs of the last serious raid, our House of Commons was destroyed by the violence of the enemy, and we have now to consider whether we should build it up again, and how, and when. We shape our buildings, and afterwards our buildings shape us. Having dwelt and served for more than forty years in the late Chamber, and having derived very great pleasure and advantage therefrom, I, naturally, should like to see it restored in all essentials to its old form, convenience, and dignity. I believe that will be the opinion of the great majority of its Members. It is certainly the opinion of His Majesty's Government, and we propose to support this Resolution to the best of our ability.

There are two main characteristics of the House of Commons which will command the approval and the support of reflective and experienced Members. They will, I have no doubt, sound odd to foreign ears. The first is that its shape should be oblong and not semi-circular. Here is a very potent factor in our political life. The semi-circular assembly, which appeals to political theorists, enables every individual or every group to move round the centre, adopting various shades of pink according as the weather changes. I am a convinced supporter of the party system in preference to the group system. I have seen many earnest and ardent Parliaments destroyed by the group system. The party system is much favoured by the oblong form of Chamber. It is easy for an individual to move through those insensible gradations from Left to Right, but the act of crossing the Floor is one which requires serious consideration. I am well informed on this matter, for I have accomplished that difficult process, not only once but twice. Logic is a poor guide compared with custom. Logic, which has created in so many countries semi-circular assemblies with buildings that give to every Member, not only a seat to sit in, but often a desk to write at, with a lid to bang, has proved fatal in Parliamentary Government as we know it here in its home and in the land of its birth.

The second characteristic of a Chamber formed on the lines of the House of Commons is that it should not be big enough to contain all its Members at once without overcrowding, and that there should be no question of every Member having a separate seat reserved for him. The reason for this has long been a puzzle to uninstructed outsiders, and has frequently excited the curiosity and even the criticism of new Members. Yet is not so difficult to understand if you look at it from a practical point of view. If the House is big enough to contain all its Members, nine-tenths of its Debates will be conducted in the depressing atmosphere of an almost empty or half-empty Chamber. The essence of good House of Commons speaking is the conversational style, the facility for quick, informal interruptions and interchanges. Harangues from a rostrum would be a bad substitute for the conversational style in which so much of our business is done. But the conversational style requires a fairly small space, and there should be on great occasions a sense of crowd and urgency. There should be a sense of the importance of much that is said, and a sense that great matters are being decided, there and then, by the House.

We attach immense importance to the survival of Parliamentary democracy. In this country this is one of our war aims. We wish to see our Parliament a strong, easy, flexible instrument of free Debate. For this purpose a small Chamber and a sense of intimacy are indispensable. It is notable that the Parliaments of the British Commonwealth have to a very large extent reproduced our Parliamentary institutions in their form as well as in their spirit, even to the Chair in which the Speakers of the different Assemblies sit. We do not seek to impose our ideas on others; we make no invidious criticisms of other nations. All the same we hold none the less tenaciously to them ourselves. The vitality and the authority of the House of Commons, and its hold upon an electorate based upon universal suffrage, depend to no small extent upon its episodes and great moments, even upon its scenes and rows, which, as everyone will agree, are better conducted at close quarters. Destroy that hold which Parliament has upon the public mind and has preserved through all these changing, turbulent times, and the living organism of the House of Commons would be greatly impaired. You may have a machine, but the House of Commons is much more than a machine; it has earned and captured and held through long generations the imagination and respect of the British nation. It is not free from shortcomings; they mark all human institutions. Nevertheless, I submit to what is probably not an unfriendly audience on that subject that our House has proved itself capable of adapting itself to every change which the swift pace of modern life has brought upon us. It has a collective personality which enjoys the regard of the public, and which imposes itself upon the conduct not only of individual Members but of parties. It has a code of its own which everyone knows, and it has means of its own of enforcing those manners and habits which have grown up and have been found to be an essential part of our Parliamentary life.

The House of Commons has lifted our affairs above the mechanical sphere into the human sphere. It thrives on criticism, it is perfectly impervious to newspaper abuse or taunts from any quarter, and it is capable of digesting almost anything or almost any body of gentlemen, whatever be the views with which they arrive. There is no situation to which it cannot address itself with vigour and ingenuity. It is the citadel of British liberty; it is the foundation of our laws; its traditions and its privileges are as lively today as when it broke the arbitrary power of the Crown and substituted that Constitutional Monarchy under which we have enjoyed so many blessings. In this war the House of Commons has proved itself to be a rock upon which an Administration, without losing the confidence of the House, has been able to confront the most terrible emergencies. The House has shown itself able to face the possibility of national destruction with classical composure. It can change Governments, and has changed them by heat of passion. It can sustain Governments in long, adverse, disappointing struggles through many dark, grey months and even years until the sun comes out again. I do not know how else this country can be governed than by the House of Commons playing its part in all its broad freedom in British public life. We have learned – with these so recently confirmed facts around us and before us – not to alter improvidently the physical structures which have enabled so remarkable an organism to carry on its work of banning dictatorships within this Island, and pursuing and beating into ruins all dictators who have molested us from outside.

'THE HOUR OF OUR GREATEST EFFORT
IS APPROACHING'

26 March 1944

Broadcast, London

In these two final paragraphs Churchill makes oblique reference to the forthcoming invasion of Normandy, which was but twelve weeks away. Britain had become a vast armed camp of British and American soldiers waiting for the word to hurl themselves against Hitler's 'Atlantic Wall' to launch the Liberation of Occupied Europe – the greatest military exploit in the history of warfare.

The hour of our greatest effort and action is approaching. We march with valiant Allies who count on us as we count on them. The flashing eyes of all our soldiers, sailors, and airmen must be fixed upon the enemy on their front. The only homeward road for all of us lies through the arch of victory. The magnificent Armies of the United States are here or are pouring in. Our own troops, the best trained and best equipped we have ever had, stand at their side in equal numbers and in true comradeship. Leaders are appointed in whom we all have faith. We shall require from our own people here, from Parliament, from the Press, from all classes, the same cool, strong nerves, the same toughness of fibre, which stood us in good stead in those days when we were all alone under the blitz.

And here I must warn you that in order to deceive and baffle the enemy as well as to exercise the forces, there will be many false alarms, many feints, and many dress rehearsals. We may also ourselves be the object of new forms of attack from the enemy. Britain can take it. She has never flinched or failed. And when the signal is given, the whole circle of avenging nations will hurl themselves upon the foe and batter out the life of the cruellest tyranny which has ever sought to bar the progress of mankind.

D-DAY

6 June 1944

House of Commons

On 4 June, Rome was liberated by British and American troops. Shortly after midnight on 6 June, the Allied invasion of Occupied Europe began.

The House should, I think, take formal cognisance of the liberation of Rome by the Allied Armies under the command of General Alexander, with General Clark of the United States Service and General Oliver Leese in command of the Fifth and Eighth Armies respectively. This is a memorable and glorious event, which rewards the intense fighting of the last five months in Italy. . . .

I have also to announce to the House that during the night and the early hours of this morning the first of the series of landings in force upon the European Continent has taken place. In this case the liberating assault fell upon the coast of France. An immense armada of upwards of 4,000 ships, together with several thousand smaller craft, crossed the Channel. Massed airborne landings have been successfully effected behind the enemy lines, and landings on the beaches are proceeding at various points at the present time. The fire of the shore batteries has been largely quelled. The obstacles that were constructed in the sea have not proved so difficult as was apprehended. The Anglo-American Allies are sustained by about 11,000 first-line aircraft, which can be drawn upon as may be needed for the purposes of the battle. I cannot, of course, commit myself to any particular details. Reports are coming in in rapid succession. So far the commanders who are engaged report that everything is proceeding according to plan. And what a plan! This vast operation is undoubtedly the most complicated and difficult that has ever taken place. It involves tides, wind, waves, visibility, both from the air and the sea standpoint, and the combined employment of land, air and sea forces in the highest degree of intimacy and in contact with conditions which could not and cannot be fully foreseen.

There are already hopes that actual tactical surprise has been attained, and we hope to furnish the enemy with a succession of surprises during the course of the fighting. The battle that has now begun will grow constantly in scale and in intensity for many weeks to come, and I shall not attempt to speculate upon its course. This I may say, however. Complete unity prevails throughout the Allied Armies. There is a brotherhood in arms between us and our friends of the United States. There is complete confidence in the supreme commander, General Eisenhower, and his lieutenants, and also in the commander of the Expeditionary Force, General Montgomery. The ardour and spirit of the troops, as I saw myself, embarking in these last few days was splendid to witness.

'THE PRICE IN BLOOD ... FOR THE LIBERATION OF THE SOIL OF FRANCE'

28 September 1944

House of Commons

The Battle of Normandy had been won. Much of France, including Paris had been liberated, as had Belgium. Following the largest ever airborne operation, British and American forces were already battling to secure the Rhine river crossings.

Little more than seven weeks have passed since we rose for the summer vacation, but this short period has completely changed the face of the war in Europe. When we separated, the Anglo-American Armies were still penned in the narrow bridgehead and strip of coast from the base of the Cherbourg Peninsula to the approaches to Caen, which they had wrested from the enemy several weeks before. The Brest Peninsula was untaken, the German Army in the West was still hopeful of preventing us from striking out into the fields of France, the Battle of Normandy, which had been raging bloodily from the date of the landing, had not reached any decisive conclusion. What a transformation now meets our eyes! Not only Paris, but practically the whole of France, has been liberated as if by enchantment. Belgium has been rescued, part of Holland is already free, and the foul enemy, who for four years inflicted his cruelties and oppression upon these countries, has fled, losing perhaps 400,000 in killed and wounded, and leaving in our hands nearly half a million prisoners. Besides this, there may well be 200,000 cut off in the coastal fortresses or in Holland, whose destruction or capture may now be deemed highly probable. The Allied Armies have reached and in some places crossed the German frontier and the Siegfried Line.

All these operations have been conducted under the supreme command of General Eisenhower, and were the fruit of the world-famous battle of Normandy, the greatest and most decisive single battle of the entire war. Never has the exploitation of victory been carried to a higher perfection. The chaos and destruction wrought by the Allied Air Forces behind the battle front have been indescribable in narrative, and a factor of the utmost potency in the actual struggle. They have far surpassed, and reduce to petty dimensions, all that our army had to suffer from the German Air Force in 1940. Nevertheless, when we reflect upon the tremendous fire-power of modern weapons and the opportunity which they give for defensive and delaying action, we must feel astounded at the extraordinary speed with which the Allied Armies have advanced. The vast and brilliant encircling movement of the American Armies will ever be a model of military art, and an example of the propriety of running risks not only in the fighting – because most of the armies are ready to do that – but even more on the Q. side, or, as the Americans put it, the logistical side. It was with great pleasure that all of us saw the British and Canadian Armies, who had so long fought against heavy resistance by the enemy along the hinge of the Allied movement, show themselves also capable of lightning advances which have certainly not been surpassed anywhere.

Finally, by the largest airborne operation ever conceived or executed, a further all-important forward bound in the North has been achieved. Here I must pay a tribute, which the House will consider due, to the superb feat of arms performed by our First Airborne Division. Full and deeply-moving accounts have already been given to the country and to the world of this glorious and fruitful operation, which will take a lasting place in our military annals, and will, in succeeding generations, inspire our youth with the highest ideals of duty and of daring. The cost has been heavy; the casualties in a single division have been grievous; but for those who mourn there is at least the consolation that the sacrifice was not needlessly demanded nor given without results. The delay caused to the enemy's advance upon Nijmegen enabled their British and American comrades in the other two airborne divisions, and the British Second Army, to secure intact the vitally important bridges and to form a strong bridgehead over the main stream of the Rhine at Nijmegen. 'Not in vain' may be the pride of those who have survived and the epitaph of those who fell.

To return to the main theme, Brest, Havre, Dieppe, Boulogne and Antwerp are already in our hands. All the Atlantic and Channel ports, from the Spanish frontier to the Hook of Holland, will presently be in our possession, yielding fine harbours and substantial masses of prisoners of war. All this has been accomplished by the joint exertions of the British and American Armies, assisted by the vehement and widespread uprising and fighting efforts of the French Maquis.

While this great operation has been taking its course, an American and French landing on the Riviera coast, actively assisted by a British airborne brigade, a British Air Force, and the Royal Navy, has led with inconceivable rapidity to the capture of Toulon and Marseilles, to the freeing of the great strip of the Riviera coast, and to the successful advance of General Patch's Army up the Rhone Valley. This army, after taking over 80,000 prisoners, joined hands with General Eisenhower, and has passed under his command. When I had the opportunity on 15th August of watching – alas, from afar – the landing at Saint Tropez, it would have seemed audacious to hope for such swift and important results. They have, however, under the spell of the victories in the North, already been gained in superabundance, and in less than half the time prescribed and expected in the plans which were prepared beforehand. So much for the fighting in France.

Simultaneously with that, very hard and successful fighting on a major scale has also proceeded on the Italian Front. General Alexander, who commands the armies in Italy with complete operational discretion, has under him the Fifth and Eighth Armies. The Fifth Army, half American and half British, with whom are serving the fine Brazilian Division, some of whose troops I had the opportunity of seeing – a magnificent band of men – is commanded by the United States General Clark, an officer of the highest quality and bearing, with a proud record of achievments behind him and his troops. The Eighth Army, under General Oliver Leese, whose qualities are also of the highest order, comprises the Polish Corps which fought so gallantly under General Anders, and a Greek Brigade which has already distinguished itself in the forefront of the battle. There is also fighting on this Front a strong force of Italians, who are ardent to free their country from the German grip and taint. This force will very soon be more than doubled in strength. The Lieutenant of the Realm is often with these troops.

The largest mass of all the troops on the Italian Front comes, of course, from the United Kingdom. Not far short of half the divisions on the whole front are from this Island. Joined with them are New Zealand, Canadian, South African and Indian Divisions, or perhaps I should say British-Indian Divisions, because, as is sometimes forgotten, one-third of them are British. The British Army in Italy includes also Palestinian units; and here I would mention the announcement, which I think will be appreciated and approved, that the Government have decided to accede to the request of the Jewish Agency for Palestine that a Jewish Brigade group should be formed to take part in active operations. I know there are vast numbers of Jews serving with our Forces and the American Forces throughout all the Armies, but it seems to me indeed appropriate that a special Jewish unit, a special unit of that race which has suffered indescribable torments from the Nazis, should be represented as a distinct formation amongst the forces gathered for their final overthrow, and I have no doubt they will not only take part in the struggle but also in the occupation which will follow.

A very hard task lies before the Army in Italy. It has already pierced at several points the strong Gothic line by which Kesselring has sought to defend the passage of the Apennines. I had an opportunity of watching and following the advance of the Eighth Army across the Metauro River, which began on August 26th. The extraordinary defensive strength of the ground held by the enemy was obvious. The mountain ridges rise one behind the other in a seemingly endless succession, like the waves of the sea, and each had to be conquered or turned by superior force and superior weapons. The process was bound to be lengthy and costly, but it is being completed, has, in fact, been practically completed. At the same time, General Clark's Fifth Army, advancing from the Florence area, has pierced deep into the mountain ranges, and, having broken the enemy's centre, now stands on the northern slopes of the Apennines at no great distance from Bologna, a place of definite strategic importance. General Alexander has now definitely broken into the basin of the Po, but here we exchange the barriers of mountain ridges for the perpetual interruption of the ground by streams and canals. Nevertheless, conditions henceforward will be more favourable for the destruction or rout of Kesselring's Army, and this is the objective to which all British and Allied Forces will be unceasingly bent. Farther than that, it is not desirable to peer at the present moment.

I am now going to give a few facts and figures about the operations in Europe. These have been very carefully chosen to give as much information as possible to the House and to the public, while not telling the enemy anything he does not already know, or only telling him too late for it to be of any service to him. The speed with which the mighty British and American Armies in France were built up is almost incredible. In the first 24 hours a quarter of a million men were landed, in the teeth of fortified and violent opposition. By the 20th day a million men were ashore. There are now between two and three million men in France. Certainly the progress in the power of moving troops and landing troops has vastly increased since the early days, when we had to plunge into the war with no previous experience. But the actual number of soldiers was only part of the problem of transportation. These armies were equipped with the most perfect modern weapons and every imaginable contrivance of modern war, and an immense artillery supported all their operations. Enormous masses of armour of the highest quality and character gave them extraordinary offensive power and mobility. Many hundreds of thousands of vehicles sustained their movements, many millions of tons of stores have already been landed – the great bulk of everything over open beaches or through the synthetic harbours which I described when last I spoke to the House.

All this constitutes a feat of organisation and efficiency which should excite the wonder and deserve the admiration of all military students, as well as the applause of the British and American nations and their Allies. I must pay my tribute to the United States Army, not only in their valiant and ruthless battle-worthy qualities, but also in the skill of their commanders and the excellence of their supply arrangements. When one remembers that the United States four or five years ago was a peace-loving Power, without any great body of troops or munitions, and with only a very small regular Army to draw their commanders from, the American achievement is truly amazing. After the intense training they have received for nearly three years, or more than three years in some cases, their divisions are now composed of regular professional soldiers whose military quality is out of all comparison with hurriedly-raised wartime levies. These soldiers, like our own from Great Britain who have been even longer under arms, are capable of being placed immediately on landing in the battle line, and have proved themselves more than a match for the so-called veteran troops of Germany, who, though fighting desperately, are showing themselves decidedly the worse for wear. When I think of the measureless output of ships, munitions and supplies of all kinds with which the United States has equipped herself and has sustained all the fighting Allies in generous measure, and of the mighty war she is conducting, with troops of our Australian and New Zealand Dominions, over the spaces of the Pacific Ocean, this House may indeed salute our sister nation as being at the highest pinnacle of her power and fame.

I am very glad to say that we also have been able to make a worthy contribution. Some time ago, a statement was made by a Senator to the effect that the American public would be shocked to learn that they would have to provide 80 per cent of the forces to invade the Continent. I then said that at the outset of the invasion of France the British and American Forces would be practically equal, but that thereafter the American build-up would give them steadily the lead. I am glad to say that after 120 days of fighting we still bear, in the cross-Channel troops, a proportion of two to three in personnel and of four to five-and-a-half in fighting divisions in France. Casualties have followed very closely the proportions of the numbers. In fact, these troops fight so level that the casualties almost exactly follow the numbers engaged. We have, I regret to say, lost upwards of 90,000 men, killed, wounded and missing, and the United States, including General Patch's Army, over 145,000. Such is the price in blood paid by the English-speaking democracies for the actual liberation of the soil of France.

'DEMOCRACY IS NO HARLOT TO BE PICKED UP IN THE STREETS BY A MAN WITH A TOMMY GUN'

8 December 1944

House of Commons

In the wake of the Allied victories in Northern Europe, Italy and the Balkans, Greece was liberated. In Greece, gangs of Communist partisans tried to seize power in the birthplace of democracy. Churchill was having none of it and committed British troops to take control until the foundations of democratic government could be restored. He himself, while bullets were still flying, spent the last Christmas of the war in Athens to supervise developments.

Democracy, I say, is not based on violence or terrorism, but on reason, on fair play, on freedom, on respecting other people's rights as well as their ambitions. Democracy is no harlot to be picked up in the street by a man with a tommy gun. I trust the people, the mass of the people, in almost any country, but I like to make sure that it is the people and not a gang of bandits from the mountains or from the countryside who think that by violence they can overturn constituted authority, in some cases ancient Parliaments, Governments and States. That is my general description of the foundation upon which we should approach the various special instances on which I am going to dwell. During the war, of course, we have had to arm anyone who could shoot a Hun. Apart from their character, political convictions, past records and so forth, if they were out to shoot a Hun we accepted them as friends and tried to enable them to fulfil their healthy instincts.

Mr McGovern (Glasgow, Shettleston): Now you are paying for it.

Mr Churchill: We are paying for it in having this Debate today, which personally I have found rather enjoyable, so far. We are paying for it also with our treasure and our blood. We are not paying for it with our honour or by defeat. But when countries are liberated it does not follow that those who have received our weapons should use them in order to engross to themselves by violence and murder and bloodshed all those powers and traditions and continuity which many countries have slowly developed and to which quite a large proportion of their people, I believe the great majority, are firmly attached. If what is called in this Amendment the action of 'the friends of democracy' is to be interpreted as carefully planned *coups d'état* by murder gangs and by the iron rule of ruffians seeking to climb into the seats of power, without a vote ever having been cast in their favour – if that is to masquerade as democracy I think the House will unite in condemning it as a mockery.

'WE DEMAND UNCONDITIONAL SURRENDER'

18 January 1945

House of Commons

Fierce fighting was under way in the Ardennes, the Russians were advancing from the East into Prussia and a British/Indian Army was making headway against the Japanese in the jungles of Burma.

I am clear that nothing should induce us to abandon the principle of unconditional surrender, or to enter into any form of negotiation with Germany or Japan, under whatever guise such suggestions may present themselves, until the act of unconditional surrender has been formally executed. But the President of the United States, and I in your name, have repeatedly declared that the enforcement of unconditional surrender upon the enemy in no way relieves the victorious Powers of their obligations to humanity, or of their duties as civilised and Christian nations. I read somewhere that when the ancient Athenians, on one occasion, overpowered a tribe in the Peloponnesus which had wrought them great injury by base, treacherous means, and when they had the hostile army herded on a beach naked for slaughter, they forgave them and set them free, and they said:

> This was not because they were men; it was done because of the nature of Man.

Similarly, in this temper, we may now say to our foes, 'We demand unconditional surrender, but you well know how strict are the moral limits within which our action is confined. We are no extirpators of nations, butchers of peoples. We make no bargain with you. We accord you nothing as a right. Abandon your resistance unconditionally. We remain bound by our customs and our nature.'

There is another reason why any abrogation of the principle of unconditional surrender would be most improvident at the present time, and it is a reason by no means inconsistent with, or contradictory to, that which I have just given. We should have to discuss with the enemy, while they still remained with arms in their hands, all the painful details of the settlement which their indescribable crimes have made necessary for the future safety of Europe and of the world; and these, when recited in detail, might well become a greater obstacle to the end of the struggle than the broad generalisation which the term 'unconditional surrender' implies.

The Germans know perfectly well how these matters stand in general. Several countries have already surrendered unconditionally to the victorious Allies, to Russia, to Britain and to the United States. Already there is a tolerable life appointed for their peoples. Take Finland, take Italy: these peoples have not all been massacred and enslaved. On the contrary, so far as Italy is concerned, there are moments when one has almost wondered whether it was they who had unconditionally surrendered to us, or whether we were about to surrender unconditionally to them. This, at least, I can say on behalf of the United Nations to Germany: 'If you surrender now, nothing that you will have to endure after the war will be comparable to what you are otherwise going to suffer during the year 1945.'

Peace, though based on unconditional surrender, will bring to Germany and Japan an immense, immediate amelioration of the suffering and agony which now lie before them. We, the Allies, are no monsters, but faithful men trying to carry forward the light of the world, trying to raise, from the bloody welter and confusion in which mankind is now plunged, a structure of peace, of freedom, of justice and of law, which system shall be an abiding and lasting shelter for all. That is how I venture to set before the Committee today the grave issue called 'unconditional surrender'.

'GREECE FOREVER, GREECE FOR ALL'

14 February 1945

Constitution Square, Athens

On his return from the Yalta Conference, Churchill stopped off in Greece to address a great crowd in the centre of Athens.

These are great days. These are days when dawn is bright, when darkness rolls away. A great future lies before your great country.

There has been much misunderstanding and ignorance of our common cause in many parts of the world, and there have been misrepresentations of issues fought out here in Athens. But now these matters are clearing, and there is an understanding of the part Greece has played and will play in the world.

Speaking as an Englishman, I am very proud of the part which the British Army played in protecting this great and immortal city against violence and anarchy. Our two countries have for long marched together along hard dusty roads in friendship and in loyalty.

Freedom and prosperity and happiness are dear to all nations of the British Commonwealth and Empire. We who have been associated with you in the very long struggle for Greek liberty, we will march with you till we reach the end of the dark valley, and we will march with you till we reach the broad highlands of justice and peace.

Let no one fail in his duty towards his country. Let no one swerve off the high road of truth and honour. Let no one fail to rise to the occasion of this great moment and of these splendid days. Let the Greek Nation stand first in every heart. Let it stand first in every man and woman. Let the future of Greece shine brightly in their eyes.

From the bottom of my heart I wish you prosperity. From the bottom of my heart I hope that Greece will take her proper place in the circle of victorious nations – of nations who have suffered terribly in war. Let right prevail. Let party hatreds die. Let there be unity, let there be resolute comradeship.

Greece forever. Greece for all.

THE YALTA CONFERENCE

27 February 1945

House of Commons

The Yalta Conference on Russia's Crimean coast took place from 4 to 11 February. This was to be the final meeting of the 'Big Three' war leaders: Churchill, Roosevelt and Stalin. The discussions centred around the future of Europe once Germany was defeated. The future of Poland, in whose defence Britain and France had drawn the sword in September 1939, was discussed at length and Stalin gave fulsome promises of democracy and fair elections. Tragically, the fate of the Polish nation was already sealed by the fact that their country had been 'liberated' by Russia's Red Army, and Stalin was determined to install his own puppet government; meanwhile Roosevelt was already a desperately sick man, and within ten weeks of death.

The recent Conference of the three Powers in the Crimea faced realities and difficulties in so exceptional a manner that the result constituted an act of State, on which Parliament should formally express their opinion. His Majesty's Government feel they have the right to know where they stand with the House of Commons. A strong expression of support by the House will strengthen our position among our Allies. The intimate and sensitive connections between the Executive Government and the House of Commons will thereby also be made plain, thus showing the liveliness of our democratic institutions, and the subordination of Ministers to Parliamentary authority. The House will not shrink from its duty of pronouncing. We live in a time when equality of decision is required from all who take part in our public affairs. In this way also, the firm and tenacious character of the present Parliament, and, generally, of our Parliamentary institutions, emerging as they do fortified from the storms of the war, will be made manifest. We have therefore thought it right and necessary to place a positive Motion on the Paper, in support of which I should like to submit some facts and arguments to the House at the opening of this three days' Debate.

The difficulties of bringing about a Conference of the three heads of the Governments of the principal Allies are only too obvious. The fact that, in spite of all modern methods of communication, fourteen months elapsed between Teheran and Yalta is a measure of those difficulties. It is well known that His Majesty's Government greatly desired a triple meeting in the Autumn. We rejoiced when, at last, Yalta was fixed. On the way there, the British and United States delegations met at Malta to discuss the wide range of our joint military and political affairs. The combined Chiefs of Staff of the two countries were for three days in conference upon the great operations now developing on the Western Front, and upon the war plans against Japan, which it was appropriate for us to discuss together. The Foreign Secretary, accompanied by high officials and assistants, some of whom unhappily perished on the way, also met Mr Stettinius there. On the morning of 2nd February the cruiser which bore the President steamed majestically into the battle-scarred harbour. A plenary meeting of the combined Chiefs of Staff was held in the afternoon, at which the President and I approved the proposals which had been so carefully worked out in the preceding days for carrying our joint war effort to the highest pitch, and for the shaping and timing of the military operations. . . .

After that, we all flew safely from Malta to the airfield in the Crimea, and motored over the mountains – about which very alarming accounts had been given, but these proved to be greatly exaggerated – until we found shelter on the Southern shore of the Crimea. This is protected by the mountains, and forms a beautiful Black Sea Riviera, where there still remain undestroyed by the Nazis a few villas and palaces of the vanished Imperial and aristocratic régime. By extreme exertions and every form of thoughtfulness and ingenuity, our Russian hosts had restored these dwellings to good order, and had provided for our accommodation and comfort in the true style of Russian hospitality. In the background were the precipices and the mountains; beyond them, the devastated fields and shattered dwellings of the Crimea, across which the armies have twice surged in deadly combat. Here on this shore, we laboured for nine days and grappled with many problems of war and policy while friendship grew. . . .

On world organisation, there is little that I can say beyond what is contained in the Report of the Conference, and, of course, in the earlier reports which emanated from Dumbarton Oaks. In the Crimea, the three Great Powers agreed on a solution of the difficult question of voting procedure, to which no answer had been found at Dumbarton Oaks. Agreement on this vital matter has enabled us to take the next step forward in the setting-up of the new world organisation, and the arrangements are in hand for the issue of invitations to the United Nations Conference which, as I have said, will meet in a couple of months at San Francisco. I wish I could give to the House full particulars of the solution of this question of the voting procedure, to which representatives of the three Great Powers, formerly in disagreement, have now wholeheartedly agreed. We thought it right, however, that we should consult both France and China, and should endeavour to secure their acceptance before the formula was published. For the moment, therefore, I can only deal with the matter in general terms.

Here is the difficulty which has to be faced. It is on the Great Powers that the chief burden of maintaining peace and security will fall. The new world organisation must take into account this special responsibility of the Great Powers, and must be so framed as not to compromise their unity, or their capacity for effective action if it is called for at short notice. At the same time, the world organisation cannot be based upon a dictatorship of the Great Powers. It is their duty to serve the world and not to rule it. We trust the voting procedure on which we agreed at Yalta meets these two essential points, and provides a system which is fair and acceptable, having regard to the evident difficulties, which will meet anyone who gives prolonged thought to the subject. . . .

The Crimea Conference leaves the Allies more closely united than ever before, both in the military and in the political sphere. Let Germany recognise that it is futile to hope for division among the Allies, and that nothing can avert her utter defeat. Further resistance will only be the cause of needless suffering. The Allies are resolved that Germany shall be totally disarmed, that Nazism and militarism in Germany shall be destroyed, that war criminals shall be justly and swiftly punished, that all German industry capable of military production shall be eliminated or controlled, and that Germany shall make compensation in kind to the utmost of her ability for damage done to Allied nations. On the other hand, it is not the purpose of the Allies to destroy the people of Germany, or leave them without the necessary means of subsistence. Our policy is not revenge; it is to take such measures as may be necessary to secure the future peace and safety of the world. There will be a place one day for Germans in the comity of nations, but only when all traces of Nazism and militarism have been effectively and finally extirpated. . . .

I now come to the most difficult and agitating part of the statement which I have to make to the House – the question of Poland. For more than a year past, and since the tide of war has turned so strongly against Germany, the Polish problem has been divided into two main issues – the frontiers of Poland and the freedom of Poland.

The House is well aware from the speeches I have made to them that the freedom, independence, integrity and sovereignty of Poland have always seemed to His Majesty's Government more important than the actual frontiers. To establish a free Polish nation with a good home to live in has always far outweighed, in my mind, the actual tracing of the frontier line, or whether these boundaries should be shifted on both sides of Poland farther to the West. . . .

But even more important than the frontiers of Poland, within the limits now disclosed, is the freedom of Poland. The home of the Poles is settled. Are they to be masters in their own house? Are they to be free, as we in Britain and the United States or France are free? Is their sovereignty and their independence to be untrammelled, or are they to become a mere projection of the Soviet State, forced against their will, by an armed minority, to adopt a Communist or totalitarian system? Well, I am putting the case in all its bluntness. It is a touchstone far more sensitive and vital than the drawing of frontier lines. Where does Poland stand? Where do we all stand on this?

Most solemn declarations have been made by Marshal Stalin and the Soviet Union that the sovereign independence of Poland is to be maintained, and this decision is now joined in both by Great Britain and the United States. Here also, the world organisation will in due course assume a measure of responsibility. The Poles will have their future in their own hands, with the single limitation that they must honestly follow, in harmony with their Allies, a policy friendly to Russia. That is surely reasonable.

The procedure which the three Great Powers have unitedly adopted to achieve this vital aim is set forth in unmistakable terms in the Crimea declaration. The agreement provides for consultations, with a view to the establishment in Poland of a new Polish Provisional Government of National Unity, with which the three major Powers can all enter into diplomatic relations, instead of some recognising one Polish Government and the rest another, a situation which, if it had survived the Yalta Conference, would have proclaimed to the world disunity and confusion. We had to settle it, and we settled it there. No binding restrictions have been imposed upon the scope and method of those consultations. His Majesty's Government intend to do all in their power to ensure that they shall be as wide as possible, and that representative Poles of all democratic parties are given full freedom to come and make their views known. Arrangements for this are now being made in Moscow by the

Commission of three, comprising M. Molotov, and Mr Harriman and Sir Archibald Clark Kerr, representing the United States and Great Britain respectively. It will be for the Poles themselves, with such assistance as the Allies are able to give them, to agree upon the composition and constitution of the new Polish Government of National Unity. Thereafter, His Majesty's Government, through their representative in Poland, will use all their influence to ensure that the free elections to which the new Polish Government will be pledged shall be fairly carried out under all proper democratic safeguards.

Our two guiding principles in dealing with all these problems of the Continent and of liberated countries, have been clear: While the war is on, we give help to anyone who can kill a Hun; when the war is over, we look to the solution of a free, unfettered, democratic election. Those are the two principles which this Coalition Government have applied, to the best of their ability, to the circumstances and situations in this entangled and infinitely varied development. . . .

The House should read carefully again and again – those Members who have doubts – the words and the terms of the Declaration, every word of which was the subject of the most profound and searching attention by the Heads of the three Governments, and by the Foreign Secretaries and all their experts. How will this Declaration be carried out? How will phrases like 'Free and unfettered elections on the basis of universal suffrage and secret ballot' be interpreted? Will the 'new' Government be 'properly' constituted, with a fair representation of the Polish people, as far as can be made practicable at the moment, and as soon as possible? Will the elections be free and unfettered? Will the candidates of all democratic parties be able to present themselves to the electors, and to conduct their campaigns? What are democratic parties? People always take different views. Even in our own country there has been from time to time an effort by one party or the other to claim that they are the true democratic party, and the rest are either Bolsheviks or Tory landlords. What are democratic parties? Obviously, this is capable of being settled. Will the election be what we should say was fair and free in this country, making some allowance for the great confusion and disorder which prevails? There are a great number of parties in Poland. We have agreed that all those that are democratic parties – not Nazi or Fascist parties or parties of collaborators with the enemy – all these will be able to take their part.

These are questions upon which we have the clearest views, in accordance with the principles of the Declaration on liberated Europe, to which all three Governments have duly subscribed. It is on that basis that the Moscow Commission of three was intended to work, and on that basis it has already begun to work.

The impression I brought back from the Crimea, and from all my other contacts, is that Marshal Stalin and the Soviet leaders wish to live in honourable friendship and equality with the Western democracies. I feel also that their word is their bond. I know of no Government which stands to its obligations, even in its own despite, more solidly than the Russian Soviet Government. I decline absolutely to embark here on a discussion about Russian good faith. It is quite evident that these matters touch the whole future of the world. Sombre indeed would be the fortunes of mankind if some awful schism arose between the Western democracies and the Russian Soviet Union, if the future world organisation were rent asunder, and if new cataclysms of inconceivable violence destroyed all that is left of the treasures and liberties of mankind.

LLOYD GEORGE

28 March 1945

House of Commons

Churchill pays tribute to the 'Greatest Welshman', who had guided Britain to victory in the First World War.

Shortly after David Lloyd George first took Cabinet office as President of the Board of Trade, the Liberals, who had been in eclipse for twenty years, obtained in January, 1906, an overwhelming majority over all other parties. They were independent of the Irish; the Labour Party was in its infancy; the Conservatives were reduced to little more than 100. But this moment of political triumph occurred in a period when the aspirations of 19th-century Liberalism had been largely achieved. Most of the great movements and principles of Liberalism had become the common property of enlightened men all over the civilised world. The chains had been struck from the slave; a free career was open to talent; the extension of the franchise was moving irresistibly forward; the advance in education was rapid and continuous, not only in this Island but in many lands. Thus at the moment when the Liberal Party became supreme, the great and beneficent impulses which had urged them forward were largely assuaged by success. Some new and potent conception had to be found by those who were called into power.

It was Lloyd George who launched the Liberal and Radical forces of this country effectively into the broad stream of social betterment and social security along which all modern parties now steer. There was no man so gifted, so eloquent, so forceful, who knew the life of the people so well. His warm heart was stirred by the many perils which beset the cottage homes: the health of the breadwinner, the fate of his widow, the nourishment and upbringing of his children, the meagre and haphazard provision of medical treatment and sanatoria, and the lack of any organised accessible medical service of a kind worthy of the age, from which the mass of the wage earners and the poor suffered. All this excited his wrath. Pity and compassion lent their powerful wings. He knew the terror with which old age threatened the toiler – that after a life of exertion he could be no more than a burden at the fireside and in the family of a struggling son. When I first became Lloyd George's friend and active associate, now more than forty years ago, this deep love of the people, the profound knowledge of their lives and of the undue and needless pressures under which they lived, impressed itself indelibly upon my mind.

Then there was his dauntless courage, his untiring energy, his oratory, persuasive, provocative, now grave, now gay. His swift, penetrating, comprehensive mind was always grasping at the root, or what he thought to be the root, of every question. His eye ranged ahead of the obvious. He was always hunting in the field beyond. I have often heard people come to him with a plan, and he would say 'That is all right, but what happens when we get over the bridge? What do we do then?'

In his prime, his power, his influence, his initiative, were unequalled in the land. He was the champion of the weak and the poor. Those were great days. Nearly two generations have passed. Most people are unconscious of how much their lives have been shaped by the laws for which Lloyd George was responsible. Health Insurance and Old Age Pensions were the first large-scale State-conscious efforts to set a balustrade along the crowded causeway of the people's life, and, without pulling down the structures of society, to fasten a lid over the abyss into which vast numbers used to fall, generation after generation, uncared-for and indeed unnoticed. Now we move forward confidently into larger and more far-reaching applications of these ideas. I was his lieutenant in those bygone days, and shared in a minor way in the work. I have lived to see long strides taken, and being taken, and going to be taken, on this path of insurance by which the vultures of utter ruin are driven from the dwellings of the nation. The stamps we lick, the roads we travel, the system of progressive taxation, the principal remedies that have so far been used against unemployment – all these to a very great extent were part not only of the mission but of the actual achievement of Lloyd George; and I am sure that as time passes his name will not only live but shine on account of the great, laborious, constructive work he did for the social and domestic life of our country.

When the calm, complacent, self-satisfied tranquillities of the Victorian era had exploded into the world convulsions and wars of the terrible twentieth century, Lloyd George had another part to play, on which his fame will stand with equal or even greater firmness. Although unacquainted with the military arts, although by public repute a pugnacious pacifist, when the life of our country was in peril he rallied to the war effort and cast aside all other thoughts and aims. He was the first to discern the fearful shortages of ammunition and artillery and all the other appliances of war which would so soon affect, and in the case of Imperial Russia mortally affect, the warring nations on both sides. . . .

Lloyd George left the Exchequer, when the Coalition Government was formed, for the Ministry of Munitions. Here he hurled himself into the mobilisation of British industry. In 1915 he was building great war factories that could not come into operation for two years. There was the usual talk about the war being over in a few months, but he did not hesitate to plan on a vast scale for two years ahead. It was my fortune to inherit the output of those factories in 1917 – the vast, overflowing output which came from them. Presently Lloyd George seized the main power in the State and the leadership of the Government. [*Hon. Members: 'Seized?'*] Seized. I think it was Carlyle who said of Oliver Cromwell:

He coveted the place; perhaps the place was his.

He imparted immediately a new surge of strength, of impulse, far stronger than anything that had been known up to that time, and extending over the whole field of wartime Government, every part of which was of equal interest to him.

I have already written about him at this time, when I watched him so closely and enjoyed his confidence and admired him so much, and I have recorded two characteristics of his which seemed to me invaluable in those days: first, his power to live in the present yet without taking short views; and secondly, his power of drawing from misfortune itself the means of future success. All this was illustrated by the successful development of the war; by the adoption of the convoy system, which he enforced upon the Admiralty and by which the U-boats were defeated; by the unified command on the Western Front which gave Marshal Foch the power to lead us all to victory; and in many other matters which form a part of the story of those sombre and tremendous years, the memory of which for ever abides with me, and to which I have often recurred in thought during our present second heavy struggle against German aggression, now drawing towards its victorious close.

Thus the statesman and guide whose gentle passing in the fullness of his years we mourn today served our country, our Island and our age, both faithfully and well in peace and in war. His long life was, from almost the beginning to almost the end, spent in political strife and controversy. He aroused intense and sometimes needless antagonisms. He had fierce and bitter quarrels at various times with all the parties. He faced undismayed the storms of criticism and hostility. In spite of all obstacles, including those he raised himself, he achieved his main purposes. As a man of action, resource and creative energy he stood, when at his zenith, without a rival. His name is a household word throughout our Commonwealth of Nations. He was the greatest Welshman which that unconquerable race has produced since the age of the Tudors. Much of his work abides, some of it will grow greatly in the future, and those who come after us will find the pillars of his life's toil upstanding, massive and indestructible; and we ourselves, gathered here today, may indeed be thankful that he voyaged with us through storm and tumult with so much help and guidance to bestow.

PRESIDENT ROOSEVELT

17 April 1945

House of Commons

Churchill had established close bonds of friendship with his comrade-in-arms, whom he salutes as 'the greatest American friend we have ever known'.

I beg to move:

> That an humble Address be presented to His Majesty to convey to His Majesty the deep sorrow with which this House has learned of the death of the President of the United States of America, and to pray His Majesty that in communicating his own sentiments of grief to the United States Government, he will also be generously pleased to express on the part of this House their sense of the loss which the British Commonwealth and Empire and the cause of the Allied nations have sustained, and their profound sympathy with Mrs Roosevelt and the late President's family, and with the Government and people of the United States of America.

My friendship with the great man to whose work and fame we pay our tribute today began and ripened during this war. I had met him, but only for a few minutes, after the close of the last war, and as soon as I went to the Admiralty in September 1939, he telegraphed inviting me to correspond with him direct on naval or other matters if at any time I felt inclined. Having obtained the permission of the Prime Minister, I did so. Knowing President Roosevelt's keen interest in sea warfare, I furnished him with a stream of information about our naval affairs, and about the various actions, including especially the action of the Plate River, which lighted the first gloomy winter of the war.

When I became Prime Minister, and the war broke out in all its hideous fury, when our own life and survival hung in the balance, I was already in a position to telegraph to the President on terms of an association which had become most intimate and, to me, most agreeable. This continued through all the ups and downs of the world struggle until Thursday last, when I received my last messages from him. These messages showed no falling off in his accustomed clear vision and vigour upon perplexing and complicated matters. I may mention that this correspondence which, of course, was greatly increased after the United States's entry into the war, comprises to and fro between us, over 1,700 messages. Many of these were lengthy messages, and the majority dealt with those more difficult points which come to be discussed upon the level of heads of Governments only after official solutions have not been reached at other stages. To this correspondence there must be added our nine meetings – at Argentia, three in Washington, at Casablanca, at Teheran, two at Quebec and, last of all, at Yalta, comprising in all about 120 days of close personal contact, during a great part of which I stayed with him at the White House or at his home at Hyde Park or in his retreat in the Blue Mountains, which he called Shangri-la.

I conceived an admiration for him as a statesman, a man of affairs, and a war leader. I felt the utmost confidence in his upright, inspiring character and outlook, and a personal regard – affection I must say – for him beyond my power to express today. His love of his own country, his respect for its constitution, his power of gauging the tides and currents of its mobile public opinion, were always evident, but added to these were the beatings of that generous heart which was always stirred to anger and to action by spectacles of aggression and oppression by the strong against the weak. It is, indeed, a loss, a bitter loss to humanity that those heart-beats are stilled for ever.

President Roosevelt's physical affliction lay heavily upon him. It was a marvel that he bore up against it through all the many years of tumult and storm. Not one man in ten millions, stricken and crippled as he was, would have attempted to plunge into a life of physical and mental exertion and of hard, ceaseless political controversy. Not one in ten millions would have tried, not one in a generation would have succeeded, not only in entering this sphere, not only in acting vehemently in it, but in becoming indisputable master of the scene. In this extraordinary effort of the spirit over the flesh, of will-power over physical infirmity, he was inspired and sustained by that noble woman, his devoted wife, whose high ideals marched with his own, and to whom the deep and respectful sympathy of the House of Commons flows out today in all fullness.

There is no doubt that the President foresaw the great dangers closing in upon the pre-war world with far more prescience than most well-informed people on either side of the Atlantic, and that he urged forward with all his power such precautionary military preparations as peacetime opinion in the United States could be brought to accept. There never was a moment's doubt, as the quarrel opened, upon which side his sympathies lay. The fall of France, and what seemed to most people outside this island, the impending destruction of Great Britain, were to him an agony, although he never lost faith in us. They were an agony to him not only on account of Europe, but because of the serious perils to which the United States herself would have been exposed had we been overwhelmed or the survivors cast down under the German yoke. The bearing of the British nation at that time of stress, when we were all alone, filled him and vast numbers of his countrymen with the warmest sentiments towards our people. He and they felt the blitz of the stern winter of 1940–41, when Hitler set himself to rub out the cities of our country, as much as any of us did, and perhaps more indeed, for imagination is often more torturing than reality. There is no doubt that the bearing of the British and, above all, of the Londoners, kindled fires in American bosoms far harder to quench than the conflagrations from which we were suffering. There was also at that time, in spite of General Wavell's victories – all the more, indeed, because of the reinforcements which were sent from this country to him – the apprehension widespread in the United States that we should be invaded by Germany after the fullest preparation in the spring of 1941. It was in February that the President sent to England the late Mr Wendell Willkie, who, although a political rival and an opposing candidate, felt as he did on many important points. Mr Willkie brought a letter from Mr Roosevelt, which the President had written in his own hand, and this letter contained the famous lines of Longfellow:

> ... Sail on, O ship of State!
> Sail on, O Union, strong and great!
> Humanity with all its fears,
> With all the hopes of future years,
> Is hanging breathless on thy fate!

At about that same time he devised the extraordinary measure of assistance called Lend-Lease, which will stand forth as the most unselfish and unsordid financial act of any country in all history. The effect of this was greatly to increase British fighting power, and for all the purpose of the war effort to make us, as it were, a much more numerous community. In that autumn I met the President for the first time during the war at Argentia in Newfoundland, and together we drew up the declaration which has since been called the Atlantic

Charter, and which will, I trust, long remain a guide for both our peoples and for other people of the world.

All this time in deep and dark and deadly secrecy, the Japanese were preparing their act of treachery and greed. When next we met in Washington, Japan, Germany and Italy had declared war upon the United States, and both our countries were in arms, shoulder to shoulder. Since then we have advanced over the land and over the sea through many difficulties and disappointments, but always with a broadening measure of success. I need not dwell upon the series of great operations which have taken place in the Western Hemisphere, to say nothing of that other immense war proceeding on the other side of the world. Nor need I speak of the plans which we made with our great ally, Russia, at Teheran, for these have now been carried out for all the world to see.

But at Yalta I noticed that the President was ailing. His captivating smile, his gay and charming manner, had not deserted him, but his face had a transparency, an air of purification, and often there was a faraway look in his eyes. When I took my leave of him in Alexandria harbour I must confess that I had an indefinable sense of fear that his health and his strength were on the ebb. But nothing altered his inflexible sense of duty. To the end he faced his innumerable tasks unflinching. One of the tasks of the President is to sign maybe a hundred or two State papers with his own hand every day, commissions and so forth. All this he continued to carry out with the utmost strictness. When death came suddenly upon him 'he had finished his mail'. That portion of his day's work was done. As the saying goes, he died in harness, and we may well say in battle harness, like his soldiers, sailors, and airmen, who side by side with ours are carrying on their task to the end all over the world. What an enviable death was his! He had brought his country through the worst of its perils and the heaviest of its toils. Victory had cast its sure and steady beam upon him.

In the days of peace he had broadened and stabilised the foundations of American life and union. In war he had raised the strength, might and glory of the great Republic to a height never attained by any nation in history. With her left hand she was leading the advance of the conquering Allied armies into the heart of Germany, and with her right, on the other side of the globe, she was irresistibly and swiftly breaking up the power of Japan. And all the time ships, munitions, supplies, and food of every kind were aiding on a gigantic scale her allies, great and small, in the course of the long struggle.

But all this was no more than worldly power and grandeur, had it not been that the causes of human freedom and of social justice, to which so much of his life had been given, added a lustre to this power and pomp and warlike might, a lustre which will long be discernible among men. He has left behind him a band of resolute and able men handling the numerous interrelated parts of the vast American war machine. He has left a successor who comes forward with firm step and sure conviction to carry on the task to its appointed end. For us, it remains only to say that in Franklin Roosevelt there died the greatest American friend we have ever known, and the greatest champion of freedom who has ever brought help and comfort from the new world to the old.

'NO WORDS CAN EVER EXPRESS THE HORROR . . .'

19 April 1945

House of Commons

As the Allied armies overran the concentration camps and death camps of the Third Reich, the full horror of the atrocities committed by the Nazis became apparent.

No words can express the horror which is felt by His Majesty's Government and their principal Allies at the proofs of these frightful crimes now daily coming into view. I do not at present, however, wish to commit myself to any special policy such as the suggestion made by my hon. Friend [to retain the captured concentration camp of Buchenwald intact as a memorial of German methods].

I have this morning received an informal message from General Eisenhower saying that the new discoveries, particularly at Weimar, far surpass anything previously exposed. He invites me to send a body of Members of Parliament at once to his Headquarters in order that they may themselves have ocular and first-hand proof of these atrocities.

The matter is of urgency, as of course it is not possible to arrest the processes of decay in many cases. In view of this urgency, I have come to the conclusion that eight Members of this House and two Members of the House of Lords should form a Parliamentary

Delegation, and should travel out at once to the Supreme Head-quarters, where General Eisenhower will make all the necessary arrangements for their inspection of the scenes, whether in American or British sectors. Members who volunteer for this extremely unpleasant but none the less necessary duty, should give their names to their Party Whips, in order that a body representative of all Parties may be selected by the usual methods during this afternoon. I should propose that they start tomorrow.

I hope that the House will approve of the somewhat rapid decision I have taken.

VICTORY IN EUROPE

8 May 1945

House of Commons and Broadcast, London

The armed forces of Germany surrendered unconditionally on 7 May. Hostilities in Europe ended officially at midnight on 8 May – almost five years to the day since Churchill, in the hour of gravest crisis, had become Prime Minister.

Yesterday morning at 2.41 a.m. at Headquarters, General Jodl, the representative of the German High Command, and Grand Admiral Doenitz, the designated head of the German State, signed the act of unconditional surrender of all German land, sea, and air forces in Europe to the Allied Expeditionary Force, and simultaneously to the Soviet High Command.

General Bedell Smith, Chief of Staff of the Allied Expeditionary Force, and General François Sevez signed the document on behalf of the Supreme Commander of the Allied Expeditionary Force, and General Susloparov signed on behalf of the Russian High Command.

Today this agreement will be ratified and confirmed at Berlin, where Air Chief Marshal Tedder, Deputy Supreme Commander of the Allied Expeditionary Force, and General de Lattre de Tassigny will sign on behalf of General Eisenhower. Marshal Zhukov will sign on behalf of the Soviet High Command. The German representatives will be Field-Marshal Keitel, Chief of the High Command, and the Commanders-in-Chief of the German Army, Navy, and Air Forces.

Victory Day broadcast from 10 Downing Street, 8 May 1945.

Hostilities will end officially at one minute after midnight tonight (Tuesday, May 8), but in the interests of saving lives the 'Cease fire' began yesterday to be sounded all along the front, and our dear Channel Islands are also to be freed today.

The Germans are still in places resisting the Russian troops, but should they continue to do so after midnight they will, of course, deprive themselves of the protection of the laws of war, and will be attacked from all quarters by the Allied troops. It is not surprising that on such long fronts and in the existing disorder of the enemy the orders of the German High Command should not in every case be obeyed immediately. This does not, in our opinion, with the best military advice at our disposal, constitute any reason for withholding from the nation the facts communicated to us by General Eisenhower of the unconditional surrender already signed at Rheims, nor should it prevent us from celebrating today and tomorrow (Wednesday) as Victory in Europe days.

Today, perhaps, we shall think mostly of ourselves. Tomorrow we shall pay a particular tribute to our Russian comrades, whose prowess in the field has been one of the grand contributions to the general victory.

The German war is therefore at an end. After years of intense preparation, Germany hurled herself on Poland at the beginning of September, 1939; and, in pursuance of our guarantee to Poland and in agreement with the French Republic, Great Britain, the British Empire and Commonwealth of Nations, declared war upon this foul aggression. After gallant France had been struck down we, from this Island and from our united Empire, maintained the struggle single-handed for a whole year until we were joined by the military might of Soviet Russia, and later by the overwhelming power and resources of the United States of America.

Finally almost the whole world was combined against the evil-doers, who are now prostrate before us. Our gratitude to our splendid Allies goes forth from all our hearts in this Island and throughout the British Empire.

We may allow ourselves a brief period of rejoicing; but let us not forget for a moment the toil and efforts that lie ahead. Japan, with all her treachery and greed, remains unsubdued. The injury she has inflicted on Great Britain, the United States, and other countries, and her detestable cruelties, call for justice and retribution. We must now devote all our strength and resources to the completion of our task, both at home and abroad. Advance, Britannia! Long live the cause of freedom! God save the King! . . .

That is the message which I have been instructed to deliver to the British Nation and Commonwealth. I have only two or three sentences to add. They will convey to the House my deep gratitude to this House of Commons, which has proved itself the strongest foundation for waging war that has ever been seen in the whole of our long history. We have all of us made our mistakes, but the strength of the Parliamentary institution has been shown to enable it at the same moment to preserved all the title-deeds of democracy while waging war in the most stern and protracted form. I wish to give my hearty thanks to men of all Parties, to everyone in every part of the House where they sit, for the way in which the liveliness of Parliamentary institutions has been maintained under the fire of the enemy, and for the way in which we have been able to persevere – and we could have persevered much longer if need had been – till all the objectives which we set before us for the procuring of the unlimited and unconditional surrender of the enemy had been achieved. I recollect well at the end of the last war, more than a quarter of a century ago, that the House, when it heard the long list of the surrender terms, the armistice terms, which had been imposed upon the Germans, did not feel inclined for debate or business, but desired to offer thanks to Almighty God, to the Great Power which seems to shape and design the fortunes of nations and the destiny of man; and I therefore beg, Sir, with your permission to move:

> That this House do now attend to the Church of St Margaret, Westminster, to give humble and reverent thanks to Almighty God for our deliverance from the threat of German domination.

This is the identical Motion which was moved in former times.

'THIS IS YOUR VICTORY'

8 May 1945

Balcony of the Ministry of Health, London

Spontaneously all London turned out into the streets to celebrate. Churchill and his principal colleagues appeared on the balcony of the Ministry of Health, above the vast crowd that thronged Whitehall.

When Churchill declared: 'This is your victory', the crowd roared back: 'No – it is yours.' As the historian, Robert Rhodes James, commented: 'It was an unforgettable moment of love and gratitude.'

God bless you all. This is your victory! It is the victory of the cause of freedom in every land. In all our long history we have never seen a greater day than this. Everyone, man or woman, has done their best. Everyone has tried. Neither the long years, nor the dangers, nor the fierce attacks of the enemy, have in any way weakened the independent resolve of the British nation. . . .

My dear friends, this is your hour. This is not victory of a party or of any class. It's a victory of the great British nation as a whole. We were the first, in this ancient island, to draw the sword against tyranny. After a while we were left all alone against the most tremendous military power that has been seen. We were all alone for a whole year.

There we stood, alone. Did anyone want to give in? [The crowd shouted 'No.'] Were we down-hearted? ['No!'] The lights went out and the bombs came down. But every man, woman and child in the country had no thought of quitting the struggle. London can take it. So we came back after long months from the jaws of death, out of the mouth of hell, while all the world wondered. When shall the reputation and faith of this generation of English men and women fail? I say that in the long years to come not only will the people of this island but of the world, whenever the bird of freedom chirps in human hearts, look back to what we've done and they will say 'do not despair, do not yield to violence and tyranny, march straight forward and die if need be – unconquered.' Now we have emerged from one deadly struggle – a terrible foe has been cast on the ground and awaits our judgment and our mercy.

But there is another foe who occupies large portions of the British Empire, a foe stained with cruelty and greed – the Japanese. I rejoice we can all take a night off today and another day tomorrow. Tomorrow our great Russian allies will also be celebrating victory and after that we must begin the task of rebuilding our health and homes, doing our utmost to make this country a land in which all have a chance, in which all have a duty, and we must turn ourselves to fulfil our duty to our own countrymen, and to our gallant allies of the United States who were so foully and treacherously attacked by Japan. We will go hand in hand with them. Even if it is a hard struggle we will not be the ones who will fail.

'FORWARD, TILL THE WHOLE TASK IS DONE'

13 May 1945

Broadcast, London

Though the war was won in Europe, the war in the Pacific against Japan was still raging. The invasion and defeat of Japan lay ahead.

It was five years ago on Thursday last that His Majesty the King commissioned me to form a National Government of all parties to carry on our affairs. Five years is a long time in human life, especially when there is no remission for good conduct. However, this National Government was sustained by Parliament and by the entire British nation at home and by all our fighting men abroad, and by the unswerving co-operation of the Dominions far across the oceans and of our Empire in every quarter of the globe. After various episodes had occurred it became clear last week that so far things have worked out pretty well, and that the British Commonwealth and Empire stands more united and more effectively powerful than at any time in its long romantic history. Certainly we are – this is what may well, I think, be admitted by any fair-minded person – in a far better state to cope with the problems and perils of the future than we were five years ago. . . .

You have no doubt noticed in your reading of British history – and I hope you will take pains to read it, for it is only from the past that one can judge the future, and it is only from reading the story of the British nation, of the British Empire, that you can feel a well-grounded sense of pride to dwell in these islands – you have sometimes noticed in your reading of British history that we have had to hold out from time to time all alone, or to be the mainspring of coalitions, against a Continental tyrant or dictator, and we have had to hold out for quite a long time: against the Spanish Armada, against the might of Louis XIV, when we led Europe for nearly twenty-five years under William III and Marlborough, and a hundred and fifty years ago, when Nelson, Pitt and Wellington broke Napoleon, not without assistance from the heroic Russians of 1812. In all these world wars our Island kept the lead of Europe or else held out alone.

And if you hold out alone long enough, there always comes a time when the tyrant makes some ghastly mistake which alters the whole balance of the struggle. On June 22, 1941, Hitler, master as he thought himself of all Europe – nay, indeed, soon to be master of the world, so he thought – treacherously, without warning, without the slightest provocation, hurled himself on Russia and came face to face with Marshal Stalin and the numberless millions of the Russian people. And then at the end of the year Japan struck a felon blow at the United States at Pearl Harbor, and at the same time attacked us in Malaya and Singapore. Thereupon Hitler and Mussolini declared war on the Republic of the United States.

Years have passed since then. Indeed every year seems to me almost a decade. But never since the United States entered the war have I had the slightest doubt but that we should be saved, and that we only had to do our duty in order to win. We have played our part in all this process by which the evil-doers have been overthrown, and I hope I do not speak vain or boastful words, but from Alamein in October, 1942, through the Anglo-American invasion of North Africa, of Sicily, of Italy, with the capture of Rome, we marched many miles and never knew defeat. And then last year, after two years' patient preparation and marvellous devices of amphibious warfare – and mark you, our scientists are not surpassed in any nation in the world, especially when their thought is applied to naval matters – last year on June 6 we seized a carefully-selected little toe of German-occupied France and poured millions in from this Island and from across the Atlantic, until the Seine, the Somme, and the Rhine all fell behind the advancing Anglo-American spearheads. France was liberated. She produced a fine army of gallant men to aid her own liberation. Germany lay open.

Now from the other side the mighty military achievements of the Russian people, always holding many more German troops on their front than we could do, rolled forward to meet us in the heart and centre of Germany. At the same time, in Italy, Field Marshal Alexander's army of so many nations, the largest part of which was British or British Empire, struck their final blow and compelled more than a million enemy troops to surrender. This Fifteenth Army Group, as we call it, British and Americans joined together in almost equal numbers, are now deep in Austria, joining their right hand with the Russians and their left with the United States armies of General Eisenhower's command. It happened, as you may remember – but memories are short – that in the space of three days we received the news of the unlamented departures of Mussolini and Hitler, and in three days also surrenders were made to Field Marshal Alexander and Field Marshal Montgomery of over two million five hundred thousand soldiers of this terrible warlike German army.

I shall make it clear at this moment that we never failed to recognise the immense superiority of the power used by the United States in the rescue of France and the defeat of Germany. For our part, British and Canadians, we have had about one-third as many men over there as the Americans, but we have taken our full share of the fighting, as the scale of our losses shows. Our Navy has borne incomparably the heaviest burden in the Atlantic Ocean, in the narrow seas and the Arctic convoys to Russia, while the United States Navy has had to use its immense strength mainly against Japan. We made a fair division of the labour, and we can each report that our work is either done or going to be done. It is right and natural that we should extol the virtues and glorious services of our own most famous commanders, Alexander and Montgomery, neither of whom was ever defeated since they began together at Alamein. Both of them have conducted in Africa, in Italy, in Normandy and in Germany, battles of the first magnitude and of decisive consequence. At the same time we know how great is our debt to the combining and unifying command and high strategic direction of General Eisenhower. . . .

I wish I could tell you tonight that all our toils and troubles were over. Then indeed I could end my five years' service happily, and if you thought that you had had enough of me and that I ought to be put out to grass, I tell you I would take it with the best of grace. But, on the contrary, I must warn you, as I did when I began this five years' task – and no one knew then that it would last so long – that there is still a lot to do, and that you must be prepared for further efforts of mind and body and further sacrifices to great causes if you are not to fall back into the rut of inertia, the confusion of aim, and the craven fear of being great. You must not weaken in any way in your alert and vigilant frame of mind. Though holiday rejoicing is necessary to the human spirit, yet it must add to the strength and resilience with which every man and woman turns again to the work they have to do, and also to the outlook and watch they have to keep on public affairs.

On the Continent of Europe we have yet to make sure that the simple and honourable purposes for which we entered the war are not brushed aside or overlooked in the months following our success, and that the words 'freedom', 'democracy', and 'liberation' are not distorted from their true meaning as we have understood them. There would be little use in punishing the Hitlerites for their crimes if law and justice did not rule, and if totalitarian or police governments were to take the place of the German invaders. We seek nothing for ourselves. But we must make sure that those causes which we fought for find recognition at the peace table in facts as well as words, and above all we must labour that the world organisation which the United Nations are creating at San Francisco does not become an idle name, does not become a shield for the strong and a mockery for the weak. It is the victors who must search their hearts in their glowing hours, and be worthy by their nobility of the immense forces that they wield.

We must never forget that beyond all lurks Japan, harassed and failing but still a people of a hundred millions, for whose warriors death has few terrors. I cannot tell you tonight how much time or what exertions will be required to compel the Japanese to make amends for their odious treachery and cruelty. We – like China, so long undaunted – have received horrible injuries from them ourselves, and we are bound by the ties of honour and fraternal loyalty to the United States to fight this great war at the other end of the world at their side without flagging or failing. We must remember that Australia and New Zealand and Canada were and are all directly menaced by this evil Power. They came to our aid in our dark times, and we must not leave unfinished any task which concerns their safety and their future. I told you hard things at the beginning of these last five years; you did not shrink, and I should be unworthy of your confidence and generosity if I did not still cry: Forward, unflinching, unswerving, indomitable, till the whole task is done and the whole world is safe and clean.

BACK TO PARTY POLITICS

4 June 1945

Broadcast, London

With the end of the war in Europe, the great wartime coalition, which had sustained Britain's democracy through more than five years of world war, came to an end. Churchill formed a Conservative Government until a General Election – the first in ten years – could be held in July. He was bitter that the Socialists had pulled the rug from under the Coalition Government before victory over Japan had been secured and, in this broadcast, made a serious misjudgment which backfired on him, when he accused the Socialists of a determination to set up in Britain 'some form of Gestapo'.

I am sorry to have lost so many good friends who served with me in the five years' Coalition. It was impossible to go on in a state of 'electionitis' all through the summer and autumn. This election will last quite long enough for all who are concerned in it, and I expect many of the general public will be sick and tired of it before we get to polling day.

My sincere hope was that we could have held together until the war against Japan was finished. On the other hand, there was a high duty to consult the people after all these years. I could only be relieved of that duty by the full agreement of the three parties, further fortified, perhaps, by a kind of official Gallup Poll, which I am sure would have resulted in an overwhelming request that we should go on to the end and finish the job. That would have enabled me to say at once, 'There will be no election for a year', or words to that effect.

I know that many of my Labour colleagues would have been glad to carry on. On the other hand, the Socialist Party as a whole had been for some time eager to set out upon the political warpath, and when large numbers of people feel like that it is not good for their health to deny them the fight they want. We will therefore give it to them to the best of our ability.

Party, my friends, has always played a great part in our affairs. Party ties have been considered honourable bonds, and no one could doubt that when the German war was over and the immediate danger to this country, which had led to the Coalition, had ceased, conflicting loyalties would arise. Our Socialist and Liberal friends felt themselves forced, therefore, to put party before country. They have departed, and we have been left to carry the nation's burden. . . .

My friends, I must tell you that a Socialist policy is abhorrent to the British ideas of freedom. Although it is now put forward in the main by people who have a good grounding in the Liberalism and Radicalism of the early part of this century, there can be no doubt that Socialism is inseparably interwoven with Totalitarianism and the abject worship of the State. It is not alone that property, in all its forms, is struck at, but that liberty, in all its forms, is challenged by the fundamental conceptions of Socialism.

Look how even today they hunger for controls of every kind, as if these were delectable foods instead of wartime inflictions and monstrosities. There is to be one State to which all are to be obedient in every act of their lives. This State is to be the arch-employer, the arch-planner, the arch-administrator and ruler, and the arch-caucus-boss.

How is an ordinary citizen or subject of the King to stand up against this formidable machine, which, once it is in power, will prescribe for every one of them where they are to work; what they are to work at; where they may go and what they may say; what views they are to hold and within what limits they may express them; where their wives are to go to queue up for the State ration; and what education their children are to receive to mould their views of human liberty and conduct in the future?

A Socialist State once thoroughly completed in all its details and its aspects – and that is what I am speaking of – could not afford to suffer opposition. Here in old England, in Great Britain, of which old England forms no inconspicuous part, in this glorious Island, the cradle and citadel of free democracy throughout the world, we do not like to be regimented and ordered about and have every action of our lives prescribed for us. In fact we punish criminals by sending them to Wormwood Scrubs and Dartmoor, where they get full employment, and whatever board and lodging is appointed by the Home Secretary.

Socialism is, in its essence, an attack not only upon British enterprise, but upon the right of the ordinary man or woman to breathe freely without having a harsh, clumsy, tyrannical hand clapped across their mouths and nostrils. A Free Parliament – look at that – a Free Parliament is odious to the Socialist doctrinaire. Have we not heard Mr Herbert Morrison descant upon his plans to curtail Parliamentary procedure and pass laws simply by resolutions of broad principle in the House of Commons, afterwards to be left by Parliament to the executive and to the bureaucrats to elaborate and enforce by departmental regulations? As for Sir Stafford Cripps on 'Parliament in the Socialist State', I have not time to read you what he said, but perhaps it will meet the public eye during the election campaign.

But I will go farther. I declare to you, from the bottom of my heart, that no Socialist system can be established without a political police. Many of those who are advocating Socialism or voting Socialist today will be horrified at this idea. That is because they are short-sighted, that is because they do not see where their theories are leading them.

No Socialist Government conducting the entire life and industry of the country could afford to allow free, sharp, or violently-worded expressions of public discontent. They would have to fall back on some form of Gestapo, no doubt very humanely directed in the first instance. And this would nip opinion in the bud; it would stop criticism as it reared its head, and it would gather all the power to the supreme party and the party leaders, rising like stately pinnacles above their vast bureaucracies of Civil servants, no longer servants and no longer civil. And where would the ordinary simple folk – the common people, as they like to call them in America – where would they be, once this mighty organism had got them in its grip?

I stand for the sovereign freedom of the individual within the laws which freely elected Parliaments have freely passed. I stand for the rights of the ordinary man to say what he thinks of the Government of the day, however powerful, and to turn them out, neck and crop, if he thinks he can better his temper or his home thereby, and if he can persuade enough others to vote with him.

GENERAL EISENHOWER

12 June 1945

*Presentation of the Freedom of the City of London,
Mansion House, London*

Many hundreds of thousands of British troops had served under the command of General Eisenhower in the liberation of Europe. The presentation to him of the Freedom of the City of London was an expression of Britain's deep appreciation of his leadership.

I have been brought very closely in contact with General Eisenhower since the day early in 1942 when we first met at the White House after the attack on Pearl Harbor, and all the grave matters of the direction of the armies to the landings in French North Africa and all the great efforts which were called for a year ago had to be discussed and examined, and I had the opportunity of seeing at close quarters General 'Ike' – for that is what I call him – in action. I saw him at all sorts of times, because in war things do not always go as we wish. Another will breaks in, and there is a clash, and questions arise. Never have I seen a man so staunch in pursuing the purpose in hand, so ready to accept responsibility for misfortune, or so generous in victory.

There is one moment I would dwell on. It was just about a little more than a year ago that he had to decide whether to go across the Channel or put it off for, it might be, eleven days. It was a terrible decision. The Army had gathered. A million men in the front line had gathered, and thousands of crafts and tens of thousands of aircraft, and the great ships were all arranged. You could not hold it. It was like trying to hold an avalanche in leash. Should it be launched or should it not be launched?

There were a great many people who had a chance of expressing their opinions. I was not one of them, because it was purely a technical matter. A great many generals and admirals were gathered in the High Command to express their opinions and views, but there was only one man on whom the awful brunt fell of saying 'Go' or 'Stay'. To say 'Stay' meant keeping hundreds of thousands of men cooped up in wired enclosures so that the plans they had been told of might not leak out. It meant the problem of hundreds of thousands of men on board ship who had to be provided for and found accommodation. It might have meant that the air could not cover the landing or that the water was too rough for the many boats that were needed.

It was one of the most terrible decisions, and this decision was taken by this man – this very great man (*prolonged applause*).

It is one of many decisions he has taken. Had he not said 'Go', and eleven days had passed, the weather would have smiled, and all the groups of meteorologists would have been happy. The expedition would have started; and two days later the worst gale for forty years at that season of the year fell upon the beaches in Normandy. Not only did he take the risk and arrive at the fence, he cleared it in magnificent style.

There are many occasions when that kind of decision falls on the Supreme Commander. Many fearful tales come from the front line. A great deal of anxiety is felt by populations at home. Do we go forward? Do we fight in this area? Are we to push on? These decisions all resolved themselves into an 'Aye' or a 'No', and all I can say about our guest is that in very many most important decisions history will acclaim his decisions as right, and that the bias, the natural bias, that moved him in these matters was very much more in favour of 'Aye' than of 'No'.

I could go on for a very long time about your guest. There is no doubt whatever that we have among us today one of the greatest

Americans who have reached our shores and dwelt a considerable time among us. We honour him very much for his invariable considerations of the British point of view, for his impartial treatment of all the officers under his command. I know he will tell you when he rises that he never gave an order to a British officer which he could not immediately obey.

We also have made our contribution to the battles on the Continent, and I am quite sure that the influence he will wield in the world will be one always of bringing our countries together in the much more difficult task of peace, in the same way as he brought them together in the grim and awful cataclysm of war. I have had personal acquaintance with him now for three years. It is not much, but three years of this sort may seem five-and-twenty. I feel we have here a great creative, constructive and combining genius, one from our sister nation across the ocean, one who will never speak evil but will always cherish his contact with the British people, and to whom I feel we should at this moment give the most cordial testimony in our power of our admiration, of our affection, and of our heartfelt good wishes for everything that may happen to him in the future.

'DEAR DESERT RATS'

21 July 1945

Opening of the 'Winston Club' for British Troops, Berlin

Churchill felt a close bond with Britain's Desert Army. The concept of defeating the enemy in the deserts of North Africa, while building up their strength and battle experience until strong enough to embark on the Liberation of Europe, had been his and he had visited them on many occasions along their path to victory.

This morning's parade brings back to my mind a great many moving incidents of these last long, fierce years. Now you are here in Berlin, and I find you established in this great centre which, as a volcano, erupted smoke and fire all over Europe. Twice in our generation as in bygone times the German fury has been unleashed on her neighbours. . . .

I have only one more word to say to the Desert Rats. You were the first to begin.

The 11th Hussars were in action in the Desert in 1940, and ever since you have kept marching steadily forward on the long road to Victory: through so many countries and changing scenes you have marched and fought your way.

I am unable to speak without emotion. Dear Desert Rats, may your glory ever shine. May your laurels never fade. May the memory of this glorious pilgrimage which you have made from Alamein to the Baltic and Berlin never die. A march – as far as my reading of history leads me to believe – unsurpassed in the whole story of war.

May fathers long tell their children the tale. May you all feel that through following your great ancestors you have accomplished something which has done good to the whole world, which has raised the honour of your country and of which every man has the right to feel proud.

RESIGNATION

26 July 1945

No. 10 Downing Street

On 25 July Churchill interrupted his participation in the Potsdam Conference outside Berlin, bidding farewell to President Truman and Marshal Stalin, to return to London for the announcement of the election results, which Conservative Party managers confidently believed would return the Conservative Party with a substantial majority. As he recounts in Triumph and Tragedy: *'Just before dawn I woke suddenly with a sharp stab of almost physical pain. A hitherto subconscious conviction that we were beaten broke forth and dominated my mind. . . . By noon it was clear that the Socialists would have a majority. At luncheon my wife said to me: "It may well be a blessing in disguise." I replied, "At the moment it seems quite effectively disguised." . . . At seven o'clock therefore, having asked for an audience, I drove to the Palace, tendered my resignation to the King, and advised His Majesty to send for Mr Attlee.' The Socialists had won a landslide victory and Churchill issued the following short but dignified statement.*

The decision of the British people has been recorded in the votes counted today. I have therefore laid down the charge which was placed upon me in darker times. I regret that I have not been permitted to finish the work against Japan. For this, however, all plans and preparations have been made, and the results may come much quicker than we have hitherto been entitled to expect. Immense responsibilities abroad and at home fall upon the new Government, and we must all hope that they will be successful in bearing them.

It only remains for me to express to the British people, for whom I have acted in these perilous years, my profound gratitude for the unflinching, unswerving support which they have given me during my task, and for the many expressions of kindness which they have shown towards their servant.

5. The Sunset Years 1945–63

The verdict of the British electorate in the summer of 1945 – in the very hour of victory – came as a rude shock to Churchill. But he took the rebuff stoically and set about restoring his strength, his finances and his political fortunes with zest and determination.

With his seminal 'Iron Curtain' speech at Fulton in 1946, warning that the West's erstwhile ally, Russia, had become her sworn enemy, and in his Zurich address, urging France to extend the hand of friendship to a defeated Germany to rebuild the European family, he set the agenda for the post-war years.

Then in 1951, against all the odds, after six years as Leader of the Opposition, he led the Conservative Party to victory, returning to office as Prime Minister, once again, at the age of 76. In 1955, soon after his 80th birthday, he retired from office in a blaze of glory and public acclaim. But even in his sunset years he was a regular attender in Parliament, sitting in his corner seat below the gangway. As the shadows lengthened, few things gave him greater pleasure than the decision of President Kennedy and the United States Congress to confer upon him Honorary Citizenship of the United States in gratitude for the part he had played in the defeat of Nazi Germany and the Liberation of Europe. His death on 22 January 1965, at the age of 90, marked the passing of an era for all who had served under his leadership in the cause of freedom.

THE ATOMIC BOMB

6 August 1945

No. 10 Downing Street

On 6 August, President Truman announced that American and British scientists had developed an atomic bomb and that the first had that day been dropped on Hiroshima. Mr Attlee then issued the following statement prepared by Churchill before he left office.

By the year 1939 it had become widely recognised among scientists of many nations that the release of energy by atomic fission was a possibility. The problems which remained to be solved before this possibility could be turned into practical achievement were, however, manifold and immense; and few scientists would at that time have ventured to predict that an atomic bomb could be ready for use by 1945. Nevertheless, the potentialities of the project were so great that His Majesty's Government thought it right that research should be carried on in spite of the many competing claims on our scientific manpower. . . .

On October 11, 1941, President Roosevelt sent me a letter suggesting that any extended efforts on this important matter might usefully be co-ordinated, or even jointly conducted. Accordingly, all British and American efforts were joined, and a number of British scientists concerned proceeded to the United States. Apart from these contacts, complete secrecy guarded all these activities, and no single person was informed whose work was not indispensable to progress.

By the summer of 1942 this expanded programme of research had confirmed with surer and broader foundations the promising forecasts which had been made a year earlier, and the time had come when a decision must be made whether or not to proceed with the construction of large-scale production plants. Meanwhile it had become apparent from the preliminary experiments that these plants would have to be on something like the vast scale described in the American statements which have been published today.

Great Britain at this period was fully extended in war production, and we could not afford such grave interference with the current munitions programmes on which our warlike operations depended. Moreover, Great Britain was within easy range of German bombers, and the risk of raiders from the sea or air could not be ignored. The United States, however, where parallel or similar progress had been made, was free from these dangers. The decision was therefore taken to build the full-scale production plants in America.

In the United States the erection of the immense plants was placed under the responsibility of Mr Stimson, United States Secretary of War, and the American Army Administration, whose wonderful work and marvellous secrecy cannot be sufficiently admired. The main practical effort and virtually the whole of its prodigious cost now fell upon the United States authorities, who were assisted by a number of British scientists. The relationship of the British and American contributions was regulated by discussion between the late President Roosevelt and myself, and a combined policy committee was set up. . . .

By God's mercy British and American science outpaced all German efforts. These were on a considerable scale, but far behind. The possession of these powers by the Germans at any time might have altered the result of the war, and profound anxiety was felt by those who were informed. Every effort was made by our Intelligence Service and by the Air Force to locate in Germany anything resembling the plants which were being created in the United States. In the winter of 1942–43 most gallant attacks were made in Norway on two occasions by small parties of volunteers from the British Commandos and Norwegian forces, at very heavy loss of life, upon stores of what is called 'heavy water', an element in one of the possible processes. The second of these two attacks was completely successful.

The whole burden of execution, including the setting-up of the plants and many technical processes connected therewith in the practical sphere, constitutes one of the greatest triumphs of American – or indeed human – genius of which there is record. Moreover, the decision to make these enormous expenditures upon a project which, however hopefully established by American and British research, remained nevertheless a heart-shaking risk, stands to the everlasting honour of President Roosevelt and his advisers.

It is now for Japan to realise, in the glare of the first atomic bomb which has smitten her, what the consequences will be of an indefinite continuance of this terrible means of maintaining a rule of law in the world.

This revelation of the secrets of nature, long mercifully withheld from man, should arouse the most solemn reflections in the mind and conscience of every human being capable of comprehension. We must indeed pray that these awful agencies will be made to conduce to peace among the nations, and that instead of wreaking measure-less havoc upon the entire globe they may become a perennial fountain of world prosperity.

SURRENDER OF JAPAN: 'THE TRUE GLORY'

15 August 1945

House of Commons

On 9 August the second atomic bomb was dropped on Nagasaki. On 14 August Japan surrendered. One of the key factors in Churchill's political defeat had been the war-weariness of British troops after five long years of war. It was assumed that the defeat of Japan would take one to two years and cost one to two million Allied casualties. Many wanted to get home and reckoned that would happen quicker under the Socialists. In the event, Japan surrendered within a month of the General Election.

This crowning deliverance from the long and anxious years of danger and carnage should rightly be celebrated by Parliament in accordance with custom and tradition. The King is the embodiment of the national will, and his public acts involve all the might and power not only of the people of this famous Island but of the whole British Commonwealth and Empire. The good cause for which His Majesty has contended commanded the ardent fidelity of all his subjects spread over one-fifth of the surface of the habitable globe. That cause has now been carried to complete success. Total war has ended in absolute victory.

Once again the British Commonwealth and Empire emerges safe, undiminished and united from a mortal struggle. Monstrous tyran-nies which menaced our life have been beaten to the ground in ruin, and a brighter radiance illumines the Imperial Crown than any which our annals record. The light is brighter because it comes not only from the fierce but fading glare of military achievement such as an endless succession of conquerors have known, but because there

Victory! The famous V-sign.

mingle with it in mellow splendour the hopes, joys, and blessings of almost all mankind. This is the true glory, and long will it gleam upon our forward path.

'GOVERNMENT OF THE PEOPLE BY THE PEOPLE, FOR THE PEOPLE'

16 August 1945

House of Commons

In those countries, torn and convulsed by war, there may be, for some months to come, the need of authoritarian government. The alternative would be anarchy. Therefore it would be unreasonable to ask or expect that liberal government – as spelt with a small 'l' – and British or United States democratic conditions, should be instituted immediately. They take their politics very seriously in those countries. A friend of mine, an officer, was in Zagreb when the results of the late General Election came in. An old lady said to him, 'Poor Mr Churchill! I suppose now he will be shot.' My friend was able to reassure her. He said the sentence might be mitigated to one of the various forms of hard labour which are always open to His Majesty's subjects. Nevertheless we must know where we stand, and we must make clear where we stand, in these affairs of the Balkans and of Eastern Europe, and indeed of any country which comes into this field. Our ideal is government of the people, by the people, for the people – the people being free without duress to express, by secret ballot without intimidation, their deep-seated wish as to the form and conditions of the Government under which they are to live.

ALAMEIN: 'THE TURNING POINT IN BRITISH MILITARY FORTUNES'

25 October 1945

Alamein Reunion Dinner, Royal Albert Hall, London

It is of Monty, as I have been for some time allowed to call him, that I speak especially tonight. The advances of the Eighth Army under his command will ever be a glittering episode in the martial annals of Britain and, not only of Britain but, as the Field Marshal has said, of the mighty array of Commonwealth and Empire which gathered around this small island and found its representation in all the desert battles. Field Marshal Montgomery is one of the greatest living masters of the art of war. Like Stonewall Jackson, he was a professor and teacher of the military science before he became an actor on the world stage. It has been my fortune and great pleasure often to be with him at important moments in the long march from Mersa Matruh to the Rhine. Either on the eve of great battles, or while the struggle was actually in progress, always I have found the same buoyant, vigorous, efficient personality with every aspect of the vast operation in his mind, and every unit of mighty armies in his grip.

He is now discharging a task of enormous responsibility and difficulty in the administration of shattered and ruined Germany and we look to him to help those misguided and now terribly smitten people through the sombre winter which is approaching. I cannot doubt that after that he has further first-rate contributions to make to the future structure of the British Army. I therefore feel it an honour that he should have proposed my health and that he should have wished to associate me here with the Eighth Army and its glorious victory.

'WE DID NOT FLINCH, WE DID NOT FAIL'

31 October 1945

Harrow School

As a youth, I always wanted to play the kettledrum, and when that could not be arranged I thought I would like to be leader of the school orchestra. That could not be arranged either, but eventually, and after a great deal of perseverance I rose to be the conductor of quite a considerable band. It was a very large band and played very strange and formidable instruments. The roar and thunder of its music resounded throughout the world. We played all sorts of tunes, and we finished up the concert with 'Rule, Britannia!' and 'God save the King.' . . . (*Cheers.*)

This is a time when the voice of youth will be welcomed in the world. We have come out of this struggle in many ways impoverished and with many burdens and the future is by no means clear. Always remember you are citizens of a country which holds its own in the very foremost ranks of the nations of the world and is entitled to receive from all of them a tribute of respect, because it was on our country that the whole brunt of the burden fell for more than a year of saving civilisation and the world. We did not flinch, we did not fail.

'THE UNNECESSARY WAR'

16 November 1945

Joint Meeting of the Belgian Parliament, Brussels

Churchill had an unwavering conviction that, had the democracies – including the United States – stood together to resist aggression in the 1930s, the Second World War could have been avoided.

The ties between Great Britain and Belgium found their culmination in the great struggle from 1914–1918. It was hoped that the wars

'An Iron Curtain has descended!' Westminster College, Fulton, Missouri, 5 March 1946.

were over. Yet we have witnessed an even more destructive world-wide struggle. Need we have done so? I have no doubt whatever that firm guidance and united action on the part of the Victorious Powers would have prevented this last catastrophe. President Roosevelt one day asked what this war should be called. My answer was, 'The Unnecessary War.' If the United States had taken an active part in the League of Nations, and if the League of Nations had been prepared to use concerted force, even had it only been European force, to prevent the rearmament of Germany, there was no need for further serious bloodshed. If the Allies had resisted Hitler strongly in his early stages, even up to his seizure of the Rhineland in 1936, he would have been forced to recoil, and a chance would have been given to the same elements in German life, which were very powerful especially in the High Command, to free Germany of the maniacal Government and system into the grip of which she was falling.

Do not forget that twice the German people, by a majority, voted against Hitler, but the Allies and the League of Nations acted with such feebleness and lack of clairvoyance, that each of Hitler's encroachments became a triumph for him over all moderate and restraining forces until, finally, we resigned ourselves without further protest to the vast process of German rearmament and war preparation which ended in a renewed outbreak of destructive war. Let us profit at least by this terrible lesson. In vain did I attempt to teach it before the war.

'AN IRON CURTAIN HAS DESCENDED'

5 March 1946

Westminster College, Fulton, Missouri

This is Churchill's famous 'Iron Curtain' speech, in which he alerts America and the world to the fact that Soviet Russia, the West's erstwhile comrade-in-arms, has become its mortal enemy. Its impact was enormous. The Soviets choose to date the Cold War from that moment, instead of from the real moment which was, of course, their occupation of the nations of Central and Eastern Europe. The reason that Churchill made the long journey to deliver this speech in the heart of the American Mid-West was that he knew he would be

speaking at the feet of the President of the United States, Harry S.
Truman. The kernel of his message to America was not to repeat the
mistake that it made in 1918 of retreating into isolation, urging her
instead to lead the free world in forging a defensive alliance that
would safeguard freedom and secure the peace. The creation of the
NATO Alliance in 1949 was everything he had hoped for.

I am glad to come to Westminster College this afternoon, and am
complimented that you should give me a degree. The name
'Westminster' is somehow familiar to me. I seem to have heard of it
before. Indeed, it was at Westminster that I received a very large part
of my education in politics, dialectic, rhetoric, and one or two other
things. In fact we have both been educated at the same, or similar, or,
at any rate, kindred establishments.

It is also a honour, perhaps almost unique, for a private visitor to
be introduced to an academic audience by the President of the United
States. Amid his heavy burdens, duties, and responsibilities –
unsought but not recoiled from – the President has travelled a
thousand miles to dignify and magnify our meeting here today and to
give me an opportunity of addressing this kindred nation, as well as
my own countrymen across the ocean, and perhaps some other
countries too. The President has told you that it is his wish, as I am
sure it is yours, that I should have full liberty to give my true and
faithful counsel in these anxious and baffling times. I shall certainly
avail myself of this freedom, and feel the more right to do so because
any private ambitions I may have cherished in my younger days have
been satisfied beyond my wildest dreams. Let me, however, make it
clear that I have no official mission or status of any kind, and that I
speak only for myself. There is nothing here but what you see.

I can therefore allow my mind, with the experience of a lifetime, to
play over the problems which beset us on the morrow of our absolute
victory in arms, and to try to make sure with what strength I have
that what has been gained with so much sacrifice and suffering shall
be preserved for the future glory and safety of mankind.

The United States stands at this time at the pinnacle of world
power. It is a solemn moment for the American Democracy. For with
primacy in power is also joined an awe-inspiring accountability to
the future. If you look around you, you must feel not only the sense
of duty done but also you must feel anxiety lest you fall below the
level of achievement. Opportunity is here now, clear and shining for
both our countries. To reject it or ignore it or fritter it away will
bring upon us all the long reproaches of the after-time. It is necessary

that constancy of mind, persistency of purpose, and the grand simplicity of decision shall guide and rule the conduct of the English-speaking peoples in peace as they did in war. We must, and I believe we shall, prove ourselves equal to this severe requirement.

When American military men approach some serious situation they are wont to write at the head of their directive the words 'over-all strategic concept'. There is wisdom in this, as it leads to clarity of thought. What then is the over-all strategic concept which we should inscribe today? It is nothing less than the safety and welfare, the freedom and progress, of all the homes and families of all the men and women in all the lands. And here I speak particularly of the myriad cottage or apartment homes where the wage-earner strives amid the accidents and difficulties of life to guard his wife and children from privation and bring the family up in the fear of the Lord, or upon ethical conceptions which often play their potent part.

To give security to these countless homes, they must be shielded from the two giant marauders, war and tyranny. We all know the frightful disturbances in which the ordinary family is plunged when the curse of war swoops down upon the breadwinner and those for whom he works and contrives. The awful ruin of Europe, with all its vanished glories, and of large parts of Asia glares us in the eyes. When the designs of wicked men or the aggressive urge of mighty States dissolve over large areas the frame of civilised society, humble folk are confronted with difficulties with which they cannot cope. For them all is distorted, all is broken, even ground to pulp.

When I stand here this quiet afternoon I shudder to visualise what is actually happening to millions now and what is going to happen in this period when famine stalks the earth. None can compute what has been called 'the unestimated sum of human pain'. Our supreme task and duty is to guard the homes of the common people from the horrors and miseries of another war. We are all agreed on that.

Our American military colleagues, after having proclaimed their 'over-all strategic concept' and computed available resources, always proceed to the next step – namely, the method. Here again there is widespread agreement. A world organisation has already been erected for the prime purpose of preventing war. UNO, the successor of the League of Nations, with the decisive addition of the United States and all that that means, is already at work. We must make sure that its work is fruitful, that it is a reality and not a sham, that it is a force for action, and not merely a frothing of words, that it is a true temple of peace in which the shields of many nations can some day be hung up, and not merely a cockpit in a Tower of Babel.

Before we cast away the solid assurances of national armaments for self-preservation we must be certain that our temple is built, not upon shifting sands or quagmires, but upon the rock. Anyone can see with his eyes open that our path will be difficult and also long, but if we persevere together as we did in the two world wars – though not, alas, in the interval between them – I cannot doubt that we shall achieve our common purpose in the end.

I have, however, a definite and practical proposal to make for action. Courts and magistrates may be set up but they cannot function without sheriffs and constables. The United Nations Organisation must immediately begin to be equipped with an international armed force. In such a matter we can only go step by step, but we must begin now. I propose that each of the Powers and States should be invited to delegate a certain number of air squadrons to the service of the world organisation. These squadrons would be trained and prepared in their own countries, but would move around in rotation from one country to another. They would wear the uniform of their own countries but with different badges. They would not be required to act against their own nation, but in other respects they would be directed by the world organisation. This might be started on a modest scale and would grow as confidence grew. I wished to see this done after the First World War, and I devoutly trust it may be done forthwith.

It would nevertheless be wrong and imprudent to entrust the secret knowledge or experience of the atomic bomb, which the United States, Great Britain, and Canada now share, to the world organisation, while it is still in its infancy. It would be criminal madness to cast it adrift in this still agitated and un-united world. No one in any country has slept less well in their beds because this knowledge and the method and the raw materials to apply it are at present largely retained in American hands. I do not believe we should all have slept so soundly had the positions been reversed and if some Communist or neo-Fascist State monopolised for the time being these dread agencies. The fear of them alone might easily have been used to enforce totalitarian systems upon the free democratic world, with consequences appalling to human imagination. God has willed that this shall not be and we have at least a breathing space to set our house in order before this peril has to be encountered: and even then, if no effort is spared, we should still possess so formidable a superiority as to impose effective deterrents upon its employment, or threat of employment, by others. Ultimately, when the essential brotherhood of man is truly embodied and expressed in a world organisation with all the necessary practical safeguards to make it effective, these powers would naturally be confided to that world organisation.

Now I come to the second danger of these two marauders which threaten the cottage, the home, and the ordinary people – namely, tyranny. We cannot be blind to the fact that the liberties enjoyed by individual citizens throughout the British Empire are not valid in a considerable number of countries, some of which are very powerful. In these States control is enforced upon the common people by various kinds of all-embracing police governments. The power of the State is exercised without restraint, either by dictators or by compact oligarchies operating through a privileged party and a political police. It is not our duty at this time when difficulties are so numerous to interfere forcibly in the internal affairs of countries which we have not conquered in war. But we must never cease to proclaim in fearless tones the great principles of freedom and the rights of man which are the joint inheritance of the English-speaking world and which through Magna Carta, the Bill of Rights, the Habeas Corpus, trial by jury, and the English common law find their most famous expression in the American Declaration of Independence.

All this means that the people of any country have the right, and should have the power by constitutional action, by free unfettered elections, with secret ballot, to choose or change the character or form of government under which they dwell; that freedom of speech and thought should reign; that courts of justice, independent of the executive, unbiased by any party, should administer laws which have received the broad assent of large majorities or are consecrated by time and custom. Here are the title deeds of freedom which should lie in every cottage home. Here is the message of the British and American peoples to mankind. Let us preach what we practise – let us practise what we preach.

I have now stated the two great dangers which menace the homes of the people: War and Tyranny. I have not yet spoken of poverty and privation which are in many cases the prevailing anxiety. But if the dangers of war and tyranny are removed, there is no doubt that science and co-operation can bring in the next few years to the world, certainly in the next few decades newly taught in the sharpening school of war, an expansion of material well-being beyond anything that has yet occurred in human experience. Now, at this sad and breathless moment, we are plunged in the hunger and distress which are the aftermath of our stupendous struggle; but this will pass and may pass quickly, and there is no reason except human folly or sub-human crime which should deny to all the nations the inauguration and enjoyment of an age of plenty. I have often used words which I learned fifty years ago from a great Irish-American orator, a friend of mine, Mr Bourke Cockran. 'There is enough for all. The earth is a generous mother; she will provide in plentiful abundance food for all her children if they will but cultivate her soil in justice and in peace.' So far I feel that we are in full agreement.

Now, while still pursuing the method of realising our overall strategic concept, I come to the crux of what I have travelled here to say. Neither the sure prevention of war, nor the continuous rise of world organisation will be gained without what I have called the fraternal association of the English-speaking peoples. This means a special relationship between the British Commonwealth and Empire and the United States. This is no time for generalities, and I will venture to be precise. Fraternal association requires not only the growing friendship and mutual understanding between our two vast but kindred systems of society, but the continuance of the intimate relationship between our military advisers, leading to common study of potential dangers, the similarity of weapons and manuals of instructions, and to the interchange of officers and cadets at technical colleges. It should carry with it the continuance of the present facilities for mutual security by the joint use of all Naval and Air Force bases in the possession of either country all over the world. This would perhaps double the mobility of the American Navy and Air Force. It would greatly expand that of the British Empire Forces and it might well lead, if and as the world calms down, to important financial savings. Already we use together a large number of islands; more may well be entrusted to our joint care in the near future.

The United States has already a Permanent Defence Agreement with the Dominion of Canada, which is so devotedly attached to the British Commonwealth and Empire. This Agreement is more effective than many of those which have often been made under formal alliances. This principle should be extended to all British Commonwealths with full reciprocity. Thus, whatever happens, and thus only, shall we be secure ourselves and able to work together for the high and simple causes that are dear to us and bode no ill to any. Eventually there may come – I feel eventually there will come – the principle of common citizenship, but that we may be content to leave to destiny, whose outstretched arm many of us can already clearly see.

There is however an important question we must ask ourselves. Would a special relationship between the United States and the

British Commonwealth be inconsistent with our overriding loyalties to the World Organisation? I reply that, on the contrary, it is probably the only means by which that organisation will achieve its full stature and strength. There are already the special United States relations with Canada which I have just mentioned, and there are the special relations between the United States and the South American Republics. We British have our twenty years Treaty of Collaboration and Mutual Assistance with Soviet Russia. I agree with Mr Bevin, the Foreign Secretary of Great Britain, that it might well be a fifty years Treaty so far as we are concerned. We aim at nothing but mutual assistance and collaboration. The British have an alliance with Portugal unbroken since 1384, and which produced fruitful results at critical moments in the late war. None of these clash with the general interest of a world agreement, or a world organisation; on the contrary they help it. 'In my father's house are many mansions.' Special associations between members of the United Nations which have no aggressive point against any other country, which harbour no design incompatible with the Charter of the United Nations, far from being harmful, are beneficial and, as I believe, indispensable.

I spoke earlier of the Temple of Peace. Workmen from all countries must build that temple. If two of the workmen know each other particularly well and are old friends, if their families are intermingled, and if they have 'faith in each other's purpose, hope in each other's future and charity towards each other's shortcomings' – to quote some good words I read here the other day – why cannot they work together at the common task as friends and partners? Why cannot they share their tools and thus increase each other's working powers? Indeed they must do so or else the temple may not be built, or, being built, it may collapse, and we shall all be proved again unteachable and have to go and try to learn again for a third time in a school of war, incomparably more rigorous than that from which we have just been released. The dark ages may return, the Stone Age may return on the glittering wings of science, and what might now shower immeasurable material blessings upon mankind, may even bring about its total destruction. Beware, I say; time may be short. Do not let us take the course of allowing events to drift along until it is too late. If there is to be a fraternal association of the kind I have described, with all the extra strength and security which both our countries can derive from it, let us make sure that that great fact is known to the world, and that it plays its part in steadying and stabilising the foundations of peace. There is the path of wisdom. Prevention is better than cure.

A shadow has fallen upon the scenes so lately lighted by the Allied victory. Nobody knows what Soviet Russia and its Communist international organisation intends to do in the immediate future, or what are the limits, if any, to their expansive and proselytising tendencies. I have a strong admiration and regard for the valiant Russian people and for my wartime comrade, Marshal Stalin. There is deep sympathy and goodwill in Britain – and I doubt not here also – towards the peoples of all the Russias and a resolve to persevere through many differences and rebuffs in establishing lasting friendships. We understand the Russian need to be secure on her western frontiers by removal of all possibility of German aggression. We welcome Russia to her rightful place among the leading nations of the world. We welcome her flag upon the seas. Above all, we welcome constant, frequent and growing contacts between the Russian people and our own people on both sides of the Atlantic. It is my duty however, for I am sure you would wish me to state the facts as I see them to you, to place before you certain facts about the present position in Europe.

From Stettin in the Baltic to Trieste in the Adriatic, an iron curtain has descended across the Continent. Behind that line lie all the capitals of the ancient states of Central and Eastern Europe. Warsaw, Berlin, Prague, Vienna, Budapest, Belgrade, Bucharest and Sofia, all these famous cities and the populations around them lie in what I must call the Soviet sphere, and all are subject in one form or another, not only to Soviet influence but to a very high and, in many cases, increasing measure of control from Moscow. Athens alone – Greece with its immortal glories – is free to decide its future at an election under British, American and French observation. The Russian-dominated Polish Government has been encouraged to make enormous and wrongful inroads upon Germany, and mass expulsions of millions of Germans on a scale grievous and undreamed-of are now taking place. The Communist parties, which were very small in all these Eastern States of Europe, have been raised to preeminence and power far beyond their numbers and are seeking everywhere to obtain totalitarian control. Police governments are prevailing in nearly every case, and so far, except in Czechoslovakia, there is no true democracy.

Turkey and Persia are both profoundly alarmed and disturbed at the claims which are being made upon them and at the pressure being exerted by the Moscow Government. An attempt is being made by the Russians in Berlin to build up a quasi-Communist party in their zone of Occupied Germany by showing special favours to groups of left-wing German leaders. At the end of the fighting last June, the American and British Armies withdrew westwards, in accordance with an earlier agreement, to a depth at some points of 150 miles upon a front of nearly 400 miles, in order to allow our Russian allies to occupy this vast expanse of territory which the Western Democracies had conquered.

If now the Soviet Government tries, by separate action, to build up a pro-Communist Germany in their areas, this will cause new serious difficulties in the British and American zones, and will give the defeated Germans the power of putting themselves up to auction between the Soviets and the Western Democracies. Whatever conclusions may be drawn from these facts – and facts they are – this is certainly not the Liberated Europe we fought to build up. Nor is it one which contains the essentials of permanent peace.

The safety of the world requires a new unity in Europe, from which no nation should be permanently outcast. It is from the quarrels of the strong parent races in Europe that the world wars we have witnessed, or which occurred in former times, have sprung. Twice in our own lifetime we have seen the United States, against their wishes and their traditions, against arguments, the force of which it is impossible not to comprehend, drawn by irresistible forces into these wars in time to secure the victory of the good cause, but only after frightful slaughter and devastation had occurred. Twice the United States has had to send several millions of its young men across the Atlantic to find the war; but now war can find any nation, wherever it may dwell between dusk and dawn. Surely we should work with conscious purpose for a grand pacification of Europe, within the structure of the United Nations and in accordance with its Charter. That I feel is an open cause of policy of very great importance.

In front of the iron curtain which lies across Europe are other causes for anxiety. In Italy the Communist Party is seriously hampered by having to support the Communist-trained Marshal Tito's claims to former Italian territory at the head of the Adriatic. Nevertheless the future of Italy hangs in the balance. Again one cannot imagine a regenerated Europe without a strong France. All my public life I have worked for a strong France and I never lost faith in her destiny, even in the darkest hours. I will not lose faith now. However, in a great number of countries, far from the Russian frontiers and throughout the world, Communist fifth columns are established and work in complete unity and absolute obedience to the directions they receive from the Communist centre. Except in the

British Commonwealth and in the United States where Communism is in its infancy, the Communist parties or fifth columns constitute a growing challenge and peril to Christian civilisation. These are sombre facts for anyone to have to recite on the morrow of a victory gained by so much splendid comradeship in arms and in the cause of freedom and democracy; but we should be most unwise not to face them squarely while time remains.

The outlook is also anxious in the Far East and especially in Manchuria. The Agreement which was made at Yalta, to which I was a party, was extremely favourable to Soviet Russia, but it was made at a time when no one could say that the German war might not extend all through the summer and autumn of 1945 and when the Japanese war was expected to last for a further 18 months from the end of the German war. In this country you are all so well informed about the Far East, and such devoted friends of China, that I do not need to expatiate on the situation there.

I have felt bound to portray the shadow which, alike in the west and in the east, falls upon the world. I was a high minister at the time of the Versailles Treaty and a close friend of Mr Lloyd George, who was the head of the British delegation at Versailles. I did not myself agree with many things that were done, but I have a very strong impression in my mind of that situation, and I find it painful to contrast it with that which prevails now. In those days there were high hopes and unbounded confidence that the wars were over, and that the League of Nations would become all-powerful. I do not see or feel that same confidence or even the same hopes in the haggard world at the present time.

On the other hand I repulse the idea that a new war is inevitable; still more that it is imminent. It is because I am sure that our fortunes are still in our own hands and that we hold the power to save the future, that I feel the duty to speak out now that I have the occasion and the opportunity to do so. I do not believe that Soviet Russia desires war. What they desire is the fruits of war and the indefinite expansion of their power and doctrines. But what we have to consider here today while time remains is the permanent prevention of war and the establishment of conditions of freedom and democracy as rapidly as possible in all countries. Our difficulties and dangers will not be removed by closing our eyes to them. They will not be removed by mere waiting to see what happens; nor will they be removed by a policy of appeasement. What is needed is a settlement, and the longer this is delayed, the more difficult it will be and the greater our dangers will become.

From what I have seen of our Russian friends and Allies during the war, I am convinced that there is nothing they admire so much as strength, and there is nothing for which they have less respect than for weakness, especially military weakness. For that reason the old doctrine of a balance of power is unsound. We cannot afford, if we can help it, to work on narrow margins, offering temptations to a trial of strength. If the Western Democracies stand together in strict adherence to the principles of the United Nations Charter, their influence for furthering those principles will be immense and no one is likely to molest them. If however they become divided or falter in their duty and if these all-important years are allowed to slip away then indeed catastrophe may overwhelm us all.

Last time I saw it all coming and cried aloud to my own fellow-countrymen and to the world, but no one paid any attention. Up till the year 1933 or even 1935, Germany might have been saved from the awful fate which has overtaken her and we might all have been spared the miseries Hitler let loose upon mankind. There never was a war in all history easier to prevent by timely action than the one which has just desolated such great areas of the globe. It could have been prevented in my belief without the firing of a single shot, and Germany might be powerful, prosperous and honoured today; but no one would listen and one by one we were all sucked into the awful whirlpool. We surely must not let that happen again. This can only be achieved by reaching now, in 1946, a good understanding on all points with Russia under the general authority of the United Nations Organisation and by the maintenance of that good understanding through many peaceful years, by the world instrument, supported by the whole strength of the English-speaking world and all its connections. There is the solution which I respectfully offer to you in this Address to which I have given the title 'The Sinews of Peace'.

Let no man underrate the abiding power of the British Empire and Commonwealth. Because you see the 46 millions in our island harassed about their food supply, of which they only grow one half, even in wartime, or because we have difficulty in restarting our industries and export trade after six years of passionate war effort, do not suppose that we shall not come through these dark years of privation as we have come through the glorious years of agony, or that half a century from now, you will not see 70 or 80 millions of Britons spread about the world and united in defence of our traditions, our way of life, and of the world causes which you and we espouse. If the population of the English-speaking Commonwealths be added to that of the United States with all that such co-operation implies in the air, on the sea, all over the globe and in science and in industry, and in moral force, there will be no quivering, precarious balance of power to offer its temptation to ambition or adventure. On the contrary, there will be an overwhelming assurance of security. If we adhere faithfully to the Charter of the United Nations and walk forward in sedate and sober strength seeking no one's land or treasure, seeking to lay no arbitrary control upon the thoughts of men; if all British moral and material forces and convictions are joined with your own in fraternal association, the highroads of the future will be clear, not only for us but for all, not only for our time, but for a century to come.

'THE TRAGEDY OF EUROPE'

9 May 1946

The States-General of the Netherlands, The Hague

Mr Speaker, the tragedy of Europe shocks mankind. Well, as you said in your Address, 'Europe is totally ravaged.' The tragedy darkens the pages of human history. It will excite the amazement and horror of future generations. Here in these beautiful, fertile and temperate lands, where so many of the noblest parent races of mankind have developed their character, their arts and their literature, we have twice in our own lifetime seen all rent asunder and torn to pieces in frightful convulsions which have left their mark in blackened devastation through the entire continent. And had not Europe's children of earlier times come back across the Atlantic Ocean with strong and rescuing arms, all the peoples of Europe might have fallen into the long night of Nazi totalitarian despotism. Upon Britain fell the proud but awful responsibility of keeping the Flag of Freedom flying in the old world till the forces of the new world could arrive. But now the tornado has passed away. The thunder of the cannons has ceased, the terror from the skies is over, the oppressors are cast out and broken. We may be wounded and impoverished. But we are still alive and free. The future stands before us, to make or mar.

Two supreme tasks confront us. We have to revive the prosperity of Europe; and European civilisation must rise again from the chaos and carnage into which it has been plunged; and at the same time we have to devise those measures of world security which will prevent disaster descending upon us again. . . .

I say here as I said at Brussels last year that I see no reason why, under the guardianship of the world organisation, there should not ultimately arise the United States of Europe, both those of the East and those of the West which will unify this Continent in a manner never known since the fall of the Roman Empire, and within which all its peoples may dwell together in prosperity, in justice and in peace.

PALESTINE

1 August 1946

House of Commons

The position which I, personally, have adopted and maintained, dates from 1919 and 1921, when as Dominions and Colonial Secretary, it fell to me to define, with the approval of the then Cabinet and Parliament, the interpretation that was placed upon our obligations to the Zionists under the Mandate for Palestine entrusted to us by the League of Nations. This was the declaration of 1922, which I, personally, drafted for the approval of the authorities of the day. Palestine was not to be a Jewish National Home, but there was to be set up a Jewish National Home in Palestine. Jewish immigration would be allowed up to the limit of the economic absorptive capacity – that was the phrase which I coined in those days and which seems to remain convenient – the Mandatory Power being, it was presumed, the final judge of what that capacity was. During the greater part of a quarter of a century which has passed, this policy was carefully carried out by us. The Jewish population multiplied, from about 80,000 to nearly 600,000. Tel Aviv expanded into the great city it is, a city which, I may say, during this war and before it, welcomed and nourished waifs and orphans flying from Nazi persecution. Many refugees found a shelter and a sanctuary there, so that this land, not largely productive of the means of life, became a fountain of charity and hospitality to people in great distress. Land

reclamation and cultivation and great electrical enterprises pro-
gressed. Trade made notable progress, and not only did the Jewish
population increase but the Arab population, dwelling in the areas
colonised and enriched by the Jews, also increased in almost equal
numbers. The Jews multiplied six-fold and the Arabs developed
500,000, thus showing that both races gained a marked advantage
from the Zionist policy which we pursued and which we were
developing over this period. . . .

Had I had the opportunity of guiding the course of events after the
war was won a year ago, I should have faithfully pursued the Zionist
cause as I have defined it; and I have not abandoned it today,
although this is not a very popular moment to espouse it; but there
are two things to say about it. First, I agree entirely with what the
President of the Board of Trade said on this point – no one can
imagine that there is room in Palestine for the great masses of Jews
who wish to leave Europe, or that they could be absorbed in any
period which it is now useful to contemplate. The idea that the
Jewish problem could be solved or even helped by a vast dumping of
the Jews of Europe into Palestine is really too silly to consume our
time in the House this afternoon. I am not absolutely sure that we
should be in too great a hurry to give up the idea that European Jews
may live in the countries where they belong. I must say that I had no
idea, when the war came to an end, of the horrible massacres which
had occurred; the millions and millions that have been slaughtered.
That dawned on us gradually after the struggle was over. But if all
these immense millions have been killed and slaughtered, there must
be a certain amount of living room for the survivors, and there must
be inheritances and properties to which they can lay claim. Are we
not to hope that some tolerance will be established in racial matters
in Europe, and that there will be some law reigning by which, at any
rate, a portion of the property of these great numbers will not be
taken away from them? It is quite clear, however, that this crude idea
of letting all the Jews of Europe go into Palestine has no relation
either to the problem of Europe or to the problem which arises in
Palestine.

A 'UNITED STATES OF EUROPE'

19 September 1946

Zurich University, Switzerland

Second only to the Fulton speech, this is probably the most important of Churchill's post-war speeches. At a time when many were still talking of grinding the Germans' face in the dust, he boldly declared: 'I am now going to say something that will astonish you. The first step in the re-creation of the European family must be a partnership between France and Germany.' Many were indeed astonished, but Churchill had set the tone for a reconciliation of the European family, and paved the way for the re-entry of a democratic West Germany (East Germany being in the Soviet sphere of influence) into the community of nations. Churchill is rightly regarded as one of the founding fathers of the cause of European unity.

I wish to speak to you today about the tragedy of Europe. This noble continent, comprising on the whole the fairest and the most cultivated regions of the earth, enjoying a temperate and equable climate, is the home of all the great parent races of the western world. It is the fountain of Christian faith and Christian ethics. It is the origin of most of the culture, arts, philosophy and science both of ancient and modern times. If Europe were once united in the sharing of its common inheritance, there would be no limit to the happiness, to the prosperity and glory which its three or four hundred million people would enjoy. Yet it is from Europe that have sprung that series of frightful nationalistic quarrels, originated by the Teutonic nations, which we have seen even in this twentieth century and in our own lifetime wreck the peace and mar the prospects of all mankind.

And what is the plight to which Europe has been reduced? Some of the smaller States have indeed made a good recovery, but over wide areas a vast quivering mass of tormented, hungry, careworn and bewildered human beings gape at the ruins of their cities and homes, and scan the dark horizons for the approach of some new peril, tyranny or terror. Among the victors there is a babel of jarring voices; among the vanquished the sullen silence of despair. That is all that Europeans, grouped in so many ancient States and nations, that is all that the Germanic Powers have got by tearing each other to pieces and spreading havoc far and wide. Indeed, but for the fact that the great Republic across the Atlantic Ocean has at length realised that the ruin or enslavement of Europe would involve their own fate as well, and has stretched out hands of succour and guidance, the Dark Ages would have returned in all their cruelty and squalor. They may still return.

Yet all the while there is a remedy which, if it were generally and spontaneously adopted, would as if by a miracle transform the whole scene, and would in a few years make all Europe, or the greater part of it, as free and as happy as Switzerland is today. What is this sovereign remedy? It is to re-create the European Family, or as much of it as we can, and provide it with a structure under which it can dwell in peace, in safety and in freedom. We must build a kind of United States of Europe. In this way only will hundreds of millions of toilers be able to regain the simple joys and hopes which make life worth living. The process is simple. All that is needed is the resolve of hundreds of millions of men and women to do right instead of wrong and gain as their reward blessing instead of cursing.

Much work has been done upon this task by the exertions of the Pan-European Union which owes so much to Count Coudenhove-Kalergi and which commanded the services of the famous French patriot and statesman, Aristide Briand. There is also that immense body of doctrine and procedure, which was brought into being amid high hopes after the First World War, as the League of Nations. The League of Nations did not fail because of its principles or conceptions. It failed because these principles were deserted by those States who had brought it into being. It failed because the Governments of those days feared to face the facts, and act while time remained. This disaster must not be repeated. There is therefore much knowledge and material with which to build; and also bitter dear-bought experience.

I was very glad to read in the newspapers two days ago that my friend President Truman had expressed his interest and sympathy with this great design. There is no reason why a regional organisation of Europe should in any way conflict with the world organisation of the United Nations. On the contrary, I believe that the larger synthesis will only survive if it is founded upon coherent natural groupings. There is already a natural grouping in the Western Hemisphere. We British have our own Commonwealth of Nations. These do not weaken, on the contrary they strengthen, the world organisation. They are in fact its main support. And why should there not be a European group which could give a sense of enlarged patriotism and common citizenship to the distracted peoples of this turbulent and mighty continent and why should it not take its rightful place with other great groupings in shaping the destinies of men? In order that this should be accomplished there must be an act of faith in which millions of families speaking many languages must consciously take part.

We all know that the two world wars through which we have passed arose out of the vain passion of a newly-united Germany to play the dominating part in the world. In this last struggle crimes and massacres have been committed for which there is no parallel since the invasions of the Mongols in the fourteenth century and no equal at any time in human history. The guilty must be punished. Germany must be deprived of the power to rearm and make another aggressive war. But when all this has been done, as it will be done, as it is being done, there must be an end to retribution. There must be what Mr Gladstone many years ago called 'a blessed act of oblivion'. We must all turn our backs upon the horrors of the past. We must look to the future. We cannot afford to drag forward across the years that are to come the hatreds and revenges which have sprung from the injuries of the past. If Europe is to be saved from infinite misery, and indeed from final doom, there must be an act of faith in the European family and an act of oblivion against all the crimes and follies of the past.

Can the free peoples of Europe rise to the height of these resolves of the soul and instincts of the spirit of man? If they can, the wrongs and injuries which have been inflicted will have been washed away on all sides by the miseries which have been endured. Is there any need for further floods of agony? Is it the only lesson of history that mankind is unteachable? Let there be justice, mercy and freedom. The peoples have only to will it, and all will achieve their hearts' desire.

I am now going to say something that will astonish you. The first step in the re-creation of the European family must be a partnership between France and Germany. In this way only can France recover the moral leadership of Europe. There can be no revival of Europe without a spiritually great France and a spiritually great Germany. The structure of the United States of Europe, if well and truly built, will be such as to make the material strength of a single state less important. Small nations will count as much as large ones and gain their honour by their contribution to the common cause. The ancient states and principalities of Germany, freely joined together for mutual convenience in a federal system, might each take their individual place among the United States of Europe. I shall not try to make a detailed programme for hundreds of millions of people who want to be happy and free, prosperous and safe, who wish to enjoy the four freedoms of which the great President Roosevelt spoke, and live in accordance with the principles embodied in the Atlantic Charter. If this is their wish, they have only to say so, and means can certainly be found, and machinery erected, to carry that wish into full fruition.

But I must give you a warning. Time may be short. At present there is a breathing-space. The cannon have ceased firing. The fighting has stopped; but the dangers have not stopped. If we are to form the United States of Europe or whatever name or form it may take, we must begin now.

In these present days we dwell strangely and precariously under the shield and protection of the atomic bomb. The atomic bomb is still only in the hands of a State and nation which we know will never use it except in the cause of right and freedom. But it may well be that in a few years this awful agency of destruction will be widespread and the catastrophe following from its use by several warring nations will not only bring to an end all that we call civilisation, but may possibly disintegrate the globe itself.

I must now sum up the propositions which are before you. Our constant aim must be to build and fortify the strength of UNO. Under and within that world concept we must re-create the European family in a regional structure called, it may be, the United States of Europe. The first step is to form a Council of Europe. If at first all the States of Europe are not willing or able to join the Union, we must nevertheless proceed to assemble and combine those who will and those who can. The salvation of the common people of every race and of every land from war or servitude must be established on solid foundations and must be guarded by the readiness of all men and women to die rather than submit to tyranny. In all this urgent work, France and Germany must take the lead together. Great Britain, the British Commonwealth of Nations, mighty America, and I trust Soviet Russia – for then indeed all would be well – must be the friends and sponsors of the new Europe and must champion its right to live and shine.

'A PROPERTY-OWNING DEMOCRACY'

5 October 1946

Conservative Party Conference, Blackpool

We have certainly had a depressing year since the General Election. I do not blame the Socialist Government – for the weather. We must also make allowances for all the difficulties which mark the aftermath of war. These difficulties would have taxed to the utmost the whole moral and physical resources of a united nation, marshalled and guided by a National Government. The Socialists broke up the national unity for the sake of their political interests, and the nation decided at the polls for a Socialist Party Government. This was their right under our well-tried Constitution. The electors, based on universal suffrage, may do what they like. And afterwards they have to like what they do. . . .

I have on other occasions set before you the immense injury which has been done to our process of recovery by the ill-considered schemes and threats of nationalisation which have cast their shadows over so many of our leading industries. The attempts to nationalise the steel industry, which was so effective in war and so buoyant in its plans for the future, is the most foolish of all the experiments in Socialism from which we have yet suffered. . . .

Look where you will, we are suffering a needless decline and contraction at a time when we had the right to brighter days. I have visited many of the smaller countries on the Continent. All are making much more of themselves and of their chances than we are. Nowhere is there the drab disheartenment and frustration which the Socialist Party have fastened on Britain. . . .

Our main objectives are: To uphold the Christian religion and resist all attacks upon it. To defend our Monarchical and Parliamentary Constitution. To provide adequate security against external aggression and safety to our seaborne trade. To uphold law and order, and impartial justice administered by Courts free from interference or pressure on the part of the executive. To regain a sound finance and strict supervision of national income and expenditure. To defend and develop our Empire trade, without which Great Britain would perish. To promote all measures to improve the health and social conditions of the people. To support as a general rule free enterprise and initiative against State trading and nationalisation of industries.

To this I will add some further conceptions. We oppose the establishment of a Socialist State, controlling the means of production, distribution and exchange. We are asked, 'What is your alternative?' Our Conservative aim is to build a property-owning democracy, both independent and interdependent. In this I include profit-sharing schemes in suitable industries and intimate consultation between employers and wage-earners. In fact we seek so far as possible to make the status of the wage-earner that of a partner rather than of an irresponsible employee. It is in the interest of the wage-earner to have many other alternatives open to him than service under one all-powerful employer called the State. He will be in a better position to bargain collectively and production will be more abundant; there will be more for all and more freedom for all when the wage-earner is able, in the large majority of cases, to choose and change his work, and to deal with a private employer who, like himself, is subject to the ordinary pressures of life and, like himself, is dependent upon his personal thrift, ingenuity and good housekeeping. In this way alone can the traditional virtues of the British character be preserved. We do not wish the people of the ancient island reduced to a mass of State-directed proletarians, thrown hither and thither, housed here and there, by an aristocracy of privileged officials or privileged Party, sectarian or Trade Union bosses. We are opposed to the tyranny and victimisation of the closed shop. Our ideal is the consenting union of millions of free, independent families and homes to gain their livelihood and to serve true British glory and world peace . . . .

How then do we draw the lines of political battle? The British race is not actuated mainly by the hope of material gain. Otherwise we should long ago have sunk in the ocean of the past. It is stirred on almost all occasions by sentiment and instinct, rather than by programmes or worldly calculation. When this new Parliament first met, all the Socialist Members stood up and sang 'The Red Flag' in their triumph. Peering ahead through the mists and mysteries of the future so far as I can, I see the division at the next election will be between those who wholeheartedly sing 'The Red Flag' and those who rejoice to sing 'Land of Hope and Glory'. There is the noble hymn which will rally the wise, the sober-minded and the good to the salvation of our native land.

THE COMMUNIST MENACE

24 October 1946

Loughton, Essex

Churchill was deeply alarmed by the fact that, with Western Europe still defenceless and devastated, the Soviet Union had established its power at the heart of Europe through a network of puppet governments and police states imposed by more than 200 divisions of the Soviet Red Army. Meanwhile the tentacles of international Communism were at work, seeking to subvert the democratic governments of Western Europe.

The British Government have rendered a very considerable service in breaking with the Communist Party. I agree with every word Mr Attlee has said. Indeed I could have added a few more words of my own. In this country the Communist Party does not bulk so largely in our minds. It is there, a venomous thing – crawling and creeping around, but it is not immediately one of the main objectives of politics.

The fact that the British Government had decisively broken with the Communists, and were fronted against them, although it did not immediately affect the course of affairs in this island, had an important and beneficial result abroad, because there were countries on the Continent of Europe, like France, quivering under the Communist attack. The fact that the Government took this stand and put its foot down on the Communists, not in any unfair way, but resisting them by argument, the fact that the Communists were banned and barred by the Labour Party and the TUC was something which added greatly to the stability of Europe. It set an example in many lands where lives and freedom hung in the balance.

In fairness he must recognise that the Government to which he was strongly opposed in so many matters had not impeded freedom of speech. They might like to but they had not; some had not wished to, others had not dared to. . . .

Mr Bevin, a sort of working-class John Bull, had maintained a continuity of policy in foreign affairs to a very considerable extent. Greece had had a fair and free plebiscite and election and had been rescued from the danger of being involved in the Communist Balkan *bloc* which was being actively fomented by the trained Communist agents who came out from the Mecca of Communism in Moscow. . . .

I had yesterday to give a serious warning in the House of Commons. I had to ask whether it was not true that there were more than 200 Soviet divisions on a war footing in the occupied territories of Europe. I did not ask that question without weighing very carefully the whole matter, and without consulting others, my friends and colleagues, and laying before them the evidence upon which I proceeded. I did not ask the question without informing the Government beforehand of my intention. The answer was neither one thing nor the other, but you may take it from me that the facts I adduced are correct.

PALESTINE: 'BLOOD AND SHAME'

31 January 1947

House of Commons

The idea that general reprisals upon the civil population and vicarious examples would be consonant with our whole outlook upon the world and with our name, reputation and principles, is, of course, one which should never be accepted in any way. We have, therefore, very great difficulties in conducting squalid warfare with terrorists. That is why I would venture to submit to the House that every effort should be made to avoid getting into warfare with terrorists; and if a warfare with terrorists has broken out, every effort should be made – I exclude no reasonable proposal – to bring it to an end.

It is quite certain that what is going on now in Palestine is doing us a great deal of harm in every way. Whatever view is taken by the partisans of the Jews or the partisans of the Arabs it is doing us harm in our reputation all over the world. I deplore very much this struggle that we have got into. I do not think we ought to have got into it. I think it could have been avoided. It could have been avoided if promises had not been made by hon. Members opposite at the Election, on a very wide scale, and if those promises had not been woefully disappointed. I must say that. All my hon. Friends on this side of the House do not agree with the views which I have held for so many years about the Zionist cause. But promises were made far beyond those to which responsible Governments should have committed themselves. What has been the performance? The performance has been a vacuum, a gaping void, a senseless, dumb abyss – nothing.

I remember so well nine or ten months ago my right hon. Friend [Mr Oliver Stanley], now sitting beside me here, talking to all of us in our councils and saying that whatever happens this delay and vacillation shall not go on. But certainly a year has gone by, and we have not advanced one single step. We have not advanced one single step either in making good our pledges to those to whom we have given them, or in reaching some broader solution, or in disembarrassing ourselves of burdens and obligations – burdens which we cannot bear, and obligations which we have shown ourselves unable or unwilling to discharge.

My right hon. Friend dealt particularly with one aspect, and one aspect only. This is a conflict with the terrorists, and no country in the world is less fit for a conflict with terrorists than Great Britain. That is not because of her weakness or cowardice; it is because of her restraint and virtues, and the way of life which we have lived so long in this sheltered island. But, sir, if you should be thrown into a quarrel, you should bear yourself so that the opponent may be aware of it. I deprecate this quarrel, and I will deal a little further with its costs. I deprecate this quarrel very much indeed, and I do not consider it was necessary. Great responsibilities rest on those who have fallen short of their opportunities. Once you are thrown into a quarrel, then in these matters pugnacity and willpower cannot be dispensed with.

This is a lamentable situation. However we may differ, it is one of the most unhappy, unpleasant situations into which we have got, even in these troublous years. Here, we are expending hard-earned money at an enormous rate in Palestine. Everyone knows what our financial difficulties are – how heavy the weight of taxation. We are spending a vast sum of money on this business. For 18 months we have been pouring out our wealth on this unhappy, unfortunate and discreditable business. Then there is the manpower of at least 100,000 men in Palestine, who might well be at home strengthening our defeated industry. What are they doing there? What good are we getting out of it?

We are told that there are a handful of terrorists on one side and 100,000 British troops on the other. . . . In my view we should definitely give notice that, unless the United States come in with us shoulder to shoulder on a fifty-fifty basis on an agreed policy, to take a half-and-half share of the bloodshed, odium, trouble, expense and worry, we will lay our Mandate at the feet of UNO. Whereas, six months ago, I suggested that we should do that in 12 months I suggest now that the period should be shortened to six months. One is more and more worried and one's anxiety deepens and grows as hopes are falsified and the difficulties of the aftermath of war, which I do not underrate, lie still heavily upon us in a divided nation, cutting deeply across our lives and feelings. In these conditions we really cannot go on, in all directions, taking on burdens which use up and drain out the remaining strength of Britain and which are beyond any duty we have undertaken in the international field. I earnestly trust that the Government will, if they have to fight this squalid war, make perfectly certain that the willpower of the British State is not conquered by brigands and bandits and that unless we are to have the aid of the United States, they will at the earliest possible moment, give due notice to divest us of a responsibility which we are failing to discharge and which in the process is covering us with blood and shame.

'UNITED EUROPE'

14 May 1947

Royal Albert Hall, London

Alarmed by the Soviet menace to Western Europe, Churchill's calls for Europe to unite had a sense of urgency to them. This, I believe, is the only one of his speeches in which he expresses the view that Britain should be a participant, rather than merely a well-wisher or godfather to a 'United States of Europe'.

All the greatest things are simple, and many can be expressed in a single word: Freedom; Justice; Honour; Duty; Mercy; Hope. We who have come together here tonight, representing almost all the political parties in our British national life and nearly all the creeds and churches of the Western world – this large audience filling a famous hall – *we also* can express our purpose in a single word – 'Europe'. At school we learned from the maps hung on the walls, and the advice of our teachers that there is a continent called Europe. I remember quite well being taught this as a child, and after living a long time, I still believe it is true. However, professional geographers now tell us that the Continent of Europe is really only the peninsula of the Asiatic land mass. I must tell you in all faith that I feel that this would be an arid and uninspiring conclusion, and for myself, I distinctly prefer what I was taught when I was a boy.

It has been finely said by a young English writer, Mr Sewell, that the real demarcation between Europe and Asia is no chain of mountains, no natural frontier, but a system of beliefs and ideas which we call Western Civilisation. 'In the rich pattern of this culture,' says Mr Sewell,

> there are many strands; the Hebrew belief in God; the Christian message of compassion and redemption; the Greek love of truth, beauty and goodness; the Roman genius for law. Europe is a spiritual conception. But if men cease to hold that conception in their minds, cease to feel its worth in their hearts, it will die.

These are not my words, but they are my faith; and we are here to proclaim our resolve that the spiritual conception of Europe shall not die. We declare, on the contrary, that it shall live and shine, and cast a redeeming illumination upon a world of confusion and woe. That is what has brought us all together here this evening, and that is what is going to keep us all together – however sharply or even deeply we may be divided – until our goal is reached and our hopes are realised.

In our task of reviving the glories and happiness of Europe, and her prosperity, it can certainly be said that we start at the bottom of her fortunes. Here is the fairest, most temperate, most fertile area of the globe. The influence and the power of Europe and of Christendom have for centuries shaped and dominated the course of history. The sons and daughters of Europe have gone forth and carried their message to every part of the world. Religion, law, learning, art, science, industry, throughout the world all bear, in so many lands, under every sky and in every clime, the stamp of European origin, or the trace of European influence.

But what is Europe now? It is a rubble-heap, a charnel-house, a breeding-ground of pestilence and hate. Ancient nationalistic feuds and modern ideological factions distract and infuriate the unhappy, hungry populations. Evil teachers urge the paying-off of old scores with mathematical precision, and false guides point to unsparing retribution as the pathway to prosperity. Is there then to be no respite? Has Europe's mission come to an end? Has she nothing to give to the world but the contagion of the Black Death? Are her peoples to go on harrying and tormenting one another by war and vengeance until all that invests human life with dignity and comfort has been obliterated? Are the States of Europe to continue for ever to squander the first fruits of their toil upon the erection of new barriers, military fortifications and tariff walls and passport networks against one another? Are we Europeans to become incapable, with all our tropical and colonial dependencies, with all our long-created trading connections, with all that modern production and transportation can do, of even averting famine from the mass of our peoples? Are we all, through our poverty and our quarrels, for ever to be a burden and a danger to the rest of the world? Do we imagine that we can be carried forward indefinitely upon the shoulders – broad though they be – of the United States of America?

The time has come when these questions must be answered. This is the hour of choice and surely the choice is plain. If the people of Europe resolve to come together and work together for mutual advantage, to exchange blessings instead of curses, they still have it in their power to sweep away the horrors and miseries which surround them, and to allow the streams of freedom, happiness and abundance to begin again their healing flow. This is the supreme opportunity, and if it be cast away, no one can predict that it will ever return or what the resulting catastrophe will be.

In my experience of large enterprises, I have found it is often a mistake to try to settle everything at once. Far off, on the skyline, we can see the peaks of the Delectable Mountains. But we cannot tell what lies between us and them. We know where we want to go; but we cannot foresee all the stages of the journey, nor can we plan our marches as in a military operation. We are not acting in the field of force, but in the domain of opinion. We cannot give orders. We can only persuade. We must go forward, step by step, and I will therefore explain in general terms where we are and what are the first things we have to do. We have now at once to set on foot an organisation in Great Britain to promote the cause of United Europe, and to give this idea the prominence and vitality necessary for it to lay hold of the minds of our fellow-countrymen, to such an extent that it will affect their actions and influence the course of national policy.

We accept without question the world supremacy of the United Nations Organisation. In the Constitution agreed at San Francisco direct provision was made for regional organisations to be formed.

United Europe will form one major Regional entity. There is the United States with all its dependencies; there is the Soviet Union; there is the British Empire and Commonwealth; and there is Europe, with which Great Britain is profoundly blended. Here are the four main pillars of the world Temple of Peace. Let us make sure that they will all bear the weight which will be imposed and reposed upon them.

There are several important bodies which are working directly for the federation of the European States and for the creation of a Federal Constitution for Europe. I hope that may eventually be achieved. There is also the movement associated with Mr Van Zeeland for the economic integration of Europe. With all these movements we have the most friendly relations. We shall all help each other all we can because we all go the same way home. It is not for us at this stage to attempt to define or prescribe the structure of constitutions. We ourselves are content, in the first instance, to present the idea of United Europe, in which our country will play a decisive part, as a moral, cultural and spiritual conception to which all can rally without being disturbed by divergencies about structure. It is for the responsible statesmen, who have the conduct of affairs in their hands and the power of executive action, to shape and fashion the structure. It is for us to lay the foundation, to create the atmosphere and give the driving impulsion.

First I turn to France. For 40 years I have marched with France. I have shared her joys and sufferings. I rejoice in her reviving national strength. I will never abandon this long comradeship. But we have a proposal to make to France which will give all Frenchmen a cause for serious thought and valiant decision. If European unity is to be made an effective reality before it is too late, the wholehearted efforts both of France and Britain will be needed from the outset. They must go forward hand in hand. They must in fact be founder-partners in this movement.

The central and almost the most serious problem which glares upon the Europe of today is the future of Germany. Without a solution of this problem, there can be no United Europe. Except within the framework and against the background of a United Europe this problem is incapable of solution. In a continent of divided national States, Germany and her hard-working people will not find the means or scope to employ their energies. Economic suffocation will inevitably turn their thoughts to revolt and to revenge. Germany will once again become a menace to her neighbours and to the whole world; and the fruits of victory and liberation will once more be cast away. But on the wider stage of a United Europe German industry and German genius would be able to find constructive and peaceful outlets. Instead of being a centre of poverty and a source of danger, the German people would be enabled to bring back prosperity in no small measure, not only to themselves, but to the whole continent.

Germany today lies prostate, famishing among ruins. Obviously no initiative can be expected from her. It is for France and Britain to take the lead. Together they must, in a friendly manner, bring the German people back into the European circle. No one can say, and we need not attempt to forecast, the future constitution of Germany. Various individual German States are at present being recreated. There are the old States and Principalities of the Germany of former days to which the culture of the world owed much. But without prejudice to any future question of German federation, these individual States might well be invited to take their place in the Council of Europe. Thus, in looking back to happier days we should hope to mark the end of that long trail of hatred and retaliation which has already led us all, victors and vanquished alike, into the pit of squalor, slaughter and ruin.

The prime duty and opportunity of bringing about this essential reunion belongs to us and to our French friends across the Channel. Strong bonds of affection, mutual confidence, common interest and similar outlook link France and Britain together. The Treaty of Alliance which has lately been signed only gives formal expression to the community of sentiment that already exists as an indisputable and indestructible fact. It is true that this task of reconciliation requires on the part of France, which has suffered so cruelly, an act of faith, sublime in character; but it is by this act of faith and by this act of faith alone that France will regain her historic position in the leadership of Europe.

There is also another leading member of our family of nations to be held in mind. There is Italy. Everything that I have said about the imperative need of reaching a reconciliation with the German race and the ending of the fearful quarrels that have ruined them, and almost ruined us, applies in a less difficult degree to the Italian people, who wish to dwell happily and industriously within their beautiful country, and who were hurled by a dictator into the hideous struggles of the North. I am told that this idea of a United Europe makes an intense appeal to Italians, who look back across the centuries of confusion and disorder to the glories of the classic age, when a dozen legions were sufficient to preserve peace and law throughout vast territories and when free men could travel freely under the sanction of a common citizenship. We hope to reach again a Europe purged of the slavery of ancient days in which men will be as proud to say 'I am a European' as once they were to say 'Civis Romanus sum'. We hope to see a Europe where men of every country will think as much of being a European as of belonging to their native land, and wherever they go in this wide domain will truly feel 'Here I am at home'. How simple it would all be, and how crowned with glory, if that should ever arise.

It will of course be asked: 'What are the political and physical boundaries of the United Europe you are trying to create? Which countries will be in and which out?' It is not our task or wish to draw frontier lines, but rather to smoothe them away. Our aim is to bring about the unity of all nations of all Europe. We seek to exclude no State whose territory lies in Europe and which assures to its people those fundamental personal rights and liberties on which our democratic European civilisation has been created. Some countries will feel able to come into our circle sooner, and others later, according to the circumstances in which they are placed. But they can all be sure that whenever they are able to join, a place and a welcome will be waiting for them at the European Council table.

When I first began writing about the United States of Europe some 15 years ago, I wondered whether the USA would regard such a development as antagonistic to their interest, or even contrary to their safety. But all that has passed away. The whole movement of American opinion is favourable to the revival and re-creation of Europe. This is surely not unnatural when we remember how the manhood of the United States has twice in a lifetime been forced to re-cross the Atlantic Ocean and give their lives and shed their blood and pour out their treasure as the result of wars originating from ancient European feuds. One cannot be surprised that they would like to see a peaceful and united Europe taking its place among the foundations of the World Organisation to which they are devoted. I have no doubt that, far from encountering any opposition or prejudice from the Great Republic of the New World, our Movement will have their blessing and their aid.

We here in Great Britain have always to think of the British self-governing Dominions – Canada, Australia, New Zealand, South Africa. We are joined together by ties of free will and affection which have stood unyielding against all the ups and downs of fortune. We are the centre and summit of a world-wide commonwealth of nations. It is necessary that any policy this island may adopt towards Europe and in Europe should enjoy the full sympathy and approval of the peoples of the Dominions. But why should we suppose that they will not be with us in this cause? They feel with us that Britain is geographically and historically a part of Europe, and that they also have their inheritance in Europe. If Europe united is to be a living force, Britain will have to play her full part as a member of the European family. The Dominions also know that their youth, like that of the United States, has twice in living memory traversed the immense ocean spaces to fight and die in wars brought about by European discord, in the prevention of which they have been powerless. We may be sure that the cause of United Europe, in which the mother country must be a prime mover, will in no way be contrary to the sentiments which join us all together with our Dominions in the august circle of the British Crown.

It is of course alleged that all advocacy of the ideal of United Europe is nothing but a manoeuvre in the game of power politics, and that it is a sinister plot against Soviet Russia. There is no truth in this. The whole purpose of a united democratic Europe is to give decisive guarantees against aggression. Looking out from the ruins of some of their most famous cities and from amid the cruel devastation of their fairest lands, the Russian people should surely realise how much they stand to gain by the elimination of the causes of war and the fear of war on the European Continent. The creation of a healthy and contented Europe is the first and truest interest of the Soviet Union. We had therefore hoped that all sincere efforts to promote European agreement and stability would receive, as they deserve, the sympathy and support of Russia. Instead, alas, all this beneficial design has been denounced and viewed with suspicion by the propaganda of the Soviet Press and radio. We have made no retort and I do not propose to do so tonight. But neither could we accept the claim that the veto of a single power, however respected, should bar and prevent a movement necessary to the peace, amity and well-being of so many hundreds of millions of toiling and striving men and women.

And here I will invoke the interest of the broad, proletarian masses. We see before our eyes hundreds of millions of humble homes in Europe and in lands outside which have been affected by war. Are they never to have a chance to thrive and flourish? Is the honest, faithful, breadwinner never to be able to reap the fruits of his labour? Can he never bring up his children in health and joy and with the hopes of better days? Can he never be free from the fear of foreign invasion, the crash of the bomb or the shell, the tramp of the hostile patrol, or what is even worse, the knock upon his door of the political police to take the loved one far from the protection of law and justice, when all the time by one spontaneous effort of his will he could wake from all these nightmare horrors and stand forth in his manhood, free in the broad light of day? The conception of European unity already commands strong sympathy among the leading statesmen in almost all countries. 'Europe must federate or perish,' said the present Prime Minister, Mr Attlee, before the late terrible war. He said that, and I have no reason to suppose that he will abandon that prescient declaration at a time when the vindication of his words is at hand. Of course we understand that until public opinion expresses itself more definitely, Governments hesitate to take positive action. It is for us to provide the proof of solid popular support, both here and abroad, which will give the Governments of Europe confidence to go forward and give practical effect to their beliefs. We cannot say how long it will be before this stage is reached. We ask, however, that in the meantime His Majesty's Government, together with other Governments, should approach the various pressing Continental problems from a European rather than from a restricted national angle. In the discussions on the German and Austrian peace settlements, and indeed throughout the whole diplomatic field, the ultimate ideal should be held in view. Every new arrangement that is made should be designed in such a manner as to be capable of later being fitted into the pattern of a United Europe.

We do not of course pretend that United Europe provides the final and complete solution to all the problems of international relationships. The creation of an authoritative, all-powerful world order is the ultimate aim towards which we must strive. Unless some effective World Super-Government can be set up and brought quickly into action, the prospects for peace and human progress are dark and doubtful.

But let there be no mistake upon the main issue. Without a United Europe there is no sure prospect of world government. It is the urgent and indispensable step towards the realisation of that ideal. After the First Great War the League of Nations tried to build, without the aid of the USA, an international order upon a weak, divided Europe. Its failure cost us dear.

Today, after the Second World War, Europe is far weaker and still more distracted. One of the four main pillars of the Temple of Peace lies before us in shattered fragments. It must be assembled and reconstructed before there can be any real progress in building a spacious superstructure of our desires. If, during the next five years, it is found possible to build a world organisation of irresistible force and inviolable authority for the purpose of securing peace, there are no limits to the blessings which all men may enjoy and share. Nothing will help forward the building of that world organisation so much as unity and stability in a Europe that is conscious of her collective personality and resolved to assume her rightful part in guiding the unfolding destinies of man.

In the ordinary day-to-day affairs of life, men and women expect rewards for successful exertion, and this is often right and reasonable. But those who serve causes as majestic and high as ours need no reward; nor are our aims limited by the span of human life. If success come to us soon, we shall be happy. If our purpose is delayed, if we are confronted by obstacles and inertia, we may still be of good cheer, because in a cause, the righteousness of which will be proclaimed by the march of future events and the judgment of happier ages, we shall have done our duty, we shall have done our best.

THE RIGHTS OF THE BRITISH

4 October 1947

Conservative Party Conference, Brighton

Confiscatory taxation has been applied to wealth to an extent only practised in Communist countries. All our daily life is increasingly subjected to ten thousand Regulations and Controls, in the enforcement of which a multitude of officials, larger than any army we have ever maintained in time of peace, is continually employed. Hundreds of new crimes have been invented for which imprisonment or penal servitude may be inflicted. In fact, on every side and by every means the machinery for the totalitarian grip upon British society is being built up and perfected. One could almost wonder whether the

Government do not reconcile themselves to the economic misfortunes of our country, to which their mismanagement has so notably contributed, because these misfortunes give the pretext of establishing even more controls and an even larger bureaucracy. They make mistakes which make things worse. As things get worse they claim more power to set them right. Thus they move ever nearer to the scheme of the All-powerful State, in which the individual is a helpless serf or pawn.

And here I come to the remark of the Prime Minister last Saturday when he said, 'Some do not understand the amount of Freedom which we rightly *give* to an Opposition to criticise.' The word that struck me in this sentence is the word 'give'. So it is Mr Attlee who *gives* us our rights to freedom of speech and political action, and we are invited to be grateful for his magnanimity. But I thought these same rights had been won for the British people beyond dispute or challenge by our forebears in bygone generations. These were the rights for which, to quote a famous Whig phrase, 'Hampden died in the field and Sidney on the scaffold.' And now it is Mr Attlee who thinks he has given them to us. Let him cherish these illusions, but let him not be so foolish as to try to take them away. Well was it said, 'the price of freedom is eternal vigilance'. Small steps and graduated stages are the means by which, in the history of many countries, the freedom of great and noble races has been slowly frittered and whittled away.

'SHABBY MONEYLENDERS!'

28 October 1947

Debate on the Address, House of Commons

At this point I must turn to the United States with whom our fortunes and interests are intertwined. I was sorry that the hon. Member for Nelson and Colne [Mr S. Silverman], whom I see in his place, said some weeks ago that they were 'shabby moneylenders'. That is no service in our country nor is it true. The Americans took but little when they emigrated from Europe except what they stood up in and what they had in their souls. They came through, they tamed the wilderness, they became what old John Bright called 'A refuge for the oppressed from every land and clime.' They have become today the greatest State and power in the world, speaking our own language, cherishing our common law, and pursuing, like our great Dominions, in broad principle, the same ideals. And the hon. Member for Nelson and Colne calls them 'shabby moneylenders'. It is true that they have lent us a great deal of money. They lent us £1,000 million in the First World War, a debt which we solemnly confirmed after the war, in time of peace. But all that they let drop. Then there was Lend-Lease, before they came into the second war, in all about £7,000 million.

Mr Sydney Silverman (Nelson and Colne): What about cash-and-carry before that?

Mr Churchill: Two years ago we borrowed another £1,000 million sterling from them, or nearly four billion dollars. I asked the other day a rhetorical question, 'What are dollars?' Dollars are the result of the toil and the skill of the American working man, and he is willing to give them on a very large scale to the cause of rebuilding our broken world. In many cases he gives them without much prospect of repayment. Shabby moneylenders!

'SOCIALISM IS THE PHILOSOPHY OF FAILURE'

28 May 1948

Scottish Unionist Conference, Perth, Scotland

Churchill here repeats the phrase 'property-owning democracy' – later to become a key tenet of Conservative Party philosophy – and follows this up by advocating the sale of council houses to their tenants. This 'Right to Buy' became a reality under Margaret Thatcher but, even in the twenty-first century, there are many in the ranks of the Labour Party who wish to deny it.

We are oppressed by a deadly fallacy. Socialism is the philosophy of failure, the creed of ignorance and the gospel of envy. Unless we free our country while time remains from the perverse doctrines of Socialism, there can be no hope for recovery. This island cannot maintain its population as a great power. The most energetic and the nimblest will emigrate, and we shall be left here with a board of state officials brooding over a vast mass of worried, hungry and broken human beings. Our place in the world will be lost forever, and not only our individual self-respect but our national independence will be gone. These hard-won privileges have been dear to us in the past. But all this structure of obstinacy and unwisdom erected for Party and not national aims must be viewed in the light of the supreme and dominating fact of our present position. The Socialist Government in London has become dependent upon the generosity of the capitalist system of the United States. We are not earning our own living or paying our way, nor do the Government hold out any prospect of our doing so in the immediate future. It is this terrible fact which glares upon us all. . . .

When I was here two years ago I got from the Scottish Unionist Association a pregnant phrase which struck me deeply: 'a property-owning democracy.' That is a broad and helpful theme for us to pursue. Owning one's own house is not a crime. Saving up to secure and maintain independence is a virtue. Why should we not make it clear that not only houses built by private enterprise – when that is again allowed – may be purchased and obtained by instalments by their tenants who will become the owners of the freehold, but that also there should be a right to purchase council houses by instalments. Here is a positive step which should be taken. It will be most bitterly opposed by the Socialist Party who want everyone to be the tenants of the State.

'WHAT WILL HAPPEN WHEN THEY GET THE ATOMIC BOMB?'

9 October 1948

Conservative Party Conference, Llandudno, Wales

Aware that the Soviets might be within months of securing their own atomic bomb, Churchill viewed it as a matter of the utmost urgency that steps be taken by the Western Allies, under the leadership of the United States, to ensure such weapons did not come into the hands of the rulers in the Kremlin. Only the United States had the power to take decisive action and the moment was lost. In consequence, the world was to live for more than forty years in the Valley of the Shadow of Death – coming more than once to the brink of nuclear holocaust – until the demise of the Soviet Union.

I hope you will give full consideration to my words. I have not always been wrong. Nothing stands between Europe today and complete subjugation to Communist tyranny but the atomic bomb in American possession. . . .

The question is asked: What will happen when they get the atomic bomb themselves and have accumulated a large store? You can judge yourselves what will happen then by what is happening now. If these things are done in the green wood, what will be done in the dry? If they can continue month after month disturbing and tormenting the world, trusting to our Christian and altruistic inhibitions against using this strange new power against them, what will they do when they themselves have large quantities of atomic bombs? What do you suppose would be the position this afternoon if it had been Communist Russia instead of free enterprise America which had created the atomic weapon? Instead of being a sombre guarantee of peace and freedom it would have become an irresistible method of human enslavement. No one in his senses can believe that we have a limitless period of time before us. We ought to bring matters to a head and make a final settlement. We ought not to go jogging along improvident, incompetent, waiting for something to turn up, by which I mean waiting for something bad for us to turn up. The Western Nations will be far more likely to reach a lasting settlement, without bloodshed, if they formulate their just demands while they have the atomic power and before the Russian Communists have got it too. . . .

As I look out upon the future of our country in the changing scene of human destiny I feel the existence of three great circles among the free nations and democracies. I almost wish I had a blackboard. I would make a picture for you. I don't suppose it would get hung in the Royal Academy, but it would illustrate the point I am anxious for you to hold in your minds. The first circle for us is naturally the British Commonwealth and Empire, with all that that comprises. Then there is also the English-speaking world in which we, Canada, and the other British Dominions and the United States play so important a part. And finally there is United Europe. These three majestic circles are co-existent and if they are linked together there is no force or combination which could overthrow them or even challenge them. Now if you think of the three interlinked circles you will see that we are the only country which has a great part in every one of them. We stand, in fact, at the very point of junction, and here in this Island at the centre of the seaways and perhaps of the airways also, we have the opportunity of joining them all together. If we rise to the occasion in the years that are to come it may be found that once again we hold the key to opening a safe and happy future to humanity, and will gain for ourselves gratitude and fame.

THE NORTH ATLANTIC TREATY

12 May 1949

House of Commons

Here at last was the Treaty of the European and North American democracies that Churchill had called for at Fulton three years earlier. Had such an organisation – with American participation – existed in the 1930s, Churchill was convinced that the Second World War (the 'unnecessary war', as he called it) could have been avoided.

We give our cordial welcome to the Atlantic Pact. We give our thanks to the United States for the splendid part they are playing in the world. As I said when over there the other day:

> Many nations have risen to the summit of world affairs, but here is a great example where new-won supremacy has not been used for self-aggrandizement, but only further sacrifices.

The sacrifices are very great. In addition to the enormous sums sent to Europe under Marshall Aid, the Atlantic Pact entails further subsidies for military supplies which are estimated at over $1,000,000,000 up to the year 1950. All this has to be raised by taxation from the annual production of the hard-working American people, who are not all Wall Street millionaires, but are living their lives in very different parts of the country than Wall Street. I say that nothing like this process of providing these enormous sums for defence and assistance to Europe – nothing like this has ever been seen in all history. We acknowledge it with gratitude, and we must continue to play our part as we are doing in a worthy manner and to the best of our abilities. . . .

I have always myself looked forward to the fraternal association of the English-speaking world and also to the union of Europe. It is only in this way, in my view, that the peace and progress of mankind can be maintained. I gave expression to these views at Fulton in March 1946, after the remarks to which I have referred had shown the differences which had arisen with Russia. Although what I said then reads very tamely today, and falls far short of what has actually been done, and far short of what the House actually has to vote at the present time, a Motion of Censure against me was placed on the Order Paper in the name of the hon. Member for Luton [Mr Warbey] in the following terms:

> World Peace and Security. – That this House considers that proposals for a military alliance between the British Commonwealth and the United States of America for the purpose of combating the spread of Communism, such as were put forward in a speech at Fulton, Missouri, USA, by the right hon. Gentleman the Member for Woodford are calculated to do injury to good relations between Great Britain, USA and the USSR, and are inimical to the cause of world peace.

That is the operative part. It is quite unusual, when a Private Member is out of office, that a Motion of that kind should be placed upon the Order Paper with regard to a speech made on his own responsibility, but no fewer than 105 hon. Members of the party opposite put their names to it. I do not see them all here today; some of them are here, but, of course, I feel that there has been a large-scale process of conversion, and, naturally, I welcome converts, and so do His Majesty's Government. They say that there is more joy over one sinner who repenteth than over ninety and nine just persons who need no repentance. Here, we have got about a hundred in a bunch, so far as I can make out, although some of them have emphasised the change of heart which they have gone through by a suitable act of penance by abstaining from attending this Debate. . . .

The situation is, therefore, from many points of view unprecedented and incalculable. Over the whole scene reigns the power of the atomic bomb, ever growing in the hands of the United States. It is this, in my view, and this alone that has given us time to take the measures of self-protection and to develop the units which make those measures possible, one of which is before us this afternoon.

THE BERLIN AIRLIFT

21 July 1949

House of Commons

In defiance of the accords reached in Potsdam in 1945, the Soviet Union established a land-blockade of Berlin. America and Britain mounted a round-the-clock airlift to succour the citizens of the city.

I was very much struck at the way in which all Germany watched the airlift, and how all Germany saw the British and American planes flying to carry food to 2,500,000 Germans whom the Soviet Government were trying to starve. I thought that was worth all the speeches that could have been made by all the peace leaders of Europe to turn the eyes of Germany to where her true destiny lies: namely, in peaceful and honourable association with the Western democracies and with the future into which they hope to lead the world under the auspices of the United Nations organisation.

'PRENEZ-GARDE! JE VAIS PARLER EN FRANÇAIS!'

12 August 1949

Open-air meeting, Place Kléber, Strasbourg, France

The packed crowds gave a roar of delight at Churchill's opening words.

Prenez-garde! Je vais parler en français.

Dans cette ville ancienne, et encore marquée par les blessures de la guerre, nous sommes réunis pour former une Assemblée qui, nous l'espérons, sera un jour le Parlement de l'Europe. Nous avons fait le premier pas et c'est le premier pas qui coûte. . . .

Nos espoirs et notre travail tendent vers une époque de paix, de prospérité, de plénitude, ou l'inépuisable richesse et génie de l'Europe feront d'elle, une fois de plus, la source même et l'inspiration de la vie du monde. Dans tout cela, nous avançons avec le soutien de la puissante République au-delà de l'Atlantique, et des Etats souverains qui sont membres de l'Empire et du Commonwealth des Nations Britanniques.

Les dangers qui nous menacent sont grands, mais grande aussi est notre force, et il n'y a aucune raison de ne pas réussir à réaliser le but et à établir la structure de cette Europe Unie dont les conceptions morales pourront recueillir le respect et la reconnaissance de l'humanité, et dont la force physique sera telle que personne n'osera la molester dans sa tranquille marche vers l'avenir.

'WATCH OUT! I AM GOING TO SPEAK IN FRENCH' (TRANSLATION)

12 August 1949

Open-air meeting, Place Kléber, Strasbourg, France

Watch out! I am going to speak in French.

In this ancient town, still marked by the wounds of war, we have gathered together to form an Assembly which, we hope, will be one day the Parliament of Europe. We have taken the first step and it is the first step which counts. . . .

Our hopes and our work are leading to a time of peace, of prosperity, of plenitude, where the inexhaustible richness and genius of Europe will make her once more the very source and inspiration of the life of the world. In all of this we are advancing with the support of the powerful Republic beyond the Atlantic and the sovereign states who are members of the Empire and the British Commonwealth of nations.

The dangers which threaten us are great, but great also is our strength and there is no reason to not succeed in realising the goal and in establishing the structure of this United Europe whose moral concepts will be able to reap the respect and recognition of humanity, and whose physical strength will be such that no one will dare molest her on her tranquil march to the future.

'ENGLISH LITERATURE IS A GLORIOUS INHERITANCE'

2 November 1949

Receiving the London Times *Literary Award,*
Grosvenor House, London

English literature is a glorious inheritance which is open to all – there are no barriers, no coupons, and no restrictions. In the English language and in its great writers there are great riches and treasures, of which, of course, the Bible and Shakespeare stand alone on the highest platform. English literature is one of our greatest sources of inspiration and strength. The English language is the language of the English-speaking people, and no country, or combination or power so fertile and so vivid exists anywhere else on the surface of the globe. We must see that it is not damaged by modern slang, adaptations, or intrusions. We must endeavour to popularise and strengthen our language in every way. Broadly speaking, short words are best, and the old words, when short, are the best of all. Thus, being lovers of English, we will not only improve and preserve our literature, but also make ourselves a more intimate and effective member of the great English-speaking world, on which, if wisely guided, the future of mankind will largely rest.

'OUR SOCIALIST MASTERS'

9 February 1950

Forum Cinema, Devonport

At 75 years of age, Churchill led the Conservative Party into the General Election, in which the Socialists' 1945 landslide majority was reduced to a threadbare margin of just seven seats. He came to Plymouth in Devon to support his son, Randolph, who was standing against Michael Foot, a future leader of the Labour Party, whom he narrowly failed to dislodge.

Electioneering in his Woodford constituency, 1951.

In this election we have had to face several grotesque untruths, the kind of thing that could not be maintained in Parliament or before any fair-minded audience, but which can be mouthed from door to door by the Socialist canvassers.

The first colossal misrepresentation of facts – 'terminological inexactitude', if you like the expression (there are shorter variants, but we have to be very careful now at this election, which we are told must be kept thoroughly genteel) – well, the first of these misrepresentations of fact was a statement that the Conservative Party meant to create unemployment in order that the need for finding a job should add a greater spur to labour. There is no truth in this. It is a monstrous suggestion. There was reference to this last night on the wireless by a Government spokesman [Mr James Griffiths].

The Socialist boast that they cured unemployment has been exploded out of their own mouths by the statements of Mr Morrison and Sir Stafford Cripps. All of them have said there would be anything up to 2,000,000 unemployed if it had not been for the American Loan. Fancy the Socialist Government in England keeping itself alive, economically and politically, by these large annual dollops of dollars from capitalist America! They seek the dollars; they beg the dollars; they bluster for the dollars; they gobble the dollars. But in the whole of their 8,000-word manifesto they cannot say 'Thank you' for the dollars.

It has also been proved that we had a joint plan in the days of the wartime Government for dealing with unemployment should it occur after the war. To this plan all the leading Socialist Ministers were party. That plan still holds good. So it is no longer a matter of dispute. We are all agreed upon it. They admit unemployment has been avoided by American dollars; and we are broadly agreed what we should do to prevent it or mitigate it should it recur. Everyone knows that any Government that comes into power as a result of this election will do its utmost to prevent unemployment. How far they will be successful will depend upon the methods they employ and the plight we are found to be in. I assure you there can be no greater safeguard against unemployment in the coming years than the return of a Government which will revive confidence in our country all over the world.

And now there is the tale of food subsidies. Sir Stafford Cripps told us on the broadcast that the Conservative Party had decided to abolish food subsidies. £406,000,000 is being spent in food subsidies, which is represented as a kindly gift by the kindly Government to the whole nation. It is not a gift. A great deal more is taken in tax by the kindly Government. Mr Morrison, evidently in collusion, repeated this whatever-you-care-to-call-it on a separate night. It is utterly untrue. We have no intention of abolishing food subsidies until and unless we are absolutely sure that the basic necessaries of life are available at prices all the people can pay down to the poorest in the land.

More than a fortnight ago Dr Edith Summerskill said at Kettering: 'The British Government could abolish rationing tomorrow if it were prepared to let the lowest income groups do without while the wealthiest bought up all available supplies. But it was not prepared to do so.' This is a very good example for the cumbrous and costly working of Socialist methods and machinery. The question immediately arises whether there is not some better way of helping the lower income groups to obtain their food at cheap prices than to keep in being for their sake the whole vast, complex, costly apparatus of rationing.

In our view the strong should help the weak. In the Socialist view the strong should be kept down to the level of the weak in order to have equal shares for all. How small the share is does not matter so much, in their opinion, so long as it is equal. They would much rather that everyone should have half rations than that anybody should get a second helping. What are called 'the lowest income groups' before the war when there were no rations in fact consumed under the 'wicked Tories' one and half times as much meat and more than twice as much sugar as Dr Summerskill doles out to all of us today.

In the years before the war the diet of London workhouses was in every way superior in meat, fats, sugar and also in variety to that which can be bought by a fully-employed wage-earner today. Yet to hear the Socialists talk on the broadcast, especially Mr Herbert Morrison and Sir Stafford Cripps, you would believe that we were living in a perfect paradise of plenty and good management. To apply the Socialist principle of equality at all costs is, in fact, to lay down the law that the pace of our advancing social army must be the pace of the slowest and the weakest man. Such a principle is, of course, destructive of all hopes of victory in social and philanthropic advance. It would undoubtedly condemn our island, with its enormous population, to a lower and more retricted standard of living than prevails anywhere else in the civilised world.

We are told: 'See what happened when sweets were derationed.' I am not at all sure that that was not a put-up job done with the hope of failure, so as to be an example. Certainly it was done in the most clumsy manner by those who had every interest to prevent its being a success. We certainly look forward to the day when we shall cease to be the only country in the civilised and free world where wartime rationing prevails. But I pledge any Conservative Government with which I am concerned not to take off rationing on any basic commodity until we are certain it will not only confer benefits upon the great mass of the people, but will protect the lower income groups from hardship.

You know, ladies and gentlemen, our Socialist masters think they know everything. They even try to teach the housewife how to buy her food. Mr Douglas Jay has said: 'Housewives as a whole cannot be trusted to buy all the right things, where nutrition and health are concerned. This is really no more than an extension of the principle according to which the housewife herself would not trust a child of four to select the week's purchases. For in the case of nutrition and health, just as in the case of education, the gentleman in Whitehall really does know better what is good for people than the people know themselves.'

That is what Mr Jay has said. Was there ever a period in the history of this island when such a piece of impertinence could have been spread about by a Minister? Let us call upon this Government to account for more of their own failures. Let us take them first on all the promises they made about housing. Before the war, under the 'wicked' Tory Government, with Mr Neville Chamberlain in charge, we were running to a thousand homes a day. There was no fuss about it. A certain amount of aid was given to local authorities, but no subsidising of private industry. They just let things work naturally. A thousand houses a day!

Now what has happened? They cannot build half what the Tories under Mr Neville Chamberlain were building without mentioning it; without it being a political question at all. The 'wicked Tories' – a thousand; the 'noble Socialists' – five hundred, each of them costing three times as much as they did before the war. Here in Plymouth I am told you have a waiting list of 11,000 houses. Randolph tells me that there are in Devonport houses which were built by private enterprise before the war in 1938 for which people paid £685. These houses sell for £2,000 today. What a sign of Socialist efficiency. What a sign of getting value for money. What a sign in the fall of the purchasing power of money, on which depends for everyone the innumerable transactions we have to carry out between man and man in any community.

If the Government had been trying to give you houses instead of playing politics; if they had been thinking in terms of bricks and mortar instead of in spite and venom, many a family in this city and many a score of thousand families in this island would today have a roof and front door and a hearth of their own. I think the Socialists should be called to account by the electors after their sorry and discreditable performance. Boasts, promises, pledges on the one hand, and the shameful underproduction on the other. No Government but this Socialist Government could have fallen so far short of public duty and of solemn obligation. . . .

Sir Stafford Cripps is reported to have said: 'You must have controls so that people cannot do just as they like.' There speaks the true voice of the Socialist. People must not do what they like. They must do what their Socialist masters (to use the word of the Attorney-General) think is good for them and tell them what to do. Thus the Socialist Party and Dr Summerskill have other reasons for wishing to keep the whole business of food rationing in full operation, besides their sympathy for the lower income groups and ignorance of the best way to help them. Mr Bottomley, the Under-Secretary for Overseas Trade, said eighteen months ago in Copenhagen: 'As long as a Socialist Government remains in office in Britain it can be expected that a rationing system will be maintained.' Thus we have not only rationing for rationing's sake, but the Food Ministry for the Food Ministry's sake. And under Socialist administration these sorts of organisations grow in cost with every month that passes.

In wartime, rationing is the alternative to famine. In peace it may well become the alternative to abundance. There is now one Food Ministry official for every 250 families in the country. There are more than 42,000 officials in all. But Dr Summerskill and her chief (I will not say her superior), Mr Strachey, exult in the feeling that they have so large an army to command. Their difficult and anxious problem is to make sure that it has enough to do to justify its existence, and give them this great mass of patronage and innumerable opportunities of interfering with other people's lives.

In the crisis of the war in 1940, when Lord Woolton was Food Minister, when the U-boats were sinking our ships and the air raids destroying our ports, the salaries paid to the Ministry of Food officials were less than £4,500,000 and the total administrative costs of the whole department were less than £8,000,000. However, the costs of all these departments tend to grow. The Socialists try to make them grow because it is part of their policy to have this vast machinery in existence. Also, they like to have as many ordinary people as possible in their power and dependent upon them as often as possible every day. In 1949 the salaries paid by the Socialists to the Ministery of Food officials had gone up from £4,500,000 in 1940 to nearly £14,000,000. The total administrative cost of running the department and working the rationing scheme had gone up from £8,000,000 to £21,000,000. It has well been said, 'The costs go up, but not the rations.'

Who do you suppose pays for all these 42,000 officials and lavish administrative expense? Every family in the country pays for it on the food they get. The food they get comes to their table weighted with this heavy charge, for which you pay as well as for the food subsidies which are given regardless of expense to millions of well-to-do people who do not need them at all. In order to pay for this and similar Socialist institutions, oppressive taxes are exacted from all, and beer and tobacco are taxed as they have never been taxed before. The purchase tax inflicts real hardships on the housewife, and particularly on those who have households and families to keep.

Income tax levied upon overtime and the highest forms of skilled craftsmanship discourages the extra effort and superior skill without which our industries cannot hold their own and compete in the modern world. Socialists pretend they give the lower income groups, and all others in the country, cheaper food through their system of rationing and food subsidies. To do it they have to take the money from their pockets first and circulate it back to them after heavy charges for great numbers of officials administering the system of rationing – which Mr Strachey and Dr Edith Summerskill are determined to keep in being whether it is needed or not – have been deducted. Little gifts have been given and came in handy for the election. We are all expected to change our political convictions and give our votes to the Government because a little extra tea and sugar has been saved up and given out. It is an insult to the intelligence of the British nation.

Sir Stafford Cripps now boasts, having first denied it, that the Socialist Government had given away to countries abroad £1,500,000,000 since they came into power to help the reconstruction of the world. They had to borrow it first from the United States or be given it by them. It was only lent or given to help Britain get on her legs again. Now it is gone. One-hundredth part of this £1,500,000,000 would have been enough to give every private motorist a reasonable ration of petrol. Conservatives are as keen as the Socialists to help revive the other countries of the world; but we believe we should be just before we are generous. It will take very strong arguments to convince me that our people should be deprived of the use of their motor vehicles, while other countries enjoy abundant supplies of petrol, largely bought with the money which we have presented to them, and for a large part of which we still remain debtors to America.

Socialism is contrary to human nature. Commerce and trade have always been a great power in this country. If difficulties have come upon them these last four and a half years it is because they have been hampered. The black patch confronting us now is due to the men at the head of the Government who have led and managed us. We must plunge into this pit of torment to rise again and overcome all perils to our life and independence as we have always done before.

The reason I ask for a strong majority is not that one party might ride roughshod, or that special favours might be granted to one class, or to vested interests. I ask for a strong majority towards that broad national unity in which our salvation will be found. Do not fail in your effort. Do not despair of your native land. No one can tell what the future will bring forth, but I believe that if we act wisely and deal faithfully with one another, and set our country, its history, glorious and inspiring, and its future – unlimited except by our own shortcomings – before our eyes, we should come through. Not only can the dangers of the present be overcome and its problems solved, but, having saved the world in war, we should save ourselves in peace.

'AN EXPERIMENT IN FREEDOM'

18 May 1950

Usher Hall, Edinburgh

I must, however, draw your attention to the characteristic remark by Dr Dalton, the new Minister of Town and Country Planning. In announcing one of his minor concessions he said, 'This is an experiment in freedom. I hope it will not be abused.' Could you have anything more characteristic of the Socialist rulers' outlook towards the public? Freedom is a favour; it is an experiment which the governing class of Socialist politicians will immediately curtail if they are displeased with our behaviour. This is language which the head of a Borstal Institution might suitably use to the inmates when announcing some modification of the disciplinary system. What an example of smug and insolent conceit! What a way to talk to the British people! As a race we have been experimenting in freedom, not entirely without success, for several centuries, and have spread the ideas of freedom throughout the world. And yet, here is this Minister, who speaks to us as if it lay with him to dole out our liberties like giving biscuits to a dog who will sit up and beg prettily. This characteristic of the official Socialist temperament and attitude in office should not pass uncensured by the British people who expect Ministers of the Crown to behave as the servants and not as the masters of the nation.

'THIS CENTURY OF TRAGEDY AND STORM'

4 July 1950

Dorchester Hotel, London

On the far side of the globe, US and British forces were battling to repel first the North Korean and, later, Chinese Communist invaders of South Korea. Churchill strongly favoured the action of the United Nations in resisting aggression.

The drawing together in fraternal association of the British and American peoples, and of all the peoples of the English-speaking world, may well be regarded as the best of the few good things that have happened to us and to the world in this century of tragedy and storm.

It was Bismarck who said in the closing years of his life that the most potent factor in human society at the end of the nineteenth century was the fact that the British and American peoples spoke the same language. He might well have added, what was already then apparent, that we had in common a very wide measure of purpose and ideals arising from our institutions, our literature and our common law. Since then, on the anvil of war, we have become so welded together that what might have remained for generations an interesting historical coincidence has become the living and vital force which preserves Christian civilisation and the rights and freedom of mankind. . . .

When I accepted your invitation I could not foresee that when the date arrived we should once again be brothers in arms, engaged in fighting for exactly the same cause that we thought we had carried to victory five years ago. The British and Americans do not war with races or governments as such. Tyranny, external or internal, is our foe whatever trappings or disguises it wears, whatever language it speaks, or perverts. We must forever be on our guard, and always vigilant against it – in all this we march together. Not only, if need be, under the fire of the enemy but also in those realms of thought which are consecrated to the rights and the dignity of man, and which are so amazingly laid down in the Declaration of Independence, which has become a common creed on both sides of the Atlantic Ocean.

The inheritance of the English-speaking world, vast and majestic though it is in territory and resources, derives its glory as a moral unity from thought and vision widely spread in the minds of our people and cherished by all of those who understand our destiny. As you may have heard (I don't want to give away any secrets) we had a General Election here a few months ago by which a Parliament was returned very evenly balanced but still more sharply divided; but divided not by small matters but by issues which cut deep into our national life. We have not developed to any extent over here the bipartisan conduct of external policy by both great parties like that which has in these later years so greatly helped the United States. Nevertheless, once the deep gong of comradeship between kindred nations strikes, resounds and reverberates, and when our obligations of the United Nations are staring us in the face, we shall allow no domestic party quarrels – grievous though they may be – to mar the unity of our national or international action. You can count on Britain, and not only Britain. Four years ago, when President Truman, whom we salute tonight, took me to Westminster College at Fulton in Missouri I ventured to offer the American people my counsel, and I said, 'Let no man underrate the abiding power of the British Empire and Commonwealth. Do not suppose that we shall not come through these dark years of privation as we came through the glorious years of agony, or that half a century from now will not see 70,000,000 or 80,000,000 Britons spread throughout the world and united in defence of our traditions, our way of life, and the world causes which you and we espouse.' In the increasing unity of the Anglo-American thought and action resides the main foundation of the freedom and progress of all men in all the lands. Let us not weary, let us not lose confidence in our mission, let us not fail in our duty in times of stress, let us not flinch if danger comes. . . .

We are told that the Kremlin oligarchy now know how to make the atomic bomb. That is the one new fact. To that extent there is a change to our disadvantage. It certainly seems to me that there is a better hope of a general settlement with Soviet Russia following on the defeat of aggression in Korea on a localised scale, than that we should drift on while large quantities of these devastating weapons are accumulated. Indeed I feel that there is nothing more likely to bring on a third world war than drift.

It is always difficult for free democracies, governed in the main by public opinion from day to day, to cope with the designs of dictator States and totalitarian systems. But hitherto we have held our own, or we should not be here tonight. We have only to be morally united and fearless, to give mankind the best hope of avoiding another supreme catastrophe. But I must say one thing before I sit down. It is of vital consequence to these hopes of world peace that what the Communists have begun in Korea should not end in their triumph. If that were to happen a third world war, under conditions even more deadly than now exist, would certainly be forced upon us, or hurled upon us before long. It is fortunate that the path of duty, and of safety, is so plainly marked out before our eyes, and so widely recognised by both our nations and governments, and by the large majority, the overwhelming majority of the member States comprised in the United Nations Organisation.

We owe it not only to ourselves, but to our faith in an institution, if not a world government at least a world protection from aggressive war, not to fail in our duty now. Thus we shall find the best hopes of peace and surest proof of honour. The League of Nations failed not because of its noble conceptions, but because these were abandoned by its members. We must not ask to be taught this hard lesson twice. Looking around this obscure, tumultuous scene, with all its uncertainties as it presents itself to us tonight, I am sure we shall not be guilty of such incurable folly; we shall go forward; we shall do our duty; we shall save the world from a third world war. And should it come in spite of all our efforts, we shall not be trampled down into serfdom and ruin.

'RENEWING THE GLORY OF OUR ISLAND HOME'

21 July 1951

Royal Wanstead School, Woodford

It is six years almost to a week since the Socialist Government came into office and we entered upon that melancholy period of eclipse and frustration which, if it continues, will lead to our decline and fall. What a contrast between our position at the end of the war and that to which we have been already reduced today. Not only were we victorious after all the hard toils and struggles but we were more honoured, respected and admired by friend and foe alike than we had ever been before.

And where do we stand today in the eyes of the world? For the time being we have lost our rank among the nations. There is hardly any country in the world where it is not believed that you have only to kick an Englishman hard enough to make him evacuate, bolt or clear out. Countries we have defended from Nazi and Fascist violence, countries we have rescued after they had been subjugated, countries which had found us strong and steadfast comrades and allies, are watching with astonishment a Britain which they think is in retreat or in decline. Egypt, Persia, Albania, the Argentine and Chile compete with each other in the insults and the humiliations they inflict upon us – and what is the cause? It is the attempt to impose a doctrinaire Socialism upon an island which has grown great and famous by free enterprise and valour and which six years ago stood in honour though not in size at the summit of the world. . . .

Devaluation was the child of wild profuse expenditure, and the evils which we suffer today from what I have called 'the money cheat' are the inevitable progeny of that wanton way of living. The greatest national misfortune which we are now entering is the ever-falling value of our money, or to put it the other way round, the ever-increasing cost measured by work and thrift of everything we buy. Taxation is higher than in any country outside the Communist world. There they take all. There no one has anything except the salaries paid them by the privileged Communist aristocracy. British taxation is higher now than it was in the height of the late war – even when we stood alone and defied all comers.

Is not that an astonishing fact? Six years of Socialist Government have hit us harder in our finance and economics than Hitler was able to do. Look at the effects you face of devaluation abroad. We are an island with a population of fifty millions living on imports of food and raw materials, which we have to buy by our exertion, ingenuity and craftsmanship. We have to pay across the dollar exchange twelve hours of work, with hand or brain, to buy what we could before have got with eight hours. We are a hard-working people. We are second to none in ability or enterprise so far as we are allowed to use these gifts. We now have to give a third more of our life strength, energy and output of every kind and quality to get the same revivifying intake as we had before devaluation two years ago. . . .

The whole social programme of which the Government boast was devised in conception and detail by a National Government resting upon a House of Commons with a Conservative majority of one hundred over all parties. Only one single new idea has been contributed by the false guides who have led us far astray, who have robbed us of the fruits of our victory and mauled our daily life. Only one. You know the one I have in mind. Nationalisation. What an awful flop! Show me the nationalised industry which has not become a burden on the public either as taxpayers or consumers or both. There is hardly an industry in which the employees are contented with changing the private employers with whom they could negotiate on equal terms through the trade unions for the hordes of all-powerful officials in Whitehall. . . .

And now I come to the worst thing of all. We had a speech the other day from the Communist Horner in which he said: 'If a Tory Government is returned it is certain that there will be a national strike of the miners. . . . It is only responsibility and loyalty to the Labour Government that has caused the miners to pull their punches.' This speech, which is, of course, only a part of the

Communist conspiracy to bring Britain under the whole of the Kremlin, would not have counted if it had only been the mouthings of a Moscow lackey. But there, sitting at his side, was a Minister of the Crown – Mr Griffiths. I give the Government credit for their hostility to Communism, though they are bringing it nearer by all they do. But fancy this Minister sitting there beside this Communist agent and not daring to open his mouth in protest or contradiction. And fancy that a week has elapsed without the Prime Minister or any other member of the Government disowning and denouncing the declaration which Mr Horner made. Let us see exactly what this declaration means. If the people of Britain should at any time be allowed to have a General Election, and if the will of the people expressed through the universal suffrage electorate should return a Conservative Government to power, Mr Horner says it is certain that there will be a national strike of the miners. This of course, if it happened, would paralyse the whole life and industry of our country.

Now I have always been a friend of the miners. Just over forty years ago I moved the Second Reading of the Mines Eight Hours Bill. I set up the system of mines inspectors drawn from the miners themselves which exists today as one of the main measures to ward off the perils of coal-mining. In 1925 as Chancellor of the Exchequer I provided £20 million to give a year for further negotiations to solve the difficulty in the mining industry and thus avoid a national or general strike. The only quarrel I have ever had with the miners was in the war when I had to forbid them from pouring out of the mines to join our armies in the field. Let them dismiss from their minds these malicious tales that a Conservative Government would be hostile to the mining community. I have always affirmed that those who work in these hard and dangerous conditions far from the light of the sun have the right to receive exceptional benefits from the nation which they serve.

But now the Communist Horner has stepped outside the sphere of industrial disputes and threatens the whole British democracy, thirty million voters, with a national strike to bring the country down if they dare express their opinion and wishes at the polls. This is an insult to the will of the people which no free democracy could endure. The idea that one section, however worthy, in our island should claim the right to deny political liberties and rights to all the rest of us, is one which would never be tolerated and one which, in my belief, the miners themselves would be the first to repudiate.

But while these shameful menaces are uttered, the Socialist Government, intent on electioneering – and false electioneering as it

Campaigning for his son, Randolph, with the editor's support,
Plymouth, 23 October 1951.

will turn out to be – remains 'mum'. Attlee doodles, Morrison gapes and only Mr Bevan grins. Well, anyhow, we are going to have a General Election as soon as we can force these office-clingers to present themselves before their fellow-countrymen. Then the people will have a chance to express their will. Great as are the difficulties of the time, ugly as the inheritance is which the Socialists will leave behind them, long as is the period of stable progressive government which will be required to remedy our misfortunes, and to rebuild our national power and fame, I have no doubt that it is the duty of all those who are here this evening, and of every man and woman in the land, to prepare themselves fearlessly and faithfully for the splendid opportunity they will have of reviving the strength and renewing the glory of our island home.

'REGAIN OUR INDEPENDENCE FINANCIALLY, ECONOMICALLY AND MORALLY'

23 October 1951

Home Park Football Ground, Plymouth

With the General Election under way, Churchill travelled down to Plymouth to support the campaign of his son, Randolph, in Devonport. I – a schoolboy of just eleven – accompanied my grandfather to lend my support as well. In spite of the cold weather, a crowd of more than 10,000 turned out to hear the Leader of the Opposition.

While we demonstrate and argue among ourselves here at home events are moving all over the world. One must not suppose that resistance to lawless outrages contrary to treaty or other obligations by Powers morally and physically not in the first rank raises the issues of a world war. A Third World War could only come if the Soviet Government calculated or miscalculated their chances of an ultimate victory and fell upon us all in ferocious aggression. That is why I am hopeful about the future. If I were a Soviet Commissar in the Kremlin tonight looking at the scene from their point of view I think I should be inclined to have a friendly talk with the leaders of the free world and see if something could not be arranged which enabled us all to live together quietly for another generation. Who can look beyond that? However, I have not yet been chosen as a Soviet Commissar – nor for any other office that I can think of – there or here. But what I cannot understand is how any of the leaders of Soviet Russia or the United States or here in Britain or France or in United Europe or anywhere else, could possibly imagine that their interests could be bettered by having an unlimited series of frightful immeasurable explosions. For another world war would not be like the Crusades or the romantic struggles in former centuries we have read about. It would be nothing less than a massacre of human beings whether in uniform or out of uniform by the hideous forces of perverted science. Science, which now offers us a Golden Age with one hand, offers at the same time with the other hand the doom of all that we have built up inch by inch since the Stone Age.

My faith is in the high progressive destiny of man. I do not believe we are to be flung back into abysmal darkness by those fearsome discoveries which human genius has made. Let us make sure that they are our servants but not our masters. Let us hold fast to the three supreme purposes. The freedom of the individual man in an ordered society; a world organisation to prevent bloody quarrels between nations by the rule of law; and for ourselves who have played so great a part in what I have called 'our finest hour,' to keep our own fifty millions alive in a small island at the high level of progressive civilisation which they have attained. Those are the three goals. To reach them we have first to regain our independence financially, economically and morally. If we are to play our part in the greater affairs of the free world, we have to gather around us our Empire and the States of the British Commonwealth, and bind them ever more closely together. We have to give our hand generously, wholeheartedly, to our Allies across the Atlantic Ocean, upon whose strength and wisdom the salvation of the world at this moment may well depend. Joined with them in fraternal association, drawn and held together by our common language and our joint inheritance of literature and custom, we may save ourselves and save the world. . . .

We are now at the final stage in this fateful election. Whatever happens on Thursday, we must all hope that we get a stable, solid Government and get out of this exhausting and distracting electioneering atmosphere, where all the forces of two great party machines have to go on working in every street and in every village week after week, to try to range the British people in opposing ranks. This is indeed a crisis in our island story. Never before in peace-time did we have so much need to judge policy on the merits and act in the true interests of our country, and of its Empire and Commonwealth of Nations. To go on like we have for the last twenty months with a Government struggling to keep its head above water from day to day and thinking of its party chances and of an election at any moment, is to give all that is strong and noble and resurgent in Britain the heaviest load to carry and the hardest battle to win.

'THE VALIANT CHAMPION OF FREEDOM'

9 November 1951

The Lord Mayor's Banquet, The Guildhall, London

The Conservatives won the election with a 17-seat majority and Churchill, nearly 77 years of age, returned as Prime Minister for a second and final term.

Though I have very often in the last forty years or so been present at your famous Guildhall banquets to salute the new Lord Mayor, this is the first occasion when I have addressed this assembly here as Prime Minister. The explanation is convincing. When I should have come here as Prime Minister the Guildhall was blown up and before it was repaired I was blown out! I thought at the time they were both disasters. But now we are all here together in a union which I hope will bring good luck. . . .

What is the world scene as presented to us today? Mighty forces armed with fearful weapons are baying at each other across a gulf which I have the feeling tonight neither wishes, and both fear to cross, but into which they may tumble or drag each other to their common ruin. On the one side stand all the armies and air forces of Soviet Russia and all their Communist satellites, agents and devotees in so many countries. On the other are what are called 'the Western Democracies' with their far superior resources, at present only partly organised, gathering themselves together around the United States with its mastery of the atomic bomb. Now there is no doubt on which side we stand. Britain and the Commonwealth and Empire still centring upon our island, are woven by ever-growing ties of strength and comprehension of common need and self-preservation to the great Republic across the Atlantic Ocean.

The sacrifices and exertions which the United States are making to deter, and if possible prevent, Communist aggression from making further inroads upon the free world are the main foundation of peace. A tithe of the efforts now being made by America would have prevented the Second World War and would have probably led to the downfall of Hitler with scarcely any blood being shed except perhaps his own. I feel a deep gratitude towards our great American Ally. They have risen to the leadership of the world without any other ambition but to serve its highest causes faithfully. I am anxious that Britain should also play her full part, and I hope to see a revival of her former influence and initiative among the Allied Powers, and indeed with all Powers.

It must not be forgotten that under the late Government we took peculiar risks in providing the principal atomic base for the United States in East Anglia, and that in consequence we placed ourselves in the very forefront of Soviet antagonism. We have therefore every need and every right to seek and to receive the fullest consideration from Americans for our point of view, and I feel sure this will not be denied us.

In order to regain our position we must do our utmost to re-establish as quickly as possible our economic and financial solvency and independence. We were shocked and surprised by the situation with which we were confronted after accepting responsibility a fortnight ago. This resulted partly from world causes, but also partly from the prolonged electioneering atmosphere in which we have dwelt for nearly two years, and especially for the past two months. We have certainly been left a tangled web of commitments and shortages, the like of which I have never seen before, and I hope and pray we may be granted the wisdom and the strength to cope with them effectively. If these conditions of furious political warfare between the two halves of our party-divided Britain are to continue indefinitely, and we are all to live under the shadow of a third General Election, it will not be at all good for the main life interests of the British nation, or for her influence in world affairs. Nevertheless, whatever way things may go, we shall not fail to do our duty however unpopular that may be. It is not cheers that we seek to win or votes we are playing to catch, but respect and confidence. This cannot come from words alone, but only from action which proves itself by results. Results cannot be achieved by the wave of a wand. Time is needed for a new Administration to grasp and measure the facts which surround us in baffling and menacing array. More time is needed for the remedies we propose and will propose to produce their curative effects. Nothing would be easier than for this country, politically rent asunder as it is, to shake and chatter itself into bankruptcy and ruin. But under grave pressures in the past we have proved ourselves to be a wise and unconquerable people, and I am sure that we shall succeed. No doubt His Majesty's Government will make mistakes. We shall not hesitate to admit them. I made many in the war. It is, however, always a comfort in times of crisis to feel that you are treading the path of duty according to the lights that are granted you. Then one need not fear whatever may happen. It was in this spirit that we all came through our worst perils eleven years ago; and I have a good and buoyant hope that the great mass of the nation will give us its ungrudging aid in all matters of truly national import. If this happens they may feel in two or three years' time that they have not been led on wrong courses and that Britain stands erect again, calm, resolute and independent, the faithful servant of peace, the valiant champion of freedom, and an honoured member of a united world instrument for preserving both.

'WE MUST NOT LOSE HOPE'

17 January 1952

United States Congress, Washington, DC

Churchill visited Washington for discussions with President Truman. This was his third address to the US Congress.

Now I come to Europe where the greatest of all our problems and dangers lie. I have long worked for the cause of a United Europe, and even of a United States of Europe, which would enable that Continent, the source of so much of our culture, ancient and modern, and the parent of the New World, to resume and revive its former splendours. It is my sure hope and conviction that European unity will be achieved, and that it will not ultimately be limited only to the countries at present composing Western Europe. I said at Zurich in 1946 that France should take Germany by the hand and lead her back into the family of nations, and thus end a thousand-year quarrel which has torn Europe to pieces and finally plunged the whole world twice over into slaughter and havoc.

Real and rapid progress is being made towards European unity, and it is both the duty and the policy of both Great Britain and her Commonwealth, and of the United States, to do our utmost, all of us, to help and speed it. As a forerunner of United Europe there is the European Army, which could never achieve its necessary strength without the inclusion of Germany. If this necessary and urgent object is being achieved by the fusion of the forces of the Continental nations outside what I have called in former times the Iron Curtain, that great operation deserves our fullest support. But, Members of Congress, fusion is not the only way in which the defence of Western Europe can be built. The system of a grand alliance such as has been created by the North Atlantic Treaty Organisation is no bar to the fusion of as many of its members as wish for this closer unity. And the United States, British and Canadian troops will stand, indeed are already standing, shoulder to shoulder with their European comrades in defence of the civilisation and freedom of the West. We stand together under General Eisenhower to defend the common cause from violent aggression.

What matters most is not the form of fusion, or melding – a word I learned over here – but the numbers of divisions, and of armoured divisions and the power of the air forces, and their weapons available for unified action under the Supreme Commander. We, in Britain, have denuded our island of military formations to an extent I have never seen before, and I cannot accept the slightest reproach from any quarter that we are not doing our full duty, because the British Commonwealth of Nations, spread all over the world, is not prepared to become a State or a group of States in any Continental federal system on either side of the Atlantic. The sooner strong enough forces can be assembled in Europe under united command the more effective will be the deterrents against a Third World War. The sooner, also, will our sense of security, and the fact of our security, be seen to reside in valiant, resolute and well-armed manhood, rather than in the awful secrets which science has wrested from nature. These are at present, it must be recognised – these secrets – the supreme deterrent against a Third World War, and the most effective guarantee of victory in it.

If I may say this, Members of Congress, be careful above all things, therefore, not to let go of the atomic weapon until you are sure, and more than sure, that other means of preserving peace are in your hands. It is my belief that by accumulating deterrents of all kinds against aggression we shall, in fact, ward off the fearful catastrophe, the fears of which darken the life and mar the progress of all the peoples of the globe. We must persevere steadfastly and faithfully in the task to which, under United States leadership, we have solemnly bound ourselves. Any weakening of our purpose, any disruption of our organisation would bring about the very evils which we all dread, and from which we should all suffer, and from which many of us would perish.

We must not lose patience, and we must not lose hope. It may be that presently a new mood will reign behind the Iron Curtain. If so it will be easy for them to show it, but the democracies must be on their guard against being deceived by a false dawn. We seek or covet no one's territory; we plan no forestalling war; we trust and pray that all will come right. Even during these years of what is called the 'cold war', material production in every land is continually improving through the use of new machinery and better organisation and the advance of peaceful science. But the great bound forward in progress and prosperity for which mankind is longing cannot come till the shadow of war has passed away. There are, however, historic compensations for the stresses which we suffer in the 'cold war'. Under the pressure and menace of Communist aggression the fraternal association of the United States with Britain and the British Commonwealth, and the new unity growing up in Europe – nowhere more hopeful than between France and Germany – all these harmonies are being brought forward, perhaps by several generations in the destiny of the world. If this proves true – and it has certainly proved true up to date – the architects in the Kremlin may be found to have built a different and a far better world structure than what they planned.

Members of the Congress, I have dwelt today repeatedly upon many of the changes that have happened throughout the world since you last invited me to address you here and I am sure you will agree that it is hardly possible to recognise the scene or believe it can truly have come to pass. But there is one thing which is exactly the same as when I was here last. Britain and the United States are working together and working for the same high cause. Bismarck once said that the supreme fact of the nineteenth century was that Britain and the United States spoke the same language. Let us make sure that the supreme fact of the twentieth century is that they tread the same path.

KING GEORGE VI

7 February 1952

Broadcast, London

King George VI died at Sandringham on the night of 5 February. He had been seriously ill for some time. Churchill's phrase 'the King walked with death, as if death were a companion' struck a deep chord with all who heard it.

My friends, when the death of the King was announced to us yesterday morning there struck a deep and solemn note in our lives which, as it resounded far and wide, stilled the clatter and traffic of twentieth-century life in many lands and made countless millions of human beings pause and look around them. A new sense of values took, for the time being, possession of human minds and mortal existence presented itself to so many at the same moment in its serenity and in its sorrow, in its splendour and in its pain, in its fortitude and in its suffering.

The King was greatly loved by all his peoples. He was respected as a man and as a prince far beyond the many realms over which he reigned. The simple dignity of his life, his manly virtues, his sense of duty alike as a ruler and a servant of the vast spheres and communities for which he bore responsibility – this gay charm and happy nature, his example as a husband and a father in his own family circle, his courage in peace or war – all these were aspects of his character which won the glint of admiration, now here, now there, from the innumerable eyes whose gaze falls upon the Throne.

We thought of him as a young naval lieutenant in the great Battle of Jutland. We thought of him, when calmly, without ambition, or want of self-confidence, he assumed the heavy burden of the Crown and succeeded his brother, whom he loved, and to whom he had rendered perfect loyalty. We thought of him so faithful in his study and discharge of State affairs, so strong in his devotion to the enduring honour of our country, so self-restrained in his judgments of men and affairs, so uplifted above the clash of party politics, yet so attentive to them; so wise and shrewd in judging between what matters and what does not. All this we saw and admired. His conduct on the Throne may well be a model and a guide to constitutional sovereigns throughout the world today, and also in future generations.

The last few months of King George's life, with all the pain and physical stresses that he endured – his life hanging by a thread from day to day – and he all the time cheerful and undaunted – stricken in body but quite undisturbed and even unaffected in spirit – these have made a profound and an enduring impression and should be a help to all. He was sustained not only by his natural buoyancy but by the sincerity of his Christian faith. During these last months the King walked with death, as if death were a companion, an acquaintance, whom he recognised and did not fear. In the end death came as a friend; and after a happy day of sunshine and sport, and after 'good night' to those who loved him best, he fell asleep as every man or woman who strives to fear God and nothing else in the world may hope to do.

The nearer one stood to him the more these facts were apparent. But the newspapers and photographs of modern times have made vast numbers of his subjects able to watch with emotion the last months of his pilgrimage. We all saw him approach his journey's end. In this period of mourning and meditation, amid our cares and toils, every home in all the realms joined together under the Crown, may draw comfort for tonight and strength for the future from his bearing and his fortitude.

There was another tie between King George and his people. It was not only sorrow and affliction that they shared. Dear to the hearts and the homes of the people is the joy and pride of a united family; with this all the troubles of the world can be borne and all its ordeals at least confronted. No family in these tumultuous years was happier, or loved one another more, than the Royal Family around the King.

My friends, I suppose no Minister saw so much of the King during the war as I did. I made certain he was kept informed of every secret matter; and the care and thoroughness with which he mastered the immense daily flow of State papers made a deep mark on my mind. Let me tell you another fact. On one of the days, when Buckingham palace was bombed, the King had just returned from Windsor. One side of the courtyard was struck, and if the windows opposite out of which he and the Queen were looking had not been, by the mercy of God, open, they would both have been blinded by the broken glass instead of being only hurled back by the explosion. Amid all that was then going on – although I saw the King so often – I never heard of this episode till a long time after. Their Majesties never mentioned it, or thought it of more significance than a soldier in their armies would of a shell bursting near him. This seems to me to be a revealing trait in the Royal character.

There is no doubt that of all the institutions which have grown up among us over the centuries, or sprung into being in our lifetime, the constitutional monarchy is the most deeply founded and dearly cherished by the whole association of our peoples. In the present generation it has acquired a meaning incomparably more powerful than anyone had dreamed possible in former times. The Crown has become the mysterious link – indeed, I may say, the magic link – which unites our loosely bound but strongly interwoven Commonwealth of nations, States and races. Peoples who would never tolerate the assertions of a written constitution which implied any diminution of their independence, are the foremost to be proud of their loyalty to the Crown.

We have been greatly blessed amid our many anxieties, and in the mighty world that has grown up all around our small island – we have been greatly blessed that this new intangible, inexpressible but for practical purposes apparently, an all-powerful element of union should have leapt into being among us. How vital it is, not only to the future of the British Commonwealth and Empire, but I believe also to the cause of world freedom and peace which we serve, that the occupant of the Throne should be equal to the august and indefinable responsibilities which this supreme office requires. For fifteen years King George VI was king; never at any moment in all the perplexities at home and abroad, in public or in private, did he fail in his duties; well does he deserve the farewell salute of all his governments and peoples.

My friends, it is at this time that our compassion and sympathy go out to his Consort and widow. Their marriage was a love match with no idea of regal pomp or splendour. Indeed, there seemed to lie before them the arduous life of royal personages denied so many of the activities of ordinary folk and having to give so much in ceremonial public service. May I say, speaking with all freedom, that our hearts go out tonight to that valiant woman with famous blood of Scotland in her veins who sustained King George through all his toils and problems and brought up, with their charm and beauty, the two daughters who mourn their father today. May she be granted strength to bear her sorrow. To Queen Mary, his mother, another of whose sons is dead – the Duke of Kent having been killed on active service – there belongs the consolation of seeing how well the King did his duty and fulfilled her hopes, and of always knowing how much he cared for her.

Now I must leave the treasures of the past and turn to the future. Famous have been the reigns of our Queens. Some of the greatest periods in our history have unfolded under their sceptres. Now that we have the Second Queen Elizabeth, also ascending the Throne in her twenty-sixth year, our thoughts are carried back nearly 400 years to the magnificent figure who presided over, and in many ways embodied and inspired, the grandeur and genius of the Elizabethan Age. Queen Elizabeth the Second, like her predecessor, did not pass her childhood in any certain expectation of the Crown. But already we know her well, and we understand why her gifts, and those of her husband, the Duke of Edinburgh, have stirred the only part of our Commonwealth she has yet been able to visit. She has already been acclaimed as Queen of Canada: we make our claim, too, and others will come forward also; and tomorrow the proclamation of her sovereignty will command the loyalty of her native land and of all other parts of the British Commonwealth and Empire.

I, whose youth was passed in the august, unchallenged and tranquil glories of the Victorian Era, may well feel a thrill in invoking, once more, the prayer and the Anthem, 'God Save the Queen!'

'THE TREACHEROUS TRAP-DOOR'

11 June 1952

Press Association Luncheon, Savoy Hotel, London

After six years of Socialist Government, Britain was burdened with debt and in dire economic straits. The £1,000 million post-war loan from the United States – and more – had all been loaned or given away to other countries.

Last week I watched the Trooping the Colour and our young Queen riding at the head of her Guards. I thought of the history of the past and the hopes of the future. Not only of the distant past – it is barely ten years since we upheld on our strong, unyielding shoulders the symbols, the honour and even perhaps the life of the free world.

Certainly no one of British race could contemplate such a spectacle without pride. But no thinking man or woman could escape the terrible question: on what does it all stand? It does indeed seem hard that the traditions and triumphs of a thousand years should be challenged by the ebb and flow of markets and commercial and financial transactions in the swaying world which has sprung up and is growing ever larger around us, and that we have to watch from month to month the narrow margins upon which our solvency and consequently our reputation and influence depend. But fifty million islanders growing food for only thirty millions, and dependent for the rest upon their exertions, their skill and their genius, present a problem which has not been seen or at least recorded before. In all history there has never been a community so large, so complex, so sure of its way of life, posed at such dizzy eminence and on so precarious a foundation. Lands and nations whom we have defeated in war or rescued from subjugation are today more solidly sure of earning their living than we, who have imparted our message of Parliamentary institutions to the civilised world, and kept the flag of freedom flying in some of its darkest days.

Around us we see the streets so full of traffic and the shops so splendidly presented, and the people, cheerful, well-dressed, content with their system of Government, proud, as they have a right to be of their race and name. One wonders if they realise the treacherous trap-door on which they stand. I would not say this to you if it was not your duty to expose any facts, however unpleasant, to them. Britain can take it.

To speak like this is not to cry despair. It is the Alert; but it is more than the Alert; it is the Alarm. We have never been beaten yet and now we fight not for vainglory or imperial pomp, but for survival as an independent, self-supporting nation. It has often been said we were approaching national bankruptcy in October last after our two-years orgy of electioneering, and certainly the figures to prove it can all be produced. But any British Government, worthy of the name, called upon to bear the burden would have taken severe, unpopular measures of one kind or another to ward off the obvious and imminent peril. In wartime we were confronted with extreme decisions. There was nothing we would not have done for our life and cause. In time of peace happily we work under more limited conditions both in risks and in remedies. The dangers do not present themselves to the mass of the people in the same acute and violent manner as in the days when London was being bombed. Now the crisis is different in form but, as it seems to me, scarcely less fateful.

Moreover there is this outstanding difference between the perils of war and peace. In war we were united, now in peace we find ourselves torn apart by quarrels which bear no relation to our dangers, and, while we brawl along, our thought and action are distracted by a vast superficial process of reciprocal calumniation. We have to live our life from day to day and give back as good as we get, but I warn you that without an intense national realisation of our position in all parties and by all classes, we shall find it very hard to reach that security without which all that we have achieved, all that we possess and all our glories may be cast away.

If I were not sure that the vital forces in our race, not only in this island, but throughout the British Empire and Commonwealth of Nations, have only to be aroused to conquer, I would not use these hard words. I use them to you because they may be a guide in the discharge of your responsible duties and also because, through your Agency, they may command the attention of our countrymen here and across the oceans. Thanks to the unpopular measures that have already been taken by the Chancellor of the Exchequer, we have reached in the last six months a position of equipoise. Our head is above water. It is not enough to float. We have to swim and we have to swim successfully against the stream. We are holding our own. That is a considerable return for the sacrifices which our people are having to make. But we cannot be satisfied with that. We must not only pay our way. We cannot be content to live from hand to mouth and from month to month in this world of change and turmoil. We must create, by long and steady systems of trade and exchange throughout our Empire and Commonwealth and throughout the wider world, reserves of strength and solvency which enable us to rise solid, steadfast and superior, above the waves of cosmopolitan speculation. Thus and thus alone can we stand firm and unbroken against all the winds that blow.

'THE SPIRIT OF ENGLAND'

23 April 1953

The Honourable Artillery Company,
St George's Day Dinner, London, and Broadcast

England has a quality which no one should overlook. England, like nature, never draws a line without smudging it. We lack the sharp logic of some other countries whom in other ways we greatly admire – in our climate, the atmosphere is veiled, there are none of these sharp presentations, and although we have our differences – especially as in a few minutes I have to go back to the House of Commons – I won't say are slaves to differences, but at any rate present the point of view which we hold. We have our differences but they do not divide us as they do in nearly all the other countries of the world. There is a great underlying spirit of neighbourliness and there is without doubt a very strong common sense of our national unity and life which, though it doesn't help us in the small matters with which we have to deal from day to day, may well be our salvation in our troubles.

Nothing can save England, if she will not save herself. If we lose faith in ourselves, in our capacity to guide and govern, if we lose our will to live, then, indeed, our story is told. If, while on all sides foreign nations are every day asserting a more aggressive and militant nationalism by arms and trade – if we remain paralysed by our own theoretical doctrines or plunged in the stupor of after-war exhaustion – but this is twenty years ago, this is not new – indeed, all that the croakers predict will come true and our ruin will be certain and final.

But why should we break up the solid structure of British power founded upon so much help, kindliness, and freedom? Why should we break it up for dreams which may some day come true, but now are only dreams, or it may be nightmares? We ought as a nation and Empire – you won't mind my mentioning that word? – I didn't get shouted down when I said it twenty years ago tonight – Empire, we might, we ought, to weather any storm that blows at least as well as any other existing system of human government.

We are at once more experienced and more truly united than any people in the world. It may well be, I say, that the most glorious chapters of our history are yet to be written. Indeed, the very problems and dangers that encompass us in our country ought to make English men and women of this generation glad to be here at such a time. We ought to rejoice at the responsibilities with which destiny has honoured us and be proud that we are the guardians of our country in an age when her life is at stake. I have lived, since then, to see our country accomplish, achieve her finest hour and I have no doubt that if this spirit of England continues, there is no reason at all why twenty years hence someone may not stand at the table of this ancient company and speak in the sense of pride and hope in which I have ventured to address you tonight.

'THE CROWN AND PARLIAMENT'

27 May 1953

Commonwealth Parliamentary Association Luncheon,
St Stephen's Hall, Westminster

This address was delivered in the presence of the new Queen, shortly before her Coronation on 2 June.

In this hall of fame and antiquity, a long story has been unfolded of the conflict of Crown *versus* Parliament, and I suppose we are most of us within a hundred yards of the statue of Oliver Cromwell. But those days are done. The vehement, passionate moral and intellectual forces that clashed in tragic violence three hundred years ago are now united. It is no longer a case of Crown *versus* Parliament, but of Crown *and* Parliament.

In our island, by trial and error, and by perseverance across the centuries, we have found out a very good plan. Here it is. 'The Queen can do no wrong.' Bad advisers can be changed as often as the people like to use their rights for that purpose. A great battle is lost. Parliament turns out the Government. A great battle is won. Crowds cheer the Queen. We have found this a very commanding and durable doctrine. What goes wrong passes away with the politicians responsible. What goes right is laid on the altar of our united Commonwealth and Empire.

Here today we salute fifty or sixty Parliaments and one Crown. It is natural for Parliaments to talk and for the Crown to shine. The oldest here will confirm me that we are never likely to run short of Members and of Ministers who can talk. And the youngest are sure they will never see the Crown sparkle more gloriously than in these joyous days.

Of course some envious people say we want to have it all ways at once. That may well be true. We seek the best of all worlds and certainly we have got the pick of this one. It is always dangerous to make comparisons about forms of government. We accept the principle that everyone should have what they like, but there can be no harm in my saying we like very much what we have got. Still, we recognise that others may prefer different solutions.

We must be very careful nowadays – I perhaps all the more because of my American forebears – in what we say about the American Constitution. I will therefore content myself with the observation that no Constitution was ever written in better English. But we have much more than that in common with the great republic. The key thought alike of the British constitutional monarchy and the republic of the United States is the hatred of dictatorship. Both here and across the ocean, over the generations and the centuries the idea of the division of power has lain at the root of our development. We do not want to live under a system dominated either by one man or one theme. Like nature we follow in freedom the paths of variety and change and our faith is that the mercy of God will make things get better if we all try our best.

I suppose it is because I have served Her Majesty's great-grandfather, grandfather, father, and now herself, that I have been accorded the honour of expressing our thanks this afternoon to her for her Royal presence here. Well do we realise the burdens imposed by sacred duty upon the Sovereign and her family. All round we see the proofs of the unifying sentiment which makes the Crown the central link in all our modern changing life, and the one which above all others claims our allegiance to the death. We feel that Her Gracious Majesty here with us today has consecrated her life to all her peoples in all her realms. We are resolved to prove on the pages of history that this sacrifice shall not be made in vain.

'SUPREME CATASTROPHE' OR
'MEASURELESS REWARD'

3 November 1953

House of Commons

The world scene had changed. Earlier that year Marshal Stalin had died. Meanwhile Churchill's friend, General Dwight D. Eisenhower, had become President of the United States and, in Korea a Truce had brought an end to the fighting.

Certain important events have happened which, rightly or wrongly, have somewhat veiled, and, it may be, actually modified the harshness of the scene. The fighting in Korea has shifted from the trenches to the tables. We do not know yet what will emerge from these stubborn and tangled discussions. But whatever else comes, or may come, as a result of the Korean War, one major world fact is outstanding. The United States have become again a heavily armed nation.

The second world event has been the death of Stalin and the assumption of power by a different régime in the Kremlin. It is on the second of these prodigious events that I wish to dwell for a moment. Nearly eight months have passed since it occurred and everywhere the question was, and still is asked, did the end of the Stalin epoch lead to a change in Soviet policy? Is there a new look?

I should not venture to ask the House, or any outside our doors to whom my words have access, to adopt positive conclusions on these mysteries. It may well be that there have been far-reaching changes in the temper and outlook of the immense populations, now so largely literate, who inhabit 'all the Russias', and that their mind has turned to internal betterment rather than external aggression. This may or may not be a right judgment, and we can afford, if vigilance is not relaxed and strength is not suffered again to dwindle, to await developments in a hopeful and, I trust, a helpful mood.

The only really sure guide to the actions of mighty nations and powerful Governments is a correct estimate of what are and what they consider to be their own interests. Applying this test, I feel a sense of reassurance. Studying our own strength and that of Europe under the massive American shield, I do not find it unreasonable or dangerous to conclude that internal prosperity rather than external conquest is not only the deep desire of the Russian peoples, but also the long-term interest of their rulers.

It was in this state of mind that six months ago I thought it would be a good thing if the heads of the principal States and Governments concerned met the new leaders of Russia and established that personal acquaintance and relationships which have certainly often proved a help rather than a hindrance. I still hope that such a meeting may have a useful place in international contacts.

On the other hand, one must not overlook the risk of such a four-Power conference ending in still a worse deadlock than exists at present. It certainly would be most foolish to imagine that there is any chance of making straight away a general settlement of all the cruel problems that exist in the East as well as in the West, and that exist in Germany and in all the satellite countries. We are not likely straight away to get them satisfactorily dealt with and laid to rest as great dangers and evils in the world by personal meetings, however friendly. Time will undoubtedly be needed – more time than some of us here are likely to see.

I am, of course, in very close touch with President Eisenhower, and my hope was that at Bermuda we might have had a talk about it all. I was sorry to be prevented by conditions beyond my control. We are at present looking forward to the four-Power conference of Foreign Secretaries, and we earnestly hope it will take place soon. If it leads to improvements those themselves might again lead to further efforts on both sides. We trust we shall soon have a favourable answer to our conciliatory invitation to the Soviet.

I have mentioned two dominant events that have happened in the last two years. But there is a third which, though it happened before, has developed so prodigiously in this period that I can treat it as if it were a novel apparition which has overshadowed both those I have mentioned. I mean the rapid and ceaseless developments of atomic warfare and the hydrogen bomb.

These fearful scientific discoveries cast their shadow on every thoughtful mind, but nevertheless I believe that we are justified in feeling that there has been a diminution of tension and that the probabilities of another world war have diminished, or at least have become more remote. I say this in spite of the continual growth of weapons of destruction such as have never fallen before into the hands of human beings. Indeed, I have sometimes the odd thought that the annihilating character of these agencies may bring an utterly unforeseeable security to mankind.

When I was a schoolboy I was not good at arithmetic, but I have since heard it said that certain mathematical quantities, when they pass through infinity, change their signs from plus to minus – or the other way round – [*laughter*]. I do not venture to plunge too much into detail of what are called the asymptotes of hyperbolae, but any hon. Gentleman who is interested can find an opportunity for an interesting study of these matters. It may be that this rule may have a novel application and that when the advance of destructive weapons enables everyone to kill everybody else nobody will want to kill anyone at all. At any rate, it seems pretty safe to say that a war which begins by both sides suffering what they dread most – and that is undoubtedly the case at present – is less likely to occur than one which dangles the lurid prizes of former ages before ambitious eyes.

I offer this comforting idea to the House, taking care to make it clear at the same time that our only hope can spring from untiring vigilance. There is no doubt that if the human race are to have their dearest wish and to be free from the dread of mass destruction, they could have, as an alternative, what many of them might prefer, namely, the swiftest expansion of material well-being that has ever been within their reach, or even within their dreams.

By material well-being I mean not only abundance but a degree of leisure for the masses such as has never before been possible in our mortal struggle for life. These majestic possibilities ought to gleam, and be made to gleam, before the eyes of the toilers in every land, and they ought to inspire the actions of all who bear responsibility for their guidance. We, and all nations, stand, at this hour in human history, before the portals of supreme catastrophe and of measureless reward. My faith is that in God's mercy we shall choose aright.

'A CALMER AND KINDLIER AGE'

9 November 1954

The Lord Mayor's Banquet, The Guildhall, London

I am one of those who believe that the powers of the West and of the East should try to live in a friendly and peaceful way with each other. It would certainly not be to anyone's disadvantage if they tried. We don't agree with Soviet Communism or with their system of one-party uniformity. We think there is a great deal to be said for nature and variety, and that governments are made for men, not men for governments. But if the Soviets really like being governed by officials in a sealed pattern, and so long as they do not endanger the safety or freedom of others, that is a matter for them to decide themselves for themselves. Nothing is final. Change is unceasing and it is likely that mankind has a lot more to learn before it comes to its journey's end.

One thing is certain: with the world divided as it is at present, the freedom of our vast international association of the free peoples can only be founded upon strength and strength can only be maintained by unity. The whole foundation of our existence stands on our alliance, friendship, and an increasing sense of brotherhood with the United States, and we are also developing increasingly intimate ties with France, Germany, Italy, and the Low Countries which are stronger and more practical than any that have yet been devised. From these solemn and important agreements we hope that we shall be able to create that peace through strength which will allow time to play its part and bring about an altogether easier relationship all over the world. We might even find ourselves in a few years moving along a smooth causeway of peace and plenty instead of roaming around on the rim of Hell. For myself I am an optimist – it does not seem to be much use being anything else – and I cannot believe that the human race will not find its way through the problems that confront it, although they are separated by a measureless gulf from any they have known before. I look forward to the time when, to use Sir Anthony Eden's words, having brought about a stability and a common purpose in the West, we shall have established the essential basis on which we can seek an understanding with the East. Thus we may by patience, courage, and in orderly progression reach the shelter of a calmer and kindlier age.

'THE NATION ... HAD THE LION-HEART'

30 November 1954

Presentation by both Houses of Parliament, Westminster Hall

On the occasion of Churchill's 80th birthday, Parliament assembled in Westminster Hall to honour him, the greatest Parliamentarian of his age or, as some would have it, of all time. I was present and recall the collective gasp when the portrait by Graham Sutherland was unveiled. Churchill, who clearly did not like it, provoked a roar of laughter when he impishly described it as 'a remarkable example of modern art'.

This is to me the most memorable public occasion of my life. No one has ever received a similar mark of honour before. There has not been anything like it in British history, and indeed I doubt whether any of the modern democracies has shown such a degree of kindness and generosity to a party politician who has not yet retired and may at any time be involved in controversy. It is indeed the most striking example I have ever known of that characteristic British Parliamentary principle cherished in both Lords and Commons 'Don't bring politics into private life.' It is certainly a mark of the underlying unity of our national life which survives and even grows in spite of vehement party warfare and many grave differences of conviction and sentiment. This unity is, I believe, the child of freedom and fair play fostered in the cradle of our ancient island institutions, and nursed by tradition and custom.

I am most grateful to Mr Attlee for the agreeable words he has used about me this morning, and for the magnanimous appraisal he has given of my variegated career. I must confess, however, that this ceremony and all its charm and splendour may well be found to have seriously affected my controversial value as a party politician. However, perhaps with suitable assistance I shall get over this reaction and come round after a bit.

The Leader of the Opposition and I have been the only two Prime Ministers of this country in the last fourteen years. There are no other Prime Ministers alive. Mr Attlee was also Deputy Prime Minister with me in those decisive years of war. During our alternating tenure, tremendous events have happened abroad, and far-reaching changes have taken place at home. There have been three general elections on universal suffrage and the activity of our Parliamentary and party machinery has been absolutely free. Mr Attlee's and my monopoly of the most powerful and disputatious office under the Crown all this time is surely the fact which the world outside may recognise as a symbol of the inherent stability of our British way of life. It is not, however, intended to make it a permanent feature of the Constitution.

I am sure this is the finest greeting any Member of the House of Commons has yet received and I express my heartfelt thanks to the representatives of both Houses for the gifts which you have bestowed in their name. The portrait is a remarkable example of modern art. It certainly combines force and candour. These are qualities which no active Member of either House can do without or should fear to meet. The book with which the Father of the House of Commons [Mr David Grenfell] has presented me is a token of the goodwill and chivalrous regard of members of all parties. I have lived my life in the House of Commons, having served there for fifty-two of the fifty-four years of this tumultuous and convulsive century. I have indeed seen all the ups and downs of fate and fortune, but I have never ceased to love and honour the Mother of Parliaments, the model to the legislative assemblies of so many lands.

The care and thought which has been devoted to this beautiful volume and the fact that it bears the signatures of nearly all my fellow-Members deeply touches my heart. And may I say that I thoroughly understand the position of those who have felt it their duty to abstain. The value of such a tribute is that it should be free and spontaneous. I shall treasure it as long as I live and my family and descendants will regard it as a most precious possession. When I read the eulogy so gracefully and artistically inscribed on the title page, with its famous quotation from John Bunyan, I must confess to you that I was overpowered by two emotions – pride and humility. I have always hitherto regarded them as opposed and also corrective of one another; but on this occasion I am not able to tell you which is dominant in my mind. Indeed both seem to dwell together hand in hand. Who would not feel proud to have this happen to him and yet at the same time I never was more sure of how far it goes beyond what I deserve.

I was very glad that Mr Attlee described my speeches in the war as expressing the will not only of Parliament but of the whole nation. Their will was resolute and remorseless and, as it proved, unconquerable. It fell to me to express it, and if I found the right words you must remember that I have always earned my living by my pen and by my tongue. It was the nation and race dwelling all round the globe that had the lion heart. I had the luck to be called upon to give the roar. I also hope that I sometimes suggested to the lion the right places to use his claws. I am now nearing the end of my journey. I hope I still have some services to render. However that may be and whatever may befall I am sure I shall never forget the emotions of this day or be able to express my gratitude to those colleagues and companions with whom I have lived my life for this superb honour they have done me.

'NEVER DESPAIR!'

1 March 1955

House of Commons

This was to be Churchill's last great speech to the House of Commons. The last two sentences were his farewell to the House of Commons and to the British people.

We live in a period, happily unique in human history, when the whole world is divided intellectually and to a large extent geographically between the creeds of Communist discipline and individual freedom, and when, at the same time, this mental and psychological division is accompanied by the possession by both sides of the obliterating weapons of the nuclear age.

We have antagonisms now as deep as those of the Reformation and its reactions which led to the Thirty Years' War. But now they are spread over the whole world instead of only over a small part of Europe. We have, to some extent, the geographical division of the Mongol invasion in the thirteenth century, only more ruthless and more thorough. We have force and science, hitherto the servants of man, now threatening to become his master.

I am not pretending to have a solution for a permanent peace between the nations which could be unfolded this afternoon. We pray for it. Nor shall I try to discuss the cold war which we all detest, but have to endure. I shall only venture to offer to the House some observations mainly of a general character on which I have pondered long and which, I hope, may be tolerantly received, as they are intended by me. And here may I venture to make a personal digression? I do not pretend to be an expert or to have technical knowledge of this prodigious sphere of science. But in my long friendship with Lord Cherwell I have tried to follow and even predict the evolution of events. I hope that the House will not reprove me for vanity or conceit if I repeat what I wrote a quarter of a century ago:

> We know enough [I said] to be sure that the scientific achievements of the next fifty years will be far greater, more rapid and more surprising than those we have already experienced. . . . High authorities tell us that new sources of power, vastly more important than any we yet

know, will surely be discovered. Nuclear energy is incomparably greater than the molecular energy which we use today. The coal a man can get in a day can easily do 500 times as much work as the man himself. Nuclear energy is at least one million times more powerful still. If the hydrogen atoms in a pound of water could be prevailed upon to combine together and form helium, they would suffice to drive a 1,000 horse-power engine for a whole year. If the electrons – those tiny planets of the atomic systems – were induced to combine with the nuclei in the hydrogen, the horse-power liberated would be 120 times greater still. There is no question among scientists that this gigantic source of energy exists. What is lacking is the match to set the bonfire alight, or it may be the detonator to cause the dynamite to explode.

This is no doubt not quite an accurate description of what has been discovered, but as it was published in the *Strand Magazine* of December, 1931 – twenty-four years ago – I hope that my plea to have long taken an interest in the subject may be indulgently accepted by the House.

What is the present position? Only three countries possess, in varying degrees, the knowledge and the power to make nuclear weapons. Of these, the United States is overwhelmingly the chief. Owing to the breakdown in the exchange of information between us and the United States since 1946 we have had to start again independently on our own. Fortunately, executive action was taken promptly by the right hon. Gentleman, the Leader of the Opposition, to reduce as far as possible the delay in our nuclear development and production. By his initiative we have made our own atomic bombs.

Confronted with the hydrogen bomb, I have tried to live up to the right hon. Gentleman's standard. We have started to make that one, too. It is this grave decision which forms the core of the Defence Paper which we are discussing this afternoon. Although the Soviet stockpile of atomic bombs may be greater than that of Britain, British discoveries may well place us above them in fundamental science.

May I say that for the sake of simplicity and to avoid verbal confusion I use the expression 'atomic bombs' and also 'hydrogen bombs' instead of 'thermo-nuclear' and I keep 'nuclear' for the whole lot. There is an immense gulf between the atomic and the hydrogen bomb. The atomic bomb, with all its terrors, did not carry us outside the scope of human control or manageable events in thought or action, in peace or war. But when Mr Sterling Cole, the Chairman of the United States Congressional Commitee, gave out a year ago – 17 February 1954 – the first comprehensive review of the hydrogen bomb, the entire foundation of human affairs was revolutionised, and mankind placed in a situation both measureless and laden with doom.

It is now the fact that a quantity of plutonium, probably less than would fill the Box on the Table – it is quite a safe thing to store – would suffice to produce weapons which would give indisputable world domination to any great Power which was the only one to have it. There is no absolute defence against the hydrogen bomb, nor is any method in sight by which any nation, or any country, can be completely guaranteed against the devastating injury which even a score of them might inflict on wide regions.

What ought we to do? Which way shall we turn to save our lives and the future of the world? It does not matter so much to old people; they are going soon anyway; but I find it poignant to look at youth in all its activity and ardour and, most of all, to watch little children playing their merry games, and wonder what would lie before them if God wearied of mankind.

The best defence would of course be bona fide disarmament all round. This is in all our hearts. But sentiment must not cloud our vision. It is often said that 'facts are stubborn things'. A renewed session of a sub-committee of the Disarmament Commission is now sitting in London and is rightly attempting to conduct its debates in private. We must not conceal from ourselves the gulf between the Soviet Government and the NATO Powers, which has hitherto, for so long, prevented an agreement. The long history and tradition of Russia makes it repugnant to the Soviet Government to accept any practical system of international inspection.

A second difficulty lies in the circumstance that, just as the United States, on the one hand, has, we believe, the overwhelming mastery in nuclear weapons, so the Soviets and their Communist satellites have immense superiority in what are called 'conventional' forces – the sort of arms and forces with which we fought the last war, but much improved. The problem is, therefore, to devise a balanced and phased system of disarmament which at no period enables any one of the participants to enjoy an advantage which might endanger the security of the others. A scheme on these lines was submitted last year by Her Majesty's Government and the French Government and was accepted by the late Mr Vyshinsky as a basis of discussion. It is now being examined in London.

If the Soviet Government have not at any time since the war shown much nervousness about the American possession of nuclear superiority, that is because they are quite sure that it will not be used against them aggressively, even in spite of many forms of provocation. On the other hand, the NATO Powers have been combined together by the continual aggression and advance of Communism in Asia and in Europe. That this should have eclipsed in a few years, and largely effaced, the fearful antagonism and memories that Hitlerism created for the German people is an event without parallel. But it has, to a large extent, happened. There is widespread belief throughout the free world that, but for American nuclear superiority, Europe would already have been reduced to satellite status and the Iron Curtain would have reached the Atlantic and the Channel.

Unless a trustworthy and universal agreement upon disarmament, conventional and nuclear alike, can be reached and an effective system of inspection is established and is actually working, there is only one sane policy for the free world in the next few years. That is what we call defence through deterrents. This we have already adopted and proclaimed. These deterrents may at any time become the parents of disarmament, provided that they deter. To make our contribution to the deterrent we must ourselves possess the most up-to-date nuclear weapons, and the means of delivering them.

That is the position which the Government occupy. We are to discuss this not only as a matter of principle; there are many practical reasons which should be given. Should war come, which God forbid, there are a large number of targets that we and the Americans must be able to strike at once. There are scores of airfields from which the Soviets could launch attacks with hydrogen bombs as soon as they have the bombers to carry them. It is essential to our deterrent policy and to our survival to have, with our American allies, the strength and numbers to be able to paralyse these potential Communist assaults in the first few hours of the war, should it come.

The House will perhaps note that I avoid using the word 'Russia' as much as possible in this discussion. I have a strong admiration for the Russian people – for their bravery, their many gifts, and their kindly nature. It is the Communist dictatorship and the declared ambition of the Communist Party and their proselytising activities that we are bound to resist, and that is what makes this great world cleavage which I mentioned when I opened my remarks.

There are also big administrative and industrial targets behind the Iron Curtain, and any effective deterrent policy must have the power to paralyse them all at the outset, or shortly after. There are also the Soviet submarine bases and other naval targets which will need early attention. Unless we make a contribution of our own – that is the point which I am pressing – we cannot be sure that in an emergency the resources of other Powers would be planned exactly as we would wish, or that the targets which would threaten us most would be given what we consider the necessary priority, or the deserved priority, in the first few hours.

These targets might be of such cardinal importance that it would really be a matter of life and death for us. All this, I think, must be borne in mind in deciding our policy about the conventional forces, to which I will come later, the existing Services.

Meanwhile, the United States has many times the nuclear power of Soviet Russia – I avoid any attempt to give exact figures – and they have, of course, far more effective means of delivery. Our moral and military support of the United States and our possession of nuclear weapons of the highest quality and on an appreciable scale, together with their means of delivery, will greatly reinforce the deterrent power of the free world, and will strengthen our influence within the free world. That, at any rate, is the policy we have decided to pursue. That is what we are now doing, and I am thankful that it is endorsed by a mass of responsible opinion on both sides of the House, and, I believe, by the great majority of the nation.

A vast quantity of information, some true, some exaggerated much out of proportion, has been published about the hydrogen bomb. The truth has inevitably been mingled with fiction, and I am glad to say that panic has not occurred. Panic would not necessarily make for peace. That is one reason why I have been most anxious that responsible discussions on this matter should not take place on the BBC or upon the television, and I thought that I was justified in submitting that view of Her Majesty's Government to the authorities, which they at once accepted – very willingly accepted.

Panic would not necessarily make for peace even in this country. There are many countries where a certain wave of opinion may arise and swing so furiously into action that decisive steps may be taken from which there is no recall. As it is, the world population goes on its daily journey despite its sombre impression and earnest longing for relief. That is the way we are going on now.

I shall content myself with saying about the power of this weapon, the hydrogen bomb, that apart from all the statements about blast and heat effects over increasingly wide areas there are now to be considered the consequences of 'fall out', as it is called, of wind-borne radio-active particles. There is both an immediate direct effect on human beings who are in the path of such a cloud and an indirect effect through animals, grass, and vegetables, which pass on these contagions to human beings through food.

This would confront many who escaped the direct effects of the explosion with poisoning, or starvation, or both. Imagination stands appalled. There are, of course, the palliatives and precautions of a courageous Civil Defence, and about that the Home Secretary will be speaking later on tonight. But our best protection lies, as I am sure the House will be convinced, in successful deterrents operating from a foundation of sober, calm, and tireless vigilance.

Moreover, a curious paradox has emerged. Let me put it simply. After a certain point has been passed it may be said, 'The worse things get, the better.'

The broad effect of the latest developments is to spread almost indefinitely and at least to a vast extent the area of mortal danger. This should certainly increase the deterrent upon Soviet Russia by putting her enormous spaces and scattered population on an equality or near-equality of vulnerability with our small densely populated island and with Western Europe.

I cannot regard this development as adding to our dangers. We have reached the maximum already. On the contrary, to this form of attack continents are vulnerable as well as islands. Hitherto, crowded countries, as I have said, like the United Kingdom and Western Europe, have had this outstanding vulnerability to carry. But the hydrogen bomb, with its vast range of destruction and the even wider area of contamination, would be effective also against nations whose population, hitherto, has been so widely dispersed over large land areas as to make them feel that they were not in any danger at all.

They, too, become highly vulnerable, not yet equally perhaps, but, still, highly and increasingly vulnerable. Here again we see the value of deterrents, immune against surprise and well understood by all persons on both sides – I repeat 'on both sides' – who have the power to control events. That is why I have hoped for a long time for a top-level conference where these matters could be put plainly and bluntly from one friendly visitor to the conference to another.

Then it may well be that we shall by a process of sublime irony have reached a stage in this story where safety will be the sturdy child of terror, and survival the twin brother of annihilation. . . .

I am anxious to repeat and to emphasise the one word which is the theme of my remarks, namely, 'Deterrent.' That is the main theme.

The hydrogen bomb has made an astounding incursion into the structure of our lives and thoughts. Its impact is prodigious and profound, but I do not agree with those who say, 'Let us sweep away forthwith all our existing defence services and concentrate our energy and resources on nuclear weapons and their immediate ancillaries.' The policy of the deterrent cannot rest on nuclear weapons alone. We must, together with our NATO allies, maintain the defensive shield in Western Europe.

Unless the NATO Powers had effective forces there on the ground and could make a front, there would be nothing to prevent piecemeal advance and encroachment by the Communists in this time of so-called peace. By successive infiltrations, the Communists could progressively undermine the security of Europe. Unless we were prepared to unleash a full-scale nuclear war as soon as some local incident occurs in some distant country, we must have conventional forces in readiness to deal with such situations as they arise.

We must, therefore, honour our undertaking to maintain our contribution to the NATO forces in Europe in time of peace. In war, this defensive shield would be of vital importance, for we must do our utmost to hold the Soviet and satellite forces at arms' length in order to prevent short-range air and rocket attack on these islands. Thus, substantial strength in conventional forces has still a vital part to play in the policy of the deterrent. It is perhaps of even greater importance in the cold war.

Though world war may be prevented by the deterrent power of nuclear weapons, the Communists may well resort to military action in furtherance of their policy of infiltration and encroachment in many parts of the world. There may well be limited wars on the Korean model, with limited objectives. We must be able to play our part in these, if called upon by the United Nations Organisation. In the conditions of today, this is also an aspect of our Commonwealth responsibility. We shall need substantial strength in conventional forces to fulfil our world-wide obligations in these days of uneasy peace and extreme bad temper. . . .

The argument which I have been endeavouring to unfold and consolidate gives us in this island an interlude. Let us not waste it. Let us hope we shall use it to augment or at least to prolong our security and that of mankind. But how? There are those who believe, or at any rate say, 'If we have the protection of the overwhelmingly powerful United States, we need not make the hydrogen bomb for ourselves or build a fleet of bombers for its delivery. We can leave that to our friends across the ocean. Our contribution should be criticism of any unwise policy into which they may drift or plunge. We should throw our hearts and consciences into that.'

Personally, I cannot feel that we should have much influence over their policy or actions, wise or unwise, while we are largely dependent, as we are today, upon their protection. We, too, must possess substantial deterrent power of our own. We must also never allow, above all, I hold, the growing sense of unity and brotherhood between the United Kingdom and the United States and throughout the English-speaking world to be injured or retarded. Its maintenance, its stimulation, and its fortifying is one of the first duties of every person who wishes to see peace in the world and wishes to see the survival of this country.

To conclude: mercifully, there is time and hope if we combine patience and courage. All deterrents will improve and gain authority during the next ten years. By that time, the deterrent may well reach its acme and reap its final reward. The day may dawn when fair play, love for one's fellow-men, respect for justice and freedom, will enable tormented generations to march forth serene and trimphant from the hideous epoch in which we have to dwell. Meanwhile, never flinch, never weary, never despair.

'THE QUEEN'

4 April 1955

No. 10 Downing Street

The day before Churchill submitted his resignation and stepped down as Prime Minister, the Queen and the Duke of Edinburgh paid my grandparents the rare honour of dining as their guests at 10 Downing Street.

I have the honour of proposing a toast which I used to enjoy drinking during the years when I was a cavalry subaltern in the reign of your Majesty's great-great-grandmother, Queen Victoria.

Having served in office or in Parliament under the four sovereigns who have reigned since those days, I felt, with these credentials, that in asking your Majesty's gracious permission to propose this toast I should not be leading to the creation of a precedent which would often cause inconvenience.

Madam, I should like to express the deep and lively sense of gratitude which we and all your peoples feel to you and to his Royal

Highness the Duke of Edinburgh for all the help and inspiration we receive in our daily lives and which spreads with ever-growing strength throughout the British realm and the Commonwealth and Empire.

Never have we needed it more than in the anxious and darkening age through which we are passing and through which we hope to help the world to pass.

Never have the august duties which fall upon the British monarchy been discharged with more devotion than in the brilliant opening of your Majesty's reign. We thank God for the gift he has bestowed upon us and vow ourselves anew to the sacred cause, and wise and kindly way of life of which your Majesty is the young, gleaming champion.

'The Queen.'

'LET US GO BOLDLY FORWARD'

21 June 1955

The Guildhall, London

Following Churchill's resignation, Sir Anthony Eden became Prime Minister and, at the General Election of 26 May, the Conservatives secured a majority of more than 50 seats. The City of London had commissioned a statue of Churchill by Oscar Nemon and had invited him to unveil it.

It has been my lot to live as a grown-up person through more than half of the most violent century in human record. I remember well the scene which spread before us at the close of the Victorian era. The vast majority of the nation looked with confidence upon our island as the centre of a vast empire spreading all over the world, as its leader in commerce, manufacture, and invention, as the model of orthodox finance and fiscal policy, as the author of Parliamentary government and all guarded by the unchallengeable power of a navy which only cost about £20 millions a year. Little did we realise how mighty was the world which was growing up around us, or how terrible and gigantic were the struggles into which all its people were to be plunged. Now we look out upon a different prospect. All the

The victorious campaigner casts his vote in Woodford,
Election Day, 1951

values and proportions are changed. We have emerged on the victorious side from two world wars in which scores of millions have perished. They were wars which in their scope and scale seemed far to surpass our resources, and at times to threaten us with doom. . . .

But now I leave the past, and I leave the present. It is to the future that we must turn our gaze. I confess that, like Disraeli, I am on the side of the optimists. I do not believe that humanity is going to destroy itself. I have for some time thought it would be a good thing if the leaders of the great nations talked freely to one another without too much of the formality of diplomacy. I am very glad that this is now going to happen. We must not count upon complete and immediate success. Whatever is the outcome, we must persevere in the maintenance of peace through strength. A period of relaxation of tension may well be all that is now within our grasp. But such a phase would not be sterile. On the contrary it would give the time for science to show the magnitude of her blessings rather than of her terrors; and this again may lead us into a more genial climate of opinion and resolve. Let us go boldly forward and play our part in all this.

HONORARY CITIZENSHIP OF THE UNITED STATES

9 April 1963

The White House, Washington, DC

Churchill, 88 years of age, was not well enough to make the journey to Washington to receive this unique honour. In his place he sent his son, Randolph who, at a ceremony in the Rose Garden of the White House, delivered his father's reply to President Kennedy. I accompanied my father to the ceremony, which was the crowning of all the many honours my grandfather had received.

Mr President, I have been informed by Mr David Bruce that it is your intention to sign a Bill conferring upon me Honorary citizenship of the United States.

I have received many kindnesses from the United States of America, but the honour which you now accord me is without parallel. I accept it with deep gratitude and affection.

US Honorary Citizenship: Randolph, supported by the editor,
delivers his father's reply to President John F. Kennedy,
The White House, Washington, DC, 9 April 1963.

I am also most sensible of the warm-hearted action of the individual States who accorded me the great compliment of their own honorary citizenships as a prelude to this Act of Congress.

It is a remarkable comment on our affairs that the former Prime Minister of a great sovereign state should thus be received as an honorary citizen of another. I say 'great sovereign state' with design and emphasis, for I reject the view that Britain and the Commonwealth should now be relegated to a tame and minor role in the world. Our past is the key to our future, which I firmly trust and believe will be no less fertile and glorious. Let no man underrate our energies, our potentialities and our abiding power for good.

I am, as you know, half American by blood, and the story of my association with that mighty and benevolent nation goes back nearly ninety years to the day of my father's marriage. In this century of storm and tragedy I contemplate with high satisfaction the constant factor of the interwoven and upward progress of our peoples. Our comradeship and our brotherhood in war were unexampled. We stood together, and because of that fact the free world now stands. Nor has our partnership any exclusive nature: the Atlantic community is a dream that can well be fulfilled to the detriment of none and to the enduring benefit and honour of the great democracies.

Mr President, your action illuminates the theme of unity of the English-speaking peoples, to which I have devoted a large part of my life. I would ask you to accept yourself, and to convey to both Houses of Congress, and through them to the American people, my solemn and heartfelt thanks for this unique distinction, which will always be proudly remembered by my descendants.

Appendix
THE CHURCHILL CENTER
AND SOCIETIES
(www.winstonchurchill.org)

The editor is pleased to be a Trustee of The Churchill Center and strongly recommends membership to anyone interested in Sir Winston.

Headquartered in Washington, DC, and active internationally, The Churchill Center was founded in 1968 to inspire leadership, statesmanship, vision, and boldness among democratic and freedom-loving peoples through the thoughts, words, works and deeds of Winston Spencer Churchill. Membership numbers over 3000 with an average age of 48, including the affiliated Churchill Societies of the UK and Canada.

The Churchill Center publishes a quarterly magazine, *Finest Hour*, a newsletter, the *Chartwell Bulletin*; and periodic collections of papers and speeches, the *Churchill Proceedings*. It sponsors international and national conferences, and Churchill tours, which have visited Britain, Australia, France, South Africa, and Morocco. Its expansive website *www.winstonchurchill.org* now includes a 'classroom' component to help educate young people on Sir Winston's life and leadership.

The Churchill Center has helped bring about republication of over twenty of Winston Churchill's long out-of-print books. In 1992, it launched a campaign for completion of the remaining document volumes to the offical biography, three of which have been published to date. More recently, it sponsored academic symposia in America and Britain; seminars where students and scholars discuss Churchill's books; scholarships for Churchill Studies at the Universities of Edinburgh and Dallas; and important reference works. In 1998 it launched the Churchill Lecture Series, in which prominent world figures apply Sir Winston's experience to the world today.

In 2003 the Churchill Center opened its first official headquarters in Washington, which houses its administrative staff, library, and computer facilities linked to the major Churchill archives. Future programmes include video aids for schoolchildren; college and graduate level courses on aspects of Churchill's career; fellowships to assist students; and visiting professorships. The overall aim is to impress Churchill's qualities of leadership firmly on the leaders of the twenty-first century.

Membership in the Churchill Center and Societies is available for a modest subscription, with special rates for students. For further information please contact:

The Churchill Center
1750 17th Street, NW (Suite 312),
Washington DC 20002 USA
Telephone: (888) WSC-1874
website: www.winstonchurchill.org

International Churchill Society,
PO Box 1257, Melksham,
Wilts, SN12 6GQ ENGLAND
Telephone: 01-380-828-609

International Churchill Society,
3256 Rymal Road, Mississauga,
Ontario, L4Y 3C1 CANADA
Telephone: (905) 279-5169

INDEX

Parliament (1950 and 1951),
453, 458, 469
Churchill, Sir Winston S.:
broadcasts, xxiii–xxiv; granted
honorary US citizenship, xxiv,
xxx–xxxi, 403, 501–3; writes
own speeches, xxiv–xxv; crosses
floor of Commons, xxvi, 1, 10,
15, 67, 87, 359; political
offices, xxvi; in Boer War, 1, 5,
7; elected MP for Oldham
(1900), 1, 7; as Home
Secretary, 1, 39, 42–3; as
President of Board of Trade
(1908), 1, 31–2; journalism, 5,
29; Commons oratory praised,
8, 91; elected as Liberal for
North-West Manchester (1906),
20–1; social concerns and
reforms, 23, 41; in Colonial
Office, 26, 67, 79, 128, 435;
authorship, 29; wins Dundee
seat (1908), 31; as First Lord of
Admiralty (1911–15), 45–6, 50,
58; and development of military
tank, 55; removed from
Admiralty (1915), 62, 67;
serves with army on Western
Front (1916), 64, 67, 69; as
Chancellor of Exchequer
(1924–9), 67, 87, 91; rejoins
Conservative Party, 67, 87;
returns to Commons (1916),
69; as Minister of Munitions
(1918), 79; loses Dundee seat
and elected for Epping (1924),
87; opposes disarmament and
appeasement, 92–3, 95, 100,
102–3, 105–10, 124–5; political
alienation (1930s), 95; supports
Edward in Abdication crisis,
156–7; fights de-selection at
Epping (1939), 185;
reappointed First Lord of
Admiralty (1939), 195, 197,
203; appointed Prime Minister
(1940), 204–5; on 'Their Finest
Hour' (1940), 219–29; wins
Commons Votes of Confidence:
(1941), 275–7; (1942), 324–9;
visits USA: (1941), 315,
317–18, 328; (1943), 350,
356–7; (1952), 473;
second anniversary of
premiership (1942), 330;
Commons Motion of Censure
defeated (May 1942), 339–41;
travels to Tripoli (1943), 347;
attends Yalta Conference
(1945), 373–8; resumes party
politics after war, 395–6;
resigns (July 1945), 401, 403;
death, 403; Fulton 'Iron
Curtain' speech (1946), 403,
413–14, 450; resumes
premiership (1951), 403; retires
(1955), 403; speaks in French,
451; given *Times* Literary
Award, 453; returns as Prime
Minister (1951), 470; 80th
birthday celebrations, 488–90;
Sutherland portrait of, 489;
final resignation (1955), 498–9;
Nemon statue of, 499
Churchill Center, Washington,
DC, 505–6
Clark, General Mark, 362, 365–6
Clough, Arthur Hugh, 266
coal miners, 39–41, 467
Cobden, Richard, 15–17
Cockran, Bourke, 418
Cold War: beginnings, 413; WSC
detests, 491
Cole, Sterling, 492
Collins, Michael, 167
Colonial Office: WSC serves at,
xxvi, 26, 67, 79, 128, 425
Colville, Sir John, xxv, 289
Commons, House of: WSC's
maiden speech in (1901), 8–9;
WSC on personality of